ENERGY EFFICIENCY IN SOUTH ASIA

OPPORTUNITIES FOR ENERGY SECTOR TRANSFORMATION

Ram M. Shrestha, Tika Ram Limbu, Bijay Bahadur Pradhan, Amnaya Paudel, and Pratik Karki

DECEMBER 2021

ASIAN DEVELOPMENT BANK

ADB

© 2021 Asian Development Bank
6 ADB Avenue, Mandaluyong City, 1550 Metro Manila, Philippines
Tel +63 2 8632 4444; Fax +63 2 8636 2444
www.adb.org

Some rights reserved. Published in 2021
Printed in the Philippines

ISBN 978-92-9262-556-6 (print); 978-92-9262-557-3 (electronic); 978-92-9262-558-0 (ebook)
Publication Stock No. TCS200435
DOI: http://dx.doi.org/10.22617/TCS200435

The views expressed in this publication are those of the authors and do not necessarily reflect the views and policies of the Asian Development Bank (ADB) or its Board of Governors or the governments they represent.

ADB does not guarantee the accuracy of the data included in this publication and accepts no responsibility for any consequence of their use. The mention of specific companies or products of manufacturers does not imply that they are endorsed or recommended by ADB in preference to others of a similar nature that are not mentioned.

By making any designation of or reference to a particular territory or geographic area, or by using the term "country" in this document, ADB does not intend to make any judgments as to the legal or other status of any territory or area.

Corrigenda to ADB publications may be found at http://www.adb.org/publications/corrigenda.

Notes:
In this publication, "$" refers to United States dollars.
ADB recognizes "Ceylon" as Sri Lanka and "Vietnam" as Viet Nam.

On the cover: Energy efficiency is an important component of sustainable energy development. Energy efficiency improvement options in the energy supply and demand sectors all play a crucial role for such development.

Cover design by Francis Manio.

Contents

Tables and Figures

Figures

About the Authors

The authors of this study are Ram M. Shrestha, Tika Ram Limbu, Bijay Bahadur Pradhan, Amnaya Paudel, and Pratik Karki. Ram M. Shrestha is an Emeritus Professor of the Asian Institute of Technology, Thailand. Tika Limbu is currently Principal Portfolio Management Specialist at the Bangladesh Resident Mission of the Asian Development Bank. Bijay Bahadur Pradhan is a doctoral candidate at Sirindhorn International Institute of Technology, Thammasat University, Thailand. Amnaya Paudel and Pratik Karki are independent researchers.

Foreword

A sustainable energy system bears special significance to the member countries of the South Asia Subregional Cooperation (SASEC) Program. Accounting for over one-fifth of the world's population, SASEC member countries still depend on fossil fuels, which have adverse effects on the environment and implications on energy security and climate change. As such, the wider deployment of renewable energy and energy-efficient technologies is a growing imperative in South Asia.

Tackling climate change, building climate and disaster resilience, and enhancing environmental sustainability is an operational priority of the Asian Development Bank (ADB) under its Strategy 2030. Through clean energy financing, ADB is actively supporting its developing member countries in their pursuit of low-carbon and climate-resilient development.

This ADB study analyzes various issues regarding energy efficiency and the development of sustainable energy systems in SASEC member countries: Bangladesh, Bhutan, India, Nepal, and Sri Lanka. It also provides an overview of the national institutions along with policies, laws, regulations, and initiatives on energy efficiency and conservation in these countries.

Recognizing the important role that regional cooperation plays in the promotion of energy efficiency, this study discusses different avenues for collaboration among governments in the national, state, and local levels. It also highlights opportunities for changes in energy mix that are beneficial to these countries and others in South Asia. Various technologies that can be developed and deployed in the region to help conserve energy and save costs are also identified.

The findings and information presented can provide national energy planners, policy makers, and other stakeholders in South Asia with a better understanding of how and why energy efficiency is essential to achieve sustainable and low-carbon economic development.

PRIYANTHA WIJAYATUNGA
Director
Energy Division
South Asia Department
Asian Development Bank

Acknowledgments

This report benefited from useful information and numerous documents on energy development, energy efficiency related regulations, policies, and programs related to the five countries in South Asia, i.e., Bangladesh, Bhutan, India, Nepal, and Sri Lanka. The lead author (Ram M. Shrestha) profoundly thanks Tilak Siyambalapitiya, Resource Management Associates (Pvt) Ltd, Colombo for sharing several useful energy audit reports on enterprises in Sri Lanka as well as to W.J.L. Shavindranath Fernando and Ananda Namal, both from the National Engineering Research and Development Centre, Colombo for sharing useful information on energy usage and technologies involved in some production activities of Sri Lanka. The lead author has greatly benefited from his years of research collaboration with the Asia-Pacific Integrated Model (AIM) team at the National Institute of Environmental Studies (NIES), Japan, particularly in the application of the AIM/Enduse model, which was used to analyze some major issues in the present study. The lead author is grateful to Toshihiko Masui, NIES, for his valuable comments and suggestions during the initial stage of this study.

The lead author wishes to thank Nazmun Nahar, Bangladesh Resident Mission, ADB, Dhaka; Tschewang Norbu, Bhutan Resident Mission, ADB, Thimphu; Jiwan Acharya, India Resident Mission, ADB, New Delhi; Ranishka Yasanga Wimalasena, Sri Lanka Resident Mission, ADB, Colombo; Priyantha Wijayatunga, ADB, Manila; and Pushkar Manandhar, Nepal Resident Mission, ADB, Kathmandu for their help in arranging his meetings with experts in different organizations during his country visits. He thankfully acknowledges the support of Bundit Limmeechokchai, Sirindhorn International Institute of Technology, Thammasat University, Thailand.

The lead author also expresses his grateful appreciation to the following persons for the helpful discussions he had with them during his country visits and for providing useful information for the study; they are, however, not responsible for the views expressed in this report:

Harsha Wickramanayake, Sri Lanka Sustainable Energy Authority; Bhasara Sirisinghe, Resource Management Associates (Pvt) Ltd, Colombo; Wijekoon Banda, Ceylon Electricity Board (CEB); Ronald Comester, CEB; Sulakshana Jayawardena, Ministry of Power and Renewable Energy, Colombo; Sherin Authukorala, Sri Lanka National Transport Commission; V.R. Rupasinghe, Sri Lanka Transport Board; and Rahula Atalage and Amal S. Kumarage, University of Moratuwa, Sri Lanka.

Al Mudabbir Bin Anam, German International Cooperation (GIZ), Dhaka; Siddique Zobair, Sustainable and Renewable Energy Development Authority (SREDA), Dhaka; Monowar Islam, Chairman, Bangladesh Energy Regulatory Commission; Ahmad Mukammeluddin, Japan International Cooperation Agency (JICA), Dhaka; and Mohammad Anis and Tanuja Bhattacharjee, World Bank, Bangladesh.

S.P. Garnaik and Banshi Shukla, Energy Efficiency Services Limited (EESL), New Delhi; Ashok Kumar, Bureau of Energy Efficiency, New Delhi; Vipin Rohila, National Productive Council, New Delhi; Manu Maudgal, GIZ, New Delhi; and Ashish Jindal, EESL, New Delhi, India.

Mewang Gyeltshen and Dawa Zangmo, Department of Renewable Energy, Thimphu; Dawa Chogyel, Department of Industries; Bhimlal Suberi, Ministry of Information and Communications; Karma Dupchu, Director, Ministry of Works and Human Settlement; and Tshewang Zam, National Environment Commission, in Bhutan, as well as Nima Tshering, Bhutan Electricity Authority; Om Bhandari, International Finance Corporation, Thimphu; and Sangay Dorji, Bhutan Chamber of Commerce, Thimphu.

Narayan Chaulagain, Nepal Energy Efficiency Programme/GIZ, Kathmandu; Madhusudhan Adhikarai and Raju Laudari, Alternative Energy Promotion Centre, Lalitpur, Nepal; Uttam Kunwar, Federation of Nepalese Chambers of Commerce and Industry/Energy Efficiency Centre, Kathmandu; Sagar Raj Goutam, Ministry of Energy, Water Resources and Irrigation, Kathmandu; Tirapeshwar Purbe and Ramji Bhandari, Nepal Electricity Authority, Kathmandu; and Shree Raj Shakya, Centre for Energy Studies, Institute of Engineering, Lalitpur, Nepal.

Abbreviations

AIC	–	average incremental cost
AICS	–	advanced improved cook stove
AIM	–	Asia-Pacific Integrated Model
BAU	–	business as usual
BEE	–	Bureau of Energy Efficiency
BIMSTEC	–	The Bay of Bengal Initiative for Multi-Sectoral Technical and Economic Cooperation
CAGR	–	compound annual growth rate
CEB	–	Ceylon Electricity Board
CFL	–	compact fluorescent lamp
DoRE	–	Department of Renewable Energy
ECBC	–	Energy Consumption Building Code
ECPG	–	energy consumption for power generation
EEC	–	energy efficiency and conservation
EECR	–	Energy Efficiency and Conservation Rules
EEG	–	energy efficiency gap
EESL	–	Energy Efficiency Services Limited
ESP	–	energy saving potential
FAME	–	Faster Adoption and Manufacturing of (Hybrid &) Electric Vehicles
FEC	–	final energy consumption
GCF	–	Green Climate Fund
GDP	–	gross domestic product
GEEREF	–	Global Energy Efficiency and Renewable Energy Fund
GHG	–	greenhouse gas
ICS	–	improved cook stove
IDCOL	–	Infrastructure Development Company Limited

IDEA	–	Integrated Development Association
INDC	–	intended nationally determined contribution
JICA	–	Japan International Cooperation Agency
LED	–	light emitting diode
LPG	–	liquefied petroleum gas
MoEA	–	Ministry of Economic Affairs
MPEMR	–	Ministry of Power, Energy and Mineral Resources
NDC	–	nationally determined contributions
NEEP	–	Nepal Energy Efficiency Programme
NEPS	–	Sri Lanka's National Energy Policy and Strategies
OECD	–	Organisation for Economic Co-operation and Development
PAT	–	Perform Achieve and Trade
R&D	–	research and development
REF	–	reference
S&L	–	standard and labeling
SAARC	–	South Asian Association for Regional Cooperation
SASEC	–	South Asia Subregional Economic Cooperation
SDA	–	state designated agencies
SEC	–	specific energy consumption
SEEC	–	specific electrical energy consumption
SEER	–	seasonal energy efficiency ratio
SLSEA	–	Sri Lanka Sustainable Energy Authority
SREDA	–	Sustainable and Renewable Energy Development Authority
SSC	–	specific steam consumption
T&D	–	transmission and distribution
TCS	–	traditional cook stove
TFEC	–	total final energy consumption
TPES	–	total primary energy supply

Weights and Measures

Unit		Abbreviation
British thermal units	–	BTU
kilogram of oil equivalent	–	kgoe
ton of carbon dioxide equivalent	–	tCO_2e
kilometer	–	km
gigawatt-hour	–	GWh
kilowatt	–	kW
megawatt	–	MW
tons of oil equivalent	–	toe
metric ton	–	t
tonne-km	–	tkm
watt	–	W

Executive Summary

This study analyzes the role of energy efficiency in the growth of energy requirements in the recent past as well as in medium to longer term future in five countries in South Asia: Bangladesh, Bhutan, India, Nepal, and Sri Lanka. It identifies the sectors that offer high potential to achieve selected energy reduction targets in a cost-effective manner during 2015–2050 in the case of Bangladesh, Bhutan, Nepal, and Sri Lanka based on a comprehensive analysis using a long-term energy system model as such analyses are lacking in these countries. Further, the study identifies the cost-optimal fuel switching needed to achieve the energy reduction targets. It also analyzes the cost and greenhouse gases (GHG) implications of the energy reduction targets. As several studies have analyzed the issue of energy efficiency in India in the context of climate change and cleaner development, this study reviews the available literature and includes the relevant findings. Another important aspect of the study is the review of institutional arrangements, regulatory frameworks, major policies, and programs focused on promotion of energy efficiency and conservation in the South Asian countries. In addition, possible areas for regional cooperation to promoted energy efficiency and conservation in these countries are discussed.

Energy Situation in South Asian Countries

The energy intensity—defined as energy use per unit of gross domestic product (GDP)—of the South Asian countries declined during 2000–2016. The energy intensity decreased by around 14% in Bangladesh, 36% in India, 13% in Nepal, and 40% in Sri Lanka; in Bhutan, there was even more rapid decline in energy intensity (approximately 54%) during 2000–2015 (World Bank 2018).

The share of fossil fuels in total primary energy supply (TPES) rose in the five South Asian countries during 2000–2016. In 2016, fossil fuels had a share of almost 75% in Bangladesh and India, while it was 57% in Sri Lanka and 21% in Nepal; in Bhutan, the share was 36% in 2014. During the same period, the share of biomass in energy consumption of the residential sector was declining in all five countries; in 2016 the share of biomass was 64% in Bangladesh, 70% in India, 95% in Nepal, and 80% in Sri Lanka. For Bhutan, biomass share in TPES decreased from 91% in 2005 to 87% in 2014. Total energy used in the productive sectors—hereafter total productive use of energy (TPUE)—has seen an annual growth rate varying from 3% in Sri Lanka to 9% in Bangladesh during 2000–2015. The growth rate of TPUE was higher than that of GDP in the South Asian countries except Sri Lanka.

The energy intensity of the industry and transport sectors has risen over time in Bangladesh, Bhutan, and Nepal but fallen in India and Sri Lanka. The commercial sector has become less energy-intensive in all countries in this study.

Assessment of the Role of Energy Efficiency in the Historical Growth of Energy Consumption

The study analyzes the role of changes in sectoral energy intensity, fuel mix, and level of production (i.e., GDP) on the growth of TPUE during 2000–2016. The analysis shows that in the case of India and Sri Lanka, improvements in energy intensity contributed toward reducing TPUE during the period. The TPUE would have been 14% higher in India and 42% in Sri Lanka if there was no improvement in sectoral energy intensities. It was the exact opposite in the other three countries—increases in energy intensity contributed to 8% increment in TPUE in Bangladesh, 12% in Bhutan, and 46% in Nepal. Changes in the fuel mix had a positive effect on growth of TPUE during 2000–2016 in all studied countries.

The study also analyzes the roles of different factors behind the growth of energy consumption for power generation (ECPG) during 2000–2016. The factors analyzed are electricity generation efficiency, transmission and distribution (T&D) losses, fuel mix in power generation, and final demand for electricity. The T&D losses decreased (i.e., T&D efficiency improved) in all countries during the period. This contributed positively to moderate the growth of energy requirement for power generation in all the countries. It is also found that ECPG would have been 4% higher in Bangladesh, 4% in Bhutan, 13% in India, and 19% in Sri Lanka, if there were no improvement in T&D efficiency. For Nepal, ECPG would have been less than 1% higher without any improvement in T&D efficiency during the period. Changes in the efficiency of electricity generation had an insignificant effect on growth of ECPG in Bangladesh, Bhutan, and Nepal. In contrast, efficiency of electricity generation had a significant role in the growth of ECPG in India and Sri Lanka; ECPG in these countries in 2016 would have been 10% and 12% higher without any improvement in electricity generation efficiency. Changes in generation mix (generation mix effect) significantly influenced the level of ECPG in Bangladesh (4%), India (7%), and Sri Lanka (51%) against the total increment in their ECPG in 2016. The large contribution of the generation mix effect in Sri Lanka was associated with the country's shift to coal-based power generation during the period.

The Energy Efficiency Gap and Energy Saving Potential

The study assesses the energy saving potential (ESP) of no-regret energy efficient technology options; the no-regret technologies are defined as efficient technologies that would be both cost- and energy-saving compared to technologies that are in use in the business as usual (BAU) case. In addition, the study also assesses the energy efficiency gap (EEG) in different end uses and subsectors in industries, which is measured as energy saving per unit service output through the use of no-regret technologies in place of corresponding BAU technologies. The sector-wise ESP of no-regret technology options in Bangladesh, Bhutan, Nepal, and Sri Lanka in 2015 is shown in Table A.

The analysis reveals the presence of highest ESP of no-regret options in the residential sector for all four countries; the sector is estimated to contribute 53% in Bangladesh, 47% in Bhutan, 66% in Nepal, and 45% in Sri Lanka of total ESP. The industry sector ranks next to the residential sector in terms of ESP in Bangladesh (42%), Bhutan (38%), and Nepal (28%). In Sri Lanka, the industry sector accounts for 27% of total ESP, which is slightly less than that for the commercial sector, with 27.5%. With the present modal structure, the transport sector has negligible ESP in the countries except Sri Lanka, where it accounts for 10% of total ESP.

Table A: Energy Saving Potential of No-regret Technology Options in 2015
(ktoe)

Sector	Bangladesh	Bhutan	Nepal	Sri Lanka
Residential	3,735	36	875	916
Industrial	2,980	29	371	546
Agricultural	173	2	13	—
Commercial	94	10	61	554
Transportation	62	—	—	—
Total	7,044	77	1,320	2,016

— = zero or negligible value; ktoe = kiloton of oil equivalent.
Source: Authors.

No-regret technologies are those that are both cost- and energy-saving. Even though these technologies are cheaper in life cycle costing, several are still not in use due to some barriers. One of the major no-regret technologies is improved cook stoves in the residential sector. Of the total ESP in the residential sector, replacing traditional with improved stoves accounts for almost 90% in Bangladesh; whereas in Bhutan and Nepal these account for 95% each, and in Sri Lanka 91%. In the industry sector of Bangladesh, there are no-regret efficient technology options in textile manufacturing and brick production. In the case of Bhutan, improved boilers are a no-regret technology for the alloy industry. In Nepal, the study identifies the four-stage cyclone suspension preheater kiln for clinker production in cement factories as a no-regret technology.

The study reveals that Bangladesh will have an ESP of 14,227 kiloton of oil equivalent (ktoe) in 2030 through the deployment of no-regret technologies. At the sectoral level, the residential sector would offer the highest ESP and would account for around 43% of total ESP in 2030. The residential sector is followed by industry, accounting for 41.5% of total ESP, transport with 10.5%, agriculture with 3.2%, and commercial with 2%.

Total ESP in Bhutan through no-regret options is estimated at 249 ktoe in 2030; the industry sector should contribute around 82% followed by the residential sector with 8%.

Total ESP of no-regret options in Nepal is estimated at 1,119 ktoe in 2030. The industry sector should have the highest ESP, accounting for around 51% of total ESP in 2030, followed by the transport (24%), commercial (13%), residential (9%), and agriculture (3%) sectors.

In Sri Lanka, the total ESP of no-regret options is estimated as 6,058 ktoe in 2030. The industry sector would contribute around 47% of total ESP in 2030; followed by the transport (43.4%), residential (5.5%), and commercial (4.1%) sectors.

For India, the study discusses EEG of eight selected industrial categories including thermal power plants as defined under Phase I of the Perform Achieve and Trade (PAT) scheme of the Bureau of Energy Efficiency (BEE). Unlike in the other four countries, the EEG in the case of the eight industrial categories represents the efficiency gap purely from the technical perspective; i.e., EEG is measured by the difference between the average specific energy consumption (SEC) of a particular type of industry in India and SEC of the corresponding best available technology in the world. In the iron and steel industry, India's most efficient plant has 5% higher SEC than the globally most efficient plant ("global best"); whereas, on average, iron and steel plants in India have 25% higher SEC than the global best. In the case of the cement industry, the specific electrical energy consumption (SEEC) of India's most efficient plant is 42% less than the global average. On average, the SEEC of cement plants in India is 14% less than the global average. Similarly, the specific thermal energy consumption of the most efficient cement plant in India is 24% less than the global average, whereas the average specific thermal energy consumption of India's cement plants is 13% less than the global average. The study also discusses EEG of some appliances in the residential sector of India based on existing analyses. One analysis shows that, at the household level, the average EEG is about 10% of total electricity demand of air-conditioners. The analysis states that, with proper awareness about cost savings, emission reduction, and payback period, the expected private EEG can decline to 2.98% from 10%. Another analysis suggests that there is ESP of almost 40% in the household sector by replacing existing appliances with five-star rating appliances, which are considered the most energy efficient.

Implications of Energy Reduction Targets

A policy to reduce total primary energy consumption would require changes in a number of respects including technology choice and energy mix at the sectoral level. These changes would affect total costs and emissions of GHG in addition to others. This study analyzes the implications of setting three different energy reduction targets, i.e., reducing TPES gradually up to 15%, 30%, and 40% by 2050 below that in the BAU scenario in the case of Bangladesh, Bhutan, Nepal, and Sri Lanka; these energy reduction scenarios are termed ER15, ER30, and ER40. It is necessary to ensure that a target set for energy reduction is feasible. This requires an assessment of the maximum limit up to which total primary energy consumption could be reduced prior to setting targets for energy reduction. The present study therefore also assesses the maximum potential for reducing primary energy consumption.

Maximum energy reduction potential. The study estimates the maximum potential of reducing total primary energy consumption in 2050 as a percentage of TPES in BAU to be 40.03% in Bangladesh, 42.5% in Bhutan, 51% in Nepal, and 56% in Sri Lanka, when a modal shift in passenger transport from car to public and mass transport vehicles of up to 70% is allowed. The corresponding figures in 2030 would be 46.5% (Bangladesh), 40.0% (Bhutan), 54.0% (Nepal), and 52.5% (Sri Lanka) when a modal shift of up to 75% is allowed.

Total primary energy supply. The study shows that the TPES in BAU would grow at a compound annual growth rate (CAGR) of 5.8% during 2015–2050 in Bangladesh. BAU would also grow in Bhutan (6.4%), Nepal (4.0%), and Sri Lanka (4.4%). Further, electricity generation requirement in BAU would increase during 2015–2050 at rates of 6.2% in Bangladesh, 6.6% in Bhutan, 9.8% in Nepal, and 4.8% in Sri Lanka.

Reduction in total final energy consumption. The reduction in TFEC in Bangladesh in 2030 in ER15, ER30, and ER40 scenarios would be 15.8, 16.4, and 22.7 Mtoe, respectively; whereas in 2050, the corresponding reductions would be 36.3, 46.5, and 71.0 Mtoe. In Bhutan, TFEC in 2030 would decrease by 0.1, 0.3, and 0.4 Mtoe in ER15, ER30, and ER40 scenarios, respectively; with corresponding reductions in 2050 of 1.2, 1.8, and 2.4 Mtoe. The TFEC in Nepal in 2030 would decrease in ER15, ER30, and ER40 scenarios by 1.9, 3.9, and 5.6 Mtoe, respectively; and in 2050, corresponding reductions would be 11.1, 18.2, and 22.9 Mtoe. In Sri Lanka, the total reduction in TFEC in ER15, ER30, and ER40 scenarios in 2030 would be 2.8, 4.5, and 6.9 Mtoe, respectively; correspondingly in 2050, reductions would be 7.3, 15.4, and 19.6 Mtoe.

Sectoral contributions to energy reduction. In Bangladesh, the residential sector would be the major contributor to reduction in TFEC for ER40 in 2030, whereas the industry sector would have a greater role in reductions for the ER15 and ER30 scenarios. In 2050, the industry sector would have the largest role in reducing energy consumption in all energy reduction scenarios. For Bhutan, the industry sector would contribute most to the reduction of TFEC in 2030 for ER15, followed by the commercial and residential sectors. For ER30 and ER40, the industry sector would have the highest contribution to reductions. In 2050, the transport sector would account for the highest energy reductions for ER15 and ER40, followed by the industry and commercial sectors. For ER30, the industry and transport sectors would have the major role in energy reduction. In the case of Nepal, the industry and residential sectors would be the two major contributors to reduction in TFEC in 2030, whereas the transport sector would also contribute significantly in 2050. In Sri Lanka, the transport sector would be the largest contributor to reduction in TFEC in 2030 and 2050, followed by the industry sector.

Changes in the energy mix. In Bangladesh, natural gas would remain the dominant fuel during 2015–2050 in BAU and energy reduction scenarios. In 2030, there would be no significant changes in the energy mix for ER15 and ER30 compared to BAU, whereas for ER40 the share of biomass and coal would decrease and that of natural gas would increase. There would be a higher share of renewables (excluding hydropower) in the primary energy mix in all energy reduction scenarios. The share of natural gas for ER15 would be lower than in BAU in 2050, whereas the share would be higher for ER30 and ER40. The share of coal would increase for ER15 but decline for ER30 and ER40 in 2050. The share of biomass would slightly increase for ER15 and ER30 but fall significantly for ER40. For ER40, both biomass and coal use would be reduced with the higher use of electricity in 2030.

In Bhutan, there would be a decrease in the use of fossil fuels and an increase in the use of hydro and renewables (except biomass) for all energy reduction scenarios during 2015–2050. The reduction in use of petroleum products and coal could cause a major reduction in TPES for all energy reduction scenarios. Decreased use of biomass would be the third highest contributor to reduction in TPES for all energy reduction scenarios.

In Nepal, hydro would have a major role in energy reduction scenarios, with increased share in the energy mix with increases in the energy reduction target. The share of biomass in the energy mix in ER15 in 2030 and 2050 would be slightly less than BAU, but would decrease significantly in ER30 and ER40. For ER15, petroleum products would have a lower share of TPES than in BAU; in contrast, the shares would be higher than in BAU in ER30 and ER40. The consumption of petroleum products would be lower in all energy reduction scenarios although their share in the energy mix would be higher than in BAU. There would be lower consumption of coal in energy reduction scenarios than in BAU. However, the share of coal in the energy mix would not change significantly for all reduction scenarios.

In Sri Lanka, reduced use of biomass and petroleum products would contribute to a major reduction in TPES for all energy reduction scenarios in 2030 and 2050. The use of coal would increase in all reduction scenarios in 2030 and 2050. There would be greater use of renewables (solar and wind) in all energy reduction scenarios.

In India, some studies have analyzed the implications of a GHG emission intensity reduction target, which results in improvements in energy efficiency and reduction in the use of fossil fuels; however, studies directly analyzing the implications of energy reduction targets are lacking. Unlike the other four countries, this study relies on existing literature to discuss the implications of energy reduction targets for India. A study on the effects of reducing GHG emission intensity under India's intended nationally determined contribution (INDC) estimates that the demand for primary energy would decline by 6% in 2030 and 10.4% in 2050 compared to the BAU scenario. The study also shows that the fuel mix in the final energy consumption under the INDC scenario would be dominated by coal and oil for 2020, 2030, and 2050 although the share of fossil fuels would be decreasing. In 2050, the combined share of coal and oil in the INDC scenario is estimated to decrease from 58% to 55% under the INDC compared to BAU scenario in 2050. The share of solar energy would increase from 1% in 2000 to 9% in 2050 for both scenarios. Electricity's share would increase by 6% in the BAU and by 8% in the INDC scenario during 2000–2050.

Cost and investment implications. In Bangladesh, the total cost of the energy system in BAU during 2015–2050 would be $3,534 billion (undiscounted). In ER15, ER30, and ER40 scenarios, the cost would be lower by 22.9%, 23.6%, and 23.0%, respectively, mainly due to the deployment of no-regret options and modal shifts considered in the transport sector. In the case of Bhutan, the total cost of the energy system during 2015–2050 would be $130 billion (undiscounted). The cost would decrease by 11.9% in ER15, 11.0% in ER30, and 4.5% in ER40. In Nepal, the total cost of the energy system in BAU during 2015–2050 would be $758 billion (undiscounted). Cost would be reduced by 4.8% in ER15 and 2.3% in ER30, and by 7.1% in ER40. In Sri Lanka, the total cost of the energy system in BAU during 2015–2050 would be $1,309 billion (undiscounted). Costs would fall by 20.0% in ER15, 27.2% in ER30, and 29.9% in ER40 scenarios.

The cumulative investment requirement under the BAU scenario during 2015–2050 is estimated at $794 billion in Bangladesh, $81 billion in Bhutan, $472 billion in Nepal, and $449 billion in Sri Lanka (all undiscounted values in 2015 prices). With the same modal shares as in BAU, the cumulative investment requirement would increase in all energy reduction scenarios in Bangladesh, Bhutan, and Nepal (Table B). Similarly, the study shows the need for additional investment under ER30 and ER40 in Sri Lanka. The cumulative investment requirement for attaining ER40 in the four countries would be in the range of 16–38% higher than the corresponding figure in BAU.

Table B: Cumulative Investment Requirement in Business as Usual and Energy Reduction Scenarios During 2015–2050, at 2015 Prices
($'000,000,000)

Country	Cumulative Investment			
	BAU	ER15	ER30	ER40
Bangladesh	794	807	964	1,096
Bhutan	81	85	90	107
Nepal	472	496	509	600
Sri Lanka	499	447	500	520

BAU = business as usual scenario; ER15 = energy reduction scenario 15% below BAU; ER30 = energy reduction scenario 30% below BAU; ER40 = energy reduction scenario 40% below BAU.
Source: Authors.

Greenhouse gas emission implications. In Bangladesh, GHG emission in BAU would increase at a CAGR of 8.4% during 2015–2050. The GHG emission in 2030 would be lower than in BAU by 20.6% in ER15, 20.8% in ER30, and 30.1% in ER40 scenarios. In 2050, GHG emissions would decrease by 17.9% in ER15, 43.6% in ER30, and 48.0% in ER40. In Bhutan, GHG emission in BAU would increase by two times in 2030 and 13.5 times in 2050 compared to 2015. In 2030, GHG emission would be reduced in the range of 11.6% in ER15 to 37.6% in ER40. In 2050, the emissions would be 13.9% lower in ER15 and 63.2% lower in ER40. In Nepal, GHG emissions in BAU would increase at a CAGR of 6.0% during 2015–2050. In 2030, the GHG emission reductions would be in the range of 15.3% in ER15 to 21.0% in ER40. In 2050, GHG emission reduction would lie in the range of 36.0%–46.2% in all energy reduction scenarios. In Sri Lanka, GHG emissions would increase by 1.2 times in 2030 and 4.7 times in 2050 from the BAU level. In 2050, GHG emissions would be lower by 17.3% in ER15, 28.2% in ER30, and 37.1% in ER40. In India, a study by Thambi et al. (2018) shows that total GHG emission would increase at a CAGR of around 11% during 2017–2032. The study also states that GHG emission in the nationally determined contributions (NDC) scenario would be only 5% lower than the BAU level.

Implications of transmission and distribution loss reduction. Reducing the T&D loss in Bangladesh from 11% to 10% during 2015–2050 would not necessarily decrease the electricity generation requirement although it would decrease the cumulative generation. In ER30, when the T&D loss is reduced from 11% to 10%, the electricity generation would increase during 2045–2050 due to a change in final energy consumption mix. However, the total cost (excluding the cost of T&D loss reduction) during 2015–2050 would decrease in BAU as well as energy reduction scenarios when T&D loss is reduced to 10% and 5%. In Bhutan, reducing the T&D loss from 6% to 5% during 2015–2050 would reduce the electricity generation requirement. The total system cost during 2015–2050 would also decrease. Similarly to the case of Bangladesh, reducing T&D loss in Nepal would not decrease the electricity generation throughout 2015–2050 due to a change in the final energy consumption mix. The total cost of the system during 2015–2050 would be lower when T&D loss is reduced. In Sri Lanka, the electricity generation would be lower when T&D is reduced from 9% to 5%. The total cost of the system would also be lower when T&D loss is reduced.

Institutional Arrangements for Energy Efficiency

The level of institutional preparedness also varies in the region. Among the South Asian countries, India is the only one with a formally dedicated nodal agency (i.e., the BEE) solely focused on energy efficiency. The BEE coordinates stakeholders, regulates energy efficiency and conservation (EEC) markets, plans strategies, implements programs, and even evaluates effectiveness of programs related to energy efficiency. Bangladesh has the Sustainable and Renewable Energy Development Authority, which is mandated to promote both renewable energy and energy efficiency. Similarly, the Sri Lanka Sustainable Energy Authority (SLSEA) has objectives to promote energy efficiency and energy sustainability in the country. The National Energy Efficiency & Conservation Policy of Bhutan has proposed the Department of Renewable Energy as the country's nodal agency for carrying out EEC and related activities. There is not yet a dedicated nodal agency for EEC in Nepal. However, the recently launched National Energy Efficiency Strategy of Nepal states that a governmental institution will be created specifically to promote, develop, and implement energy-efficiency measures in the country.

In addition to the BEE, India also has a dedicated public sector institution for expanding the energy-efficiency market in different sectors of the economy. Energy Efficiency Services Limited in India has been actively involved in developing the market for energy efficiency in the country's residential, commercial, industrial, building, as well as railway sectors.

In Bangladesh, Infrastructure Development Company Limited (IDCOL) is a nonbank finance institution created to bridge the finance gap for developing infrastructure and renewable energy projects. The main objective of IDCOL is to stimulate and optimize private sector investment in renewable energy and energy efficiency through public–private partnership initiatives. In Nepal, Rastriya Banijya Bank (a commercial bank) serves as an intermediary bank to provide finance to EEC projects. Several energy service companies (ESCOs) operate in India. They are specialized in the development and implementation of energy-efficiency projects. The ESCOs offer technical services such as identifying ESPs and designing, retrofitting, and implementing projects. There are no significant ESCO operations in the other South Asian countries.

Energy Efficiency Acts and Regulatory Frameworks

India enacted the Energy Conservation Act 2001 and Bangladesh enacted the Energy Efficiency and Conservation Rules 2016. Sri Lanka has taken a slightly different approach by enacting the Sustainable Energy Authority Act No. 35 of 2007 to establish SLSEA as the government body to carry out functions related to EEC and sustainable growth of the energy sector. Other South Asian countries do not have dedicated acts or rules on energy efficiency. All South Asian countries except Bhutan and Nepal have building energy codes. Bangladesh, India, and Sri Lanka are revising their existing codes to incorporate best available technologies.

Policies, Programs, and Initiatives

There is a wide variation in the region in terms of EEC policies, programs, and initiatives. India has implemented several effective strategies and measures, while other counties are at the initial stages of development of energy-efficiency programs and policies.

The PAT scheme in India is a highly successful program that uses regulatory as well as market-based approaches to create a robust incentive-based scheme for the industry sector. The first cycle of PAT (2012–2015) covered over 400 energy-intensive utilities and industries, and managed to reduce energy consumption by 5.3%. The second PAT cycle operated during 2016–2019.

There are some innovative schemes for promotion of energy efficiency in the region. The Unnat Jyoti by Affordable LEDs for All Program in India is one such example. The program involves an innovative business model which includes demand aggregation, mass campaigning, and bulk procurement for promotion of the use of efficient lamps and fans. The approach drove down light emitting diode (LED) lamp prices in India well below the market price and made LED lamps ubiquitous. This scheme was even replicated for energy-efficient tube lights and fans. This approach also holds promise for adoption in other South Asian countries and similar schemes could be applicable for promoting other energy-efficient appliances.

Financing schemes on energy efficiency in the form of grants or loan are found in all five countries in the present study. The Japan International Cooperation Agency recently provided a concessional loan to the Government of Bangladesh and the government in turn provides loans to the energy-intensive industry sector at a nominal rate. In the case of Nepal, the Government of Germany has made funds available to the Government of Nepal to provide conditional grants to industrial enterprises willing to adopt energy-efficiency measures. Loan and grant schemes have also been implemented in India. However, key takeaways from the Indian financing success stories are related to the initiation of finance instruments to support participating entities. The Partial Risk Guarantee Fund for Energy Efficiency in India provides risk-sharing services to financing institutions providing loans for EEC projects. The Venture Capital Fund for Energy Efficiency has also been initiated in India to provide equity support for EEC projects.

Voluntary building efficiency schemes also operate in India, including Green Rating for Integrated Habitat Assessment, Leadership in Energy and Environmental Design, and the BEE's scheme for star rating of office buildings. These schemes help to further enhance energy efficiency in the building sector.

Regional Cooperation on Energy Efficiency

There are possibilities for regional cooperation for enhancing energy efficiency in South Asian countries in several areas. Potential areas of regional collaboration include exchange of know-how, sharing of experience, capacity building, regional funding mechanisms, research and development among the participating nations, and establishing a regional center on EEC. The idea of regional cooperation was started in early 2000 for harmonization of energy-efficiency standards and certification related to most of the commonly used appliances. However, there has been little progress so far. As countries like Bangladesh, Bhutan, and Nepal are in early stages of setting energy-efficiency standards, cooperation for harmonization of standards and labeling could prove beneficial and effective at the regional level.

Establishment of a regional organization could help not only in harmonization of energy-efficiency standards and regulations, it could also serve as a regional platform for research and development on energy efficiency and for sharing relevant knowledge and technology data.

There could also be a regional mechanism for funding energy-efficiency investments in the region. Establishment of a regional fund could help bridge the investment gap in the region and also mobilize financial resources by linking itself with global climate funds.

1 Introduction

The South Asian countries of Bangladesh, Bhutan, India, Nepal, and Sri Lanka house over 1.5 billion people, i.e., over 20% of the global population in 2017 (World Bank 2018). However, these countries together accounted for only about 6% of the total primary energy supply in the world in 2016. With growing economy and urbanization, the situation is likely to change; energy consumption per capita has been rising in all five countries and the trend is expected to continue.

The South Asian countries face several energy-related challenges; these are mainly related to provision of universal access to cleaner energy, energy security and sustainability, climate policy commitments, and improvement of environmental quality.

According to the International Energy Agency, 439 million people in Asia, most of them in South Asia, do not have access to electricity. Similarly, 64%–94% of people in South Asian countries lack access to clean cooking services. Universal access to electricity and clean energy services at affordable prices is therefore a key energy policy problem for the governments in these countries.

The economies of the South Asian countries have been growing rapidly in recent years. Associated with the economic growth, the countries are facing rising consumption of energy; during 2000–2015, total energy consumption grew at the rate of 2%–6%. More importantly, dependence of the countries on fossil fuels has been growing; for example, in 2000 the share of fossil fuels in total energy consumption was 59% in Bangladesh and 64% in India. By 2016, the fossil fuel dependence of both countries had reached almost 75%. Even in the less developed economy of Nepal, dependence on fossil fuels increased from 12% to 21% during 2000–2016. The growing dependence on fossil fuels poses a challenge to both national energy security and energy sustainability.

Many urban areas in South Asian countries—especially Bangladesh, India, and Nepal—suffer from severe air pollution, mainly caused by combustion of dirty fuels and inefficient use of other forms of energy. This problem is likely to get worse with the growing use of fossil fuels if corrective measures are not implemented. The use of sustainable energy resources and energy-efficient technologies thus form an integral part of the solution to the air quality problem in South Asian countries.

Following the Paris Agreement on Climate Change in 2015, there is growing international pressure on countries to contribute toward greenhouse gas (GHG) mitigation. In this context, countries in South Asia have declared their commitments for climate change mitigation through various activities as a part of their nationally determined contributions. For example, India has included a target to achieve a 33%–35% reduction in its GHG emission intensity by 2030 compared to the 2005 value, while Nepal has set a target of reducing its dependence on fossil fuels by 50% by 2050. Obviously, the climate policy commitments by the countries imply low-carbon development strategies, which include renewable energy and efficient use of energy as key elements.

Furthermore, most South Asian countries suffer from relatively low efficiency of energy use. To address the aforementioned challenges, it is imperative to identify the energy efficient and climate resilient measures for long-term sustainable energy development in these countries. As most energy supply and utilization technologies involve assets with long lives, early adoption of efficient and low-carbon technologies would also save these countries from costly technological lock-ins for a long period in the future.

This study analyzes different energy resources and technology options to meet the future demand for energy services in different sectors of Bangladesh, Bhutan, India, Nepal, and Sri Lanka. Additionally, it identifies the cost-optimal energy resource and efficient technology options to achieve selected energy reduction targets in these countries during the planning horizon of 2015–2050. The study also reviews energy institutions, energy efficiency and conservation (EEC) policies and programs, as well as possible areas for regional cooperation on energy efficiency.

The study is part of an activity of the Asian Development Bank (ADB) regional technical assistance program for Demonstration of an Assisted Broker Model for Transfer of Low Carbon Technologies to Asia and the Pacific (ADB 2012) in view of the growing importance of EEC for sustainable and low-carbon development.

The study focuses on addressing the following energy-efficiency related questions:

(i)   (a)   What has been the role of changes in sectoral energy intensity, fuel mix, and structural change in production in the growth of the total productive use of energy in the selected South Asian countries?

       (b)   What has been the contribution of power generation efficiency as well as transmission and distribution losses in the growth of energy use for power generation in the countries?

(ii)   (a)   Are there cost-saving energy-efficient technology options (or no-regret technology options) that are not presently in use due to various non-cost barriers?

       (b)   What are the energy efficiency gaps (EEGs) between the no-regret options and the less efficient technologies presently in use?

       (c)   What is the energy saving potential (ESP) of the no-regret efficient technology options in different sectors?

(iii) How big is the potential for reducing energy consumption in the entire economy during 2015–2050 as compared to energy use in the business as usual (BAU) scenario?

(iv)   (a)   Which sectors need to be targeted if the countries are to achieve certain targets for energy reduction from the BAU level?

       (b)   What types of energy-efficient technologies and fuel-switching strategies should be adopted to achieve the energy reduction targets?

(v)   What types of regulatory frameworks, policies, and programs are there in the South Asian countries to promote EEC?

(vi)   What are the possible areas for regional cooperation among the South Asian countries to improve energy efficiency and promote energy conservation?

A factor decomposition model has been developed and used to analyze the issue raised in Question (i) for each of the five South Asian countries under this study. A long-term national energy system model (i.e., AIM/ Enduse model) was used in the case of Bangladesh, Bhutan, Nepal, and Sri Lanka to analyze the issues raised by Questions (ii), (iii), and (iv). In the case of India, these issues are addressed through a review of the relevant available literature primarily because a relatively large number of energy studies already exist for the country.

The study mainly used secondary data from national and international sources for energy modeling. Also, discussions were held on data availability as well as energy-efficiency related policies and programs with key experts in relevant organizations and other stakeholders during the country visits.

Chapter 2 presents an overview of the energy situation in the five South Asian countries under the study.

Chapter 3 presents the results of factor decomposition analyses and highlights the role of energy intensity and other factors in the growth of total energy consumption by productive sectors during a recent period. It also discusses the role of energy efficiency in the growth of total energy consumption for power generation (ECPG) in the countries.

Chapter 4 discusses the no-regret energy efficient technologies and EEGs associated with technologies presently in use relative to the no-regret technologies. It also presents the ESP in the countries due to no-regret technologies. Furthermore, the chapter discusses energy development under the BAU and reference scenarios during 2015–2050.

In Chapter 5, the implications of setting targets for reduction of overall energy consumption during 2015–2050 in Bangladesh, Bhutan, Nepal, and Sri Lanka are discussed. It also includes a review of available relevant literature in the case of India.

A review of institutions involved directly or indirectly in EEC in each of the countries is presented in Chapter 6.

Chapter 7 briefly reviews the regulatory frameworks, policies, as well as major programs and initiatives related to EEC in the five countries.

In Chapter 8, possible areas for regional cooperation on promotion of energy efficiency are briefly highlighted. It also gives a brief description of existing agreements and mechanisms in the South Asian countries for regional cooperation in the energy sector.

2 Review of the Energy Situation and Energy Efficiency in South Asian Countries

This chapter discusses the evolution of the energy sector during 2000–2016 for countries in South Asia except Bhutan, for which the coverage is for the period of 2005–2014 due to data constraints. It also discusses the changes in energy intensity at the aggregate national and sectoral levels. At the national level, energy intensity is defined as energy consumption per unit of gross domestic product (GDP); and at sectoral level, it is energy consumption per unit of value added. Moreover, it discusses energy efficiencies of power generation, transmission and distribution, gas distribution, and the oil sector in the countries.

2.1 Status of the Energy Situation

Primary Energy Supply Side

Figure 2.1 shows the increase in total primary energy supply (TPES) and energy mix of TPES in Bangladesh, India, Nepal, and Sri Lanka during 2000–2016. In 2000, biomass was the major source of energy in all countries under this study. The TPES of Bangladesh more than doubled during the period and increased by around 96% in India, 58% in Nepal, and 41% in Sri Lanka.

Also, the combined share of fossil fuels in TPES increased in all countries during the period. In 2000, fossil fuels had the share of 59% in Bangladesh and 64% in India; by 2016 this increased to almost 75% in both countries. In Sri Lanka, the share increased from 43% in 2000 to 57% in 2016. Among the five countries, Nepal had the lowest share of fossil fuels in TPES (i.e., 12% in 2000 and 21% in 2016). For Bhutan, fossil fuel share in TPES increased from 25% in 2005 to 36% in 2014.

Figure 2.1 indicates that the four countries had reduced their relative dependence on biomass energy because its share in TPES decreased during 2000–2016; there was a similar case in Bhutan during 2005–2014 (Figure 2.2). Consumption of coal increased more rapidly than that of oil and gas during 2000–2016 in India; this was also the case in Bangladesh, Bhutan, and Sri Lanka although their share of coal in TPES was relatively small. In the case of Nepal, consumption of oil grew more rapidly than that of other fossil fuels. The main source of energy supply was natural gas in Bangladesh, coal in India, and biomass in Bhutan, Nepal, and Sri Lanka. Biomass played the predominant role in Nepal, accounting for about 75% of TPES in 2016, 36% for Bhutan in 2014, and 40% for Sri Lanka in 2016.

Figure 2.1: Total Primary Energy Consumption Based on Fuel Types, 2000–2016

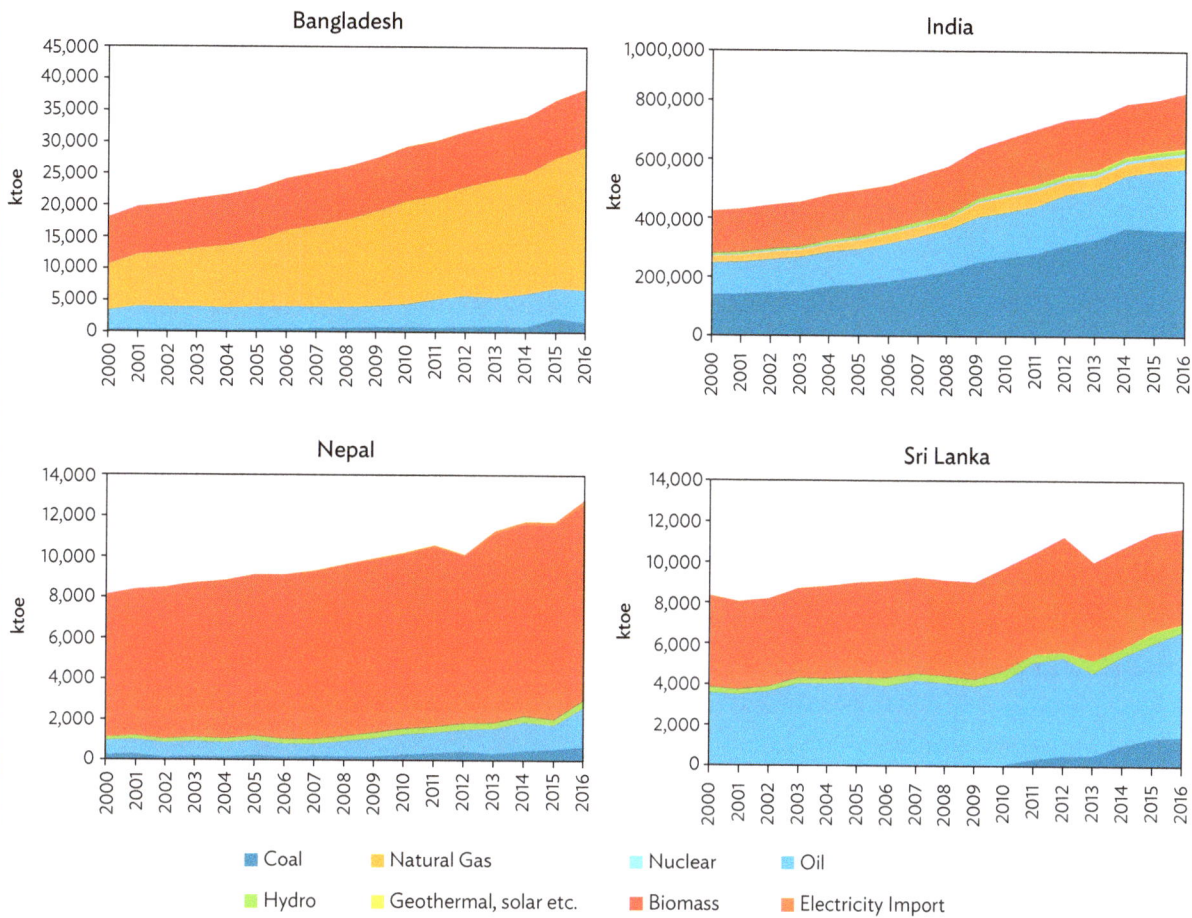

Bangladesh, India, Nepal, Sri Lanka

Legend: Coal, Natural Gas, Nuclear, Oil, Hydro, Geothermal, solar etc., Biomass, Electricity Import

ktoe = kiloton of oil equivalent.

Note: Biomass comprises liquid biofuels, solid biofuels, biogas, municipal waste, and industrial waste.

Source: International Energy Agency (IEA). 2018. IEA Online Database. Paris. https://www.iea.org/data-and-statistics/data-tables? (accessed 18 August 2019).

Figure 2.2: Total Primary Energy Consumption by Fuel Type for Bhutan, 2005 and 2014

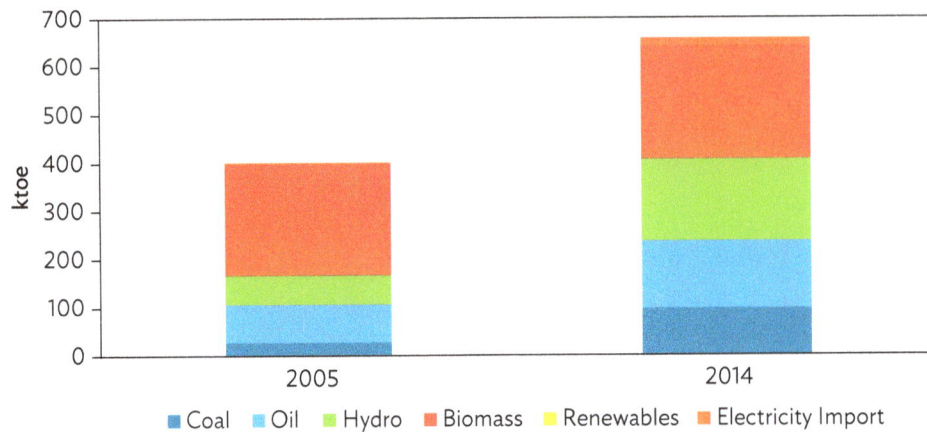

ktoe = kiloton of oil equivalent.

Sources: Government of Bhutan, Department of Energy. 2007. Bhutan Energy Data Directory 2005. Thimphu; and Government of Bhutan, Department of Renewable Energy. 2016. Bhutan Energy Data Directory 2015. Thimphu. https://www.moea.gov.bt/wp-content/uploads/2018/07/Bhutan-Energy-Data-Directory-2015.pdf.

Structure of Power Generation

Figure 2.3 shows the change in the structure of electricity generation in Bangladesh, India, Nepal, and Sri Lanka during 2000–2016. Hydropower was the major source for electricity generation in Bhutan and Nepal, accounting for almost 100% of total generation in 2014 and 99% in 2016. Natural gas was the dominant source of electricity generation in Bangladesh; its share in total power generation decreased from 89%[1] in 2000 to 82% in 2016. Coal's share in electricity generation in India rose from 69% in 2000 to 77% by 2016. The coal share in electricity generation also increased from 0% to 2% in Bangladesh and 0% to 36% in Sri Lanka during 2000–2016. The oil share in electricity generation decreased in India and Sri Lanka during the period but increased in Bangladesh. The share of natural gas in electricity generation decreased in Bangladesh and India. Share of net electricity import in total domestic electricity supply of Nepal rose from 9% to 35% during the period (Nepal Electricity Authority [NEA] 2001 and 2017).

Final Demand for Energy in South Asian Countries

Table 2.1 presents the compound annual growth rate (CAGR) of total final energy consumption (TFEC) in individual sectors of Bangladesh, India, Nepal, and Sri Lanka during 2000–2016. The industry sector had the highest growth of energy consumption in Bangladesh and Bhutan during the period. For India and Nepal, the transport sector recorded the highest CAGR during 2000–2016; and in Sri Lanka, CAGR was highest in the commercial sector.

---

[1]   According to the annual report of the Bangladesh Power Development Board (BPDB) for 2015–2016, the share of natural gas in total power generation was 69% in 2016. However, due to lack of complete BPDB time series data from 2000 to 2007, IEA data has been used hereafter.

Figure 2.3: Electricity Generation Mix, 2000–2016

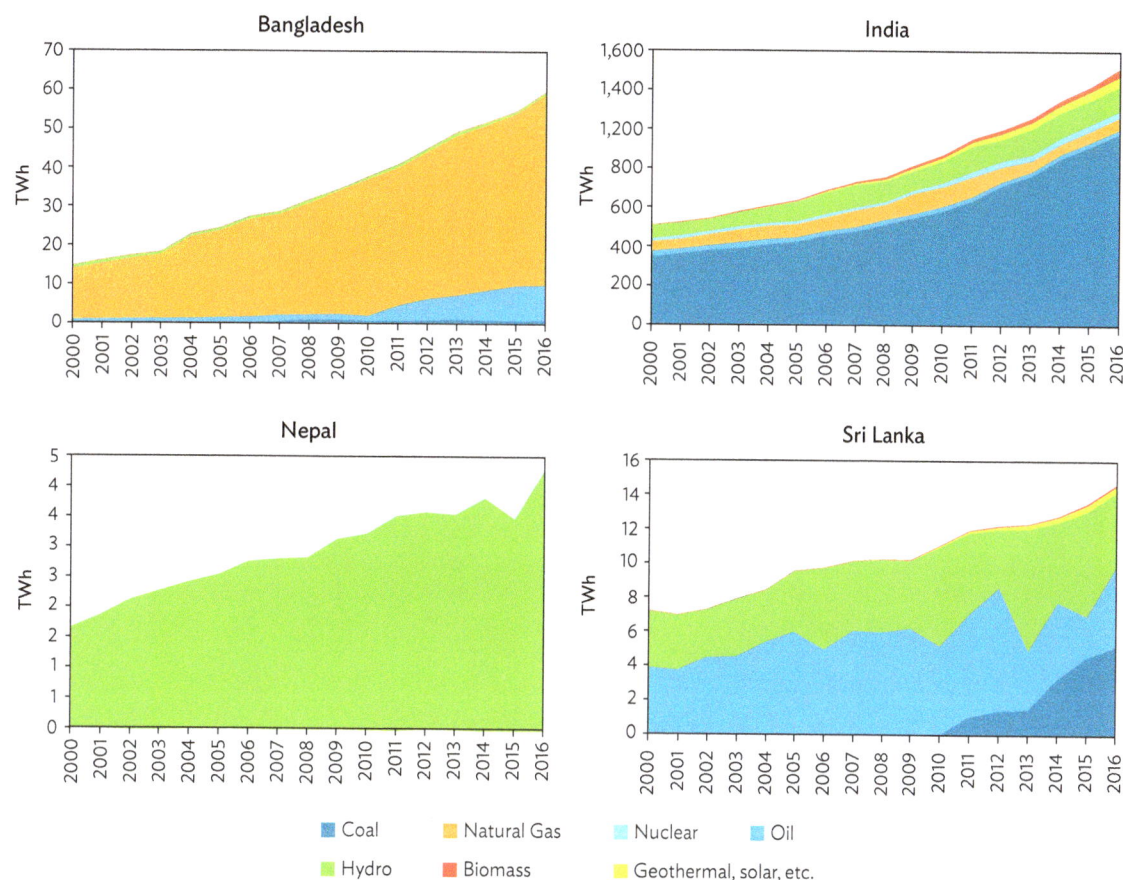

Bangladesh

India

Nepal

Sri Lanka

■ Coal   ■ Natural Gas   ■ Nuclear   ■ Oil

■ Hydro   ■ Biomass   ■ Geothermal, solar, etc.

TWh = terawatt-hour.

Source: International Energy Agency (IEA). 2018. IEA Online Database. Paris. https://www.iea.org/data-and-statistics/data-tables? (accessed 18 August 2019).

Table 2.1: Sector-Wise CAGR of Energy Consumption, 2000–2016
(%)

	Bangladesh	Bhutan[a]	India	Nepal	Sri Lanka
Industry	9.38	10.57	5.37	5.66	2.71
Transport	8.08	8.95	6.69	10.21	3.88
Residential	2.82	1.23	1.47	2.03	0.19
Commercial	6.93	3.97	5.50	7.20	4.29
Agricultural	5.58	9.93	3.56	7.20	—[b]
TFEC	4.09	5.77	3.82	2.88	1.80

CAGR = compound annual growth rate; TFEC = total final energy consumption.

[a] During 2005–2014.

[b] The agriculture sector shows no consumption in 2016.

Sources: International Energy Agency (IEA). 2018. IEA Online Database. Paris. https://www.iea.org/data-and-statistics/data-tables? (accessed 18 August 2019); Government of Bhutan, Department of Energy. 2007. Bhutan Energy Data Directory 2005. Thimphu; and Government of Bhutan, Department of Renewable Energy. 2016. Bhutan Energy Data Directory 2015. Thimphu. https://www.moea.gov.bt/wp-content/uploads/2018/07/Bhutan-Energy-Data-Directory-2015.pdf.

Figure 2.4 shows the growth of TFEC and contributions of different sectors to TFEC during 2000–2016 in Bangladesh, India, Nepal, and Sri Lanka; Figure 2.5 shows the same for Bhutan in 2005 and 2014. The residential sector accounted for the highest share in TFEC in Bangladesh, Nepal, and Sri Lanka, followed by the industry sector. In the case of Bhutan and India, the industry sector had the highest share in TFEC followed by the residential sector. The share of the transport sector was about 30% in Sri Lanka but was below 20% in other countries.

Figure 2.4: Sector-Wise Total Final Energy Consumption, 2000–2016

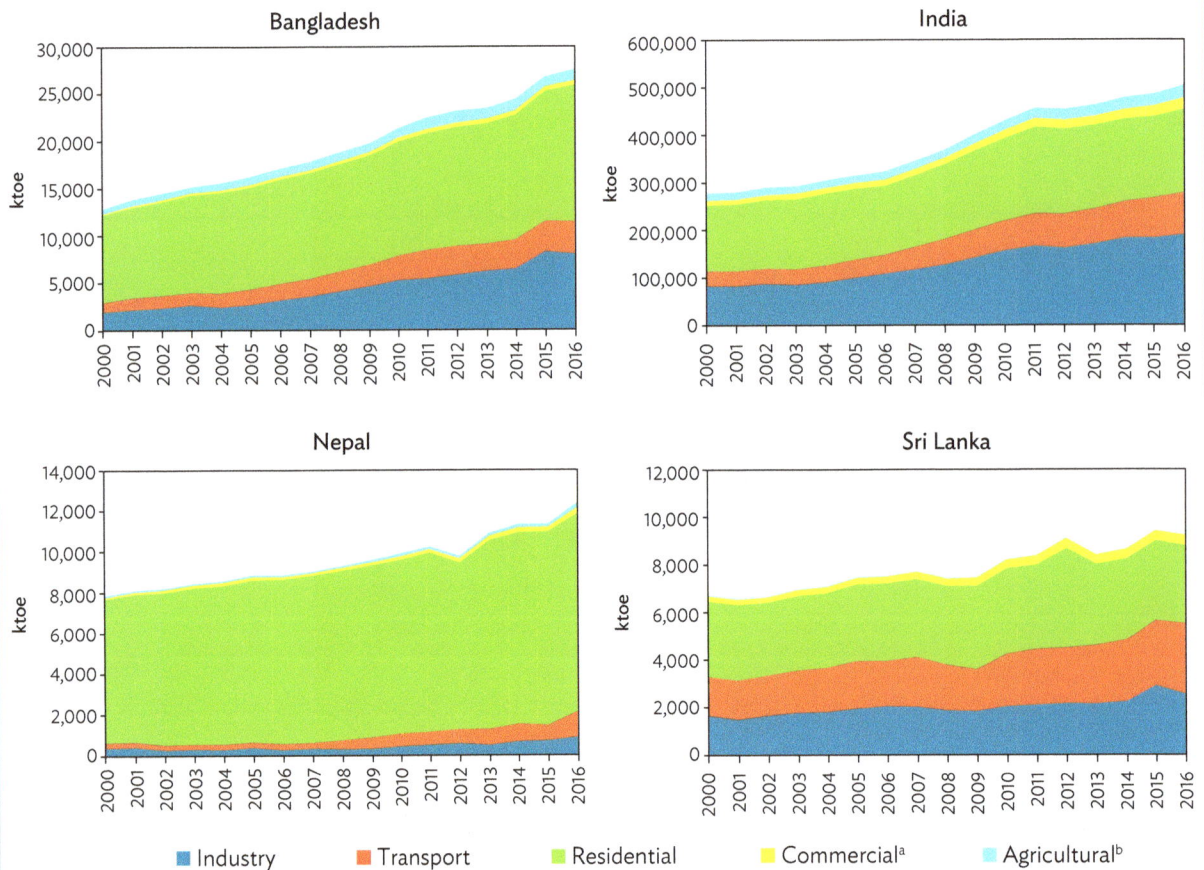

ktoe = kiloton of oil equivalent.

[a] Commercial comprises public services and commercial.

[b] Agriculture includes forestry and fishing.

Source: International Energy Agency (IEA). 2018. IEA Online Database. Paris. https://www.iea.org/data-and-statistics/data-tables? (accessed 18 August 2019).

Figure 2.5: Sector-Wise Total Final Energy Consumption for Bhutan, 2005 and 2014

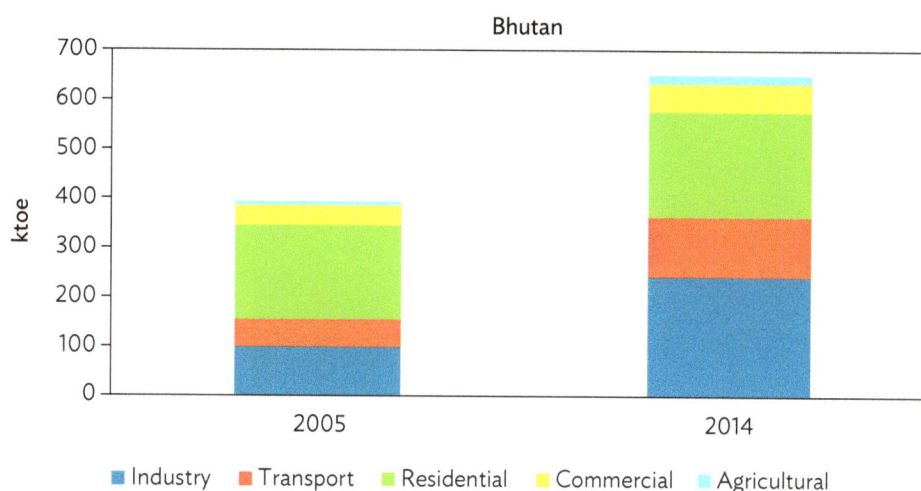

ktoe = kiloton of oil equivalent.

Sources: Government of Bhutan, Department of Energy. 2007. Bhutan Energy Data Directory 2005. Thimphu; and Government of Bhutan, Department of Renewable Energy. 2016. Bhutan Energy Data Directory 2015. Thimphu. https://www.moea.gov.bt/wp-content/uploads/2018/07/Bhutan-Energy-Data-Directory-2015.pdf.

At the sectoral level, the structure of energy use in the countries changed over time. Table 2.2 shows the fuel mix of sectoral energy consumption in the different countries in 2000 and 2016. The share of electricity grew while that of biomass declined in every sector in all countries (except the commercial sector of Bhutan) during 2000–2016. The share of oil decreased in all sectors except transport by 2016. There was growing use of coal in the industry sector of all countries. In India, the share of fuel use in the residential and commercial sectors decreased. Natural gas use grew in the energy mix of the transport and residential sectors of Bangladesh and continued to dominate its industry sector.

2.2 Energy Intensity

Figure 2.6 shows overall energy intensity (defined as energy consumption per national GDP) and expressed in kgoe/1000 $ 2011 PPP GDP (defined as kilogram of oil equivalent per $1,000 GDP at purchasing power parity at constant 2011 $) of five selected countries in South Asia along with that of the world and the Organisation for Economic Co-operation and Development (OECD) as a group during 2000–2016. There was a large variation in energy intensity across the countries with the lowest in Sri Lanka and highest in Bhutan. The high energy intensity in the case of Bhutan and Nepal was mainly due to their heavy reliance on biomass energy. Overall, as for the OECD, the energy intensity showed a decreasing trend in all the countries.

Table 2.2: Sector-Wise Energy Mix, 2000 and 2016
(%)

	Sectors	Coal 2000	Coal 2016	Oil 2000	Oil 2016	Natural Gas 2000	Natural Gas 2016	Biomass 2000	Biomass 2016	Electricity 2000	Electricity 2016
Bangladesh	Industry	17	18	9	3	49	47	—	—	25	32
	Transport	—	—	100	68	—	32	—	—	—	—
	Residential	—	—	6	2	8	23	81	64	5	11
	Commercial	—	—	—	—	49	42	—	—	51	58
	Agriculture	—	—	91	86	3	2	—	—	6	12
Bhutan[a]	Industry	28	40	5	1	—	—	31	2	36	57
	Transport	—	—	100	100	—	—	—	—	—	—
	Residential	—	—	5	5	—	—	91	86	4	9
	Commercial	—	—	15	5	—	—	59	78	25	16
	Agriculture	—	—	25	6	—	—	56	—	19	94
India	Industry	31	46	20	15	2	4	31	16	16	19
	Transport	—	—	98	95	—	3	—	1	2	2
	Residential	2	1	13	15	—	—	80	70	5	14
	Commercial	25	18	—	9	—	3	53	29	22	41
	Agriculture	—	—	52	37	1	1	—	—	47	62
Nepal	Industry	68	75	8	2	—	—	12	7	12	16
	Transport	—	—	100	100	—	—	—	—	—	—
	Residential	—	—	3	2	—	—	96	96	1	2
	Commercial	—	—	52	62	—	—	40	20	8	18
	Agriculture	—	—	97	96	—	—	—	—	3	4
Sri Lanka	Industry	—	2	15	17	—	—	74	67	11	14
	Transport	—	—	100	100	—	—	—	—	—	—
	Residential	—	—	3	7	—	—	93	80	4	13
	Commercial	—	—	15	13	—	—	51	25	34	62
	Agriculture	—	—	100	—	—	—	—	—	—	—

— = zero or negligible value.

[a] In the case of Bhutan, the figures are given for 2005 and 2014.

Sources: International Energy Agency (IEA). 2018. IEA Online Database. Paris. https://www.iea.org/data-and-statistics/data-tables? (accessed 18 August 2019); Government of Bhutan, Department of Energy. 2007. Bhutan Energy Data Directory 2005. Thimphu; and Government of Bhutan, Department of Renewable Energy. 2016. Bhutan Energy Data Directory 2015. Thimphu. https://www.moea.gov.bt/wp-content/uploads/2018/07/Bhutan-Energy-Data-Directory-2015.pdf.

Figure 2.6: Overall Energy Intensity Change, 2000–2016

Energy intensity change

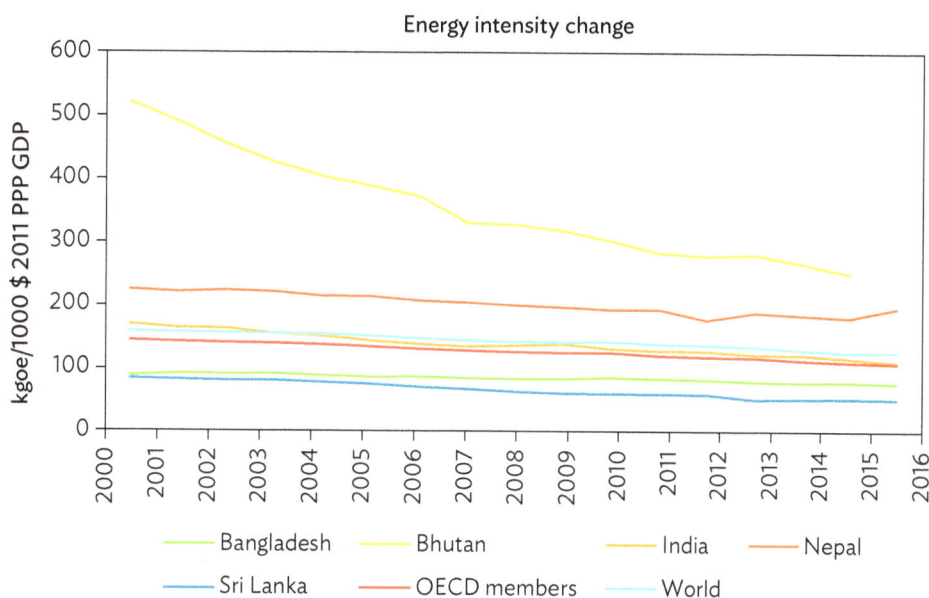

GDP = gross domestic product; kgoe = kilogram of oil equivalent; OECD = Organisation of Economic Co-operation and Development; PPP = purchasing power parity.

Source: World Bank. World Bank Database. https://data.worldbank.org/ (accessed 3 September 2019).

The energy intensities of the industry, transport, commercial, and agriculture sectors in Bangladesh, India, Nepal, and Sri Lanka during 2000–2016 are shown in Figure 2.7. The energy intensities of all sectors except commercial increased in Bangladesh and Nepal. The energy intensities fell in almost all sectors in Sri Lanka. In India, energy intensity fell in all sectors except agriculture. The sectoral energy intensities of Bhutan during 2005–2014 increased in all sectors except commercial (Figure 2.8).

Figure 2.7: Sectoral Energy Intensities, 2000–2016

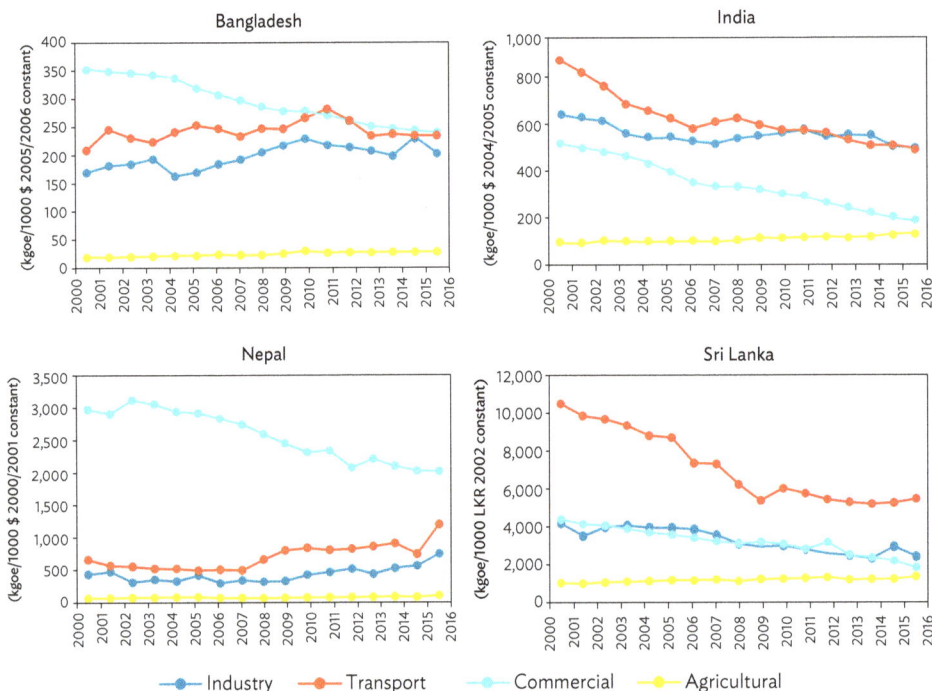

kgoe = kilogram of oil equivalent; LKR = Sri Lanka rupee.

Sources: Asian Development Bank. 2018. Key Indicators for Asia and the Pacific 2017. Manila. https://www.adb.org/publications/key-indicators-asia-and-pacific-2017; and International Energy Agency (IEA). 2018. IEA Online Database. Paris. https://www.iea.org/data-and-statistics/data-tables? (accessed 18 August 2019).

Figure 2.8: Sectoral Energy Intensity Change for Bhutan, 2005 and 2014

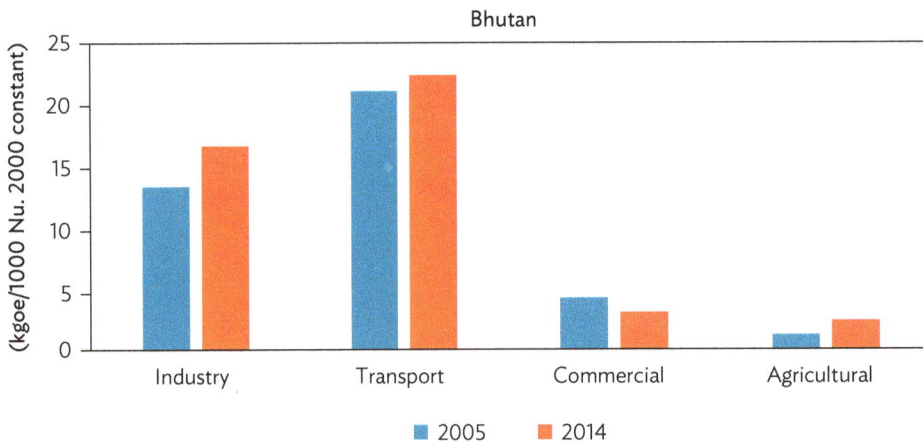

kgoe = kilogram of oil equivalent; Nu. = ngultrum.

Sources: Asian Development Bank. 2018. Key Indicators for Asia and the Pacific 2017. Manila. https://www.adb.org/publications/key-indicators-asia-and-pacific-2017; Government of Bhutan, Department of Energy. 2007. Bhutan Energy Data Directory 2005. Thimphu; and Government of Bhutan, Department of Renewable Energy. 2016. Bhutan Energy Data Directory 2015. Thimphu. https://www.moea.gov.bt/wp-content/uploads/2018/07/Bhutan-Energy-Data-Directory-2015.pdf.

2.3 Efficiency in the Power Sector

Efficiency of Power Generation

Table 2.3 shows the efficiency of power plants using fossil fuel in the studied countries (except Bhutan) along with that of the OECD as a group and developing Asia (i.e., all developing countries in Asia except the People's Republic of China) in 2000 and 2016. Efficiency improved for coal-fired power generation in all countries where such generation occurred. The efficiency of coal-fired power plants in the South Asian countries was comparable to that in developing Asia; however, it was still much below the efficiency in the OECD as a whole. The efficiency of oil-fired power generation increased over time in Bangladesh and Sri Lanka, but decreased in India—efficiency in the South Asian countries was lower than that in the OECD as a whole. The efficiency of gas-fired power generation, which is limited to Bangladesh and India, exhibited some decline by 2016 and was relatively low in both countries compared to the OECD figure. In the case of Bangladesh, efficiency was also lower than that of developing Asia.

Efficiency of Transmission and Distribution

Transmission and distribution (T&D) of electricity is also an integral part of the power sector. Table 2.4 shows the T&D loss of South Asian countries along with that of the OECD as a group and developing Asia. The T&D loss had a decreasing trend (i.e., improving T&D efficiency) during 2000–2018 in all countries. Except for Bhutan, the losses were higher than in the OECD. The T&D loss in India and Nepal was also higher than that in developing Asia. This indicates potential to improve T&D efficiency in these countries.

Efficiency of Oil Refining and Gas Supply

Among the South Asian countries, natural gas is produced and used in Bangladesh and India. In the case of Bangladesh, the loss in gas supply decreased from 3% in 2000 to 2% in 2016 (International Energy Agency [IEA] 2018a). Losses in the gas sector are generally associated with loss in gas transportation.

Among the studied countries, only Bangladesh, India, and Sri Lanka have oil refineries. Refinery loss increased from 5% in 2000 to 8% in 2016 in Bangladesh (IEA 2018a), from 6% in 2000 (Government of India, Central Statistics Office [CSO] 2012) to 9% in 2016 in India (CSO 2018), and from 1% in 2000 to 5% in 2016 in Sri Lanka (IEA 2018a).

Table 2.3: Power Generation Efficiency in Years 2000 and 2016 in South Asian Countries, Except Bhutan
(%)

Fuel Type	Bangladesh		India		Nepal		Sri Lanka		OECD		Developing Asia[a]	
	2000	2016	2000	2016	2000	2016	2000	2016	2000	2016	2000	2016
Coal	NA	35	33	37	NA	NA	NA	31	40	42	35	37
Oil	25	38[b]	28	25	39	—	33	40	36	48	35	35
Natural Gas	37	34	52	43	NA	NA	NA	NA	58	61	41	44

NA = not applicable, OECD = Organisation for Economic Co-operation and Development.

[a] All developing countries in Asia except the People's Republic of China.

[b] Bangladesh Power Development Board. 2017. Annual Report 2016–2017. Dhaka. http://www.bpdb.gov.bd/download/annual_report/Annual%20Report%202016-17%20(2).pdf.

Source: International Energy Agency (IEA). 2018a. IEA Online Database. Paris. https://www.iea.org/data-and-statistics/data-tables? (accessed 18 August 2019).

Table 2.4: Transmission and Distribution Loss in South Asian Countries, OECD, and Developing Asia
(%)

Country	2000	2016	2018
Bangladesh[a]	15	12	12
Bhutan[b]	15[c]	4	6
India[d]	27	18	17[e]
Nepal[f]	24	26	15
Sri Lanka[g]	21	10	9[e]
OECD countries[d]	6	6	6[e]
Developing Asia[d,h]	18	13	12[e]

OECD = Organisation for Economic Co-operation and Development.

[a] Bangladesh Power Development Board. 2019. Annual Report 2018-19. Dhaka. https://www.bpdb.gov.bd/bpdb_new/resourcefile/annualreports/annualreport_1574325376_Annual_Report_2018-19.pdf.

[b] Government of Bhutan, Department of Energy (DoE). 2007. Bhutan Energy Data Directory 2005. Thimphu. BPC. 2017. Annual Report. Bhutan Power Company Limited (BPC). Thimphu. https://www.bpc.bt/wp-content/uploads/2018/06/Final-BPC-Report-2017.pdf; Bhutan Power Company Limited. 2018. Meeting Bhutan's Electricity Needs. Thimphu. https://www.bpc.bt/wp-content/themes/2020/assets/downloads/BPC-Annual-Report-2018.pdf?

[c] 2005 figure.

[d] International Energy Agency (IEA). 2018a. IEA Online Database. Paris. https://www.iea.org/data-and-statistics/data-tables? (accessed 18 August 2019).

[e] 2017 figure.

[f] Nepal Electricity Authority (NEA). 2001. Annual Report FY 2000/2001: A Year in Review. Kathmandu. http://www.nea.org.np/admin/assets/uploads/supportive_docs/Nepal%20Electricity-compressed.pdf; NEA. 2019. A Year in Review: Fiscal Year 2018/2019. Kathmandu: Nepal Electricity Authority (NEA). http://www.nea.org.np/admin/assets/uploads/supportive_docs/90599295.pdf.

[g] Government of Sri Lanka, Ministry of Power and Energy. 2017. Performance 2017 and Programmes for 2018. Sri Lanka. http://powermin.gov.lk/english/wp-content/uploads/2017/10/MoPRE-2017.2018-03-English.pdf.

[h] All developing countries in Asia except the People's Republic of China.

Source: Compiled by the authors.

3 Growth in Energy Consumption: What Role Have Energy Efficiency and Other Factors Played?

This chapter discusses the growth in the total productive use of energy (TPUE) in South Asian countries during 2000–2016. The growth of TPUE (i.e., the total use of energy by all production sectors) can depend on several factors including the level and structure of production, sectoral energy intensities (defined as energy consumption per unit of value added by the sector), as well as energy mix in the sectors. More importantly, the chapter assesses the roles of energy intensities as well as growth in gross domestic product (GDP), structural change, and energy mix behind the growth in total TPUE in South Asian countries during 2000–2016. Furthermore, it examines the role of energy efficiency, energy mix, and demand for electricity behind the growth of total energy consumption for power generation (ECPG) in these countries. Due to non-availability of disaggregated data on energy use in different types of industries, detailed analyses of factors specifically behind the growth of energy consumption in the industry sector could not be carried out. For a similar reason, assessment of the role of energy intensities and other factors in the growth of energy consumption specific to the transport sector was also not carried out.

The methodological framework for analyzing the role of the key factors (or drivers) behind the growth of TPUE has been discussed in Section 2 of the chapter; that section also discussed the framework to analyze the role of the factors behind the growth in energy use in power generation and transport sectors. This is followed by a discussion on the changes in the key drivers of TPUE in 2000 and 2016 in Section 3. Section 4 presents an assessment of the contributions of different factors behind the growth of TPUE during 2000–2016, and Section 5 discusses the role of different factors behind the increase in ECPG. The contributions of key drivers behind transport sector energy consumption during 2000–2016 are discussed in Section 6. The final section presents a summary of the major findings.

3.1 Methodological Frameworks

Framework for Assessing the Contributions of Energy Intensity and Other Factors Behind the Productive Use of Energy

A factor decomposition model is used for analyzing the factors behind changes in total productive use of energy (TPUE). TPUE is defined as the sum of energy used by different production sectors of an economy. In this study, the following five productive sectors of an economy are considered:

- Industry sector
- Transportation and communication sector (hereafter transport sector)
- Commercial and public services sector (hereafter commercial sector)
- Power sector
- Agriculture, forestry, fishing, and other nonspecified sectors (hereafter agriculture sector)

The total use of energy in the productive sectors of economy (E) can be expressed in terms of the following identity:

$$E = \sum_{j} \sum_{i} \begin{pmatrix} \text{Total} \\ \text{production} \\ \text{or GDP} \end{pmatrix} \times \begin{pmatrix} \text{Share of} \\ \text{sector } j \\ \text{in GDP} \end{pmatrix} \times \begin{pmatrix} \text{Energy} \\ \text{intensity of} \\ \text{sector } j \end{pmatrix} \times \begin{pmatrix} \text{Consumption} \\ \text{of fuel type } i \\ \text{in sector } j \end{pmatrix} \quad (3.1)$$

where,

j = Index for a productive sector

i = Index for a fuel type

Note that the right-hand side of Equation 3.1 consists of the four different factors (or drivers) that affect the level of TPUE in an economy: total production or productive activity level (measured by GDP), structure of production (measured by the shares of different production sectors in GDP), energy intensity of individual production sectors, and fuel mix (or energy mix) in each production sector. Hereafter, the contribution of the total production or activity level to a change in TPUE is called the "activity effect." Similarly, a change in TPUE due to a change in the structure of GDP is the "structural change effect" (or simply "structural effect") and the contribution of a change in the sectoral energy intensities to the change in TPUE is the "energy intensity effect." Likewise, the contribution of changes in the fuel mix of the production sectors in TPUE is the "fuel mix effect."

A factor decomposition model has been used to assess the contributions of different factors affecting the growth of the total energy use in the productive sectors. A detailed description of the model is presented in Appendix 1.

Framework for Assessing the Contributions of Factors Behind Growth of Energy Consumption in the Power Generation Sector

In the power generation sector, the level of energy consumption depends on the level of electricity demand, efficiency of electricity generation, efficiency of transmission and distribution (T&D), and structure of power generation or "generation mix" (i.e., shares of different power generation options in total electricity generation). Hereafter, the contribution of an increase in electricity demand to growth in ECPG is termed the "electricity demand effect," and the contributions of changes in the efficiencies of power generation and T&D are the "Electricity generation efficiency effect" and "T&D efficiency effect," respectively. Similarly, the contribution of changes in the generation mix to the change in ECPG is termed the "generation mix effect." A factor decomposition model has been used to assess the different factors behind the growth in ECPG during 2000–2016 in the South Asian countries. The model details are presented in Appendix 2.

3.2 Key Drivers Behind the Productive Use of Energy: Changes During 2000–2016

The level of economic activity within a country (measured by GDP), structure of GDP, sectoral energy intensities, and energy mix of different sectors are the key drivers behind the growth of TPUE during a period. The larger the economic activity, the higher would be the expected TPUE if other things remain the same, such as the structure of the economy (or production), sectoral energy intensities, and energy mix. If the structure of production changes over time such that the shares in GDP of more energy-intensive sectors (e.g., manufacturing) increase and the shares of less energy-intensive sectors decline, this would result in a higher TPUE. If the sectoral energy intensities increase over time, the total TPUE would also increase if other things remain the same; the opposite would happen if sectoral energy intensities decrease. Similarly, all other things remaining the same, a change in the energy mix could result in a change in total TPUE. Changes in each of these key drivers from 2000 to 2016 are discussed next in this section.

Level of Productive Activity

The level of national productive activity is normally measured by the GDP of a country. The growth in GDP in the South Asian countries during 2000–2016 (except for Bhutan for which GDP figures correspond to 2005 and 2014) is presented in Table 3.1. Among these countries, GDP growth was highest in India and lowest in Nepal; GDP in 2016 was 3.1 times that in 2000 in India while it was 1.8 times in Nepal.

Table 3.1: Gross Domestic Product of South Asian Countries, 2000 and 2016

S.N.	Country	Currency Unit	GDP 2000	GDP 2016	Ratio GDP2016/ GDP2000
1	Bangladesh	billion $ (2005/2006 prices)	54	136	2.53
2	Bhutan	billion $ (2000 prices)	0.6[a]	1.2[b]	1.93
3	India	billion $ (2004/2005 prices)	551	1,718	3.12
4	Nepal	billion $ (2000/2001 prices)	6	11	1.83
5	Sri Lanka	billion $ (2002 prices)	17	41	2.45

GDP = gross domestic product.
[a] 2005 figure.
[b] 2014 figure.
Source: Asian Development Bank. 2018. *Key Indicators for Asia and the Pacific 2017*. Manila. https://www.adb.org/publications/key-indicators-asia-and-pacific-2017.

Structure of Production

Table 3.2 shows the changes in the structure of production in South Asian countries between 2000 and 2016. In Bangladesh, the commercial sector (which is relatively less energy intensive) accounted for the largest share (over 44%) in the GDP. Shares in GDP of energy-intensive sectors like industry and transport increased during 2000–2016, whereas shares of the commercial and agriculture sectors declined. The commercial sector was also the largest production sector in Bhutan, accounting for about one-third of GDP. The shares of all sectors except agriculture increased during 2000–2016. In India, the share in GDP of the commercial sector increased from 48% in 2000 to 55% by 2016. The transport sector also showed an increment in its share of GDP, whereas shares of other sectors (most significantly agriculture) declined during this period. In Nepal, the commercial sector accounted for over 45% of GDP and its share increased during 2000–2016. Agriculture contributed about one-third of GDP in 2000; however, its share declined. The transport sector share in GDP increased while that of industry fell during the period. In Sri Lanka, the commercial and industry sectors were the largest and second largest contributors to GDP. The shares of commercial, industry, and transport grew, whereas that of agriculture declined.

Table 3.2: Structure of Gross Domestic Product in South Asian Countries
(%)

S.N.	Country	Year	Industry	Transport	Commercial	Agriculture	Power
1	Bangladesh	2000	21	9	48	21	1
		2016	29	11	44	15	1
2	Bhutan	2000	26	9	33	21	11
		2016	27	10	34	12	17
3	India	2000	23	7	48	20	2
		2016	22	10	55	11	2
4	Nepal	2000	15	7	41	35	2
		2016	12	10	45	31	2
5	Sri Lanka	2000	27	10	46	15	2
		2016	30	15	52	10	3

Source: Asian Development Bank. 2018. *Key Indicators for Asia and the Pacific 2017*. Manila. https://www.adb.org/publications/key-indicators-asia-and-pacific-2017.

Sectoral Energy Intensities

Table 3.3 presents the energy intensity of different sectors in South Asian countries (defined as energy consumption per monetary unit of the sectoral value added at constant prices) in 2000 and 2016. The energy intensities of the industry and transport sectors increased in Bangladesh, Bhutan, and Nepal during the period but fell in India and Sri Lanka. The commercial sector became less energy intensive in Bhutan, India, and Sri Lanka, while the opposite happened in Bangladesh and Nepal.

Table 3.3: Sectoral Energy Intensities in South Asian Countries

S.N.	Country	Unit	Year	Industry	Transport	Commercial	Agriculture	Power
1	Bangladesh	kgoe/$1,000[a]	2000	210	207	7	45	4,215
			2016	216	233	9	59	4,926
2	Bhutan	kgoe/$1,000[b]	2005	588	941	188	56	145
			2014	743	998	148	104	14
3	India	kgoe/$1,000[c]	2000	854	901	40	188	8,526
			2016	661	508	25	230	7,915
4	Nepal	kgoe/$1,000[d]	2000	446	648	40	41	469
			2016	765	1,192	60	72	635
5	Sri Lanka	kgoe/$1,000[e]	2000	412	1,046	31	120	2,075
			2016	250	541	25	38	1,543

kgoe = kilogram of oil equivalent.
[a] 2005–2006 prices.
[b] 2000 prices.
[c] 2004–2005 prices.
[d] 2000–2001 prices.
[e] 2002 prices.

Sources: Asian Development Bank. 2018. *Key Indicators for Asia and the Pacific 2017*. Manila. https://www.adb.org/publications/key-indicators-asia-and-pacific-2017; International Energy Agency (IEA). 2018. IEA Online Database. Paris. https://www.iea.org/data-and-statistics/data-tables? (accessed 18 August 2019); Government of Bhutan, Department of Energy (DoE). 2007. Bhutan Energy Data Directory 2005. Thimphu; and Government of Bhutan, Department of Renewable Energy (DoRE). 2016. Bhutan Energy Data Directory 2015. Thimphu. https://www.moea.gov.bt/wp-content/uploads/2018/07/Bhutan-Energy-Data-Directory-2015.pdf.

Energy Mix at the Sectoral Level

Table 3.4 shows the energy mix of industry, transport, commercial, and agriculture sectors of South Asian countries in 2000 and 2016, and Table 3.5 presents the mix of different types of energy used for power generation. There have been significant changes in the energy mix at the sectoral level for several countries, the most noticeable being the increased share of electricity and coal in total energy consumption of the industry sector during 2000–2016. The role of oil in the industry sector decreased in all countries except Sri Lanka, and the role of biomass energy diminished. Natural gas was the most important source of energy in industry in Bangladesh, while it was electricity in Bhutan, coal in India and Nepal, and biofuel and waste in Sri Lanka. The transport sector was almost entirely dependent on oil in Bhutan, Nepal, and Sri Lanka, but decreased over time in Bangladesh (owing to a growing shift to gas) and India (some shift to gas and electricity). There were also significant variations in the energy mix of the commercial sector across the countries. Electricity use in the commercial sector grew in all countries. Its share in the commercial sector energy consumption in 2000 varied widely from 8% in Nepal to 51% in Sri Lanka; by 2016 the share had increased to 18% in Nepal and 62% in Sri Lanka. In the case of agriculture, oil was the main source of energy in Bangladesh, Nepal, and Sri Lanka. In Bhutan, there was a major shift in the sector's energy dependence, from bioenergy in 2005 to electricity in 2014. In India, electricity and oil collectively represented over 80% of the energy use in the agriculture sector with the share of electricity growing over time.

The energy mix in the power sector showed no significant change in the South Asian countries except Sri Lanka, where there was a dramatic decrease in the share of oil and an increase in use of coal for power generation during 2000–2016 (Table 3.5). The share of coal in power generation also slightly increased in Bangladesh and India.

Table 3.4: Sector-Wise Final Energy Mix in South Asian Countries, 2000–2016
(%)

Country	Sub-Sector	Year	Coal	Oil	Natural Gas	Biofuels and Waste	Electricity
Bangladesh	Industry	2000	14	13	48	6	20
		2016	17	5	46	2	31
	Transport	2000	—	100	—	—	—
		2016	—	68	32	—	—
	Commercial	2000	—	—	49	—	51
		2016	—	—	42	—	58
	Agriculture	2000	—	88	3	—	9
		2016	—	83	2	—	16
Bhutan	Industry	2005	28	4	—	31	36
		2014	40	1	—	2	57
	Transport	2005	—	100	—	—	—
		2014	—	100	—	—	—
	Commercial	2005	—	15	—	59	25
		2014	—	—	—	71	29
	Agriculture	2005	—	24	—	59	18
		2014	—	6	—	—	94
India	Industry	2000	31	24	5	27	13
		2016	45	23	3	14	15
	Transport	2000	—	97	—	—	2
		2016	—	95	3	—	2
	Commercial	2000	29	—	—	51	21
		2016	18	9	3	29	41
	Agriculture	2000	13	44	1	—	43
		2016	11	30	1	—	59
Nepal	Industry	2000	64	11	—	14	11
		2016	72	4	—	8	16
	Transport	2000	—	100	—	—	—
		2016	—	100	—	—	—
	Commercial	2000	—	52	—	40	8
		2016	—	62	—	20	18
	Agriculture	2000	—	86	—	—	14
		2016	—	90	—	—	10

continued on next page

Table 3.4 *continued*

Country	Sub-Sector	Year	Coal	Oil	Natural Gas	Biofuels and Waste	Electricity
Sri Lanka	Industry	2000	—	18	—	71	10
		2016	2	21	—	65	13
	Transport	2000	—	100	—	—	—
		2016	—	100	—	—	—
	Commercial	2000	—	15	—	52	34
		2016	—	13	—	25	62
	Agriculture	2000	—	100	—	—	—
		2016	—	100	—	—	—

— = zero or negligible value.

Sources: International Energy Agency (IEA). 2018. IEA Online Database. Paris. https://www.iea.org/data-and-statistics/data-tables? (accessed 18 August 2019); Government of Bhutan, Department of Energy (DoE). 2007. Bhutan Energy Data Directory 2005. Thimphu; and Government of Bhutan, Department of Renewable Energy (DoRE). 2016. Bhutan Energy Data Directory 2015. Thimphu. https://www.moea.gov.bt/wp-content/uploads/2018/07/Bhutan-Energy-Data-Directory-2015.pdf.

Table 3.5: Fuel Mix in Power Generation in South Asian Countries, 2000–2016
(%)

Country	Year	Coal	Oil	Natural Gas	Nuclear	Hydro	Renewables	Biofuel and Waste
Bangladesh	2000	—	9	89	—	2	—	—
	2016	2	8	90	—	—	—	—
Bhutan	2005	—	—	—	—	100	—	—
	2014	—	—	—	—	100	—	—
India	2000	77	6	7	3	5	1	1
	2016	78	2	4	3	4	2	7
Nepal	2000	—	4	—	—	96	—	—
	2016	—	—	—	—	100	—	—
Sri Lanka	2000	—	78	—	—	22	—	—
	2016	50	35	—	—	13	1	2

— = zero or negligible value.

Sources: International Energy Agency (IEA). 2018. IEA Online Database. Paris. https://www.iea.org/data-and-statistics/data-tables? (accessed 18 August 2019); Government of Bhutan, Department of Energy (DoE). 2007. Bhutan Energy Data Directory 2005. Thimphu; and Government of Bhutan, Department of Renewable Energy (DoRE). 2016. Bhutan Energy Data Directory 2015. Thimphu. https://www.moea.gov.bt/wp-content/uploads/2018/07/Bhutan-Energy-Data-Directory-2015.pdf.

3.3 Roles of Energy Intensities and Other Factors Behind the Growth of Productive Use of Energy

Bangladesh

The TPUE in Bangladesh increased by 16,424 kilotons of oil equivalent (ktoe) during 2000–2016. All factors—i.e., level of total output (or activity), fuel mix, energy intensity, and structure of GDP—contributed positively to the increase in energy consumption (Figure 3.1). Of the increase in TPUE during the period, 69% was associated purely with the growth in GDP. Structural change (mainly the increased shares of industry and transport sectors in GDP) was responsible for 18% of the increase. The energy intensity effect contributed to 8% of the increase. Moreover, the increased energy intensity of the power sector was the most influential force behind this change (Figure 3.2). The fuel mix effect had a relatively small influence of 4%, mainly due to the increment in the share of coal in the industry and power sectors in 2016.

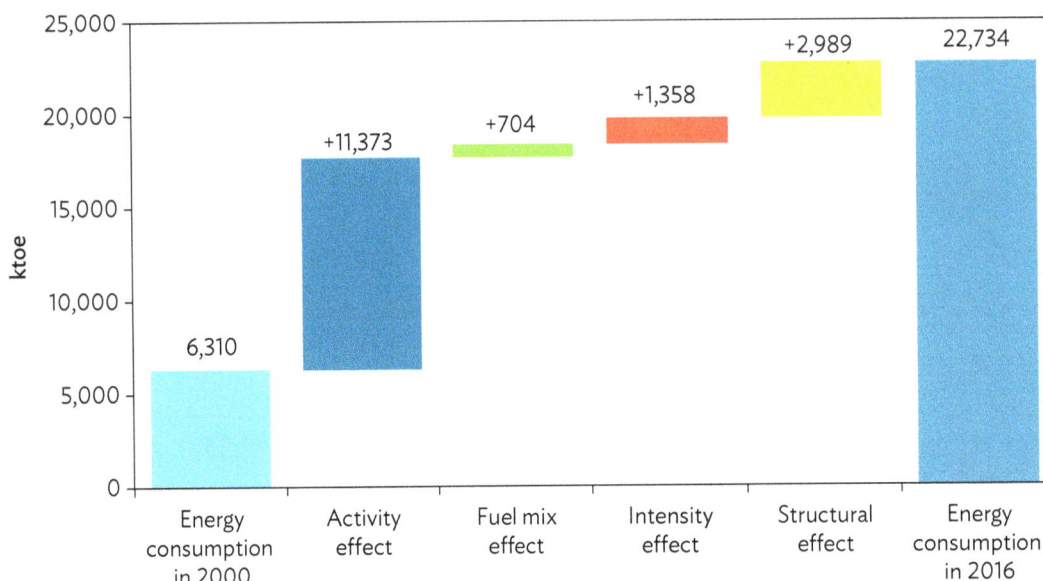

Figure 3.1: Decomposition of Total Productive Use of Energy Change in Productive Sectors of Bangladesh, 2000–2016

ktoe = kiloton of oil equivalent.
Source: Authors.

Figure 3.2: Energy Intensity Effect per Sector in Bangladesh, 2000–2016

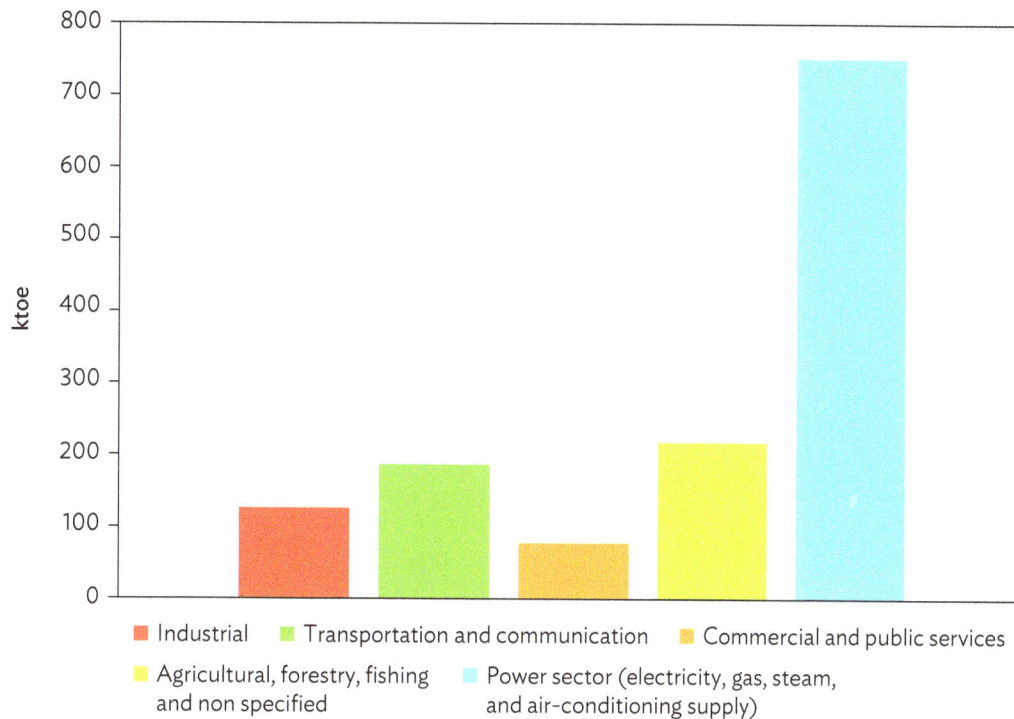

- Industrial
- Transportation and communication
- Commercial and public services
- Agricultural, forestry, fishing and non specified
- Power sector (electricity, gas, steam, and air-conditioning supply)

ktoe = kiloton of oil equivalent.
Source: Authors.

Bhutan

Due to limitations in data availability, analysis of factors behind the change in TPUE of Bhutan was carried out for the changes that occurred between 2005 and 2014.

TPUE in Bhutan increased by 235 ktoe (i.e., by 111%) between 2004 and 2015. All factors (i.e., activity, energy intensity, structural change, and fuel mix effects) contributed positively to the increase (Figure 3.3). The activity effect (due to increased GDP) was responsible for 80% of the increase, whereas the energy intensity effect only contributed 12%. In the case of the energy intensity effect, the industry sector played a largest role, followed by the agriculture and transport sectors (Figure 3.4). Energy intensities of the power and commercial sectors in 2015 were lower than in 2004; without the decrease in their energy intensities, the total TPUE would have been even higher than the 2015 figure. The positive fuel mix effect on TPUE in 2015 was due to the increased shares of bioenergy use in the commercial sector and coal use in the industry sector.

Figure 3.3: Decomposition of Total Productive Use of Energy Change of Productive Sectors of Bhutan, 2005–2014

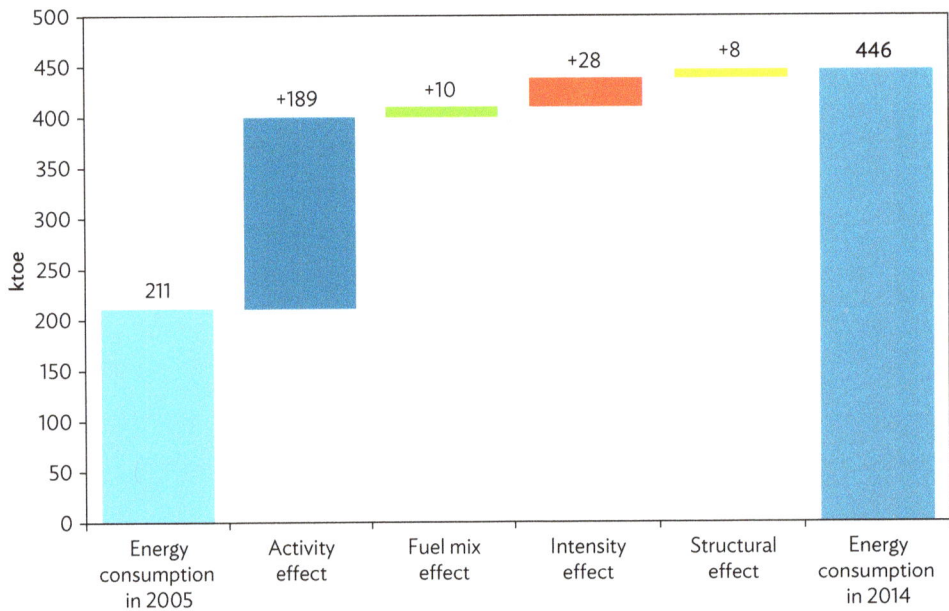

ktoe = kiloton of oil equivalent.
Source: Authors.

Figure 3.4: Energy Intensity Effect per Sector in Bhutan, 2000–2015

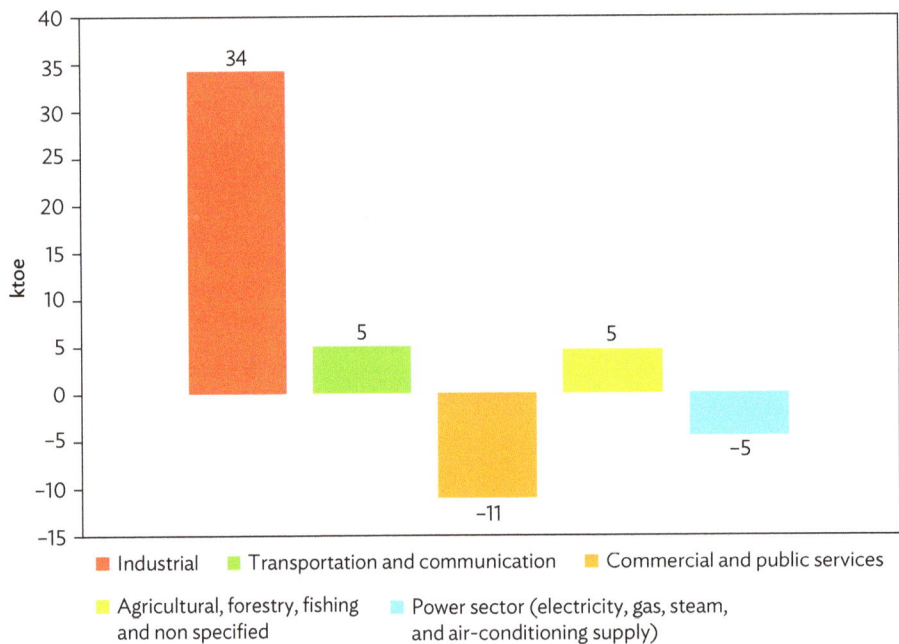

ktoe = kiloton of oil equivalent.
Source: Authors.

Figure 3.5: Decomposition of Total Productive Use of Energy Change of Productive Sectors of India, 2000–2016

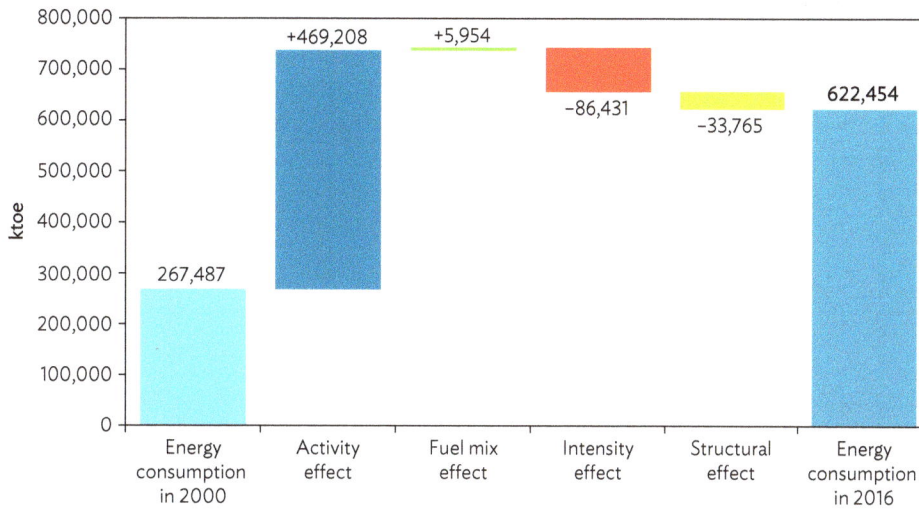

ktoe = kiloton of oil equivalent.
Source: Authors.

Figure 3.6: Energy Intensity Effect per Sector in India, 2000–2016

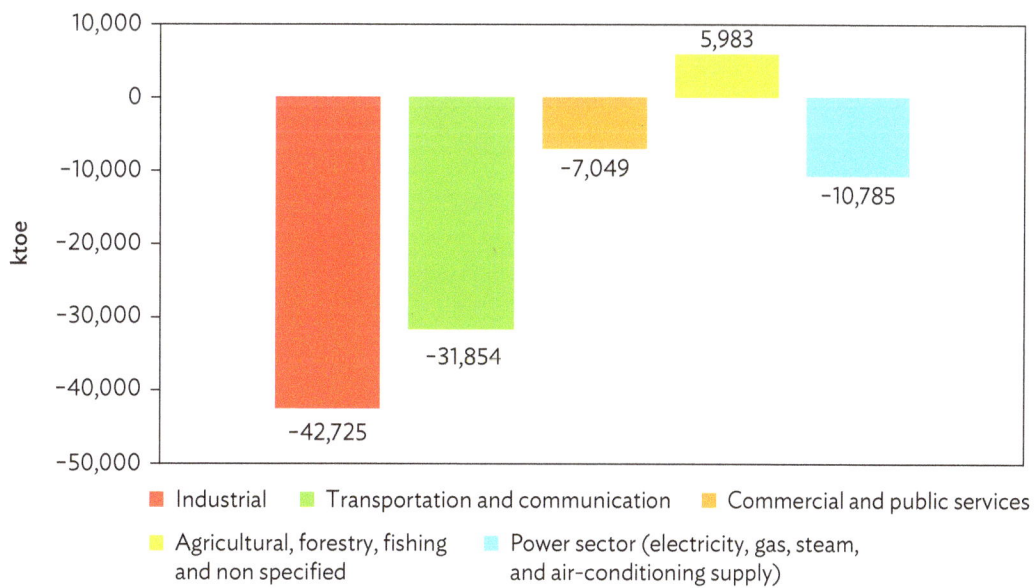

ktoe = kiloton of oil equivalent.
Source: Authors.

India

In India, the TPUE in 2016 was 354,967 ktoe higher (i.e., 133% more) than that in 2000. The activity and fuel mix effects acted to increase the TPUE during 2000–2016. The fuel mix effect was slightly positive due to an increased share of coal use in the industry and power sectors (Figure 3.5). The energy intensity effect acted toward a reduction of TPUE in 2016. This was because energy intensities of all sectors except agriculture had declined by 2016; in particular, the industry and transport sectors had a major influence on the energy intensity effect (Figure 3.6). Were it not for the improvements in sectoral energy intensities (except in the agriculture sector), the TPUE in 2016 would have been 14% higher. Similarly, structural change acted to reduce the TPUE, mainly because of the reduced share of agriculture and the increased share of the commercial sector in GDP. The TPUE in 2016 would have been about 5% higher if there had been no change in the structure of production in the economy.

Nepal

Nepal's TPUE increased by 1,997 ktoe between 2000 and 2016. Growth in the economic output as well as changes in the fuel mix, energy intensity, and structure of GDP all contributed positively to the increase in TPUE (Figure 3.7). In particular, the increase in TPUE was mostly associated with the growth of GDP and increased sectoral energy intensities. Increase in GDP was responsible for 51% of the increase in TPUE in 2016, while the intensity effect contributed 46% of the increment; with the latter caused by increased energy intensities of all sectors—most noticeably the transport sector (Figure 3.8). The slightly positive contribution of the structural change in the increase of TPUE was mainly associated with the increased share of the transport sector in GDP. The small positive contribution of the fuel mix effect to the increase in TPUE was due to the increased share of coal in the energy consumption of the industry sector.

Sri Lanka

During 2000–2016, TPUE increased by 3,196 ktoe in Sri Lanka, i.e., TPUE in 2016 was 66% higher than in 2000. All factors except the intensity effect contributed to the growth in TPUE (Figure 3.9). Notably, the decline in all sectoral energy intensities acted toward significantly moderating the growth of TPUE during the period. Had it not been for the large negative intensity effect, TPUE in 2016 would have been 42% higher. Changes in all sectoral energy intensities contributed to the reduction in TPUE, but the transport and industry sectors were the two largest contributors (Figure 3.10). Structural change in GDP (i.e., increased shares of the transport and industry sectors in GDP) acted toward increasing the TPUE in 2016.

Figure 3.7: Decomposition of Total Productive Use of Energy Change of Productive Sectors of Nepal, 2000–2016

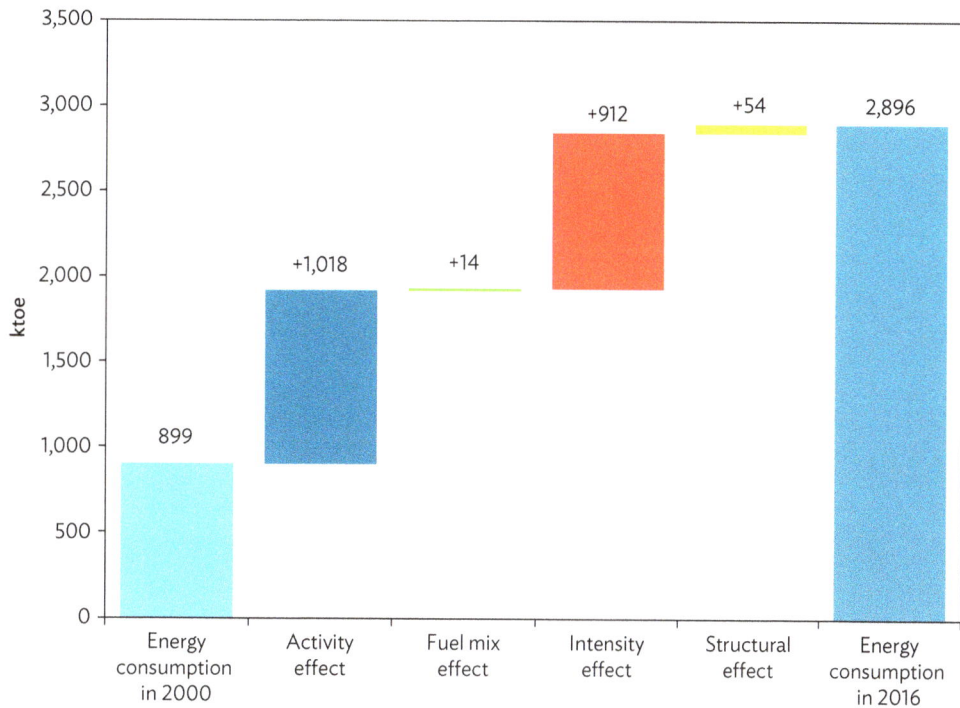

ktoe = kiloton of oil equivalent.
Source: Authors.

Figure 3.8: Energy Intensity Effect per Sector in Nepal, 2000–2016

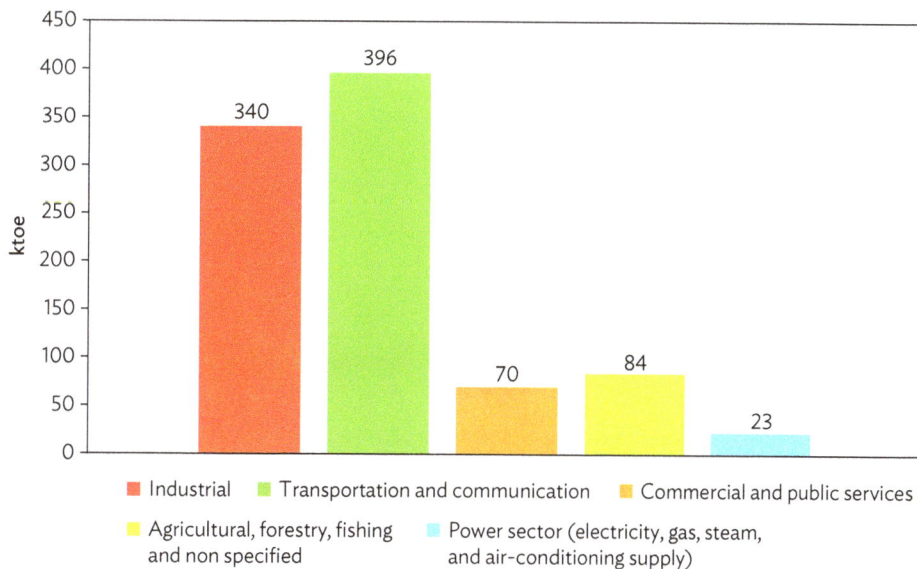

ktoe = kiloton of oil equivalent.
Source: Authors.

Figure 3.9: Decomposition of Total Productive Use of Energy Change of Productive Sectors of Sri Lanka, 2000–2016

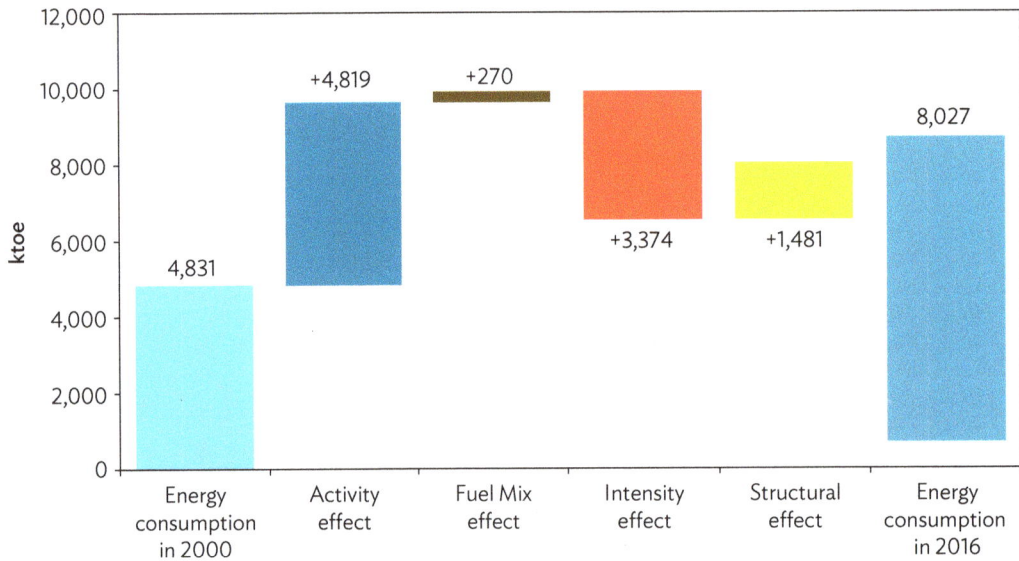

ktoe = kiloton of oil equivalent.
Source: Authors.

Figure 3.10: Energy Intensity Effect per Sector in Sri Lanka, 2000–2016

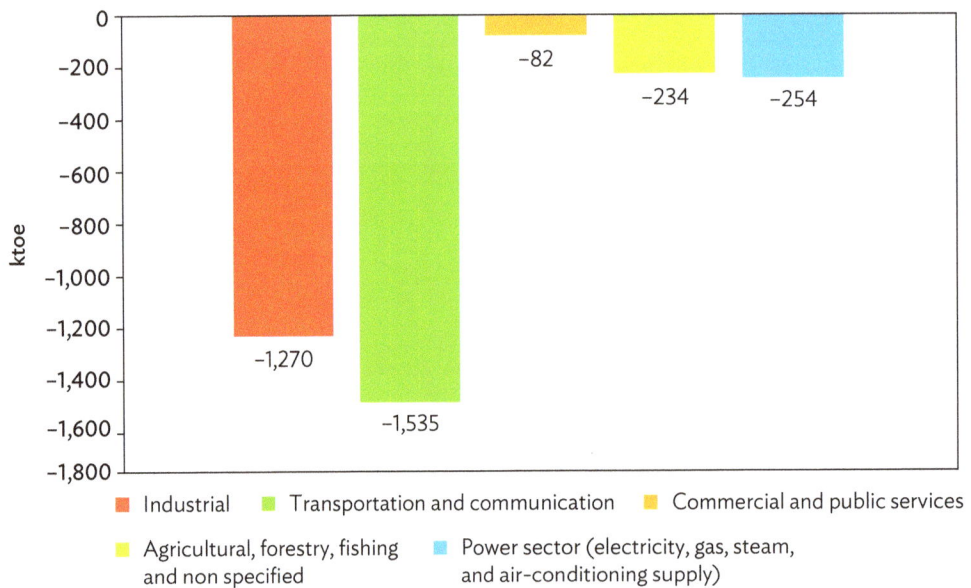

ktoe = kiloton of oil equivalent.
Source: Authors.

3.4 Analysis of Factors Affecting Change in Total Energy Use for Power Generation

Total energy consumption for power generation (ECPG) increased along with the growth of electricity generation in all countries. Figure 3.11 shows the growth in electricity generation and the structure of generation. Various factors could affect the growth of energy use for power generation. The key factors include the following:

- Change in generation efficiencies (electricity generation efficiency effect)
- Change in generation mix (generation mix effect)
- Change in transmission and distribution losses (T&D efficiency effect)
- Change in the demand for electricity (electricity demand effect)

The role of different factors behind the growth in ECPG in South Asian countries is discussed in this section.

Figure 3.11: Energy Consumption for Electricity Generation, 2000–2016

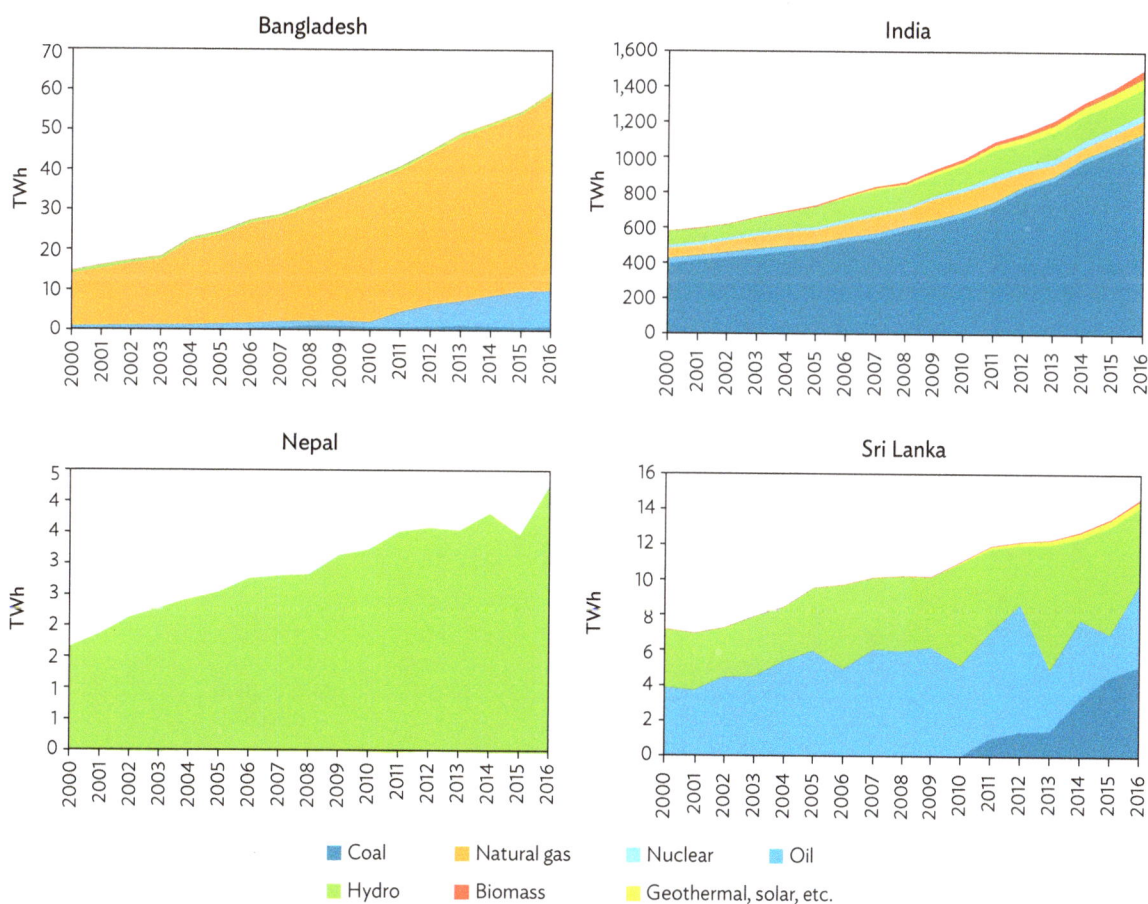

TWh = terawatt-hour.

Source: International Energy Agency (IEA). 2018. IEA Online Database. Paris. https://www.iea.org/data-and-statistics/data-tables? (accessed 18 August 2019).

Bangladesh

Power generation recorded a compound annual growth rate (CAGR) of 9.8% during 2000–2016. Final demand for electricity increased by 4.5 times, i.e., from 12,468 gigawatt-hour (GWh) to 56,188 GWh. In 2000, natural gas accounted for 88% of electricity generation while the shares of oil- and hydro-based generation were 10% and 2%, respectively. By 2016 the generation mix was diversified to include coal-fired generation, which accounted for 2% of total power generation (Table 3.5). In 2016, the efficiency of gas-fired power generation was lower than in 2000, whereas the efficiency of oil-based generation had improved. The T&D efficiency improved during 2000–2016, with T&D loss decreasing from 15% to 12%.

Between 2000 and 2016, ECPG increased by 12,831 ktoe. In addition to the activity effect (i.e., final electricity demand effect), the fuel mix effect was responsible for an increase in ECPG in 2016 (Figure 3.12). A deterioration in generation efficiency of natural gas-fired power generation in 2016 contributed to the increase in ECPG while the increased share of coal was also responsible for the positive fuel mix effect (Figure 3.12). The decline in percentage T&D losses (i.e., improved T&D efficiency) from 15% in 2000 to 12% in 2016 moderated the growth in ECPG in 2016. If the T&D efficiency in 2016 was the same as in 2000, ECPG in 2016 would have increased by another 4%.

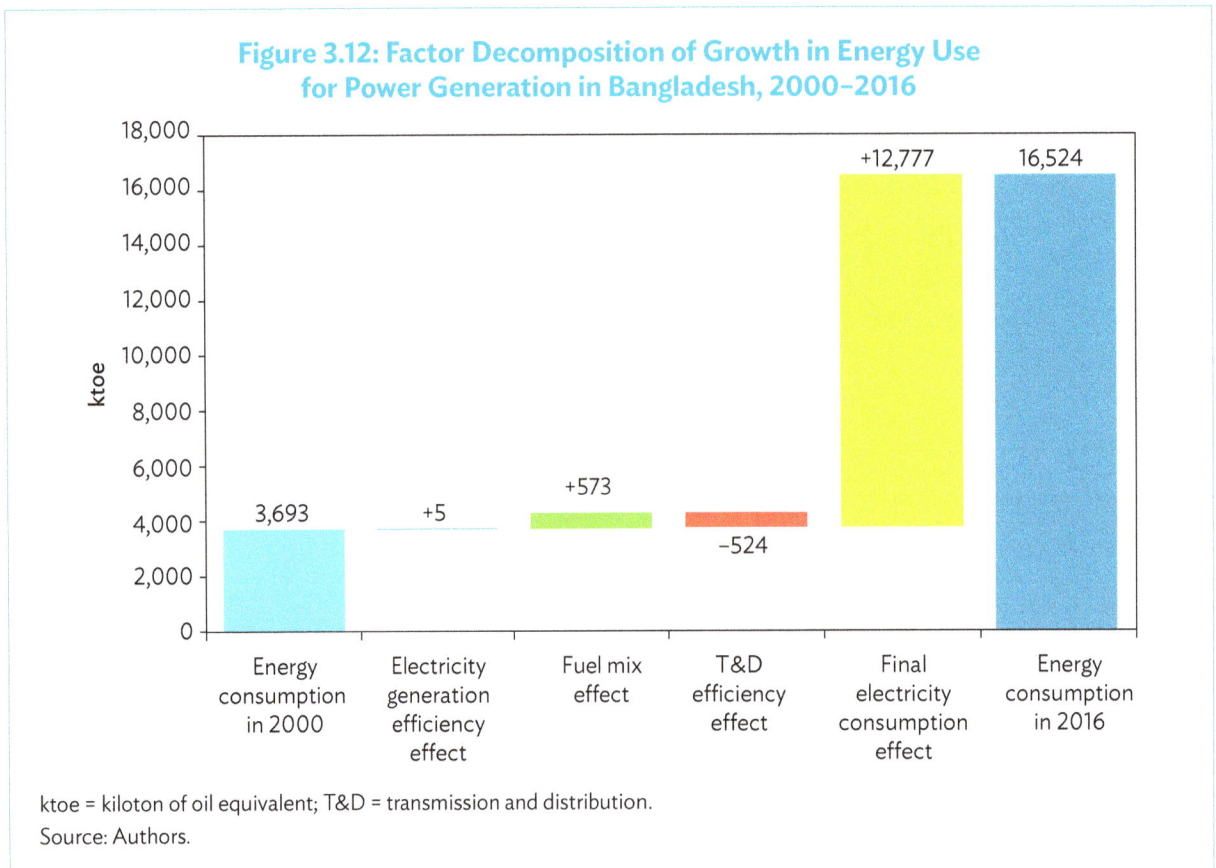

Figure 3.12: Factor Decomposition of Growth in Energy Use for Power Generation in Bangladesh, 2000–2016

ktoe = kiloton of oil equivalent; T&D = transmission and distribution.
Source: Authors.

Table 3.6: Electricity Generation Efficiency in Bangladesh in 2000 and 2016
(%)

	2000	2016
Coal	NA	35
Oil	25	38[a]
Natural Gas	37	36

NA = not applicable.

[a] Bangladesh Power Development Board. 2017. Annual Report 2016–2017. Dhaka. http://www.bpdb.gov.bd/download/annual_report/Annual%20Report%202016-17%20(2).pdf.

Source: International Energy Agency (IEA). 2018. IEA Online Database. Paris. https://www.iea.org/data-and-statistics/data-tables? (accessed 18 August 2019).

Bhutan

Final demand for electricity in Bhutan increased by two times during 2005–2014, at a CAGR of 13%. During this period, ECPG for meeting the national electricity demand increased from 217 to 616 ktoe. Because the country's power generation is almost entirely hydro-based, there was almost no change in generation efficiency and fuel mix for power generation during the period. The T&D losses significantly fell from 15% in 2005 to 4% in 2014.

During 2005–2014, ECPG increased from 217 ktoe to 616 ktoe. This was almost entirely due to increased demand for electricity. The improvement in efficiency of generation and fuel mix acted toward reducing ECPG in 2014; however, their effect was negligible (Figure 3.13). The improvement in T&D efficiency contributed to moderating the growth in ECPG; in the absence of such improvement, ECPG in 2014 would have increased further by 3.7%.

Figure 3.13: Factor Decomposition of Growth in Energy Use
for Power Generation in Bhutan, 2005–2014

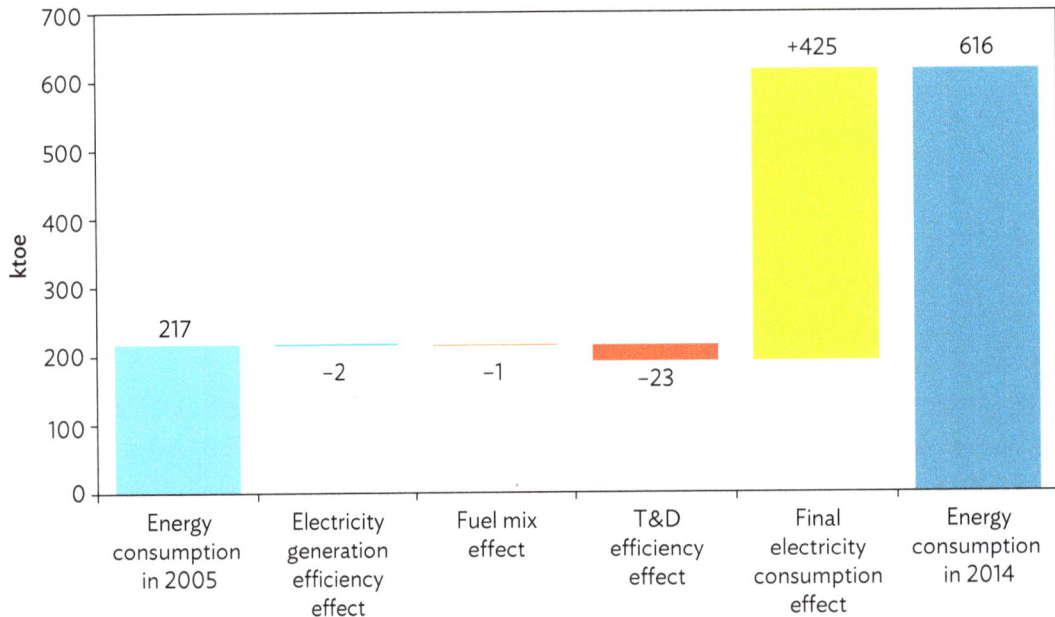

ktoe = kiloton of oil equivalent; T&D = transmission and distribution.
Source: Authors.

India

Total demand for electricity in India during 2000–2016 increased from 376 terawatt-hour (TWh) to 1,131 TWh, with a CAGR of 7%. Coal-fired plants continued to dominate power generation in the country; the share of coal-based generation increased from 77% to 78% during 2000–2016 (Table 3.5). During the period, efficiency of coal-based generation improved whereas that of oil- and gas-based generation deteriorated (Table 3.7). The T&D loss decreased from 27% to 18% during 2000–2016.

The ECPG in India increased by 195,549 ktoe during 2000–2016, from 133,069 ktoe to 328,618 ktoe. While electricity demand (i.e., activity effect) and fuel mix effects were responsible for increases in ECPG, improvements in generation and T&D efficiencies acted to counter this in 2016. If there was no improvement in generation efficiency, ECPG would have increased further by 10%. Similarly, if there was no improvement in T&D efficiency, ECPG would have increased further by 13%.

Figure 3.14: Factor Decomposition of Growth in Energy Use for Power Generation in India, 2000–2016

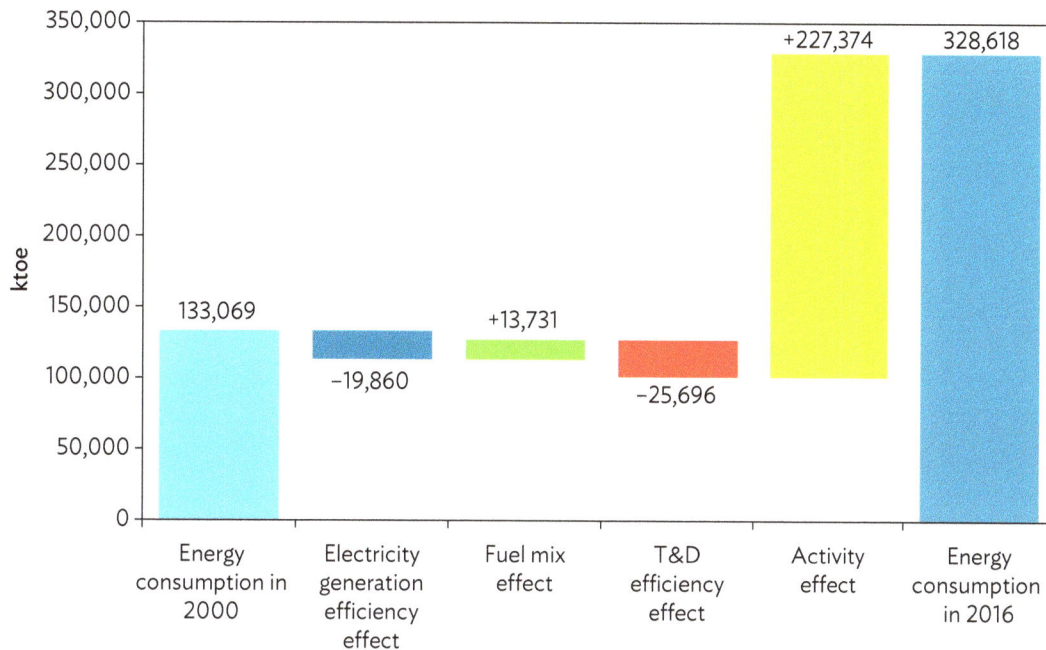

ktoe = kiloton of oil equivalent; T&D = transmission and distribution.
Source: Authors.

Table 3.7: Power Generation Efficiency in 2000 and 2016 in India
(%)

	2000	2016
Coal Fired Power Plant	33	37
Oil Fired Power Plant	28	25
Natural Gas Fired Power Plant	52	43

Source: IEA. 2018a. IEA Online Database. Paris. Accessed 18 August 2019. https://www.iea.org/data-and-statistics/data-tables?

Nepal

Nepal generated 4,244 GWh of electricity in 2016; this was 2.56 times the generation in 2000. Over 96% was hydro during 2000–2016. The increase in ECPG was almost entirely associated with increased demand for electricity. There were minor changes in the generation mix and generation efficiencies whereas T&D losses increased from 24% to 26% during the period. There was no significant change in electricity generation efficiency and choice of fuel selection for electricity generation.

Figure 3.15: Factor Decomposition of Growth in Energy Use for Power Generation in Nepal, 2000–2016

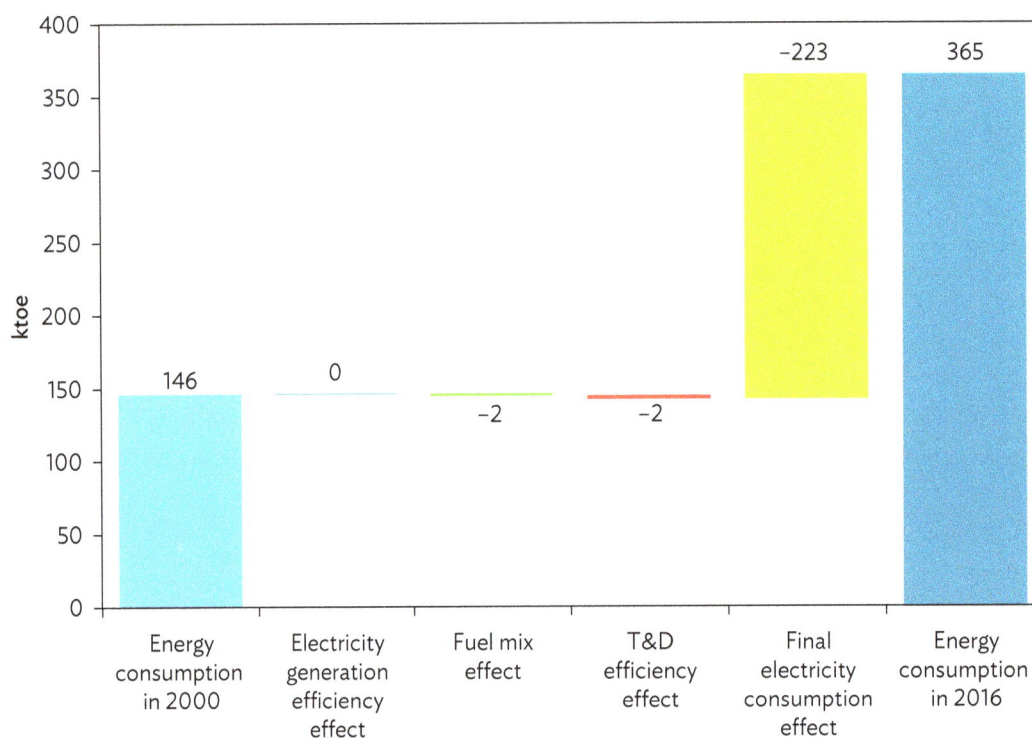

ktoe = kiloton of oil equivalent; T&D = transmission and distribution.
Source: Authors.

Sri Lanka

During 2000–2016, the total generation of electricity in Sri Lanka increased from 4,004 GWh to 14,284 GWh, while demand for electricity grew from 4,849 GWh to 12,715 GWh. In 2000, oil (diesel) accounted for 78% of the generation and the rest came from hydro. The structure of electricity generation changed greatly by 2016 in that coal contributed to about half and there was a decline in the share of oil- and hydro-based generation (Table 3.5). The efficiency of oil-based power generation improved significantly from 33% to 40% during the period. There was also a huge reduction in T&D losses, from 21% in 2000 to 7% in 2016.

The ECPG increased from 1,271 ktoe to 2,828 ktoe during 2000–2016. As expected, the increase in electricity demand was the largest contributor to the increase in ECPG. Structural change in generation (or generation mix), mainly the increased share of coal, significantly contributed to the increased ECPG in 2016. In contrast, improvements in efficiencies of generation and T&D acted against the increase in ECPG. If there were no efficiency improvement in generation, ECPG in 2016 would have increased further by 12.5%. Similarly, if there were no improvement in T&D efficiency, ECPG in 2016 would have increased another 19%.

Figure 3.16: Factor Decomposition of Growth in Energy Use for Power Generation in Sri Lanka, 2000–2016

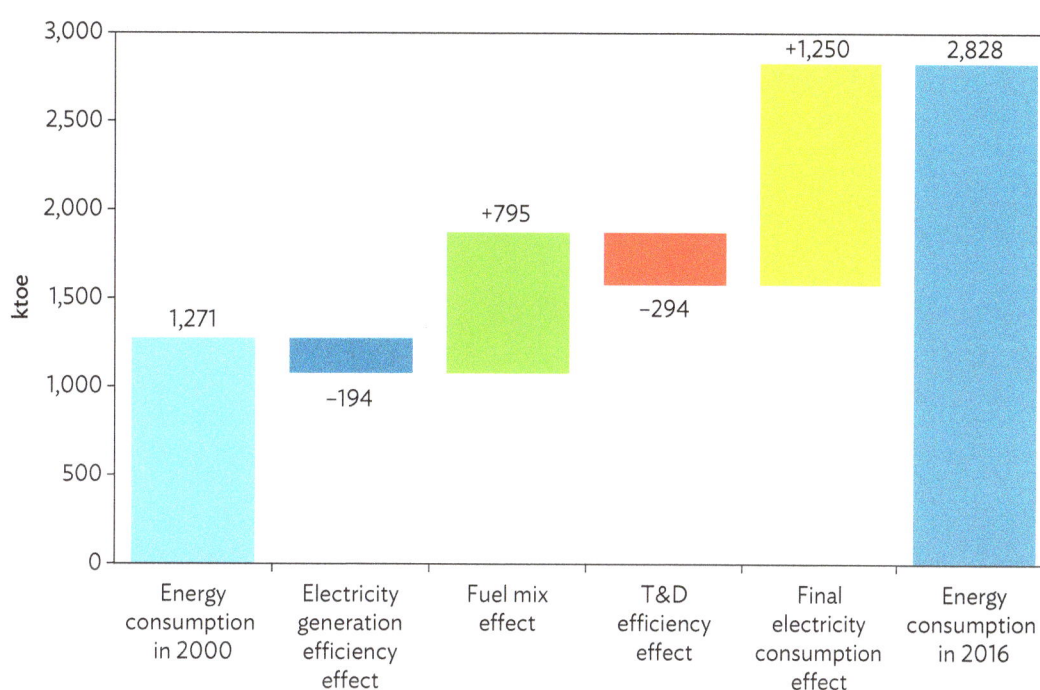

ktoe = kiloton of oil equivalent; T&D = transmission and distribution.
Source: Authors.

Table 3.8: Power Generation Efficiency in 2000 and 2016 in Sri Lanka
(%)

	2000	2016
Coal Fired Power Plant	NA	31
Oil Fired Power Plant	33	40

NA = not applicable.
Source: International Energy Agency (IEA). 2018. IEA Online Database. Paris. https://www.iea.org/data-and-statistics/data-tables? (accessed 18 August 2019).

Transmission and Distribution Efficiency Effect

Figure 3.17 shows the improvement in efficiency of the T&D system during 2000–2016, which helped avoid a 19% increment in ECPG.

Figure 3.17: Transmission and Distribution Loss in Sri Lanka, 2000–2016
(%)

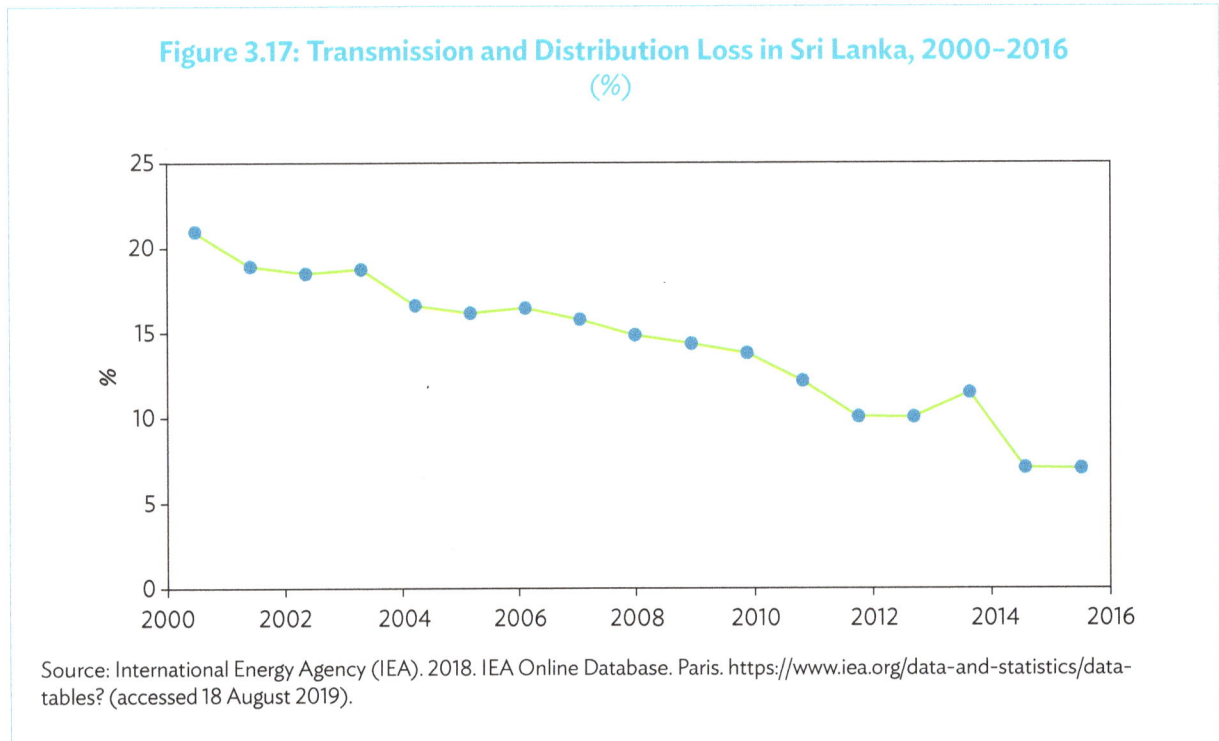

Source: International Energy Agency (IEA). 2018. IEA Online Database. Paris. https://www.iea.org/data-and-statistics/data-tables? (accessed 18 August 2019).

3.5 Key Findings

The analysis in this chapter shows that the historical increase in the total TPUE in the economy during 2000–2016 is mostly due to the positive contributions of the activity and fuel mix effects. The structural effect also contributed positively to the increase in all countries except India. The energy intensity effect contributed differently in different countries. In India and Sri Lanka, the intensity effect acted toward a decrease in TPUE whereas in Bangladesh, Bhutan and Nepal, the intensity effect contributed to increase TPUE.

In the power sector for all studied countries, the activity effect (i.e., the increase in electricity demand) played a vital role in the increment in energy consumption for power generation (ECPG) during 2000–2016, while the T&D efficiency effect played an opposite role. Overall efficiency of electricity generation improved in all countries except in Bangladesh and Nepal. The electricity generation efficiency effect acted toward increasing the total ECPG in Bangladesh; however, this had no significant effect in the case of Nepal. Total ECPG increased in Bangladesh, India, and Sri Lanka due to the fuel mix effect. In Bhutan and Nepal, where hydro is the major source of electricity, the fuel mix effect acted toward decreament in ECPG but has minor effect.

4 The Energy Efficiency Gap and Energy Saving Potential

4.1 Introduction

This chapter presents an analysis of the energy efficiency gap (EEG) and energy saving potential (ESP) in Bangladesh, Bhutan, India, Nepal, and Sri Lanka. An EEG from an economic perspective refers to the improvement potential of energy efficiency or the difference between the cost-minimizing level of energy efficiency and the level of energy efficiency actually realized.

4.2 Concept of the Energy Efficiency Gap

Most studies on EEG broadly define it as the difference between the actual and optimal level of energy efficiency. The optimal level of energy efficiency is defined at the societal level (weighing social costs against social benefits) and the private level (weighing private costs against private benefits). A number of EEG studies have compared the difference between the energy efficiency of the technologies in actual use and that of the least-cost technology, which is also one of the more efficient technologies available. Such studies identify the technologies actually used and determine their respective energy consumption based on a sample survey of energy-using units—e.g., households in the case of residential sector EEG studies and firms (or production plants) in the case of industry sector EEG studies. Bhardwaj and Gupta (2017) carried out such a study concerning household air-conditioners in Delhi, India. Some studies define EEG as being the difference between the *ex ante* market and techno-economic energy savings potentials and measure the gap using top-down and bottom-up models (Broin et al. 2015).

Carrying out a sample survey of households and industry firms is not within the scope of the present study. In this study, the overall EEG at a subsectoral level under each sector is estimated; for example in the case of the industry sector the overall EEG in each of cement, iron and steel, brick, and other manufacturing subsectors is estimated. The EEG is represented in terms of the difference between specific energy consumption of a subsector in the business as usual (BAU) case when technology shares are fixed at the same level as that in the reference year and specific energy consumption of the subsector in the reference case (i.e., without restriction on technology shares). The total ESP of a subsector will be estimated as the difference between the energy consumption of the subsector in the BAU and the reference (REF) cases; note that these two values are obtained by running the energy system model of a country for BAU and REF cases.

4.3 Methodology

The EEG and ESP are assessed using a long-term national energy system model. For this purpose, separate long-term national energy system models were developed for Bangladesh, Bhutan, Nepal, and Sri Lanka.

The Energy System Modeling Approach

National energy system models were developed for Bangladesh, Bhutan, Nepal, and Sri Lanka using the framework of the AIM/Enduse model, where AIM stands for Asia-Pacific Integrated Model (Kainuma et al. 2003). The AIM/Enduse modeling framework considers the possible flow of different types of energy and technology options and determines the optimal energy and technology options to meet the future demand for energy services in each sector of the economy (Figure 4.1). The model has four modules: primary energy supply, conversion processes, end-use service demand, and environmental emissions. The primary energy supply module deals with the availability and use of indigenous resources (e.g., solar, hydro, and biomass) as well as electricity and other energy imports (e.g., petroleum products and coal). The module on conversion processes handles the secondary energy generation (e.g., heat and electricity generation) and transmission and distribution of electricity from power plants to end-use services. The end-use service demand module covers five energy-use sectors: agriculture, commercial, industry, transport, and residential. The emissions of greenhouse gases (GHGs) and other local pollutants are dealt with in the environmental emission module. In this study, GHGs include carbon dioxide (CO_2), methane (CH_4), and nitrous oxide (N_2O).

The AIM/Enduse Model is an optimization model; it determines the technology and fuel options that minimize the total energy system cost year by year. The inputs to the model are energy data, technology data, emission factors by fuel or technology type, and service demands. The model includes several practical constraints, such as energy resources constraints (e.g., resource availability), technology constraints (e.g., maximum share of technology that can be deployed), and emission constraints (e.g., maximum permissible emission limits). In this study, the planning horizon is 2015–2050.

Figure 4.1: Structure of the AIM/Enduse Model

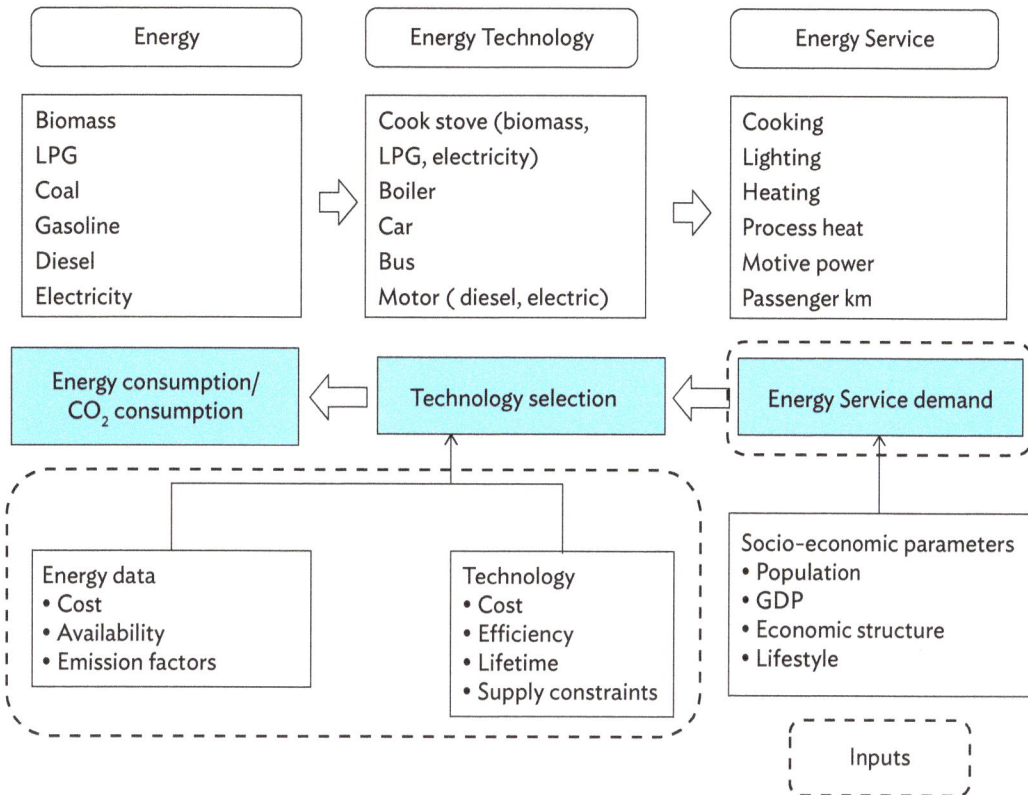

CO$_2$ = carbon dioxide, GDP = gross domestic product, km = kilometer, LPG = liquefied petroleum gas.
Source: Adapted from M. Kainuma, Y. Matsuoka, and T. Morita, eds. 2003. Climate Policy Assessment: Asia-Pacific Integrated Modeling. Springer, Tokyo. https://doi.org/10.1007/978-4-431-53985-8.

Inputs to the AIM/Enduse Model

The development of an energy system model requires intensive energy as well as technology data. The energy and technology data used in this study are based on various country reports, journals, as well as national and international literature. Various energy audit reports are also used.

Start Year, End Year, and Discount Rate

The start year for all countries under study is 2015. The effects of energy-efficiency improvement are studied for the period 2015–2050. A discount rate of 10% is considered throughout the study.

Classification of Energy, Sectors, and Services

The energy system in the model comprises energy supply, energy conversion, and sectoral energy service demand activities. In the energy supply side, the supply of coal, petroleum products, natural gas, hydro, other renewables, and imported energy are considered. The demand-side considers end-use services in the residential, commercial, transport, industry, and agriculture sectors. Furthermore, the residential sector is classified into rural and urban categories. Likewise, the industry sector is categorized into various subsectors. Transport is categorized into passenger transport and freight transport. Appendix 3 shows the classification of energy services considered in each of the countries under this study along with the corresponding service units. Technology options in different sectors, gross domestic product (GDP), and population growth rates as well as share of urban population during 2015–2050 as considered in the models of the countries are presented in Appendix 4.

Energy Sources

The study considered all forms of traditional and modern fuels in the energy model development. Primary energy includes fossil fuels and renewable energy. In the case of renewable energy, the maximum potential has been considered. In addition, production of secondary forms of energy such as electricity, biogas, and hydrogen are also considered in the reference energy system of the models. In all countries, petroleum refineries are not considered. Fossil fuels are represented directly as ready to use fuels in primary energy supply. Biofuels (biodiesel and ethanol) for transport are also represented directly in primary energy supply. In the case of hydro, wind, and solar power plants, energy input for electricity generation is considered equal to the electricity output from the plant and is represented in primary energy supply. In nuclear power plants, the energy input is estimated assuming power plant efficiency of 33%.

Emission Factors

The study estimates GHG emissions including CO_2, CH_4, and N_2O. The emission factors considered in the study are those compiled in Shrestha et al. (2012). The emission factors for various fuels are classified by sector.

Projection of Service Demand

The end-use service demand in various sectors is projected using econometric methods following various publications. The total cooking service demand in year Y ($SD_{c,Y}$) is estimated as follows:

$$SD_{c,Y} = SD_{c,0} \text{ per capita} \times Population_Y \qquad (4.1)$$

where,

$SD_{c,0}$ per capita = per capita demand for cooking service in the base year

$Population_Y$ = population in year Y

The total service demand in the residential sector and passenger transport are estimated following Shakya and Shrestha (2011) as follows:

$$SD_{c,Y} = SD_{j,0} \text{ per capita} \times \left(\frac{GDP_Y \text{ per capita}}{GDP_0 \text{ per capita}} \right)^{\lambda j} \times Population_Y \qquad (4.2)$$

where,

$SD_{j,0}$ per capita = per capita service demand for service type j in the base year

GDP_0 = GDP in the base year

GDP_Y = GDP in year Y

λ_j = income elasticity of service demand for service type j

Following van de Riet et al. (2008), the total freight service demand in year Y ($SD_{f,Y}$) is estimated as:

$$SD_{f,Y} = SD_{f,0} \times \left(\frac{GDP_Y}{GDP_0} \right)^{\lambda_f} \qquad (4.3)$$

where,

$SD_{f,0}$ = total service demand for freight service in the base year

λ_f = GDP elasticity of freight transport demand

Similarly, the total demand for service type j in year Y ($SD_{j,Y}$) in the agriculture, commercial, and industry sectors is estimated based on the following equation (Shrestha and Rajbhandari 2010):

$$SD_{j,Y} = SD_{j,0} \times \left(\frac{VA_Y}{VA_0} \right)^{\lambda_j} \qquad (4.4)$$

where,

$SD_{j,0}$ = total demand for service type j in the base year
VA_0 = value added by sector j in the base year
VA_Y = value added by sector j in year Y
λ_j = sectoral value-added elasticity of demand for service type j

There are some limitations in the demand projection in this study. The price elasticity in the demand projection is ignored due to unavailability of the elasticity values. Also, when sectoral value-added data are not available, GDP of the country is used as a proxy for value added. Likewise, income elasticity is used when sectoral value-added elasticity is not available.

Calculation of Energy Efficiency Gap

In this study, ESP is measured by the difference between the energy consumption by technologies in use in the BAU and those that would be cost-effective in the REF scenario. The BAU scenario represents the continuation in the usage of fuels and technologies in the base year (2015) during the entire planning period, assuming a reasonable trend considering economic growth and demographic changes during 2015–2050, while the REF scenario is more flexible in that it allows the possibility of using alternative fuel and technology options. The approach for measuring EEG is that, once the model runs with the constraint of existing technology in the base year and is run again with no constraint for technology, the model can choose the technology most cost-effective to meet that particular demand. Thus, cost-effective technology is identified. Furthermore, EEG is measured by the difference in gap between the performance of the existing technology and cost-effective technology selected by the model for the base year.

4.4 Description of Scenarios

Two different scenarios, BAU and REF, are considered for the assessments of EEG and ESP.

The BAU scenario is developed to analyze the changes in energy supply and technology use during 2015–2050. This scenario follows the historical patterns of energy and technology usage in each country. For example, in the case of cooking end-use services in residential and commercial sectors, solid fuel-based cooking is expected to decrease over time. Also, the use of traditional cook stoves (TCS) is considered to decrease over time. The share of passenger cars in total passenger demand in the transport sector is assumed to grow with the increase in income.

The REF scenario has been developed to identify more cost-effective technology and energy options by allowing more flexibility in the choice of efficient technologies than the BAU scenario. In the REF scenario, the shares of technologies are not constrained during 2015–2050. The technology shares are also not constrained in the base year (2015) to identify the presence of no-regret technology options and ESP in that year. However, the maximum share of solid fuels and the minimum share of passenger cars remain constrained as in the BAU case.

Comparison of the technology choice for end uses between the BAU and REF scenarios allows assessment of the EEG at the end-use level in different sectors and of the sector ESP.

4.5 Energy Usage, Efficiency Gaps, and Saving Potential

This section presents a country-wise discussion of energy usage as well as EEGs and ESP in different sectors. The total primary energy supply (TPES) as well as total final energy consumption (TFEC) in the BAU scenario during 2015–2050 are discussed. The TPES is defined as the sum of domestic energy production, energy imports, and stock changes minus energy exports. The TFEC measures total energy used by the final demand sectors for all end-use services; the final demand sectors considered in the study are industry, transport, households, services, and agriculture. This section also identifies cost-saving energy efficient technologies (no-regret technologies) in different sectors of each country under this study. The no-regret technologies are not only more energy efficient but also less expensive over their lifetime compared to their counterpart technologies in use in BAU. This section also analyzes EEG and ESP in each sector in 2015. Furthermore, it presents the estimates of ESP offered by the no-regret technology options in 2030. In the case of India, the findings are presented based on a review of literature.

Bangladesh

Energy Development in Business as Usual Scenario

Total Primary Energy Supply:
Figure 4.2 shows the growth of TPES in Bangladesh during 2015–2050 in the BAU scenario. It also shows the growth of individual energy sources. The TPES in 2030 would grow to 2.4 times the TPES level of 2015 and 7.1 times in 2050, i.e., compound annual growth rate (CAGR) of 5.8% during 2015–2050. The CAGR would be 2.1% for biomass, 5.7% for natural gas, 4.0% for petroleum products, and 11.2% for coal. In 2015, natural gas was the predominant source of energy, accounting for over 50% of TPES. The shares of petroleum products and coal were 19.8% and 4.7%, respectively. The share of biomass would decrease from 24.9% in 2015 to 19.8% in 2030, whereas petroleum products and coal would account for 12.6% and 15.3% of TPES, respectively. Other renewables would have a share of 1.4%. Natural gas would continue to be the most important energy source until 2050, with a 49.8% share in TPES. The role of coal in TPES would increase during 2015–2050 and would have the second highest share (26.9%) followed by petroleum products (11.1%), biomass (7.1%), nuclear (3.4%), and other renewables (1.6%). The share of hydro would be negligible.

Figure 4.2: Total Primary Energy Supply in Bangladesh, 2015–2050

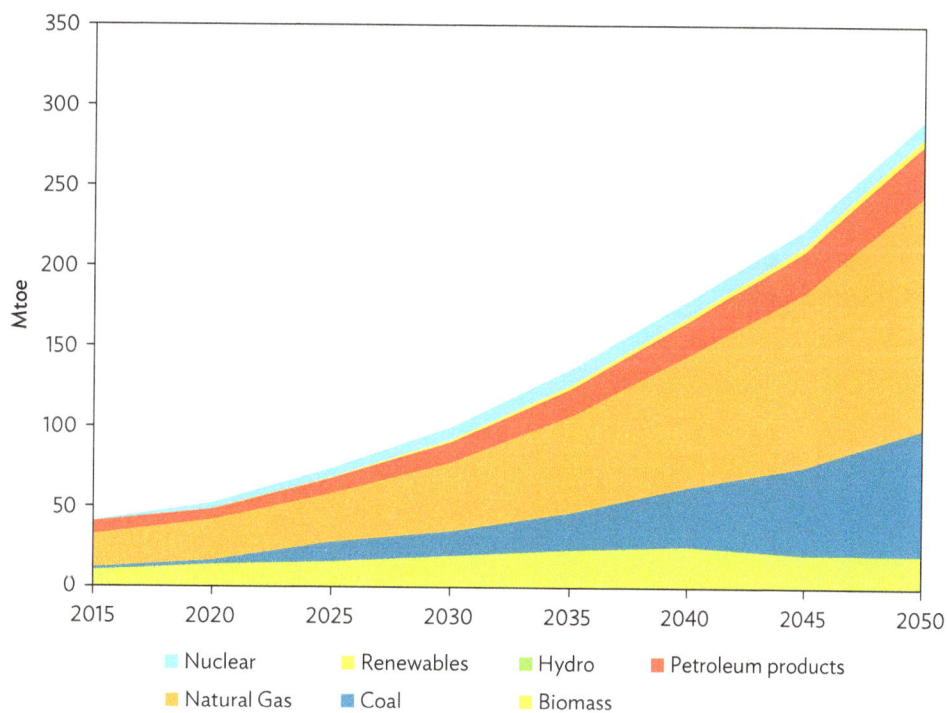

Mtoe = million tons of oil equivalent.
Source: Authors.

Table 4.1: Final Energy Mix during 2015–2050 in Bangladesh
(%)

Fuel type	2015	2025	2030	2040	2050
Biomass	33.1	27.0	24.3	18.0	9.1
Natural Gas	32.4	36.1	37.1	40.7	45.6
Petroleum products	12.7	15.5	15.5	14.8	14.2
Coal	5.3	6.5	7.4	9.7	12.8
Electricity	16.5	14.9	15.6	16.7	18.3
Total	100	100	100	100	100

Source: Authors.

Figure 4.3: Fuel Mix and Sector Contributions in Total Final Energy Consumption in Bangladesh, 2015–2050

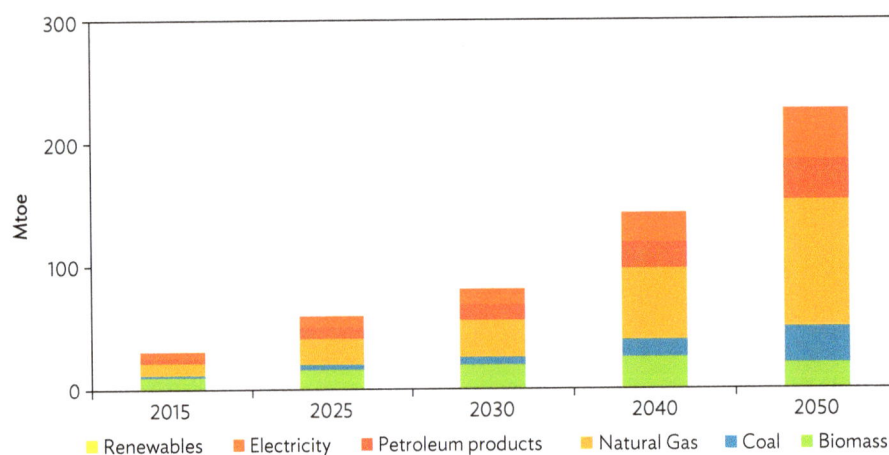

a. Fuel Mix

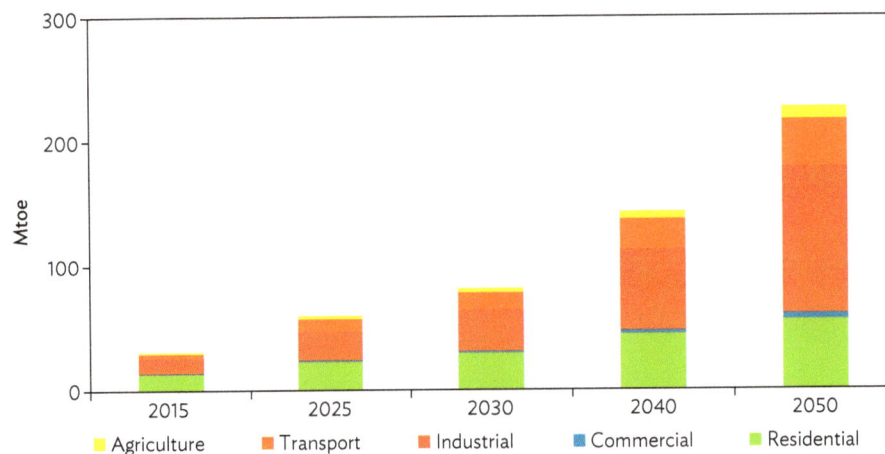

b. Sector Contributions

Mtoe = million tons of oil equivalent.
Source: Authors.

Final Energy Consumption:

The TFEC would increase at CAGR of 5.9% during 2015–2050 (Figure 4.3), from 30.6 to 81.0 million tons of oil equivalent (Mtoe) during 2015–2030 and reaching 226.9 Mtoe in 2050. Biomass consumption would increase at a modest rate of 2.1% during 2015–2050. However, the consumption of natural gas, petroleum products, coal, and electricity would increase at 6.9%, 6.2%, 8.6%, and 6.2%, respectively. The share of biomass in TFEC would decrease during 2015–2050.[2] The shares of natural gas and coal would increase significantly. The TFEC mix during 2015–2050 is presented in Table 4.1.

Energy mix in the residential sector. Final energy consumption (FEC) of the sector would increase from 13.4 kilotons of oil equivalent (ktoe) in 2015 to 29.5 ktoe in 2030 and 55.9 ktoe in 2050 (Figure 4.4). Use of biomass would increase at CAGR of 2.1% during 2015–2020, while consumption of modern fuels (i.e., natural gas and electricity) would increase considerably at CAGR of 7.6% and 6.6%, respectively. The share of biomass in the FEC of the sector would decrease during 2015–2050 because of the assumption that the use of traditional fuels and technologies would gradually decrease over time in the sector with an increase in the household income. The share of natural gas and electricity would increase during 2015–2050 (Figure 4.4).

Energy mix in the commercial sector. The FEC of the commercial sector would increase from 0.49 Mtoe in 2015 to 1.4 Mtoe in 2030, representing a 185% increase, and then up to 4.5 Mtoe in 2050, with an 824% increase. The only fuels used in the sector would be natural gas, with a growth in use at 6.6%, and electricity, with a 6.5% increase in usage. There would be no significant changes in the share of natural gas and electricity in the sector's FEC (Table 4.2).

Energy mix in the transport sector. The FEC of the transport sector would rise from 3.5 Mtoe in 2015 to 14.0 Mtoe in 2030 and 38.4 Mtoe in 2050 (i.e., CAGR of 7.1%). In 2015, petroleum products had the dominant share (over 70%) in the sector's FEC; however, this would decline to about 53% by 2050. Use of natural gas would increase significantly over time, reducing the sector's dependence on petroleum products. There would also be an increase in the use of electric vehicles over time; however, electricity's share in transport sector FEC would increase only marginally during 2015–2050 (Figure 4.4).

Energy mix in the industry sector. The FEC of the industry sector would increase from 12.2 Mtoe in 2015 to 33.1 Mtoe in 2030 and 118.2 Mtoe in 2050 (i.e., CAGR of 6.7%). Natural gas would remain the dominant fuel with a share of over 50% in the FEC of the sector and its consumption would increase at a CAGR of 5.9% during the period. There would be an increase in the use of coal (8.6%), electricity (5.9%), and petroleum (6.1%). The share of coal would increase during 2015–2050, but the shares of natural gas, electricity, and petroleum products would decrease (Figure 4.4).

Energy mix in the agriculture sector. The agriculture sector had a low share of 3.5% in TFEC in 2015. Although the sector's FEC would increase from 1.1 Mtoe in 2015 to 3.0 Mtoe in 2030 and 9.8 Mtoe in 2050, the sector's share in TFEC would decrease further during 2015–2050. Petroleum products would be the predominant energy source, accounting for over 86% of the sector's FEC during the period, while electricity and natural gas would account for the rest.

---

[2]   It is assumed that biomass would be gradually replaced by modern fuels in the residential sector.

Figure 4.4: Final Energy Consumption by Sector in Bangladesh

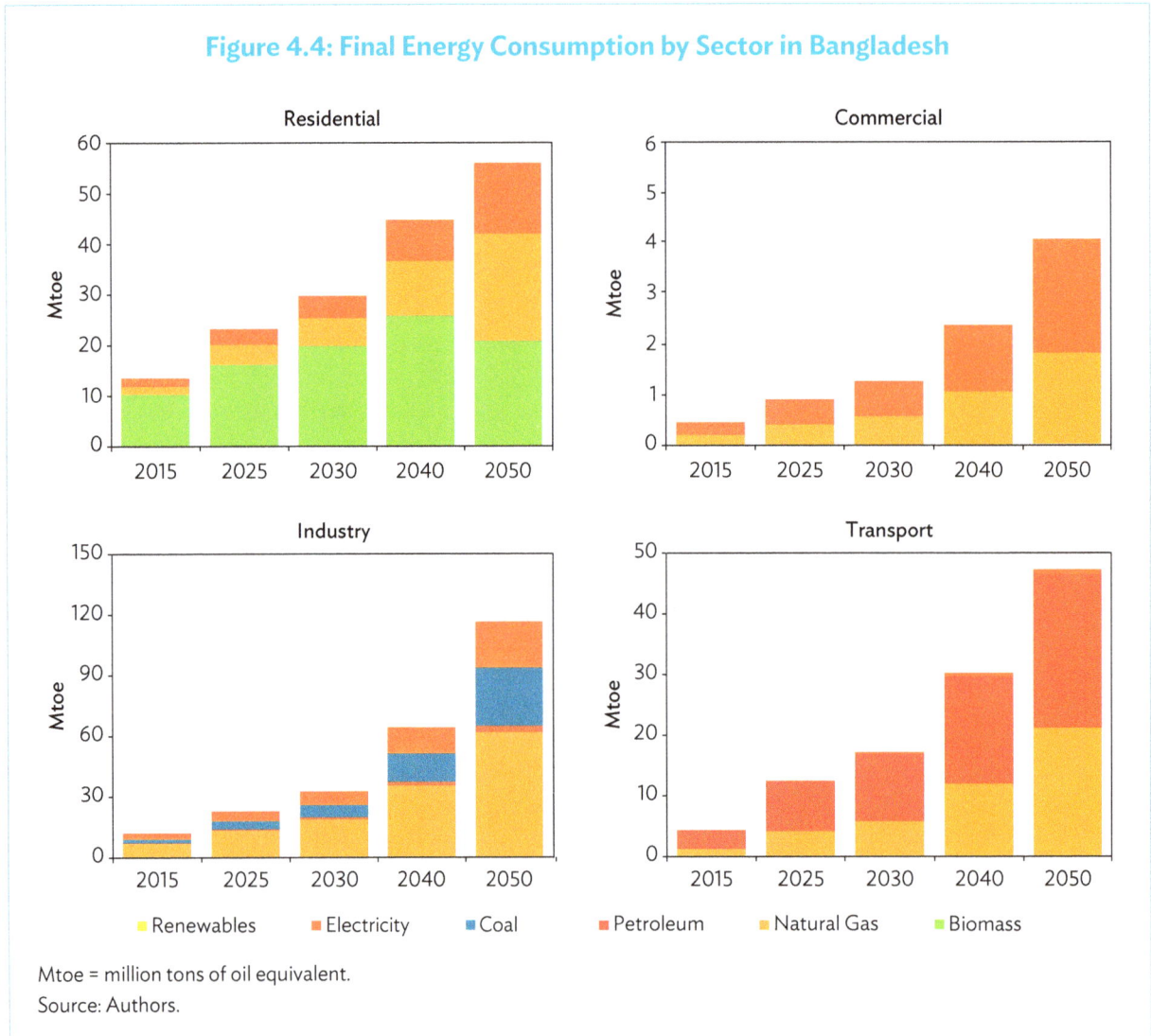

Mtoe = million tons of oil equivalent.
Source: Authors.

Table 4.2: Fuel Shares in Different Sectors in Bangladesh
(%)

Fuel Type	Residential			Commercial			Industry			Transport			Agriculture		
	2015	2030	2050	2015	2030	2050	2015	2030	2050	2015	2030	2050	2015	2030	2050
Biomass	75.8	66.8	37.0	0.0	0.0	0.0	0.0	0.0	0.0	0.0	0.0	0.0	0.0	0.0	0.0
Natural Gas	12.1	18.6	38.0	44.2	44.5	44.5	57.8	57.9	53.1	29.1	33.9	44.9	1.8	1.8	1.8
Petroleum	0.8	0.0	0.0	0.0	0.0	0.0	3.3	2.9	2.7	70.5	64.3	53.5	86.5	86.5	86.5
Coal	0.0	0.0	0.0	0.0	0.0	0.0	13.3	18.2	24.5	0.0	0.0	0.0	0.0	0.0	0.0
Electricity	11.3	14.6	25.0	55.8	55.5	55.5	25.6	21.0	19.7	0.5	1.8	1.6	11.7	11.7	11.7

Source: Authors.

Cost-Saving Energy Efficient Technologies in 2015

Based on the comparative analysis of the results of the BAU and REF scenarios, Table 4.3 presents a list of no-regret technologies in the base year (2015), as well as the EEG and ESP in different sectors. The EEG and ESP are discussed in detail in the subsequent sector subsections.

Energy Efficiency Gap and Energy Saving Potential in 2015

Figure 4.5 presents the ESP of no-regret technology options in 2015. In the figure, the blue colored bar represents FEC in the BAU whereas the green colored bar represents the FEC in REF scenario; the difference between the two measures the ESP and is shown by the orange bar (it is also shown by the number above the green bar). The analysis shows that the residential sector would offer the highest ESP followed by the industry, agriculture, commercial, and transport sectors. The total ESP is 17.3% of TFEC in BAU in 2015. The ESP of the residential and industry sectors accounts for 9.2% and 7.3% of the TFEC in BAU in 2015, respectively, while that of the other sectors would account for less than 1%.

Figure 4.5: Energy Saving Potential in Different Sectors of Bangladesh, 2015

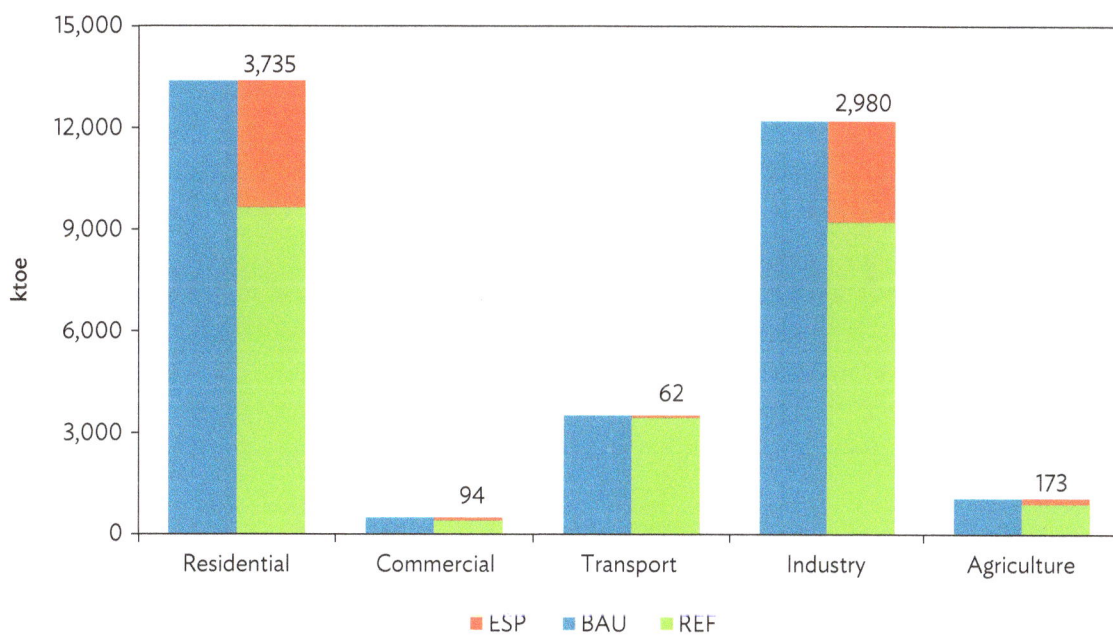

BAU = business as usual scenario; ESP = energy saving potential; ktoe = kiloton of oil equivalent; REF = reference scenario.
Source: Authors.

Table 4.3: No-regret Technologies, EEG and ESP in Different Sectors in Bangladesh in 2015

Sector	Type of End-use or Product	Technology in BAU	No-regret Technology	BAU	REF	Unit	EE Gap	Energy Saving Potential (ktoe)
Residential	Lighting	Incandescent bulb	LED	6.30	0.90	toe/billion lumen-hour	5.40	138
		CFL bulb		1.90	0.90		1.00	24
		Fluorescent bulb		1.90	0.90		1.00	43
	Cooling	Air-conditioner SEER 13	Air-conditioner SEER 20.5	0.26	0.17	Watt/Watt	0.10	71
	Cooking	TCS	ICS	7.70	4.30	toe/toe	3.30	3,294
		Kerosene stove	NG stove	2.90	1.70	toe/toe	1.20	45
Commercial	Cooling	Air-conditioner SEER 13	Air-conditioner SEER 20.5	0.26	0.17	Watt/Watt	0.10	9
	Lighting	Incandescent bulb	LED	6.30	0.90	toe/billion lumen-hour	5.40	52
		CFL bulb		1.90	0.90		1.00	12
		Fluorescent bulb		1.90	0.90		1.00	21
Transport	Passenger transport	CNG 3Ws	LPG 3Ws	7.00	4.80	toe/million pass-km	2.20	11
		Diesel 3Ws	LPG 3Ws	7.10	4.80		2.40	27
		Diesel bus	CNG bus	5.90	5.70		0.14	13
		Diesel Mini-bus	CNG Micro-bus	4.00	3.90		0.10	3
		Diesel Micro-bus	CNG Mini-bus	11.10	10.80		0.30	5
		Gasoline car	CNG car	16.70	16.30		0.40	3
	Freight transport	Diesel pick-up truck	CNG pick-up truck	12.50	12.20	toe/million ton-km	0.30	1
Industry	Brick	Clamp Kiln	Improved Fixed Chimney BTK	114.40	46.70	toe/million bricks	67.30	8
		Fixed Chimney Bull Trench Kiln (BTK)		60.60	46.70		13.90	109
		Hoffman Kiln		60.60	46.70		13.90	3
	Fertilizer	Existing Technology[a]	EE improvement in Existing Technology[b]	87.60	51.70	toe/1000 tons	35.90	68
	(Fabric) Textile and Garment	Exiting Technology[a]	EE improvement in Existing technology[b]	18.30	13.70	toe/million meters	4.60	948
	Steel	Exiting Technology[a]	EE improvement in Existing technology[b]	5,45.80	1,516.20	toe/1000 tons	970.40	146

BAU = business as usual; CFL = compact fluorescent lamp; CNG = compressed natural gas; EE = energy efficient; ICS = improved cook stove; ktoe = kiloton of oil equivalent; LED = light emitting diode; LPG = liquefied petroleum gas; REF = reference; SEER = seasonal energy efficient ratio; TCS = traditional cook stove; toe = tons of oil equivalent; W = watt; km = kilometer.

[a] The technology here refers to the existing technologies used in the respective industries based on the audit reports.

[b] The technology here refers to the energy efficiency measures in the existing technologies as mentioned in the audit report.

Source: Authors.

Residential Sector

In the residential sector, EEG in using improved cook stoves (ICS) versus TCS is 3.3 toe per toe of useful energy. Likewise, EEG for cooking based on natural gas stoves over kerosene stoves is 1.2 toe per toe of useful energy. In lighting, light emitting diode (LED) lamps are a no-regret option. The EEG in using LED over incandescent lamps is 5.4 toe per billion lumen-hour. Similarly, EEG between LED and compact fluorescent lamps (CFLs) is 1.0 toe per billion lumen-hour. In the case of cooling, the EEG between the use of conventional (seasonal energy efficiency ratio [SEER] 13 British thermal units (BTU)/watt (Wh)) and energy efficient (SEER 2.5 BTU/Wh) air-conditioners is 0.1 watt (W) input per watt of cooling.

Figure 4.6 presents the ESP in major end-use services in the residential sector. The ICS and natural gas stoves are the cost-saving efficient technologies for cooking in the REF scenario. Replacement of TCS with ICS would result in an energy saving of 3,294 ktoe in cooking, while switching to natural gas stoves would save 45 ktoe. In the case of lighting, 205 ktoe (i.e., 2,384 Gigawatt hours (GWh)) of energy could be saved (representing 64.0% of total energy consumption for lighting) by replacing CFLs and incandescent lamps with LED lamps. The use of efficient air-conditioners in cooling would save 71 ktoe (i.e., 826 GWh), which is 36.7% of the total electricity consumption for cooling in 2015.

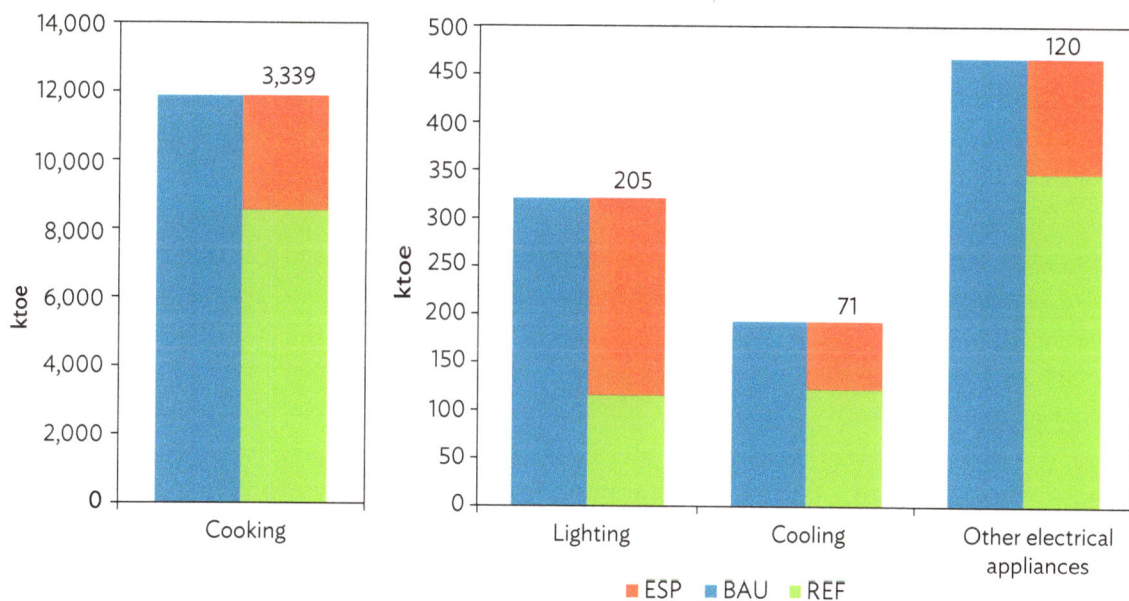

Figure 4.6: Energy Saving Potential in the Residential Sector of Bangladesh

BAU = business as usual scenario; ESP = energy saving potential; ktoe = kiloton of oil equivalent; REF = reference scenario.
Source: Authors.

Commercial Sector

The present analysis shows the presence of no-regret energy saving technologies in the case of lighting and cooling in the commercial sector. The EEG in lighting and cooling are the same as in the residential sector. For lighting, the EEG in using LED versus incandescent lamps is 5.4 toe per billion lumen-hour and EEG between LED lamps and CFLs is 1.0 toe per billion lumen-hour. Similarly, EEG between conventional (SEER 13 BTU/Wh) and energy efficient (SEER 6 BTU/Wh) air-conditioners is 0.1 W per unit watt of cooling.

The sector has the potential for saving 85.6 ktoe (i.e., 999.5 GWh) of energy in lighting in 2015; corresponding to 61.1% of electricity use in lighting in the sector. Use of efficient air-conditioners in the sector would save 8.8 ktoe of energy (equivalent to 103 GWh) in the same year (Figure 4.7).

Figure 4.7: Energy Saving Potential in the Commercial Sector of Bangladesh

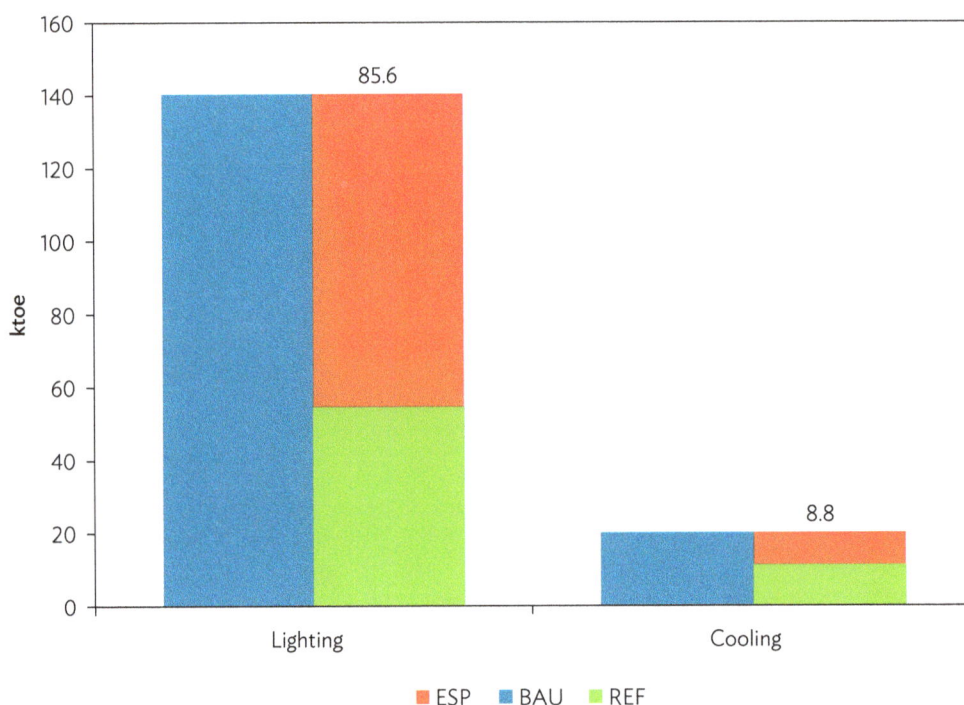

BAU = business as usual scenario; ESP = energy saving potential; ktoe = kiloton of oil equivalent; REF = reference scenario.
Source: Authors.

Industry Sector
The no-regret energy technology options in the industry sector as well as the corresponding EEG and ESP in 2015 are presented in Table 4.3. Figure 4.8 presents the ESP in selected industries. The ESP of the entire industry sector is 26% of the FEC of the sector. Among industries, the textile industry offers the highest ESP of 948 ktoe in 2015, representing 25% of energy consumption in the industry sector. The steel industry has the second highest ESP of 416 ktoe, while the brick industry has the potential to save 245 ktoe, i.e., 19.1% of energy consumed by this industry in BAU. The cement industry has the potential to save 11 ktoe, i.e., 2.9% of its total energy consumption in BAU. Other remaining industries together have ESP of 1,292 ktoe.

Transport Sector
Figure 4.9 shows the ESP of different types of vehicles in the transport sector. Several cost-saving energy efficient technology options existed in the sector in 2015; the cost saving would occur with a switch from oil-based vehicles to those based on natural gas or liquefied petroleum gas (LPG). Cars, buses, mini-buses, micro-buses, and trucks based on natural gas are found to be a no-regret option compared to their counterparts operating on gasoline or diesel. The ESP was highest in the case of three-wheelers with fuel switching from diesel to LPG. The EEG between three-wheelers based on LPG and diesel is 2.4 toe per million passenger km. The EEGs for other modes of transport are presented in Table 4.3.

Figure 4.8: Energy Saving Potential in the Industry Sector of Bangladesh

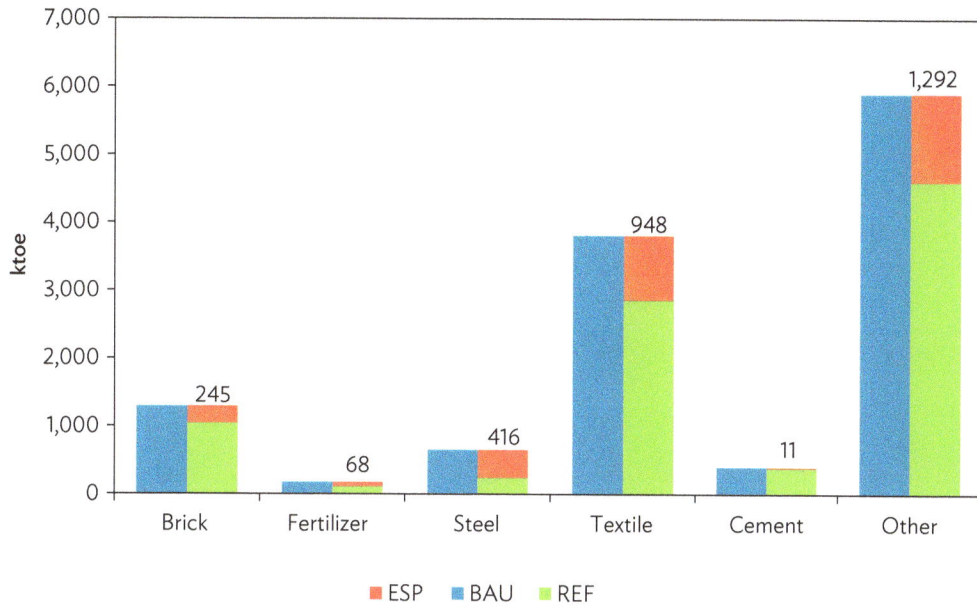

BAU = business as usual scenario; ESP = energy saving potential; ktoe = kiloton of oil equivalent; REF = reference scenario.
Source: Authors.

Figure 4.9: Energy Saving Potential in the Transport Sector of Bangladesh

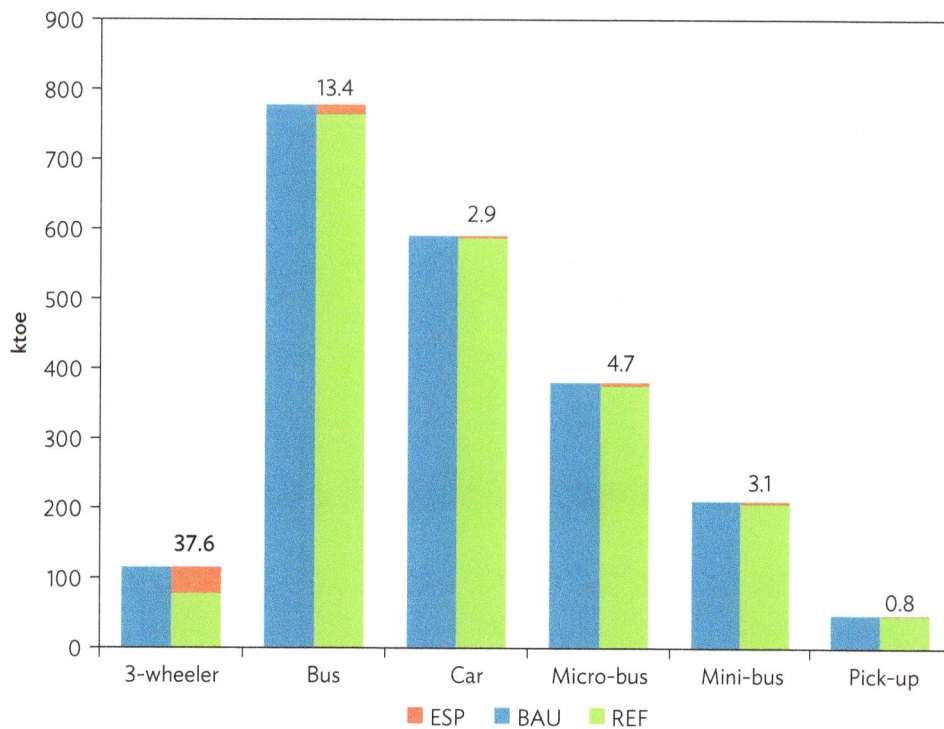

BAU = business as usual scenario; ESP = energy saving potential; ktoe = kiloton of oil equivalent; REF = reference scenario.
Source: Authors.

Agriculture Sector

In the agriculture sector, ESP was found in irrigation and tilling. The level of ESP from use of energy efficient pumps and tillers is estimated to be 146 ktoe and 27 ktoe, respectively, representing 15.7% of energy use for irrigation and 20% for tilling in BAU.

Sensitivity Analysis

In the residential sector, increasing the cost of ICS by 75% would still make it more cost-competitive than TCS. In the case of lighting, the initial cost of LED lamps up to 20% higher would still make them a no-regret option compared to CFLs, whereas they would still be a no-regret option compared to incandescent lamps if initial cost was 10 times higher. Efficient air-conditioners would be more cost-effective than existing ones if the initial cost was up to 33% higher. The sensitivity analysis shows that no-regret options in the textile industry would be cost-competitive with existing ones if the initial cost were up to 14% higher. Sensitivity analysis shows that improved fixed-chimney bull trench kilns would be cost-effective if the initial cost was up to 10% higher.

Energy Saving Potential in 2030

This study also estimates the ESP for 2030 with no-regret options (Figure 4.10). In 2030, total ESP would be 13,765 toe, representing 17.7% of the FEC in 2030 in BAU. Residential and industry sectors would offer the major savings, with both sectors contributing more than 40% of total ESP. The transport sector would offer nearly 11% of the total ESP; and the shares of commercial and agriculture sectors would be 2.0% and 3.6%, respectively.

Figure 4.10: Energy Saving Potential in Different Sectors of Bangladesh, 2030

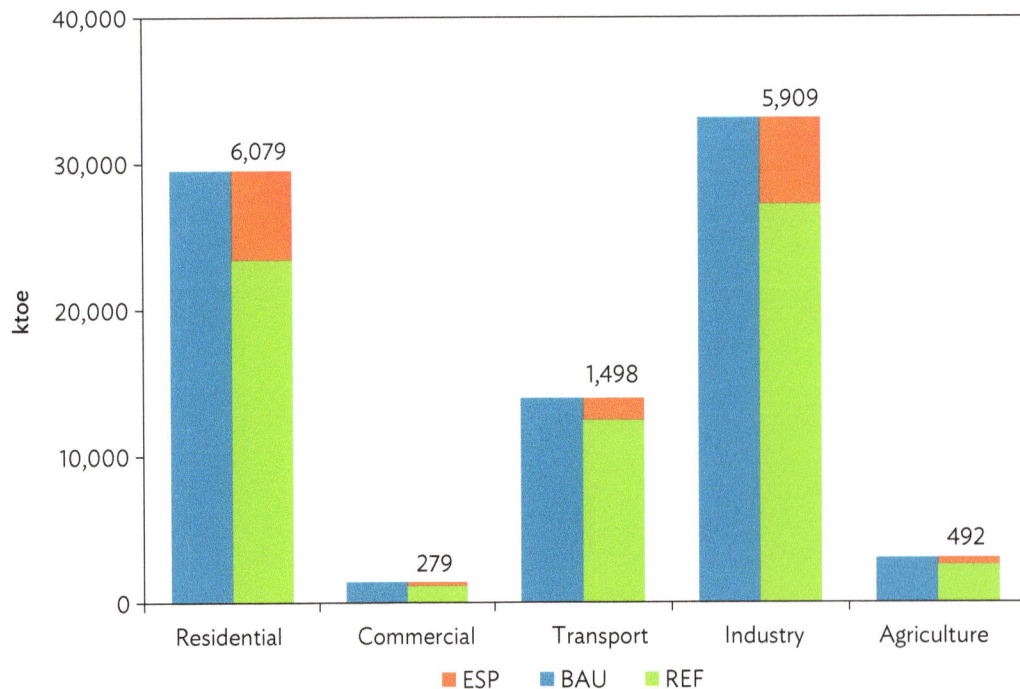

BAU = business as usual scenario; ESP = energy saving potential; ktoe = kiloton of oil equivalent; REF = reference scenario.
Source: Authors.

Bhutan

Energy Development in Business as Usual

Total Primary Energy Supply:
In the BAU scenario, total primary energy supply (TPES) would increase by 100% during 2015–2030 and 700% during 2015–2050 (Figure 4.11). The compound annual growth rate (CAGR) of TPES during 2015–2050 would be 6.4%. Biomass, petroleum products, coal, hydro, and other renewables would grow at CAGR of 1%, 8.2%, 7.4%, 6.9%, and 17.4%, respectively.

In BAU, biomass would experience a decreased share in TPES from 33.5% in 2015 to 17.3% in 2030 and 5.5% in 2050. The shares of coal, petroleum products, and hydro would increase during 2015–2050. Petroleum products would have the highest share (35.3%) in TPES in 2050, followed by hydro (31.6%), coal (27.6%), biomass (5.5%), and other renewables (0.1%). The shares of other renewables would remain negligible throughout the period.

Figure 4.11: Total Primary Energy Supply in Bhutan, 2015–2050

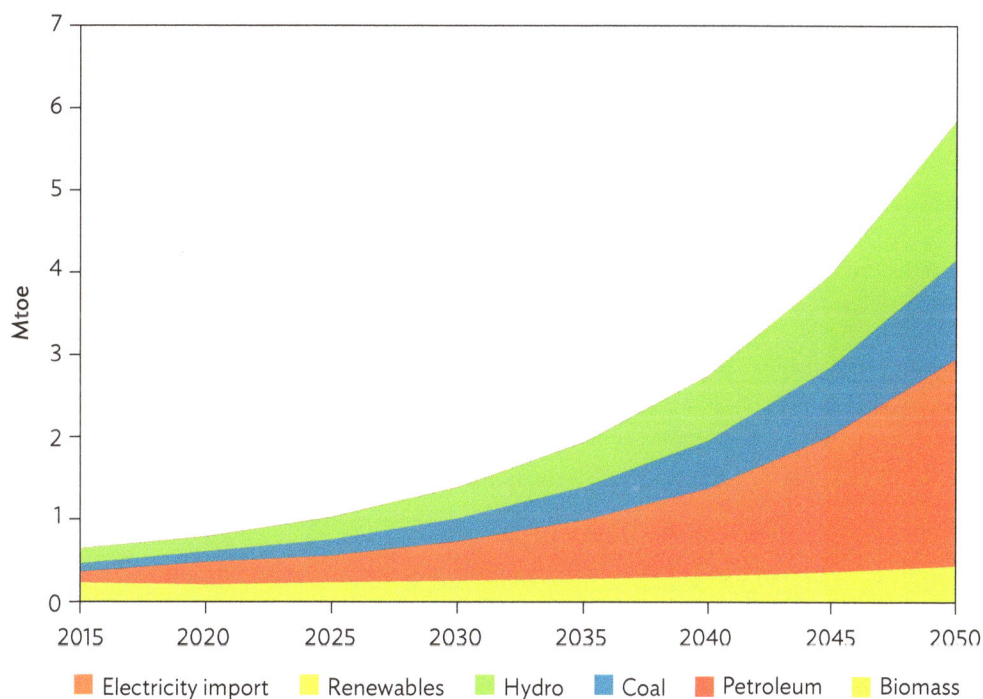

Mtoe = million tons of oil equivalent.
Source: Authors.

Final Energy Consumption:

Total final energy consumption (TFEC) would increase at CAGR of 4.1% during 2015–2050. It would increase from 0.7 Mtoe in 2015 to 1.5 Mtoe in 2030 and reach 6.1 Mtoe in 2050 (Figure 4.12). Biomass consumption would increase at 1.0% during 2015–2050. However, modern fuels like petroleum products, coal, and electricity would increase at CAGR of 8.8%, 7.4%, and 6.6%, respectively.

The share of biomass in TFEC would decrease from more than one-third in 2015 to 16.7% in 2030 and 5.3% in 2050 (Figure 4.12), because it is assumed that the use of traditional biomass in the residential sector would be replaced with modern fuels with increasing household income in the country. The shares of other modern fuels and renewables (i.e., solar and biogas) would increase significantly. The share of petroleum products would increase from 19.6% in 2015 to 30.4% in 2030 and 40.9% in 2050; correspondingly, the share of coal would increase from 20.3% (2015), 26.3% (2030), and 26.7% (2050). The share of electricity would remain in the range of 26%–28% during 2015–2050 and the share of renewables would remain negligible.

Energy mix in the residential sector. Final energy consumption in the residential sector would decrease during 2015–2050 (Figure 4.13). The FEC would decrease from 210 ktoe in 2015 to 198 ktoe in 2030 and 199 ktoe in 2050. This decrease in FEC would be due to an increase in the use of modern fuels and a decrease in the use of biomass during the period. Modern fuels like petroleum products, electricity, and renewables would increase at CAGR of 1.3%, 2.8%, and 17.4% during the period, respectively. In BAU, the share of biomass would decrease from 88.3% in 2015 to 82.0% in 2030 and 69.6% in 2050. The shares of petroleum products, electricity, and renewables would increase during 2015–2050, with the share of electricity increasing significantly from 8.7% to 23.9%.

Energy mix in the commercial sector. The FEC in the commercial sector would increase from 50 ktoe in 2015 to 110 ktoe in 2030 and 380 ktoe in 2050—an increase of almost six times during 2015–2050. The use of biomass would increase almost five-fold during the same period, while the use of petroleum products and electricity would increase by 9 and 20 times, respectively. As for the residential sector, the share of biomass in FEC of the commercial sector would decrease during 2015–2050, from 80.0% in 2015 to 75.0% in 2030 and 66.2% in 2050. The share in FEC of petroleum products was 3.1% in 2015, and would be 17.0% in 2030 and 9.5% in 2050; with corresponding values for electricity of 16.9%, 8.1%, and 24.2%.

Energy mix in the transport sector. The FEC of the transport sector would increase from 0.12 Mtoe in 2015 to 0.42 Mtoe in 2030 and 2.5 Mtoe in 2050, i.e., a 9.6-fold increase during 2015–2050. The sector depended almost entirely on petroleum products in 2015. However, there would be some use of electricity in the sector during 2015–2050, with its share increasing to over 3% by 2050.

Energy mix in the industry sector. The FEC in the industry sector would increase almost ten-fold during 2015–2050. Electricity would remain the dominant fuel in the sector, followed by coal. The use of biomass and petroleum products would remain insignificant during the period.

Energy mix in the agriculture sector. The agriculture sector had a low share in TFEC in 2015 in Bhutan; however, the sector's FEC would increase significantly during 2015–2050: from 20 ktoe in 2015 to 40 ktoe in 2030 and 160 ktoe in 2050; i.e., a seven-fold increase during 2015–2050.

Figure 4.12: Fuel Mix and Sector Contributions in Total Final Energy Consumption in Bhutan, 2015–2050

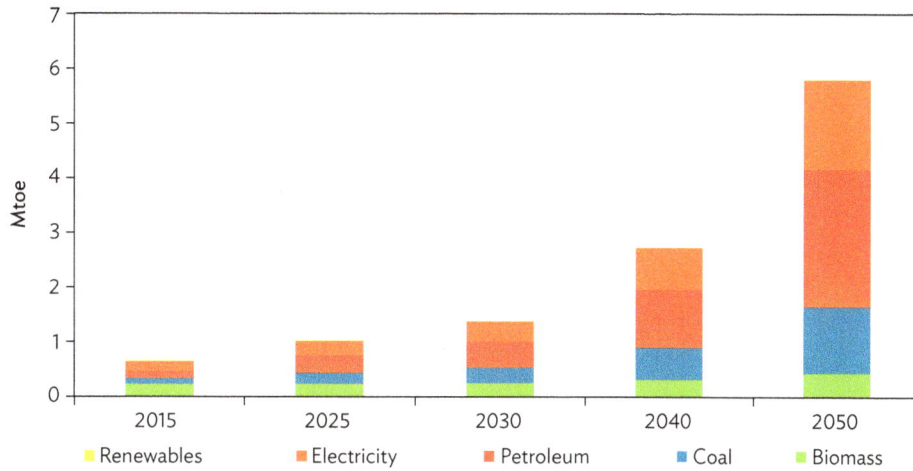

a. Fuel Mix

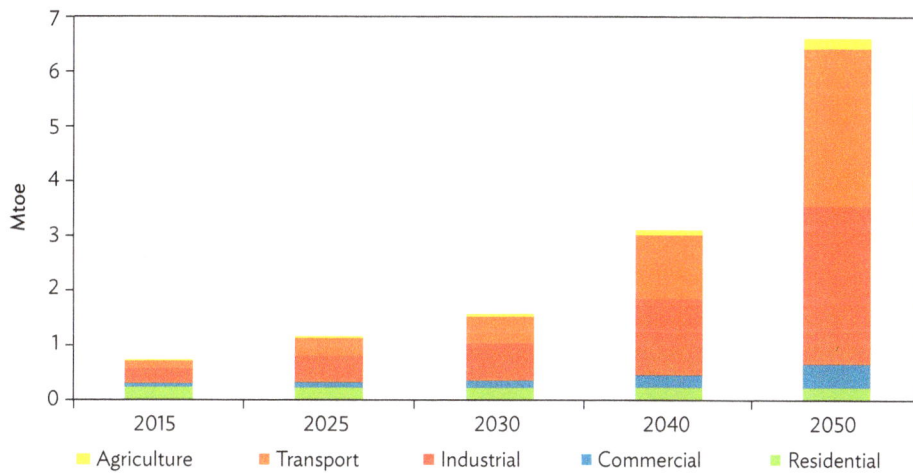

b. Sector Contributions

Source: Authors.

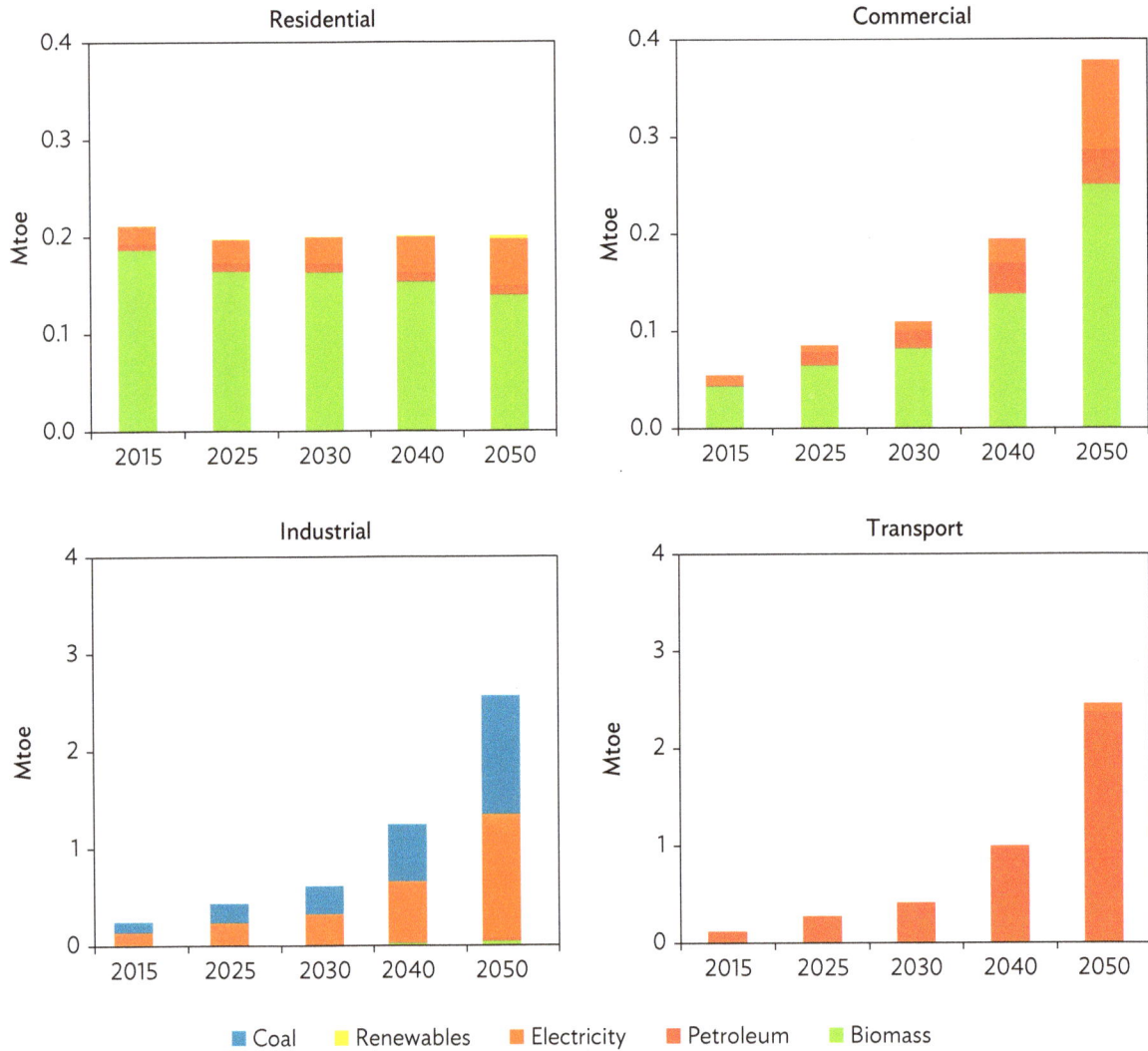

Figure 4.13: Final Energy Consumption by Sector in Bhutan

Source: Authors.

Cost-Saving Energy Efficient Technologies in 2015

Table 4.4 presents a list of no-regret technologies in the base year (2015). In addition, it presents the EEG and ESP in different sectors in 2015. In the residential sector, energy-efficiency improvement in biomass-based cooking, mostly in rural areas, has a high ESP. In the case of lighting, the replacement of incandescent lamps offers the highest ESP and this is similarly so for the commercial sector. In the industry sector, alloy industries have the highest ESP. In industries that use boilers for thermal application, energy efficiency improvement in boilers also offers significant ESP. The EEG and ESP in each sector are discussed in subsequent sections.

Energy Efficiency Gap and Energy Saving Potential in 2015

Figure 4.14 presents the ESP in 2015 for different sectors. The residential sector offers the highest ESP of 36 ktoe in 2015; followed by industry (29 ktoe), commercial (10 ktoe), and agriculture (2 ktoe) sectors. No ESP was found in the transport sector at a lower cost than that in BAU.

Figure 4.14: Energy Saving Potential in Different Sectors for Bhutan, 2015

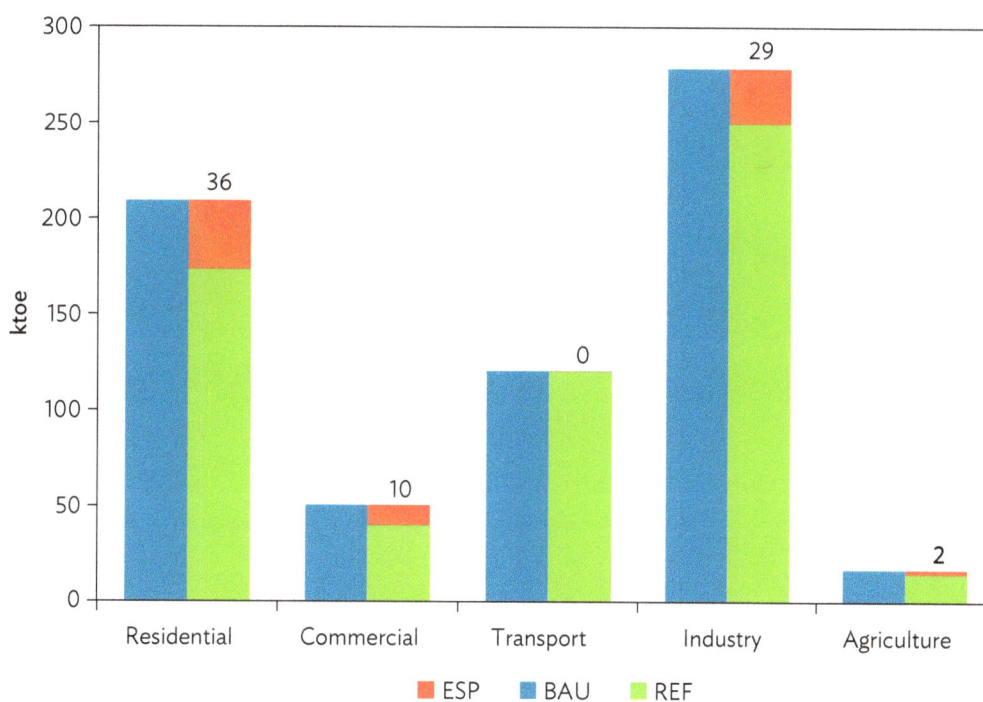

BAU = business as usual scenario; ESP = energy saving potential; ktoe = kiloton of oil equivalent; REF = reference scenario.
Source: Authors.

Table 4.4: No-regret Technologies, EEG and ESP in Different Sectors in Bhutan in 2015

Sector	Type of End-use or Product	Technology in BAU	No-regret Technology	Energy Intensity (Input/Output)			EE gap	Energy Saving Potential (ktoe)
				BAU	REF	Unit		
Residential	Lighting	Incandescent bulb	LED	6.30	0.90	toe/billion lumen–hour	5.40	0.56
		CFL bulb		1.90	0.90		1.00	0.05
		Fluorescent bulb		1.90	0.90		1.00	0.05
	Space Cooling/Heating	Air-conditioner SEER 13	Air-conditioner SEER 20.5	0.26	0.17	Watt/Watt	0.10	0.80
	Cooking	TCS	ICS	7.70	4.30	toe/toe	3.30	31.90
		LPG stove	Efficient electric stove	1.90	1.50	toe/toe	0.30	1.10
		Conventional electric stove	Efficient electric stove	1.90	1.50	toe/toe	0.30	1.30
	Space Cooling/Heating	Air-conditioner SEER 13	Air-conditioner SEER 20.5	0.26	0.17	Watt/Watt	0.10	0.50
	Cooking	TCS	Advance ICS	7.70	3.40	toe/toe	4.20	7.30
		ICS	Advance ICS	4.30	3.40	toe/toe	0.90	1.50
		LPG stove	Efficient electric stove	1.90	1.50	toe/toe	0.30	0.10
		Electric stove	Efficient electric stove	1.90	1.50	toe/toe	0.30	0.20
	Lighting	Incandescent bulb	LED	6.30	0.90	toe/billion lumen–hour	5.40	0.33
		CFL bulb		1.90	0.90		1.00	0.12
		Fluorescent bulb		1.90	0.90		1.00	0.25

continued on next page

Table 4.4 *continued*

Sector	Type of End-use or Product	Technology in BAU	No-regret Technology	Energy Intensity (Input/Output)				Energy Saving Potential (ktoe)
				BAU	REF	Unit	EE gap	
Industry	Alloy	Existing technology	Advance Technology	735.00	638.00	toe/1000 tons	97.00	12.90
	Carbide	Existing Technology	Advance Technology	638.00	565.00	toe/1000 tons	41.00	1.00
	Silicon	Existing Technology	Advance Technology	1,445.00	1,380.00	toe/1000 tons	65.00	0.20
	Cement-raw material grinding	Ball Mill	Vertical Mill	4.30	2.30	toe/1000 tons	2.00	1.60
		Without high efficiency fan and VSD	With high efficiency fan and VSD			toe/1000 tons	0.03	0.02
	Cement-clinker grinding	Ball Mill	Vertical Mill	3.10	2.30	toe/1000 tons	0.80	0.60
	Boiler	Conventional Technology	EE improvement in Existing technology	1.83	1.57	toe/toe	0.26	12.50

BAU = business as usual; CFL = compact fluorescent lamp; CNG = compressed natural gas; EE = energy efficient; ICS = improved cook stove; ktoe = kiloton of oil equivalent; LED = light emitting diode; LPG = liquefied petroleum gas; REF = reference; SEER = seasonal energy efficient ratio; TCS = traditional cook stove; toe = tons of oil equivalent; VSD = variable speed drives.

Source: Authors.

Residential Sector

In the residential sector, the EEG in solid fuel-based cooking when replacing TCS with ICS is 3.3 toe per toe of useful energy. Likewise, for cooking based on modern fuels, the EEG is 0.3 toe per toe of useful energy when LPG stoves are replaced by efficient electric stoves. The EEG is the same (0.3 toe per toe of useful energy) when replacing conventional electric with efficient electric stoves. In lighting, LED lamps are the no-regret option. The EEG between LED and incandescent lamps is 5.4 toe per billion lumen-hour. Similarly, EEG between LED and CFL lamps is 1.0 toe per billion lumen-hour. In the case of air-conditioners, the EEG between use of conventional (seasonal energy efficiency ratio [SEER] 13) and energy-efficient (SEER 20.5) air-conditioners is 2.2 W per unit watt of cooling or heating.

Figure 4.15 shows the ESP in the residential sector. In the reference (REF) scenario, ICS and induction cookers are the cost-saving efficient technologies for cooking. Replacement of TCS with ICS offers the highest potential for energy saving of 31.9 ktoe, while switching from LPG and conventional electric cookers to induction electric cookers offers ESP of 2.4 ktoe. In percentage terms, the total energy saving from cooking based on solid fuels with the use of ICS is 31.6%, while from cooking based on modern fuels the saving is 17.1%. In the case of lighting, ESP is 0.67 ktoe, representing 77.4% of total energy consumption in the lighting sector; the ESP can be achieved by replacing incandescent and compact fluorescent lamps (CFLs) with LEDs. The use of efficient rather than standard air-conditioners for cooling would save 0.8 ktoe, which is 36.7% of the total electricity consumption for cooling in 2015.

Figure 4.15: Energy Saving Potential in Residential Sector in Bhutan

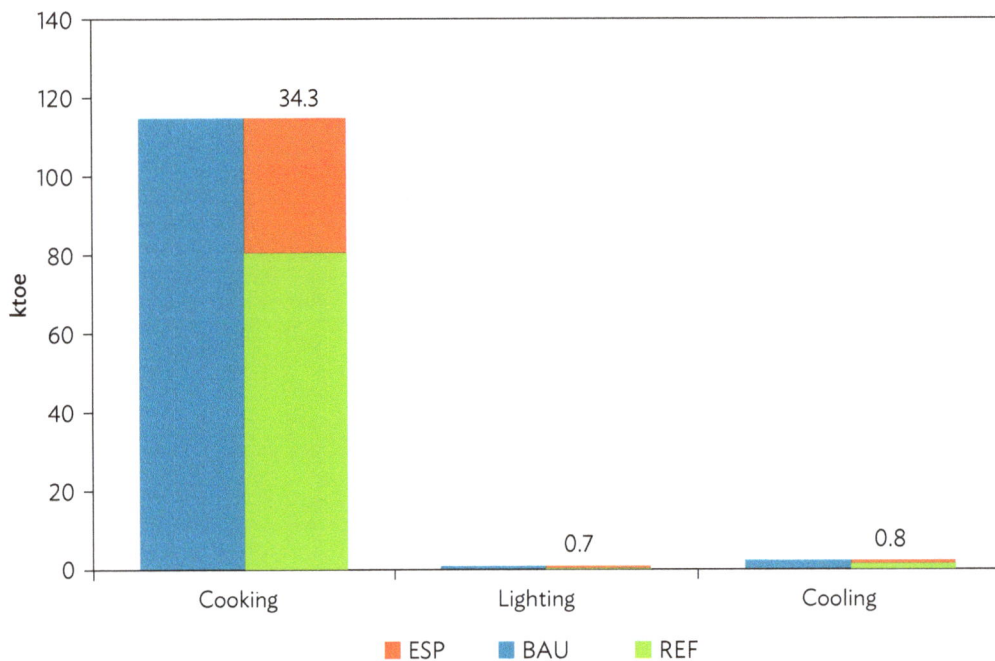

BAU = business as usual scenario; ESP = energy saving potential; ktoe = kiloton of oil equivalent; REF = reference scenario.
Source: Authors.

Commercial Sector

Similar to the residential sector, the commercial sector also has no-regret ESP mainly in three end uses: cooking, lighting, and cooling. The ESP from cooking based on solid fuels is 8.8 ktoe, which represents 43.1% in energy consumption savings; on modern fuels, ESP is 0.3 ktoe and energy savings is 18.3% (Figure 4.16). The energy saving in lighting in the sector is 0.7 ktoe, corresponding to 56.0% of electricity use in lighting. The use of efficient air-conditioners in the sector can save 0.5 ktoe.

The no-regret options are the same as for the residential sector. The EEG in using LED versus incandescent lamps is 5.4 toe per billion lumen-hour and the EEG for LED versus CFLs is 1 toe per billion lumen-hour. The EEG in space heating and cooling using air-conditioners is 2.2 W per unit watt of heating or cooling. In the case of cooking based on solid fuel, the average EEG is 2.6 toe per toe of useful energy. Similarly, in the case of cooking using modern fuel, the average EEG is 0.34 toe per toe of useful energy.

Figure 4.16: Energy Saving Potential in the Commercial Sector in Bhutan

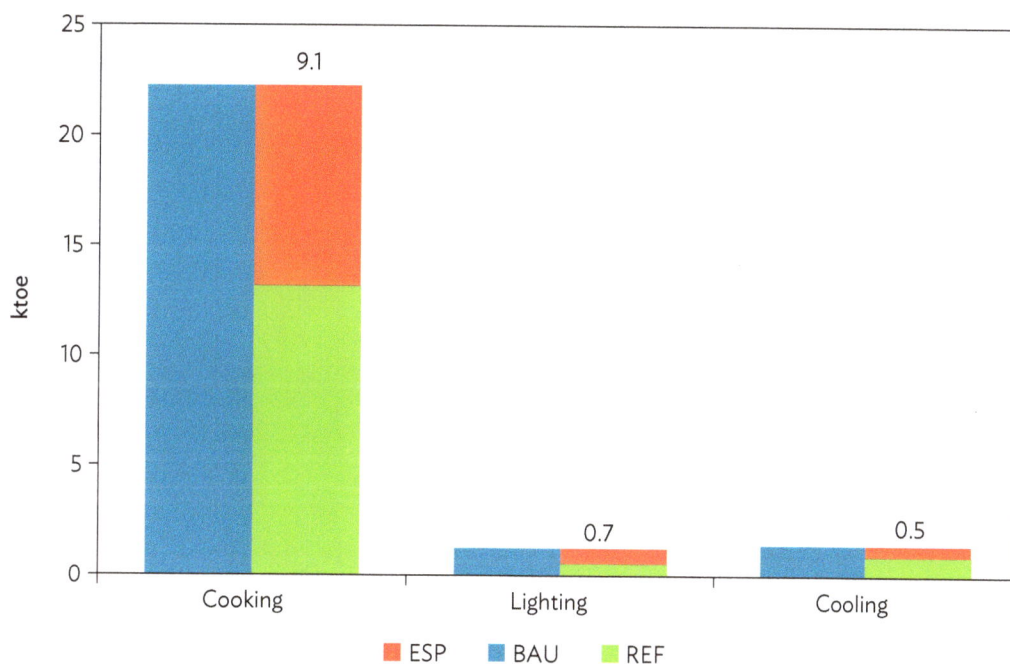

BAU = business as usual scenario; ESP = energy saving potential; ktoe = kiloton of oil equivalent; REF = reference scenario.
Source: Authors.

Industry Sector

In the alloy industries, EEG is 97.0 toe per thousand t alloy. In carbide industries, the EEG is 41.2 toe per 1,000 t of carbide. The EEG in steam generation (from boilers) is 0.4 toe per unit toe of useful energy. The EEG in silicon production is 65 toe per 1,000 t of silicon. In the cement industry, EEG is 2.8 toe per 1,000 t of cement production. There were no options of no-regret technology for the clinker production process in the cement industry.

The ESP in major industries is shown in Figure 4.17. The industry sector has ESP with no-regret measures in alloy, carbide, cement, and silicon manufacturing industries and process heat end-use. Alloy industries have the potential to save 12.9 ktoe of electricity consumption with energy-efficiency improvement, corresponding to 13.2% reduction in their total electricity use. The energy-efficiency improvement in boilers for process heat could save 12.5 ktoe of thermal energy and accounts for nearly 20% of energy consumption. The cement industry has the potential to save 2.2 ktoe mainly from energy-efficiency improvement in raw material preparation and cement grinding. In the silicon industry, ESP is 0.2 ktoe, representing 4.5% of the total energy consumption in the subsector.

Figure 4.17: Energy Saving Potential in the Industry Sector in Bhutan

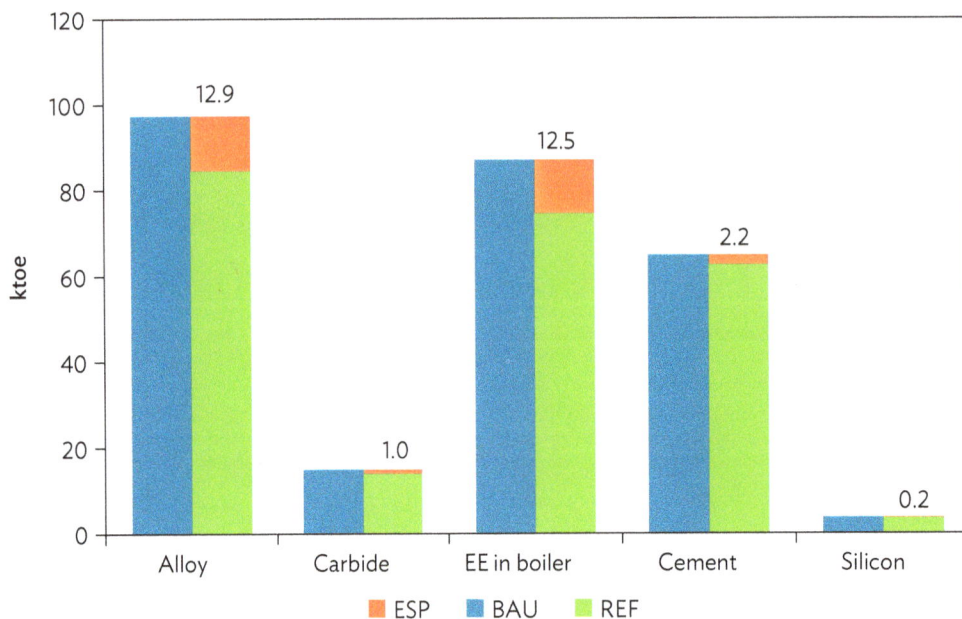

BAU = business as usual scenario; ESP = energy saving potential; EE = energy efficient; ktoe = kiloton of oil equivalent; REF = reference scenario.
Source: Authors.

Transport Sector

There was no option of no-regret technology for the transport sector in 2015.

Agriculture Sector

In the agriculture sector, ESP was found in irrigation only. The ESP is 2.3 ktoe, representing 14% of energy consumption for irrigation. The EEG is 0.2 toe per toe output.

Implications of Reference Scenario on Electricity Generation Power

With improvements in energy efficiency of end-use devices, the total electricity generation requirement in Bhutan would decrease by 8.5% in the REF case.

Sensitivity Analysis

This subsection presents the analysis on the sensitivity of the no-regret technologies in the foregoing discussion with respect to the variation in their respective initial costs. In the residential and commercial sectors, the use of LED lamps is more cost-effective than incandescent lamps even if the initial cost of LED lamps was 15 times higher than that considered in the BAU and REF cases. Similarly, compared to CFLs, LED lamps would still be a no-regret option if their cost was 50% more. In the case of cooking, an efficient electric stove is cost-effective compared to a conventional electric stove even when the initial cost is eight times that considered in this study. Also, efficient electric stoves are a no-regret option compared to LPG stoves even if their initial cost increased to 2.6 times. For solid fuel-based cooking, ICS would still be a no-regret option if its initial cost increased 2.65 times. These results show that for cooking and lighting, energy cost plays a higher role than the initial cost of the devices in the total life-cycle cost comparison of the options and hence their cost-effectiveness.

In the alloy industry, the best available technology would be more cost-effective than the existing conventional option even if the initial cost was 9.25 times higher. Likewise, in the silicon industry, the best available technology would be more cost-effective than its conventional counterpart even if the initial cost was 9.5 times higher. In the carbide industry, the best available technology would still be the no-regret option for an initial cost up to 6.75 times higher.

In process heating, energy-efficient coal boilers would be cost-effective compared to conventional boilers even if the initial cost increased 10 times. Likewise, energy-efficient diesel boilers would still be a no-regret option even if their cost increased up to 12 times.

In the cement industry, the use of high-efficiency fans and variable-speed drives for mill vents in raw material grinding would remain the no-regret options even if their costs were 2.1 times higher than what is considered in the REF case. Vertical mills in raw material grinding remain cost-effective for up to 51% higher investment cost. In clinker grinding, vertical mills are a no-regret technology compared with ball mills even if investment cost of the former was 4.6% higher.

Energy Saving Potential in 2030

The ESP of different sectors in 2030 in the REF case is shown in Figure 4.18. The industry sector would have the highest ESP of 205 ktoe in that year. Note that the no-regret energy efficient options are similar to those in 2015. In the industry sector, the use of electricity-based heat pump boilers would replace conventional boilers (diesel, coal, or biomass) in 2030. The ESP in the residential sector would be 20 ktoe and in the commercial sector it would be 24 ktoe. There would be no ESP in the transport and agriculture sectors. Technologies based on electricity are economical in residential, commercial, as well as industry sectors, therefore, there is switching from technologies based on LPG to technologies based on electricity. This would increase electricity demand for REF compared to BAU. Electricity generation would increase by 8% in 2030 due to a switch from petroleum products to electricity options in the industry and residential sectors.

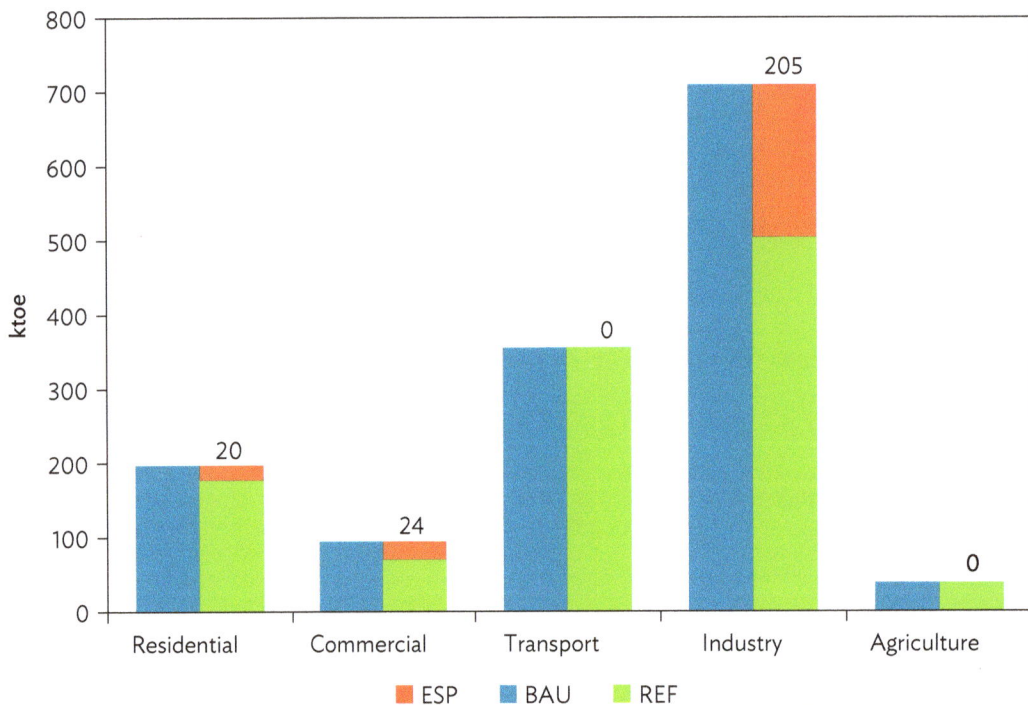

Figure 4.18: Energy Saving Potential in Different Sectors in Bhutan, 2030

BAU = business as usual scenario; ESP = energy saving potential; ktoe = kiloton of oil equivalent; REF = reference scenario.
Source: Authors.

Nepal

Energy Development in Business as Usual

Total Primary Energy Supply:
Figure 4.19 shows the growth of total primary energy supply (TPES) in Nepal during 2015–2050 in the BAU scenario. It also shows the growth of individual energy sources. The TPES would increase by 40% in 2030 and almost 300% in 2050 compared to 2015, with a compound annual growth rate (CAGR) of 4% during 2015–2050. Biomass, petroleum products, coal, hydro, and other renewables (e.g., solar and wind) would grow at CAGR of 1.7%, 6.3%, 6.9%, 11.1%, and 25%, respectively. Biomass was the predominant source of energy in 2015, accounting for 80% of TPES. It would continue to have the highest share of TPES during 2015–2050. The share of biomass would, however, decrease to 59.8% in 2030 and 34.6% in 2050. The decline is partly due to the assumption that traditional biomass would be replaced by modern fuels such as petroleum, biogas, and electricity. The roles of petroleum products, coal, and hydro in TPES would increase during 2015–2050. In 2030, petroleum products, coal, and hydro would account for 16.0%, 10.4%, and 13.2% of TPES, respectively, while the share of other renewables would be below 1%. Hydroelectricity would have the second highest share (26.8%) in TPES in 2050, followed by petroleum products (21.1%), coal (14.5%), and other renewables (1.1%). The shares of other renewables would remain negligible throughout the period.

Figure 4.19: Total Primary Energy Supply for Nepal, 2015–2050

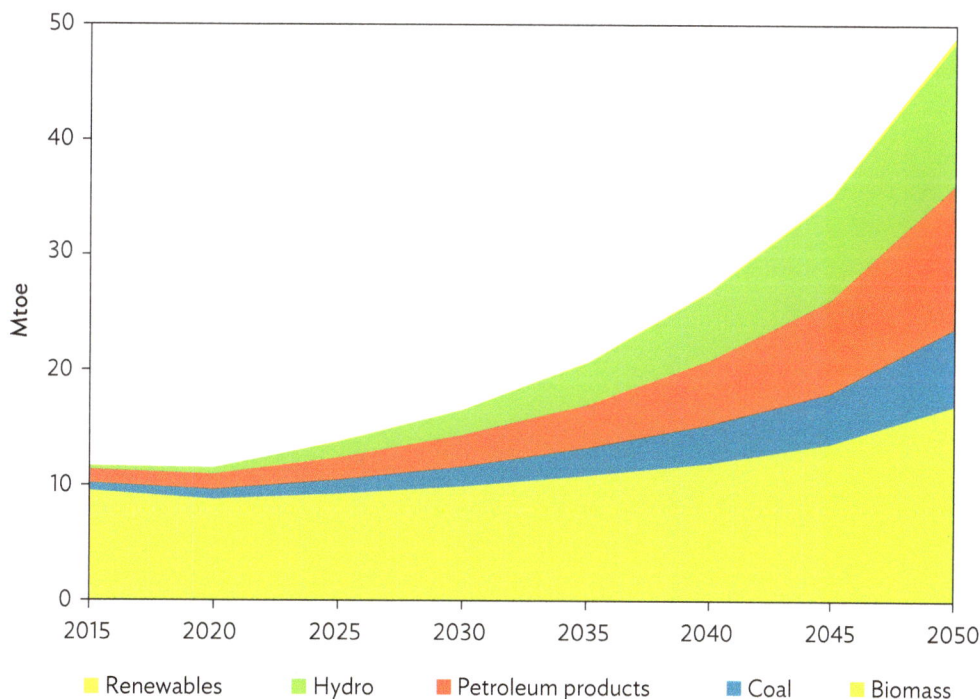

Mtoe = million tons of oil equivalent.
Source: Authors.

Final Energy Consumption:

The TFEC would increase from 11.7 Mtoe to 16.6 Mtoe during 2015–2030 and would reach 46.2 Mtoe in 2050, a CAGR of 4.0% during 2015–2050 (Figure 4.20). Biomass consumption would increase at a modest rate of 1.8% during this period. However, the use of petroleum products, coal, and electricity would increase at 6.3%, 6.9%, and 10.4%, respectively.

The share of biomass in the final energy mix would decrease during 2015–2050, from more than 80% in 2015 to about 62% in 2030 and 38% in 2050. The shares of modern fuels and renewables would increase significantly; the share of petroleum products would increase from 9.9% in 2015 to 15.9% in 2030 and 21.3% in 2050. Similarly, the share of coal would increase from 5.6% in 2015 to 10.3% in 2030 and 14.6% in 2050. Electricity, which had a share of just 3.1% in 2015, would have its share in TFEC increase to 11.9% in 2030 and 24.8% in 2050. The share of renewables would be 1% in 2050.

The residential sector had the highest contribution in TFEC in 2015. It would continue to do so during 2015–2050 although its share in TFEC would decrease from 80.3% in 2015 to 66.3% in 2030 and 47.4% in 2050. Industry and transport sectors had the second and third largest contributions in TFEC in 2015 and would maintain these positions until 2050. The industry sector's share was 10.3% in 2015 and would increase to 18.5% in 2030 and 27.1% in 2050. The share of the transport sector would grow from 5.4% in 2015 to 9.1% in 2030 and 14.9% in 2050. The share of the commercial sector in TFEC would increase from 3.1% to 5.2% during the period, whereas the agriculture sector's share would increase from 1.0% to 5.4%.

Energy mix in the residential sector. Final energy consumption of the sector would increase during 2015–2050 (Figure 4.21), from 9.4 ktoe in 2015 to 11.0 ktoe in 2030 and 21.8 ktoe in 2050. Use of biomass would decrease during 2015–2020, mainly due to the use of ICS. However, the use of biomass would increase after 2020 due to increased final energy demand; the CAGR during 2015–2050 would be 1.2%. Modern fuels like petroleum products and electricity would increase considerably by 4.3% and 11.5%, respectively. The share of biomass would decrease from 97.0% in 2015 to 84.9% in 2030 and 64.0% in 2050. This is partly due to the assumption that the cooking based on traditional fuels and technologies would gradually decrease over time in the sector with the increase in household income. As a result, the share of modern fuels (petroleum products, electricity, and renewables) would increase during 2015–2050. In particular, the share of electricity would increase significantly from 1.7% in 2015 to 32.3% by 2050. The share of petroleum products in the final energy mix would increase from 1.4% in 2015 to 5.4% in 2030 and then decrease to 2.6% in 2050. The share of renewables, which was negligible in 2015, would exceed 1% in 2050.

Energy mix in the commercial sector. The FEC of the commercial sector would increase from 0.4 Mtoe in 2015 to 0.7 Mtoe in 2030 and 2.4 Mtoe in 2050, increases of 80% and 570%, respectively. Biomass use would increase at the CAGR of 2.8% during 2015–2050, whereas the use of petroleum products, coal, and electricity would increase at 4.8%, 3.7%, and 10.2%, respectively. As for the residential sector, the share of biomass would decrease during 2015–2050, from 57.7% in 2015 to 39.6% in 2030 and 23.0% in 2050. In 2015, petroleum products, coal, and electricity accounted for 21.9%, 8.1%, and 12.3% of TFEC, respectively. The share of petroleum products would increase to 25.0% in 2030 and decrease to 17.0% in 2050, whereas the share of electricity would increase to 29.0% in 2030 and 55.6% in 2050. The contribution of coal in TFEC would be 6.1% in 2030 and 4.3% in 2050.

Energy mix in the transport sector. The FEC in the transport sector would increase from 0.6 Mtoe in 2015 to 1.6 Mtoe in 2030 and 9.4 Mtoe in 2050, by 1.6 and 14 times, respectively. In 2015, petroleum products accounted for over 99% of the sector's FEC, and this share would be maintained during 2015–2050.

Energy mix in the industry sector. The FEC of the industry sector would increase from 1.2 in 2015 to 3.1 Mtoe in 2030 and 12.4 Mtoe in 2050, i.e., a CAGR of 6.9% during 2015–2050. Coal would remain the dominant fuel in the sector, followed by biomass and electricity. The use of petroleum products would remain insignificant during the period.

Coal contributed to 52%–54% of FEC of the sector during 2015–2050. Electricity's share in the FEC would increase from 12.2% in 2015 to 22.9% in 2030 and 21.1% in 2050. Similarly, the share of biomass would also increase from 18.8% in 2015 to 21.2% in 2030 and 25.6% in 2050. The share of petroleum would be reduced to almost zero by 2050.

Energy mix in the agriculture sector. The agriculture sector had a low share of 1.0% in FEC in 2015 in Nepal; however, the sector's FEC would increase significantly during 2015–2050, from 0.1 Mtoe in 2015 to 0.4 Mtoe in 2030 and 2.5 ktoe in 2050; i.e., increases of 2.1 and 19.5 times, respectively. Petroleum products and electricity are the energy commodities used in the sector. Petroleum products accounted for almost 94% of the FEC in 2015 and would decrease to 89.7% in 2030 and 83.6% in 2050.

Figure 4.20: Fuel Mix and Sector Contributions in Total Final Energy Consumption for Nepal, 2015–2050

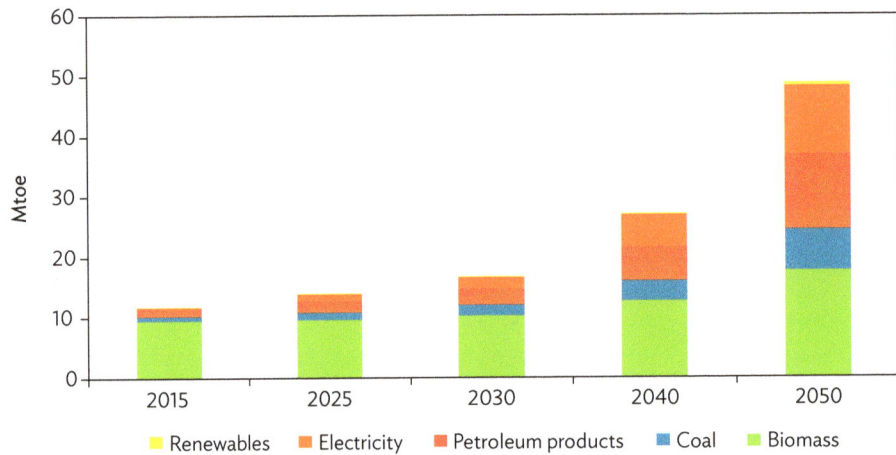

a. Fuel Mix

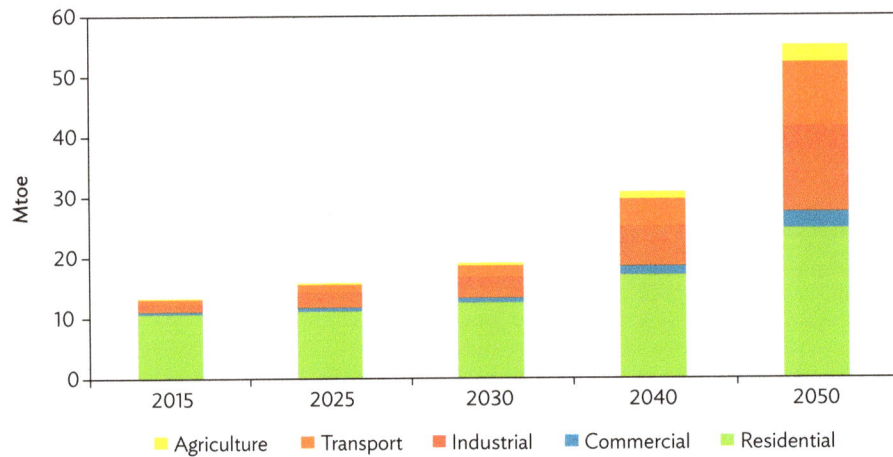

b. Sector Contributions

Mtoe = million tons of oil equivalent.
Source: Authors.

Figure 4.21: Final Energy Consumption by Sector for Nepal

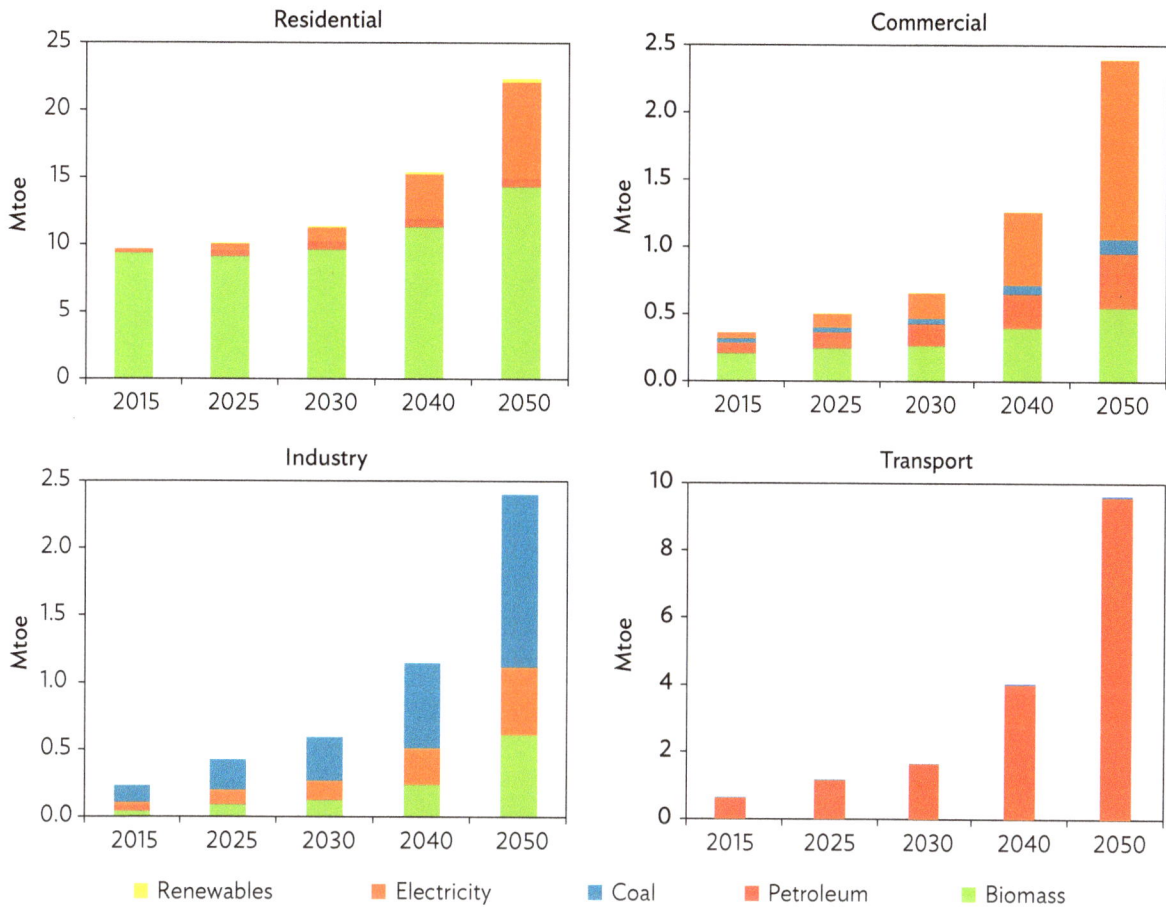

Mtoe = million tons of oil equivalent.
Source: Authors.

Cost-Saving Energy Efficient Technologies in 2015

Table 4.5 presents a list of no-regret efficient technology options in the base year (2015) for the reference (REF) scenario. The table also shows the corresponding technologies used in the BAU scenario. No option of no-regret technology found in the REF scenario in the transport sector.

Energy Efficiency Gap and Energy Saving Potential in 2015

Figure 4.22 presents the overall ESP at the sector levels in 2015 with the use of the no-regret efficient technology options. The analysis shows that the residential sector offered the highest ESP of 875 ktoe in 2015, followed by the industry (371 ktoe), commercial (61 ktoe), and agriculture (13 ktoe) sectors. Because there was no difference in technology choice between BAU and REF scenarios in the transport sector, the sector did not offer any ESP in 2015.

Figure 4.22: Energy Saving Potential in Different Sectors for Nepal, 2015

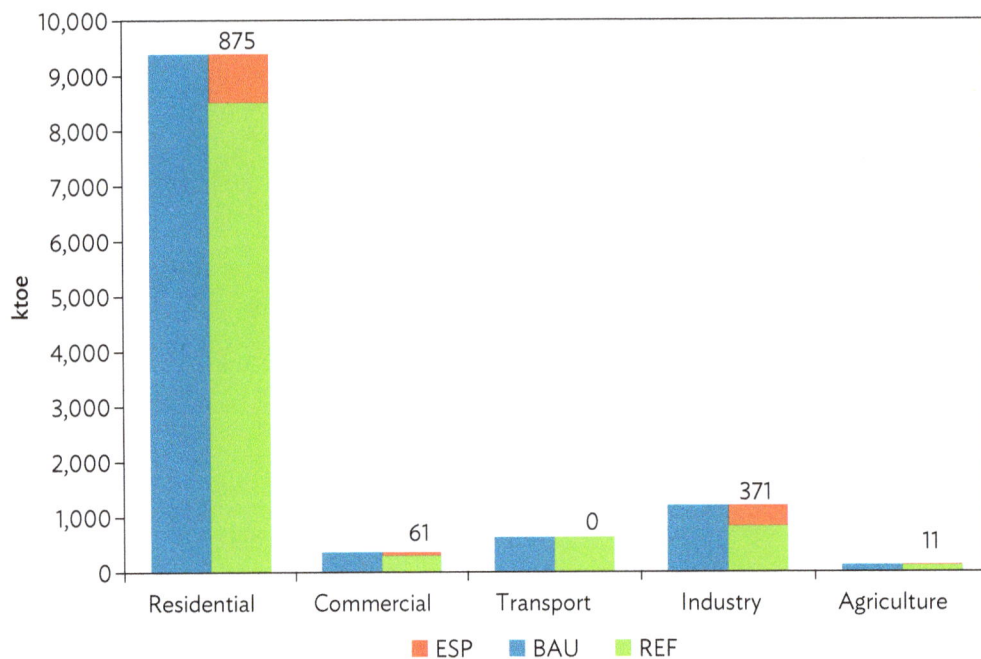

BAU = business as usual scenario; ESP = energy saving potential; ktoe = kiloton of oil equivalent; REF = reference scenario.
Source: Authors.

Table 4.5: No-regret Technologies, EEG and ESP in Different Sectors in Nepal in 2015

Sector	Type of End-use or Product	Technology in BAU	No-regret Technology	Energy Intensity (Energy Input/Output)			EE gap	Energy saving Potential (ktoe)
				BAU	REF	Unit		
Residential	Lighting	Incandescent bulb	LED	6.30	0.90	toe/billion lumen-hour	5.4	20.6
		CFL bulb		1.90	0.90		1.0	0.6
		Fluorescent bulb		1.90	0.90		1.0	4.6
	Cooling	Air-conditioner SEER 13	Air-conditioner SEER 20.5	0.26	0.17	Watt/Watt	0.1	7.5
	Cooking	TCS	ICS	7.70	4.30	toe/toe	3.3	778.0
	Cooking	LPG stove	Energy-efficient LPG stove	1.90	1.70	toe/toe	0.2	57.0
Commercial	Cooking	TCS	AICS	7.70	3.40	toe/toe	4.3	35.2
		ICS	AICS	4.30	3.40	toe/toe	0.9	13.6
		ICCS	AICS	3.60	3.40	toe/toe	0.2	1.0
		LPG stove	Energy-efficient LPG stove	1.90	1.70	toe/toe	0.2	6.4
	Lighting	Incandescent bulb	LED	6.30	0.90	toe/billion lumen-hour	5.4	2.9
		CFL bulb		1.90	0.90		1.0	0.2
		Fluorescent bulb		1.90	0.90		1.0	0.7
	Water heating	LPG geyser	Energy-efficient LPG geyser	1.70	1.30	toe/toe	0.4	1.2
Industry	Brick	Hoffmann Kiln	Improved Fixed Chimney BTK	60.60	46.70	toe/million bricks	13.8	0.1
		Fixed Chimney Bull Trench Kiln (BTK)		53.30	46.70		6.7	8.3
		Moving Chimney Bull Trench Kiln (BTK)		60.60	46.70		13.9	25.5
	Process heat	Coal boiler	Energy-efficient coal boiler	1.80	1.50	toe/toe	0.3	26.1
		Diesel boiler	Energy-efficient diesel boiler	1.50	1.40	toe/toe	0.1	2.5
		Fuelwood boiler	Heat-pump boiler	2.50	0.20	toe/toe	2.3	50.4
		Electric boiler	Heat-pump boiler	1.00	0.20	toe/toe	0.8	16.6
		Fuel Oil boiler	Heat-pump boiler	1.50	0.20	toe/toe	1.3	0.8

continued on next page

Table 4.5   *continued*

Sector	Type of End-use or Product	Technology in BAU	No-regret Technology	Energy Intensity (Energy Input/ Output)			Energy saving Potential (ktoe)
				BAU	REF	Unit	EE gap
	Motive power	IE1 motor–small size (< 0.75 kW)	IE5 motor small size	1.50	1.10	toe/toe	0.3	3.3
		IE1 motor–medium size (0.75 kW–375 kW)	IE5 motor medium size	1.30	1.10	toe/toe	0.2	7.6
		IE1 motor–large size (>375 kW)	IE5 motor large size	1.10	1.00	toe/toe	0.1	3.2
	Cement–raw material grinding	Ball Mill	Vertical Mill	4.30	2.30	toe/1000 tons	2.0	4.7
	Cement–clinker production	Wet kiln	4-stage cyclone suspension preheater type rotary kiln	145.80	77.50	toe/1000 tons	68.3	48.7
		Long dry kiln	4-stage cyclone suspension preheater type rotary kiln	112.40	77.50	toe/1000 tons	34.9	133.0
	Cement–finish grinding	Ball Mill	Vertical Mill	3.10	2.30	toe/1000 tons	0.8	5.4
	Industrial lighting	Incandescent bulb	LED	6.30	1.30	toe/billion–lumen hour	5.1	5.0
		Fluorescent	LED	1.90	1.30	toe/billion–lumen hour	0.6	0.6

AICS = advanced improved cook stove; CFL = compact fluorescent lamp; ICS = improved cook stove; IE1 = standard efficiency motor; IE5 = ultra premium efficiency motor; ktoe = kiloton of oil equivalent; kW = kilowatt; LED = light emitting diode; LPG = liquefied petroleum gas; SEER = seasonal energy efficient ratio; TCS = traditional cook stove; toe = tons of oil equivalent.

Source: Authors.

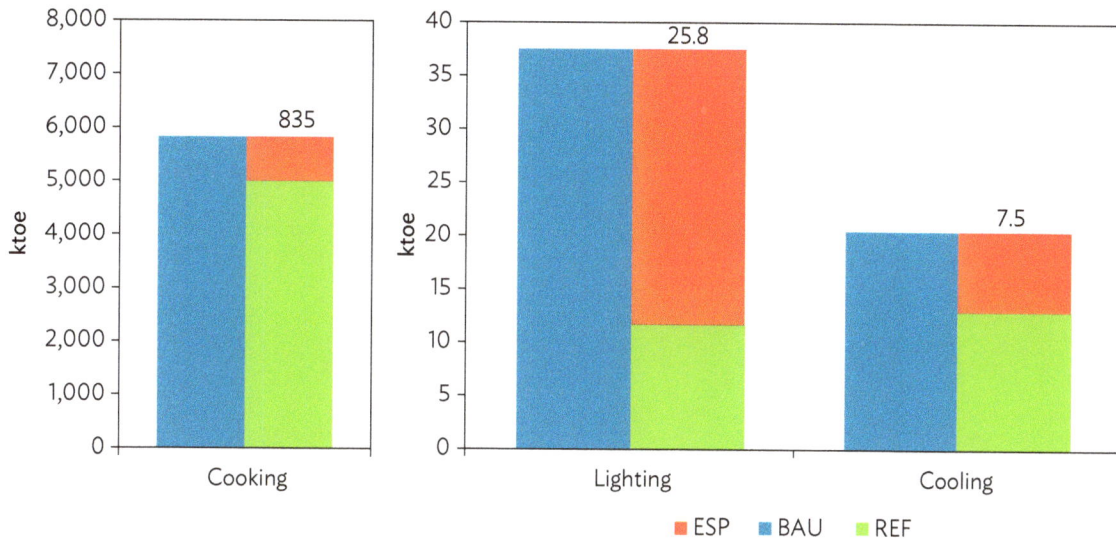

Figure 4.23: Energy Saving Potential in the Residential Sector of Nepal, 2015

BAU = business as usual scenario; ESP = energy saving potential; ktoe = kiloton of oil equivalent; REF = reference scenario.
Source: Authors.

Residential Sector

The estimated EEG in different end-use services in the residential and other sectors is shown in Figure 4.23 to Figure 4.25. Figure 4.23 presents the ESP in major end-use services in the residential sector. The ICS and energy-efficient LPG stoves are the cost-saving efficient technologies for cooking in the sector in the REF scenario. In 2015, replacement of TCS with ICS would result in an energy saving of 777.6 ktoe in cooking; and switching to using energy-efficient LPG stoves would save 57.5 ktoe. In the case of lighting, 25.8 ktoe (300 GWh) of electricity could be saved (representing 68.9% of total energy consumption for lighting) with the use of light emitting diode (LED) lamps in place of incandescent and compact fluorescent lamps (CFLs). The use of efficient air-conditioners for space cooling would save 7.5 ktoe (87.2 GWh), which is 36.7% of the total sector electricity consumption for cooling in 2015.

Commercial Sector

Similar to the residential sector, the commercial sector has no-regret ESP for mainly three end uses: cooking, lighting, and space cooling. The ESP in cooking based on biomass is 49.8 ktoe representing 31.5% savings in energy consumption in BAU, while it is 6.4 ktoe on LPG accounting for 11.7% savings (Figure 4.24). The no-regret technology options in the commercial sector have ESP of 3.8 ktoe (44.2 GWh) in lighting, corresponding to 71.3% of electricity use in the end-use. Efficient air-conditioners have the potential to save 1.2 ktoe (12.8 GWh) in the sector.

Figure 4.24: Energy Saving Potential in the Commercial Sector of Nepal, 2015

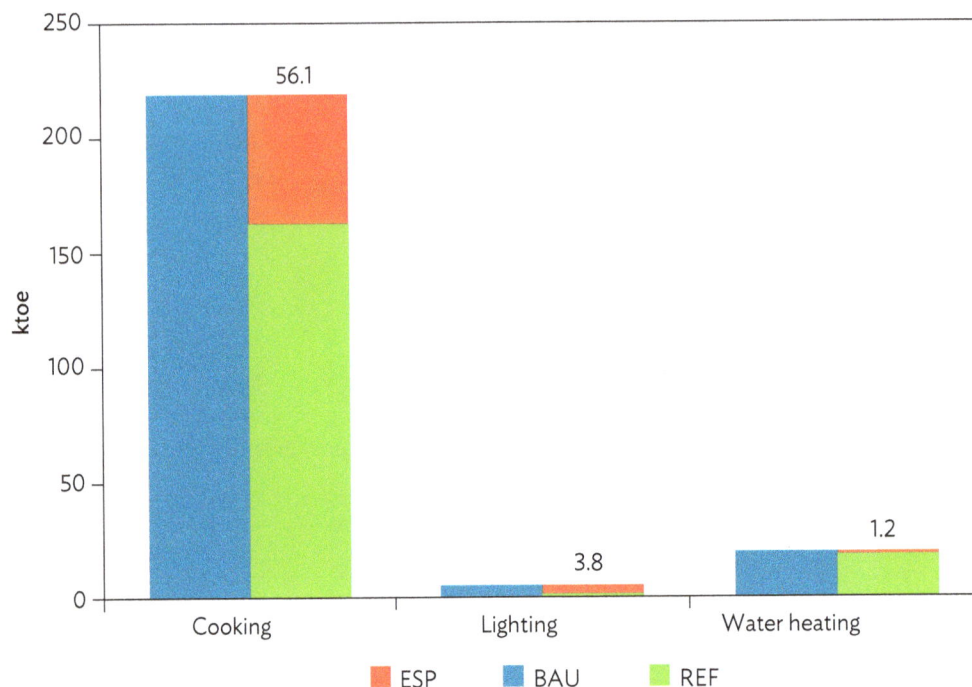

BAU = business as usual scenario; ESP = energy saving potential; ktoe = kiloton of oil equivalent; REF = reference scenario.
Source: Authors.

Transport

No cost-saving technology option was found for the transport sector in 2015. It should be noted that modal shift from private cars to public transport, such as buses and mini-buses, could offer significant ESP; however, this analysis does not consider the modal shift option in the BAU and REF cases.

Industry

Figure 4.25 presents ESP in selected industries in 2015. The ESP of efficient lighting in the entire industry sector is 5.6 ktoe (65.1 GWh), representing 58.1% of the total electricity consumed in lighting in the sector. In the case of motive power, ESP of energy-efficient motors in the sector as a whole is 14.1 ktoe (164 GWh). This analysis also identified cost-saving efficient boilers in the industry sector in the REF scenario; such boilers would save 96.5 ktoe compared to 2015. In the cement industry, there would be a saving of 102.7 ktoe of thermal energy, representing 36.9% of total thermal energy consumption in the industry; likewise there is potential to save 6.6 ktoe of electrical energy in the industry, representing 28.5% of its total electricity consumption. The brick industry has ESP of 32.5 ktoe, which is almost 18% of the industry's FEC.

Figure 4.25: Energy Saving Potential in the Industry Sector of Nepal, 2015

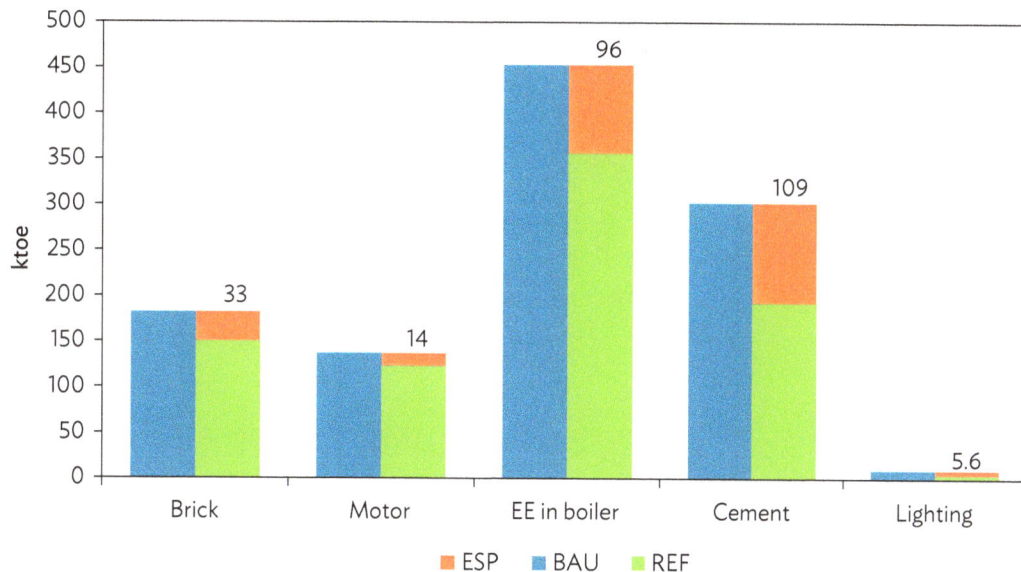

BAU = business as usual scenario; ESP = energy saving potential; ktoe = kiloton of oil equivalent; REF = reference scenario.
Source: Authors.

Agriculture

In the agriculture sector, average EEG in irrigation pumping is 0.69 toe electricity per toe of water lifted. Diesel pumps are highly prevalent in irrigation in BAU. The use of energy-efficient pumps in off-grid areas and electric pumps in grid-connected areas offer high ESP. The use of these efficient options would result in energy saving of 2.3 ktoe (i.e., 14% of energy consumption) in irrigation.

Implications of No-Regret Energy Efficient Technologies for Electricity Generation

Electricity generation in the REF scenario would decrease due to improvements in the energy efficiency of end-use devices and to fuel switching. In industry and agriculture sectors, electricity consumption would increase due to switching from petroleum and biomass to electricity. However, overall, there would be a net decrease in electricity consumption. Energy-efficiency improvement in 2015 can reduce electricity generation by 913 GWh in the residential sector and 135 GWh in the commercial sector. In the agriculture sector, fuel switching from gasoline- and diesel-based technologies to electricity-based technologies in irrigation and threshing increases electricity use by 195 GWh. In industry, the use of heat pumps in process use increases electricity use by 109 GWh. Adoption of cost-saving energy technology options would reduce the total electricity generation requirement in Nepal by 17.8% in 2015.

Sensitivity Analysis

Sensitivity analyses were carried out with the variation of the initial cost of the no-regret technologies with significant ESP in key end uses and major industry subsectors. In the residential sector, the analysis found that ICS would still be a no-regret option even if its cost increased by 1.4 times. In the case of modern cooking, efficient LPG stoves would be a cost-efficient option even if the initial cost increased 3.9 times. In the residential and commercial sectors, the use of LED lamps would be less expensive than incandescent lamps even if the initial cost of LED lamps was 15 times that considered in the BAU and REF cases. Similarly, LED lamps would still be more cost-competitive than fluorescent lamps even if the initial cost of LED lamps increased by 200%; also LED lamps would be a cost and energy-saving option compared to CFLs even if the LED lamp cost was 150% higher than that considered in the BAU and REF cases. In the case of cooling, energy-efficient air-conditioners (seasonal energy efficiency ratio [SEER] 20.5) would still be a no-regret option compared to conventional air-conditioners (SEER 13) even if the initial cost of energy-efficient air-conditioners was 50% higher than that considered in the BAU and REF cases.

In the commercial sector, the use of advanced improved cook stoves (AICS) would be cheaper than ICS even if the initial cost of AICS was 15% higher. Similarly, compared to TCS, AICS would still be a no-regret option if the initial cost of AICS increased by 3.5 times. It should be noted that in this study the biomass fuel price considered is higher in the commercial than in the residential sector; therefore, the no-regret options differ for the two sectors. In the commercial sector, the market price of biomass fuel is considered but in the residential sector the biomass price is considered as the shadow price. The shadow price is based on fuel wood collection time from the forest and the minimum wage rate of Nepal.

In the brick industry, the improved fixed-chimney bull trench kiln would be a no-regret technology compared to fixed-chimney and moving-chimney bull trench kilns even if its initial investment cost was 20% and 65% higher, respectively.

In the case of motive power in industry, motors are classified as small (<0.75 kW), medium (0.75–375 kW), and large (375–1,000 kW). The sensitivity analysis in the case of motors in industry showed that ultra-premium efficiency type of motors would remain a no-regret option even if their cost increased by 3.5 times in the case of small motors, by 2.3 times for medium motors, and by 1.2 times for large motors.

In the cement industry, the clinker production process is the most energy-intensive process. The four-stage cyclone suspension preheater type kiln is a no-regret option compared to both wet and long dry types of kilns. The four-stage cyclone suspension preheater type would still be a no-regret option compared to the wet kiln if the former's initial cost increased by 12% and compared to the long dry kiln if its cost increased by 3%.

In industries requiring process heat, different types of boilers are considered in this study. Efficient coal boilers are cost-effective compared to conventional coal boilers. Similarly, energy-efficient diesel boilers are also more cost-effective than conventional counterparts. Heat-pump boilers are also considered as an option in the study, assuming that waste heat is available in the industries; however, it is assumed that heat pumps would supply less than 50% of the total industry process heat requirement. Heat-pump boilers were the most cost-effective among all the technology options. The energy-efficient coal boilers would be a no-regret option compared to conventional coal boilers even if the cost rose 9.5 times. Likewise, energy-efficient diesel boilers are cheaper to use than conventional diesel boilers even if the former's cost were 10 times higher. Heat-pump boilers are cost-effective compared to fuelwood boilers even if their cost rises by 3.5 times.

Energy Saving Potential in 2030

Comparative analysis of the results for the BAU and REF scenarios provides information concerning the ESP of no-regret efficient technologies in 2030 (Figure 4.26). The industry sector would have the highest ESP of 568 ktoe in 2030, representing 52.2% of total ESP. The residential and commercial sectors would offer ESP of 106 ktoe and 141 ktoe, respectively, through the deployment of no-regret options. Similarly, the ESP of the transport and agriculture sectors in 2030 would be 273 ktoe and 21 ktoe, respectively. It should also be noted that electricity generation in the REF scenario would be 8.2% higher than in BAU.

Figure 4.26: Energy Saving Potential in Different Sectors for Nepal, 2030

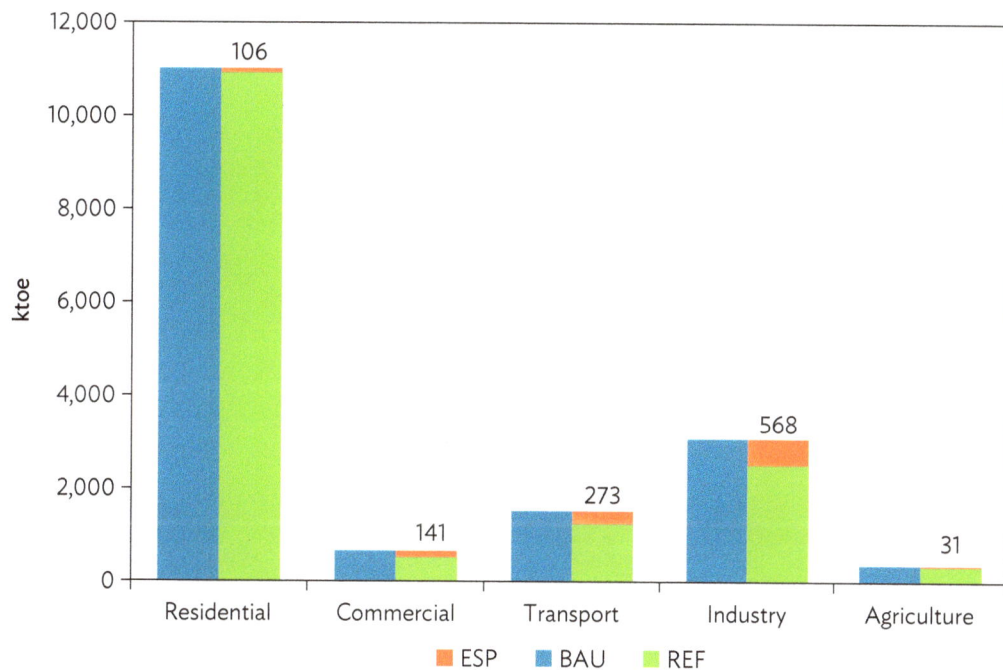

BAU = business as usual scenario; ESP = energy saving potential; ktoe = kiloton of oil equivalent; REF = reference scenario.
Source: Authors.

Sri Lanka

Energy Development for Business as Usual

Total Primary Energy Supply:
Figure 4.27 shows the growth of total primary energy supply (TPES) in Sri Lanka during 2015–2050 in the BAU scenario, as well as the growth of individual energy sources. The TPES would increase by 97% in 2030 and by 360% in 2050 compared to 2015, i.e., a compound annual growth rate (CAGR) of 4.4% during 2015–2050. Biomass, petroleum products, hydro, and other renewables would grow at a CAGR of 3.0%, 4.9%, 0.6%, and 7.7%, respectively. The use of coal would increase by 5.6% during 2015–2050. In 2015, biomass was the predominant source of energy and accounted for over 40% of TPES. The shares of petroleum products and coal were 42.7% and 11.0%, respectively. The share of biomass would decrease to 32.9% in 2030 and would further decrease to 25.4% by 2050, whereas petroleum products and coal would account for 45.7% and 10.7% of TPES in 2030, respectively. Other renewables would have a combined share of 1.7% in 2030. The role of petroleum products in TPES would increase during 2015–2050 and have the highest share (50.0%) in TPES in 2050, followed by biomass (25.4%), coal (16.2%), hydro (1.2%), and other renewables (0.7%).

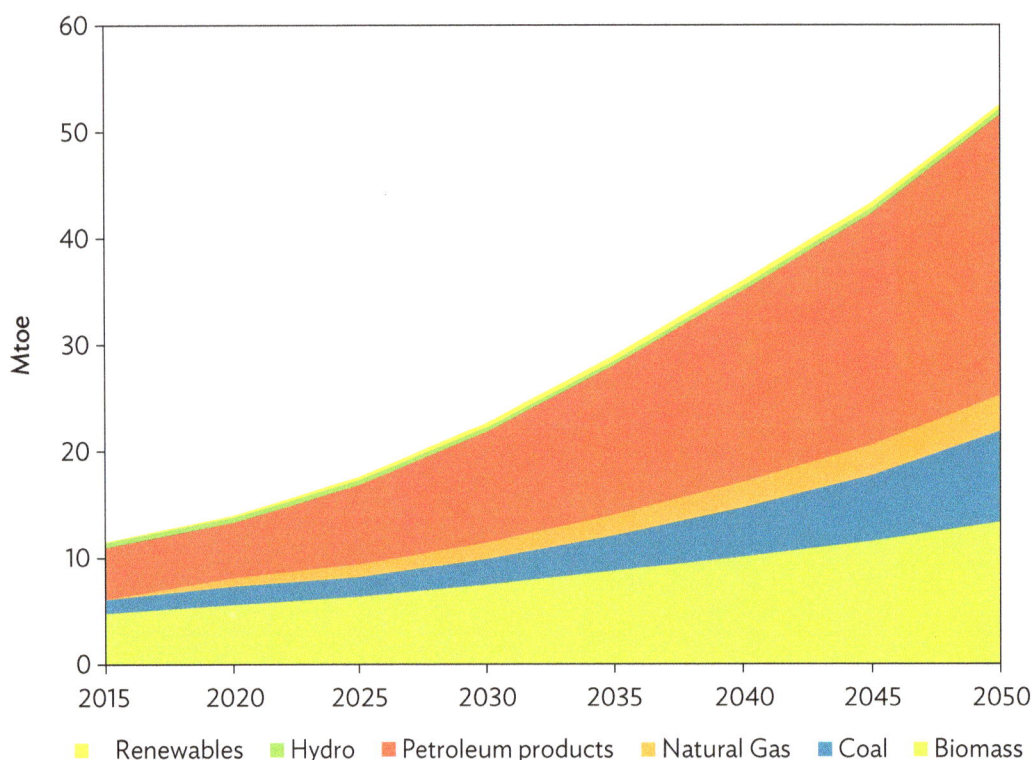

Figure 4.27: Total Primary Energy Supply in Sri Lanka, 2015–2050

Mtoe = million tons of oil equivalent.
Source: Authors.

Final Energy Consumption:
The TFEC would increase at the CAGR of 4.4% during 2015–2050 (Figure 4.28), from 9.9 Mtoe to 20.2 Mtoe during 2015–2030, an reaching 44.8 Mtoe in 2050. Biomass consumption would increase at a modest rate of 3.0% during 2015–2050. However, consumption of modern fuels like petroleum products, coal, and electricity would increase at 5.5%, 3.4%, and 4.8% during the period, respectively.

The share of biomass in TFEC would decrease from nearly 50% in 2015 to 36.8% in 2030 and 29.8% in 2050. The shares of other petroleum products would increase significantly, from 41.5% in 2015 to over 50% in 2030 and nearly 60% in 2050. Electricity's share in TFEC would be around 10%–12% during this period. The share of coal and renewables would not be significant.

The residential sector had the highest contribution in TFEC in 2015; however, its share would decrease from 31.6% in 2015 to 14.2% in 2030 and 7.0% in 2050. The transport sector's share was 28.8% in 2015 and would increase to 41.8% in 2030 and 48.3% in 2050. The share of the industry sector would grow from 30.6% in 2015 to 36.1% in 2030 and 37.2% in 2050. The share of the commercial sector in TFEC would decrease from 9.0% to 7.5% during 2015–2050.

Energy mix in the residential sector. Final energy consumption in the residential sector is shown in Figure 4.29. The use of biomass would decrease during 2015–2020, but consumption of modern fuels like petroleum products and electricity would both increase considerably at CAGR of 3.2% and 4.6%, respectively. The share of biomass in the FEC of the sector would decrease from over 80% in 2015 to below 20% in 2050. This is due to the assumption made in the study that the use of traditional fuels and technologies would gradually decrease over time in the residential sector with an increase in household income. The share of electricity would increase significantly from 12.8% in 2015 to 63.0% by 2050, whereas the share of petroleum products would increase from 5.9% in 2015 to 9.5% in 2030 and to 17.8% in 2050.

Energy mix in the commercial sector. The FEC of the commercial sector would increase from 0.9 Mtoe in 2015 to 1.6 Mtoe in 2030 and 3.3 Mtoe in 2050, i.e., increases of 80% and 275%, respectively. The sector would use biomass, petroleum products, and electricity. The use of petroleum products and electricity would grow at 5.6% and 4.9%, respectively. There would be no significant changes in the share of electricity in the FEC of the commercial sector. Petroleum products would play a higher role in the sector's FEC by 2050, but the role of biomass would diminish.

Energy mix in the transport sector. The FEC of the transport sector would rise from 2.9 Mtoe in 2015 to 8.4 Mtoe in 2030 and 21.6 Mtoe in 2050 (i.e., a CAGR of 6.0%). In 2015, petroleum products accounted for more than 99% of the sector's FEC and their share would be almost the same during 2015–2050, while electricity accounted for less than 1%.

Energy mix in the industry sector. The FEC of the industry sector would increase from 3.0 Mtoe in 2015 to 7.3 Mtoe in 2030 and to 16.7 Mtoe in 2050; i.e., a CAGR of 5.1% during 2015–2050. Biomass would remain the dominant fuel in the sector and would increase at the highest CAGR of 5.6% during the period. Brick and tile, tea, and rubber industries are some of the major industries that rely on fuelwood to meet their energy needs. Use of coal, electricity, and petroleum products would increase at 3.4%, 5.1%, and 3.3%, respectively. The contribution of biomass in the sector's FEC during 2015–2050 would increase from 58% in 2015 to 73% in 2050. Electricity's share would remain almost constant at around 10%–11% during 2015–2050, whereas the share of petroleum products and coal would decrease. The share of petroleum products would decrease from nearly 30% in 2015 to 16.6% in 2050.

Figure 4.28: Fuel Mix and Sector Contributions in Total Final Energy Consumption in Sri Lanka, 2015–2050

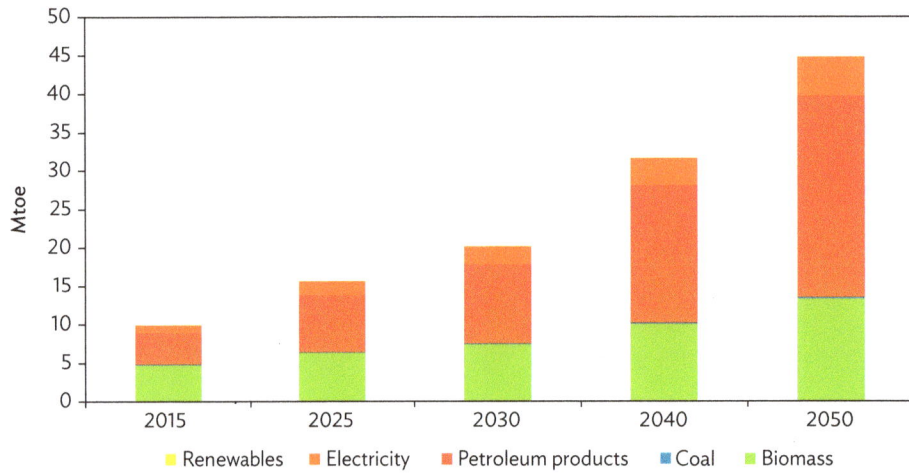

a. Fuel Mix

Renewables   Electricity   Petroleum products   Coal   Biomass

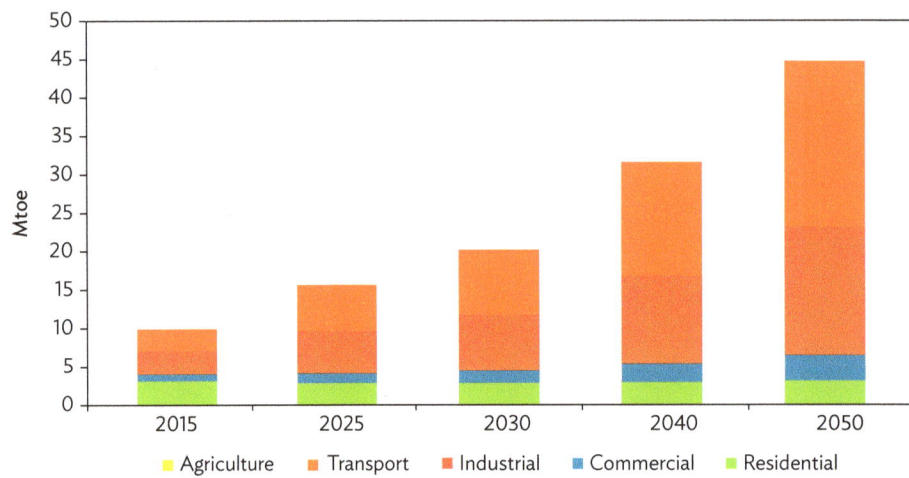

b. Sector Contributions

Agriculture   Transport   Industrial   Commercial   Residential

Mtoe = million tons of oil equivalent.
Source: Authors.

Figure 4.29: Final Energy Consumption by Sector in Sri Lanka, 2015–2050

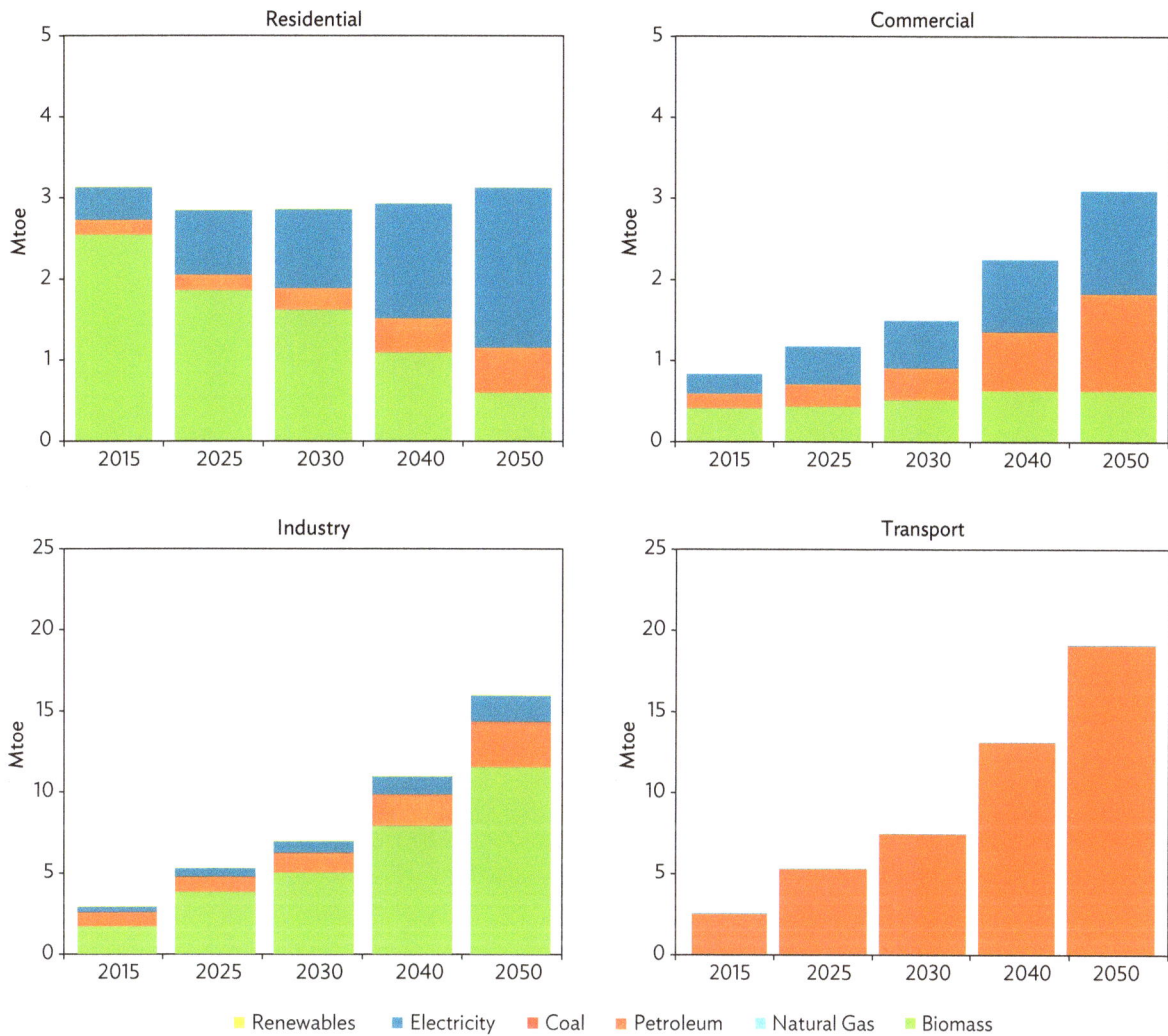

Mtoe = million tons of oil equivalent.
Source: Authors.

Energy Efficiency Gap and Energy Saving Potential in 2015

Figure 4.30 presents the FEC of different sectors in the BAU and REF scenarios as well as the ESP of no-regret technology options in each of the sectors in 2015. The residential sector offers the highest ESP with 916 ktoe, followed by the commercial (554 ktoe) and industry (546 ktoe) sectors. The ESP in the transport sector was negligible in 2015. For EEG analysis in the transport sector, only fuel-shift options are considered. This is because there is high range of values for the specific energy consumption MegaJoule (MJ)/passenger km) of the vehicles and the technology data are not available. In addition, specific energy consumption depends on the quality of roads and speed of the vehicles, which is not modeled in detail in this study. This study also ignores the modal shift in the transport sector in EEG analysis.

Figure 4.30: Energy Saving Potential in Different Sectors in Sri Lanka, 2015

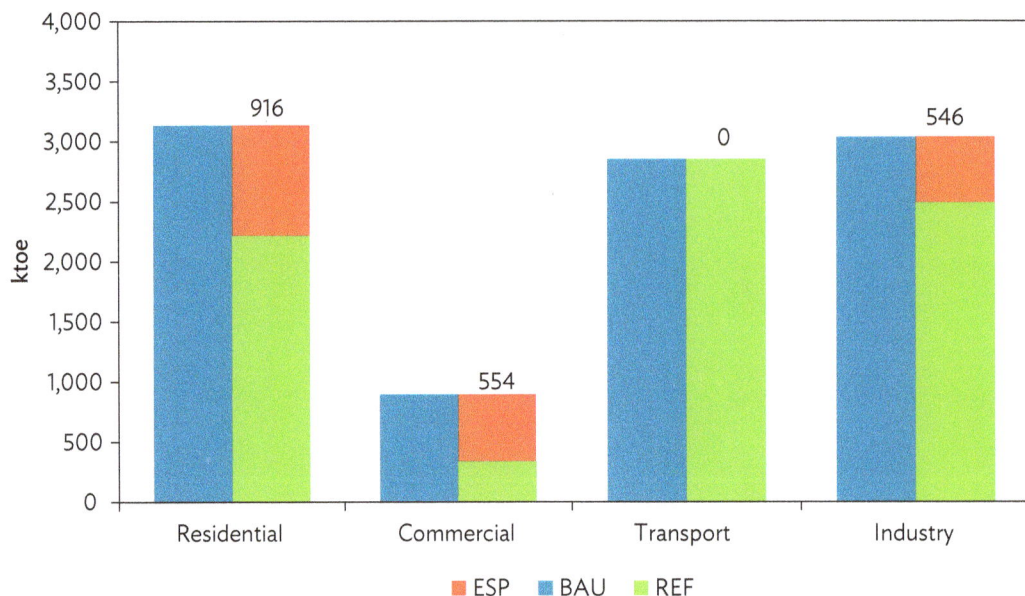

BAU = business as usual scenario; ESP = energy saving potential; ktoe = kiloton of oil equivalent; REF = reference scenario.
Source: Authors.

Cost-Saving Energy Efficient Technologies in 2015

Table 4.6 presents a list of no-regret technologies in the base year (2015). There is huge ESP by replacing traditional cook stoves (TCS) with improved cook stoves (ICS) in the residential sector. The use of LED bulbs offers the highest ESP in the residential sector, while in the commercial sector the use of more efficient air-conditioners offers the highest ESP. The tea and apparel industries are the sectors with major ESPs. The EEG and ESP by energy-efficiency improvement in each sector and subsector (in the case of industry) are presented in Table 4.6.

Table 4.6: No-regret Technologies, EEG and ESP in Different Sectors in Sri Lanka in 2015

Sector	Type of End-use or Product	Technology in BAU	No-regret Technology	Energy Intensity (Input/Output)			EE gap	Energy Saving Potential (ktoe)
				BAU	REF	Unit		
Residential	Lighting	Incandescent bulb	LED	6.30	0.90	toe/billion lumen–hour	5.4	16.9
		CFL bulb		1.90	0.90	lumen–hour	1.0	4.8
		Fluorescent bulb		1.90	0.90		1.0	9.8
	Cooling	Air-conditioner SEER 13	Air-conditioner SEER 20.5	0.26	0.17	Watt/Watt	0.1	17.0
	Cooking	TCS	ICS	7.70	4.30	toe/toe	3.3	829.4
		LPG stove	Efficient LPG stove	1.90	1.50	toe/toe	0.3	15.1
Commercial	Cooling	Air-conditioner SEER 13	Air-conditioner SEER 20.5	0.26	0.17	Watt/Watt	0.1	69.6
	Cooking	TCS	ICS	7.70	3.40	toe/toe	4.2	4.2
		LPG stove	Efficient LPG stove	1.90	1.50	toe/toe	0.3	0.2
	Lighting	Incandescent bulb	LED	6.30	0.90	toe/billion lumen–hour	5.4	5.4
		CFL bulb		1.90	0.90	lumen–hour	1.0	0.4
		Fluorescent bulb		1.90	0.90		1.0	1.0
Industry	Apparel industry	Existing boilers[a]	Efficiency improvement in existing boilers[b]	2.50	1.50	toe/toe	1.0	213.8
	Tea industry	Existing heater[a]	Efficiency improvement in existing heater[b]	2.50	1.50	toe/toe	1.0	199.3
		Existing dryer[a]	Efficiency improvement in existing dryer[b]	1.30	0.30	toe/toe	1.0	73.1
	Process heat	Existing boilers[a]	Energy efficiency improvement in existing boilers[b]	1.50	1.40	toe/toe	0.1	14.4
	Brick	Downdraft Brick Kiln	Improved Fixed Chimney Bull Trench Kiln (IFCBTK)	83.50	46.70	toe/1000 bricks	36.9	15.6

BAU = business as usual scenario; CFL = compact fluorescent lamp; ICS = improved cook stove; ktoe = kiloton of oil equivalent; LED = light emitting diode; REF = reference scenario; SEER = seasonal energy efficient ratio; TCS = traditional cook stove; toe = tons of oil equivalent.

[a] The technology here refers to the existing technologies used in the respective industries based on the audit reports.

[b] The technology here refers to the energy efficiency measures in the existing technologies as mentioned in the audit report.

Source: Authors.

Residential Sector

There is an EEG of 3.3 toe per unit toe of useful energy between ICS and TCS, i.e., for every 1 toe of useful energy delivered by a TCS, 3.3 toe of energy would be saved by the use of ICS without any additional cost. Similarly, the study found an EEG of 0.3 toe per unit toe of useful energy between an energy-efficient LPG cook stove and a conventional LPG stove. In the case of lighting, LED lamps were a no-regret option. The EEG in lighting would be highest for incandescent bulbs with EEG of 5.4 toe per billion lumen-hour and lowest for compact fluorescent lamps (CFLs) and fluorescent lamps with 1.0 toe per billion lumen-hour each. In the case of air-conditioning, EEG between efficient (Seasonal Energy Efficiency Ratio [SEER] of 20.5) and conventional (SEER of 13) air-conditioners was 0.1 W per unit watt of cooling.

Figure 4.31 presents the ESP in major end-use services in the residential sector. The ICS would be the major energy-saving efficient technology in the REF scenario. Replacement of TCS with ICS would result in an energy saving of 829.4 ktoe in cooking. Using efficient instead of conventional LPG stoves would save 15.1 ktoe. In the case of lighting, 32.5 ktoe (i.e., 376 GWh) of energy could be saved (amounting to 53.7% of total electricity consumed for lighting). Electricity savings by replacement of incandescent, fluorescent, and CFLs by more efficient LED lamps are presented in Table 4.6; of total lighting electricity demand, these lamps represent 10%, 30%, 40%, and 20%, respectively. The use of efficient air-conditioners for cooling would save 17.1 ktoe (i.e., 198 GWh), which is 53.9% of total electricity consumption for air-conditioning in 2015. The use of other efficient electrical devices would save 22.3 ktoe (259 GWh) of electricity.

Figure 4.31: Energy Saving Potential by End-Use in the Residential Sector in Sri Lanka, 2015

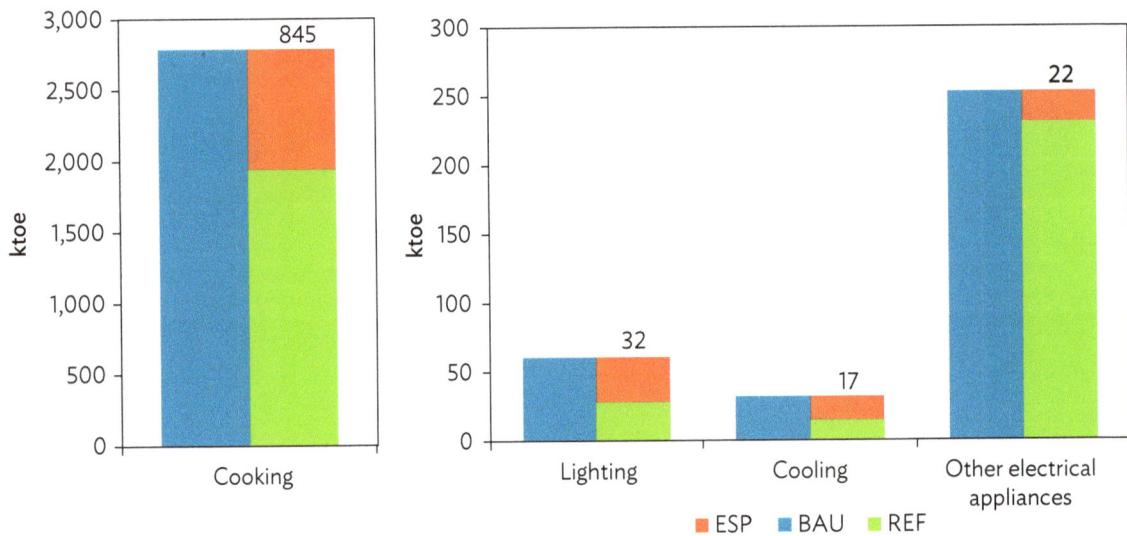

BAU = business as usual scenario; ESP = energy saving potential; ktoe = kiloton of oil equivalent; REF = reference scenario.
Source: Authors.

Commercial Sector

The commercial sector also has no-regret energy saving technologies in two end uses: lighting and cooling (Figure 4.32). The EEG for different end-use devices in the sector is the same as for the residential sector.

The sector has ESP of 301 ktoe in cooking. Furthermore, the sector has potential for saving 27.3 ktoe (i.e., 317 GWh) of energy in lighting, corresponding to 51.7% of electricity use for lighting in the sector. Efficient air-conditioners have ESP of 69.6 ktoe (equivalent to 810 GWh) in the sector.

Figure 4.32: Energy Saving Potential by End-Use in the Commercial Sector in Sri Lanka, 2015

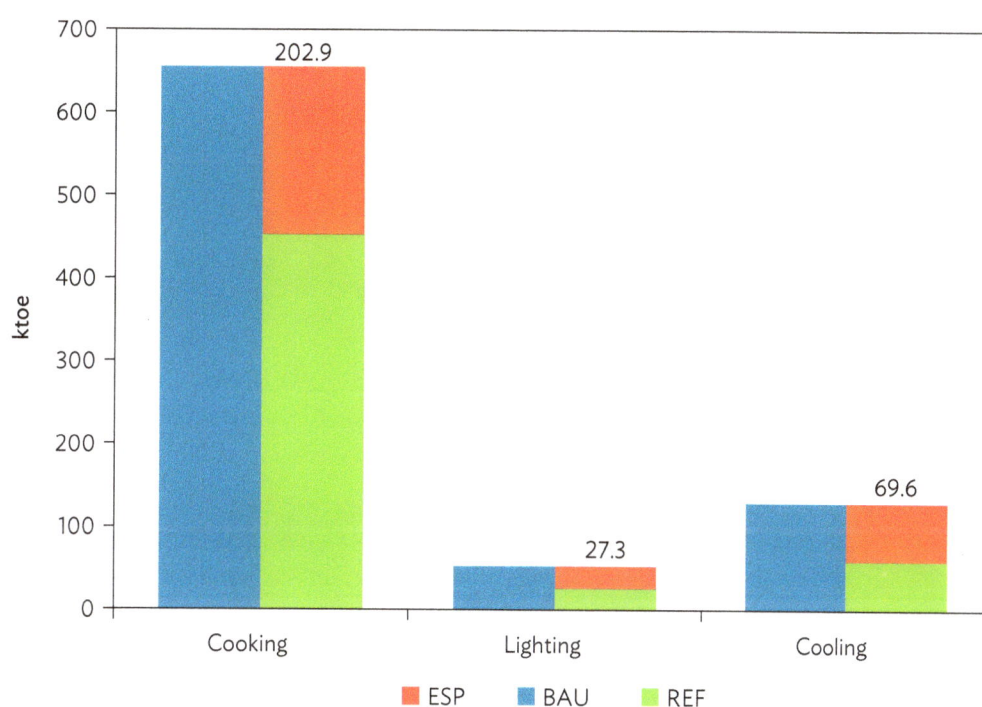

BAU = business as usual scenario; ESP = energy saving potential; ktoe = kiloton of oil equivalent; REF = reference scenario.
Source: Authors.

Industry Sector

In the industry sector, EEG is estimated based on energy-efficiency improvement in the existing facilities in case of apparel, tea, textile and fabric, rice processing, water treatment, and ceramicware industries. The EEG for boilers in the apparel industry is 1.0 toe per unit toe of process heat produced. In the tea industry, EEG is 1.0 toe per unit toe of heat output for both heaters and dryers. In other industries that use diesel boilers for process heat, EEG by energy-efficiency improvement is 0.1 toe per unit toe heat output. The EEG potential is lower for diesel compared to fuelwood boilers. In the brick industry, EEG is 36.9 toe per 1,000-unit bricks produced when downdraft brick kilns are replaced by improved fixed-chimney bull trench kilns.

The ESP in selected industries is presented in Figure 4.33. The ESP of the entire industry sector was 546 ktoe (i.e., 18.0% of the FEC of the sector) in 2015. Among industries, the tea industry offers the highest ESP of 272.4 ktoe, representing 49.3% of energy consumption in the industry in 2015. The apparel industry has the second highest ESP of 214 ktoe. The brick industry has the potential to save 15.6 ktoe, representing 40.2% of energy consumed by the industry in BAU. Together, other industries have an ESP of 44 ktoe.

Figure 4.33: Energy Saving Potential by End-Use in the Industry Sector in Sri Lanka, 2015

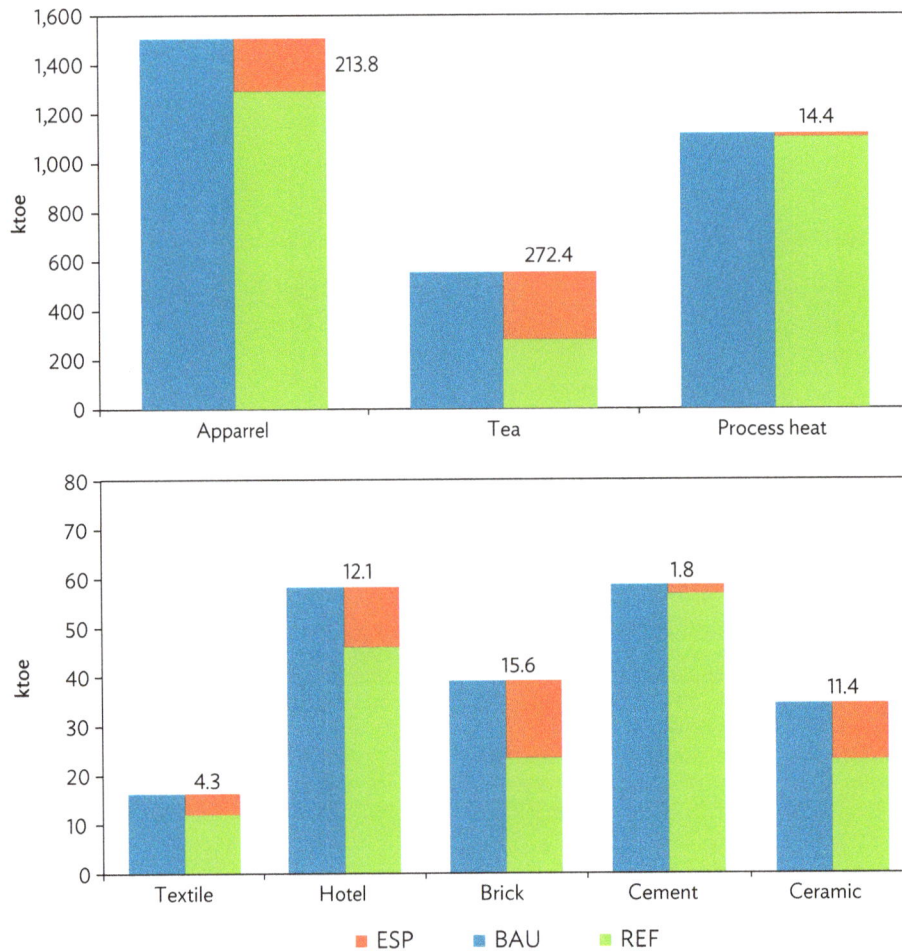

BAU = business as usual scenario; ESP = energy saving potential; ktoe = kiloton of oil equivalent; REF = reference scenario.

Source: Authors.

Transport Sector

The transport sector offers no ESP from no-regret technologies. As explained earlier, energy-efficiency improvement in vehicles and modal shifts are not considered in EEG analysis.

Implications for Electricity Generation

Electricity generation in the REF scenario is 18.2% less than that in BAU. This is mainly due to improvements in energy efficiency in end-use devices.

Sensitivity Analysis

In residential and commercial sectors, LED bulbs are the no-regret option over incandescent and CFL bulbs. The LED bulbs would still be more cost-effective than incandescent bulbs if the initial cost of LED bulbs was 18 times the considered cost, and more cost-effective compared to CFL bulbs even if their initial cost was 70% higher. Efficient air-conditioners (SEER 20.5) would still be cost-competitive with low-efficiency air-conditioners (SEER 13) if initial cost was 65% higher.

In cooking, ICS is the no-regret option over TCS even if the initial cost was 1.5 times the initial considered cost. Efficient LPG stoves are more cost-effective than conventional ones even if the initial cost increased by three times.

In the brick industry, improved fixed-chimney bull trench kilns would be a no-regret option over downdraft kilns if the initial cost was three times the given cost.

Energy Saving Potential in 2030

Comparative analysis of the results of BAU and REF scenarios also provides information on the ESP of no-regret efficient technologies in 2030. The total ESP of final demand sectors in 2030 would be 6,393 ktoe, equivalent to 31.7% of FEC in 2030 in BAU (Figure 4.34). The FEC of different sectors in the BAU and REF scenarios as well as the corresponding ESP values are shown in Figure 4.34. The industry sector would have the highest ESP in 2030, representing 47.2% of total ESP. The transport, residential, and commercial sectors would contribute 41.9%, 6.4%, and 4.4% to the total ESP in final energy consumption, respectively. Accordingly, the TPES in 2030 would decrease by 23.0%. Note that the percentage reductions in TFEC and TPES would differ due to differences in energy consumption in the power sector since electricity demand would be 32.4% higher in the REF than the BAU scenario.

Figure 4.34: Energy Saving Potential in Different Sectors in Sri Lanka, 2030

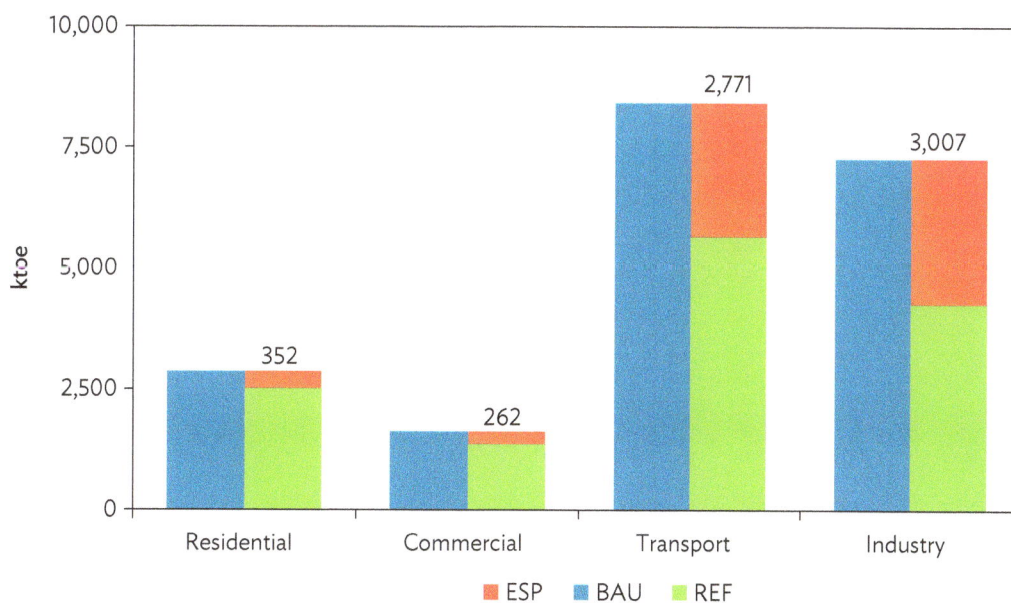

BAU = business as usual scenario; ESP = energy saving potential; ktoe = kiloton of oil equivalent; REF = reference scenario.
Source: Authors.

India

As no modeling of energy systems was carried out in the case of India, EEG estimates in the present study are based on information available in the existing literature. The EEGs of the industry and thermal power plants are based upon the Perform Achieve and Trade (PAT) scheme (BEE 2018e), while those of selected devices in the residential sector are based on existing studies. Note, however, that EEG estimates for the industry and power sectors in India based on information in the PAT scheme represent EEGs from a technical perspective unlike those for the four countries discussed earlier, which represent an economic perspective.

The industry, power, and residential sectors in India collectively accounted for around 66% of TPES in 2017. Thus, the discussion here focuses on EEG in these sectors. Note that the approaches used for estimating the EEG in these two sectors also differ to those discussed in previous sections.[3]

Industry and Power Sector

The Bureau of Energy Efficiency (BEE) launched the PAT scheme in 2008, with an objective to increase the overall efficiency of the industry sector (including thermal power plants) in a cost-effective manner (BEE 2011). The scheme imposes legal obligations for designated consumers to reduce specific energy consumption (SEC) within a pre-specified time frame. The first cycle of the PAT scheme was implemented during 2012–2015. More details about the PAT scheme are discussed in BEE (2018e). In this section, the discussion of EEG in India is based on results of the evaluation of Cycle 1 of the PAT scheme. The EEG discussed here is purely from the technical perspective in that EEG is measured as the difference between the SEC of the technology employed by a particular type of Indian industry (average) in the baseline year and the SEC of the corresponding best available technology in the world (except in the case of the cement industry).[4,5]

In the iron and steel industry, India's most efficient plant has SEC of 5.67 gigacalorie/tonne or (Gcal)/t of crude steel, which is 5% higher than that of the most efficient plant globally ("global best"), where, on average, iron and steel plants in India have 25% higher SEC than the global best. In the case of the cement industry, India's most efficient plant has a specific electrical energy consumption (SEEC) of 64 kilowatt hour (kWh)/t of cement, which is 42% less than the global average. On average, the SEEC of cement plants in India is 14% less than the global average. The specific thermal energy consumption of the most efficient cement plant in India is 24% less than the global average; the average for India's cement plants is 13% less than the global average.

In the pulp and paper industry, mills are divided into four categories: wood-based mills, recycled fiber-based mills producing unbleached grade products, agro-based mills, and recycled fiber-based mills producing bleached grade products. In wood-based mills, the average SEEC is 27%–29% above the global average SEEC and 14%–20% higher than the industry benchmark; moreover, specific steam consumption (SSC) is 31%–42% higher than that of global average. The SEEC and SSC of agro-based mills are both 17%–29% higher than the industry benchmark.

---

[3] Authors' calculation based on the International Energy Agency (IEA) database. IEA. Data and Statistics. https://www.iea.org/data-and-statistics (accessed 18 August 2019).

[4] Baseline year for the PAT scheme is 2007–2010 and assessment year is 2015 (BEE 2018e).

[5] In case of the cement industry, India's best and average SEC and SEEC values are better than global average values.

In the case of recycled fiber-based mills producing unbleached grade products, the average SEEC ranges from 11% less than to 9% higher than the global average and 11%–27% higher than the industry benchmark. The average SSC is 38%–50% above the global average and 13%–30% above the industry benchmark. In recycled fiber-based mills producing bleached grade products, the average SEEC is 12%–19% higher than the global average and 16%–29% higher than the industry benchmark. The average SSC of the mills is 33%–36% higher than the global average and 17%–29% above the industry benchmark.

The aluminum industry is divided into two categories: refining and smelting. In the case of refining, India's most efficient plant has an SEC of 0.23 tons of oil equivalent (toe)/t of alumina which is 13% higher than the SEC of the global best; on average, alumina refineries in India have 39% higher SEC than the global best. Likewise, in smelting, India's most efficient plant has an SEEC of 14,558 kWh/t of molten aluminum, which is 7% higher than the global best; an average alumina refinery in India has 5% higher SEC than the global best.

The fertilizer industry is divided into two types: urea and ammonia. India's most efficient urea plant has an SEC of 5.16 Gcal/t, which is 3% higher than the global best; on average urea plants in India have 16% higher SEC than the global best. Likewise, India's most efficient ammonia plant has an SEC of 7.1 Gcal/t, which is 3% above the SEC of the global best; on average, ammonia plants in India have 17% higher SEC than the global best (BEE 2018e).

In the context of the thermal power sector, BEE (2018e) gives the difference in gross unit heat rate and net heat rate between the national average and the national best (Table 4.7). For gas-fired power plants, the national average of gross unit heat rate is 18% higher than the national best, while the net heat rate of the national average gas-fired plant is 19% higher than the national best. In the case of other thermal plants, the difference in gross unit heat rate between the national average and the national best ranges from 6% for large power plants (300–600 megawatts [MW]) to 18% for small power plants (below 100 MW). Similarly, the difference in net heat rate between the national average and the national best ranges from 6% for large to 19% for small power plants.

Table 4.7: Gross and Net Heat Rates of Thermal Power Plants of Different Sizes
(kcal/kWh)

Size (MW)	Gross Unit Heat Rate		Net Heat Rate	
	National Best	National Average	National Best	National Average
<100	2,606	3,082	2,908	3,470
100–150	2,450	2,718	2,687	3,070
150–300	2,274	2,554	2,496	2,757
300–600	2,244	2,386	2,419	2,556
Gas	1,837	2,161	1,881	2,239

kcal = kilocalorie; kWh = kilowatt hour; MW = megawatt.
Source: Government of India, Bureau of Energy Efficiency. 2018. Enhancing Energy Effiency Through Industry Partnership (Outcome & Way Forward). (BEE). New Delhi. https://beeindia.gov.in/sites/default/files/press_releases/Consolidated%20Report.pdf.

Residential Sector

A number of studies on EEG have assessed the difference between the energy efficiency of the technologies in actual use and that of the least-cost technology (which is one of the more efficient technologies available) in different countries. Such studies identify the technologies actually used and determine their respective energy consumption based on a sample survey of energy-using units (e.g., households in the residential sector, and firms or production plants in the industry sector). Following this approach, Bhardwaj and Gupta (2017) carried out a study of household air-conditioners in Delhi, India. The study shows that the average EEG in households is about 10% of total electricity demand of air-conditioners. The study states that, with proper awareness of cost saving, emission reduction, and payback period, the expected private EEG could decline from 10% to 2.98% (Bhardwaj and Gupta 2017). However, it should be noted that this study focused on a specific appliance in a particular urban area and does not give a complete picture on EEG and ESP in the household sector of India.

A study (Parikh and Parikh 2016) on ESP in households of India considered a scenario of replacing all existing energy-consuming appliances by five-star rated appliances. The study showed the potential for saving nearly 40% of energy consumption in the household sector through these efficient appliances. Since the study considered replacement of the existing technologies by the most energy-efficient appliances, this finding also implies an EEG of 40% for the household sector. Note, however, that EEG here is measured from the technical perspective.

5 Implications of Energy Reduction Targets

5.1 Introduction

This chapter presents the implications of selected energy reduction targets in the case of four countries in South Asia (Bangladesh, Bhutan, Nepal, and Sri Lanka) based on the national energy system model developed for this study. A key objective of the analysis in this chapter is to assess the potential that different sectors offer to achieve the overall energy reduction targets as well as to find out the changes in technology-mix and energy mix needed in different sectors as well as the cost implications in meeting the energy reduction targets. The chapter also discusses the maximum possible levels of energy reduction in 2030 and 2050 in these countries. Furthermore, it discusses the implications of energy reduction targets for electricity sector development in terms of the level of power generation required, generation mix, and efficiency of generation.

The next section of the chapter describes the methodology used in the analysis. This is followed by a description of the business as usual (BAU) and energy reduction scenarios considered. The next section discusses the long-term implications of the energy reduction targets considered for total primary energy supply (TPES), structure of TPES, energy intensity, and electricity generation, as well as the final energy consumption, technological mix, costs, and emissions in the case of Bangladesh, Bhutan, Nepal, and Sri Lanka. This section also includes a discussion on targets for reduction of specific energy consumption, overall energy reduction of selected designated consumers, and energy intensity improvement projection until 2030 set under the PAT scheme of the BEE for India.[6] Furthermore, the section discusses the estimated energy consumption of India in future years under the emission reduction targets of the intended nationally determined contributions (INDCs) scenario based on the findings of an existing study. The concluding section discusses some policy implications and includes final remarks.

5.2 Methodology

The AIM/Enduse model, where AIM stands for Asia-Pacfic Integrated Model, was used for analysis of the implications of selected energy reduction targets. The details of the model were discussed in Chapter 4. At first, TPES, total final energy consumption (TFEC), energy mix, technology-mix, and costs are determined in the BAU scenario using the model. For the analysis of the implications of energy reduction targets, energy constraints are given exogenously to the model in the energy reduction scenarios. The energy reduction constraints are imposed based on desired reduction in the TPES in different years from the corresponding energy consumption

---

[6]   The Energy Conservation Act authorizes the Central Government to select the designated consumers based on the yearly energy consumption of the industry and compared to the prescribed sector-wise threshold limit.

levels in BAU. The model then determines the desired levels of energy consumption, energy mix, technology-mix, and costs in the energy reduction scenarios. Comparison of the model results for the BAU and energy reduction scenarios gives the estimated changes required in energy mix, technology-mix, and costs to achieve the reduction targets.

This study also estimates the maximum potential for the reduction of TPES in selected years, i.e., 2030 and 2050.[7] This is done iteratively by gradually increasing the energy reduction target in the AIM/Enduse model and running the model until it is found no longer feasible to meet the target. Note that in BAU it is assumed that some of the existing low-efficiency technologies would still be in use in the future and this would restrict the extent to which efficient technologies could be used. However, in determining the maximum energy-reduction potential, the model is not restricted in the choice of efficient technologies except that some limits are imposed on some technologies to make the scenarios more realistic; this is also done in BAU. For example, in the urban-residential sector, solid fuel-based cooking technologies are not allowed to completely substitute modern cooking technologies based on gas and electricity. In the transport sector, there is one major difference in the assumption made in the BAU scenario and in determining the maximum energy-reduction potential—in the BAU scenario it is assumed that the minimum shares of passenger cars would reach 35% by 2050; however, in determining the maximum energy-reduction potential, the minimum share of passenger cars is limited to 20% (thus allowing for the possibility of having sharing of passenger cars up to 80%). This assumption is made to capture higher energy-reduction possibilities that could be allowed for by a modal shift in the sector. Note that this study does not consider the possibility of modal shift in freight transport in determining the maximum energy-reduction potential. Thus, to that extent, the estimate of the maximum energy-reduction potential in this study will be somewhat underestimated.

This study estimates the average incremental cost (AIC) of energy reduction under the selected energy reduction targets. The AIC is measured as the ratio of the difference in total discounted cost between energy reduction and BAU scenarios to the total discounted value of energy reduction under an energy reduction scenario from the levels of total energy consumption in BAU. The AIC is expressed as follows:

$$\text{AICC of energy reduction} = (TC_i - TC_0)/\sum_i^T \frac{\Delta E_t^i}{(1+r)^t} \qquad (5.1)$$

where,

TC_0 is the present value of total cost in BAU

TC_i is the present value of total costs in energy reduction case i

$\Delta E_t^i = E_t^0 - E_t^i$

E_t^0 is energy consumption in year t in BAU

E_t^i is energy consumption in year t in energy reduction case i

The study also calculates the overall energy conversion efficiency, which is measured as the ratio of TFEC to the TPES.

---

[7] The maximum energy reduction potential in this study is defined as the maximum feasible level of reduction in the TPES from its BAU level and is expressed as a percentage of the TPES in BAU.

5.3 Scenario Descriptions

This study analyzes energy development and technology choice under four scenarios: a BAU scenario and three energy reduction scenarios. The BAU scenario is the same as discussed in Chapter 4. The BAU and energy reduction scenarios are similar, with the exception that the latter include constraints related to reduction in overall energy consumption in future years by some predetermined levels compared to BAU. Furthermore, the technological shares are not constrained in energy reduction scenarios. However, it should be noted that in residential and commercial sectors, minimum shares of modern fuel-based cooking are constrained. For example, it is assumed that at least a certain percentage of cooking would be based on modern fuels like liquefied petroleum gas (LPG), electricity, or kerosene. Furthermore, the minimum share of cars in the BAU has been defined in the transport sector. The minimum share of cars is assumed to reach 35% by 2050.

The study formulates different energy-reduction scenarios taking into account the maximum energy-reduction potential in the case of Bangladesh, Bhutan, Nepal, and Sri Lanka. The maximum energy-reduction potential in each of these countries is determined first. The maximum energy-reduction potential in Bangladesh is less than 41% of the TPES in BAU in 2050. In the case of other countries, the reduction potential is higher. Therefore, in the highest energy reduction scenario, the maximum reduction target of 40% of the TPES in BAU was set in 2050. Two more energy reduction scenarios were constructed with lower energy reduction targets. The three energy reduction scenarios considered in this study are (i) minimum 15% reduction in TPES by 2050 (ER15 scenario), (ii) minimum 30% reduction in TPES by 2050 (ER30 scenario), and (iii) minimum 40% reduction in TPES by 2050 (ER40 scenario). The temporal profiles of energy reduction in different years during 2020–2050 under the energy reduction scenarios are shown in Figure 5.1. In the ER15 scenario, TPES in 2020 is 1% less than that in the BAU scenario. The target for energy reduction would increase over time and by 2050 TPES is reduced by 15% under ER15. Similarly, in the ER30 scenario, TPES is 2.5% less in 2020 and 30% less by 2050. In the ER40 scenario, TPES is reduced by 5% in 2020 and by 40% in 2050. The transmission and distribution (T&D) losses in BAU and energy reduction scenarios during 2015–2050 for each country are presented in Appendix 5.

From practical considerations, minimum and maximum allowable shares are introduced in some cases in the residential and transport sectors. In rural residential, the minimum share of solid fuel-based cooking is constrained; similarly, the maximum share is constrained in urban residential. The minimum shares of passenger cars considered in different years are given in Table 5.1. The minimum share of passenger cars in total passenger service demand (passenger kilometer) in any particular year is considered to be smaller for a higher energy-reduction target to allow for a greater possibility for modal shift under higher energy-reduction targets. Note that passenger cars here refer to cars and jeeps used for private purposes. Public passenger cars such as taxis are not included. Furthermore, the minimum share would increase gradually over time under each energy reduction target. The study also analyzes the cost implications without modal shifts, i.e., when the minimum share of passenger cars is the same as in BAU.

This study also analyzes the implications of a reduction in T&D loss for electricity generation and installed capacity requirements. An additional analysis assesses the impacts of lower T&D losses (i.e., 10% and 5%) on the electricity generation sector. The base case and two T&D loss cases are hereafter named TDL-B, TDL-10%, and TDL-5%, respectively. The T&D loss in each case is presented in Table 5.2. It should be noted that electricity demand is not fixed in the T&D loss reduction analysis, therefore electricity demand during 2015–2050 might change as a result of T&D reduction.

Figure 5.1: Minimum Percent Energy Reduction Profile

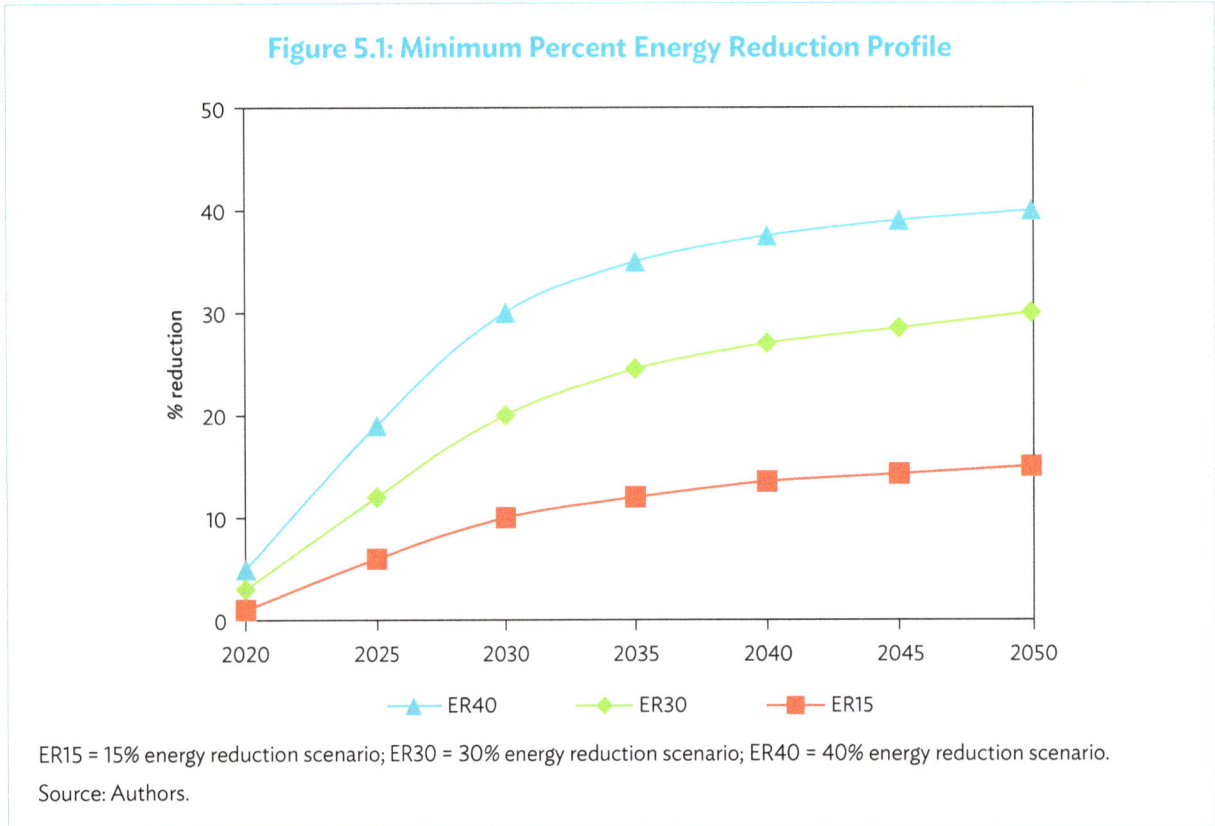

ER15 = 15% energy reduction scenario; ER30 = 30% energy reduction scenario; ER40 = 40% energy reduction scenario.

Source: Authors.

Table 5.1: Minimum Share of Passenger Cars in Passenger Transport Demand
(%)

Scenario	2020	2025	2030	2035	2040	2045	2050
BAU	12	12.5	15	20	25	30	35
ER15	10	13.0	15	18	20	25	30
ER30	10	13.0	15	18	20	23	25
ER40	8	10.0	12	14	16	18	20

BAU = business as usual scenario; ER15 = 15% energy reduction scenario; ER30 = 30% energy reduction scenario; ER40 = 40% energy reduction scenario.

Source: Authors.

Table 5.2: Transmission and Distribution Loss Considered During 2020–2050 in Different Cases in Four Countries
(%)

Country	TDL-B	TDL-10%	TDL-5%
Bangladesh	11	10	5
Bhutan	6	NA	5
Nepal	15	10	5
Sri Lanka	10	NA	5

NA = not applicable; TDL-B = transmission and distribution loss baseline; TDL-10% = transmission and distribution loss 10%; TDL-5% = transmission and distribution loss 5%.

Source: Authors.

5.4 Implications of Energy Reduction Targets in Individual Countries

This section discusses the implications of setting energy reduction targets for energy development and technology choices as well as costs during 2020–2050 in the individual studied countries. It first discusses the maximum energy-reduction potential for 2030 and 2050. This is followed by comparison between the BAU and energy reduction scenarios in terms of TPES, final energy consumption (FEC), electricity generation, overall energy conversion, technology selection, and cost implications. The study focuses on two snapshot years, 2030 and 2050, for comparison. The study also analyzes the effect of T&D loss reduction in the power sector. In addition, this section includes policy implications of energy reduction targets for each country.

Bangladesh

Determination of Maximum Energy-Reduction Potential by 2030 and 2050

This study determines the maximum energy-reduction potential for 2030 and 2050.[8] The maximum reduction is determined for two cases: a modal shift in the transport sector in ER40 (Table 5.1) and without the modal shift, i.e., with the same modal share as in BAU. The maximum energy-reduction potential with the modal shift would be 46.5% in 2030 and 40.03% in 2050. Without the modal shift, the maximum reduction potential would be 46.0% in 2030 and 38.2% in 2050.

Total Primary Energy Supply

Figure 5.2 (a) presents the TPES by fuel type as well as the structure of TPES in terms of the percentage shares of different fuels (fuel mix) in various scenarios. There would be less use of oil (crude and petroleum products) and coal, and more use of other renewables, in all energy reduction scenarios during 2020–2050 compared with BAU. The cumulative energy consumption during 2015–2050 would be 2,292 Mtoe and would decrease by 19.1% in ER15, 41.4% in ER30, and 58.2% in ER40 compared to BAU.

---

[8] This was done iteratively by gradually increasing the energy reduction target in the AIM/Enduse Model and running the model with each increment in the target until it was found no longer feasible to meet the target.

In 2030, the major reduction in TPES in both ER15 and ER30 scenarios would take place due to lower use of oil and coal; whereas, in ER40, the major reduction would come from decreased use of traditional biomass and coal. The use of advanced improved cook stoves (AICS)[9] in cooking would have an important role in reducing the consumption of biomass in ER40. Coal use would decrease significantly in ER30 and ER40 due to energy-efficiency improvement in the industry and a shift from coal to natural gas in power generation. There would also be a decrease in the use of natural gas in all energy reduction scenarios except ER40 in 2030. In 2030, there would be a lower usage of other renewables (solar and wind) and nuclear in energy reduction scenarios than in BAU due to decrease in electricity demand.

In 2050, there would be a lower level of coal and oil use in TPES in all energy reduction scenarios compared with BAU. There would also be lower natural gas consumption in all reduction scenarios compared with BAU. Biomass usage would increase in ER15 (due to its increased use in the industry sector); however, its use would decline in ER30 and ER40. There would be higher usage of renewables in all reduction scenarios than in BAU.

Figure 5.2 (b) shows the shares of different types of fuels in TPES under the scenarios considered. The biomass share would decrease significantly in BAU during 2015–2050, while the share of coal and other renewables would increase. In 2030, natural gas would have the highest share in TPES in BAU, followed by biomass, coal, petroleum products, nuclear, and other renewables. The share of hydro would be less than 1%. In energy reduction scenarios, natural gas would have a higher share in TPES than in BAU, while biomass and oil shares would be lower. The share of coal in 2030 under ER15 and ER30 would be slightly higher than in BAU. In contrast, coal share in ER40 would be significantly lower than in BAU; likewise, biomass share would be considerably reduced.

In 2050, the share of biomass in TPES would increase in ER15 and ER30 scenarios compared with BAU, whereas in ER40 the share would decline to below 1%. The share of oil would decrease in ER15 and ER30 scenarios compared to its BAU level, whereas the share would rise for ER40. The share of other renewables would increase in all energy reduction scenarios: by 2.3% in ER15, 7.5% in ER30, and 13.5% in ER40. The share of natural gas would be lower in ER15 compared with BAU, whereas it would be higher in ER30 and ER40. The share of coal for ER15 would be higher than that in BAU but would be lower for ER30 and ER40.

Energy Intensity

Figure 5.3 presents the changes in overall energy intensity in various scenarios. The overall energy intensity in BAU would decrease from 0.19 toe/$ in 2015 to 0.15 toe/$ in 2030 and 0.14 toe/$ in 2050. In 2030, energy intensity would be 0.12 toe/$ in ER15, 0.12 toe/$ in ER30, and 0.10 toe/$ in ER40; the corresponding values in 2050 would be 0.12 toe/$ in ER15, 0.10 toe/$ in ER30, and 0.09 toe/$ in ER40. According to Energy Efficiency and Conservation Master Plan, the government's target is to reduce energy intensity by 20% in 2030, from the 2013 level (SREDA 2015). Note that in BAU, the EI in 2030 would be lower than the 2013 level (i.e., 0.174 toe/$) by 13.4%. The target would not be achieved by 2030 in the BAU scenario. As such, in ER15, ER30, and ER40 scenarios, EI by 2030 would be lower by 30.2%, 30.8%, and 39.8%, respectively. Therefore, a larger reduction in EI than the target set in the Energy Efficiency and Conservation Master Plan would be achieved in all ER scenarios.

---

[9]   AICS are highly efficient biomass cook stoves with an efficiency of 35%.

Figure 5.2: Total Primary Energy Supply in Different Scenarios

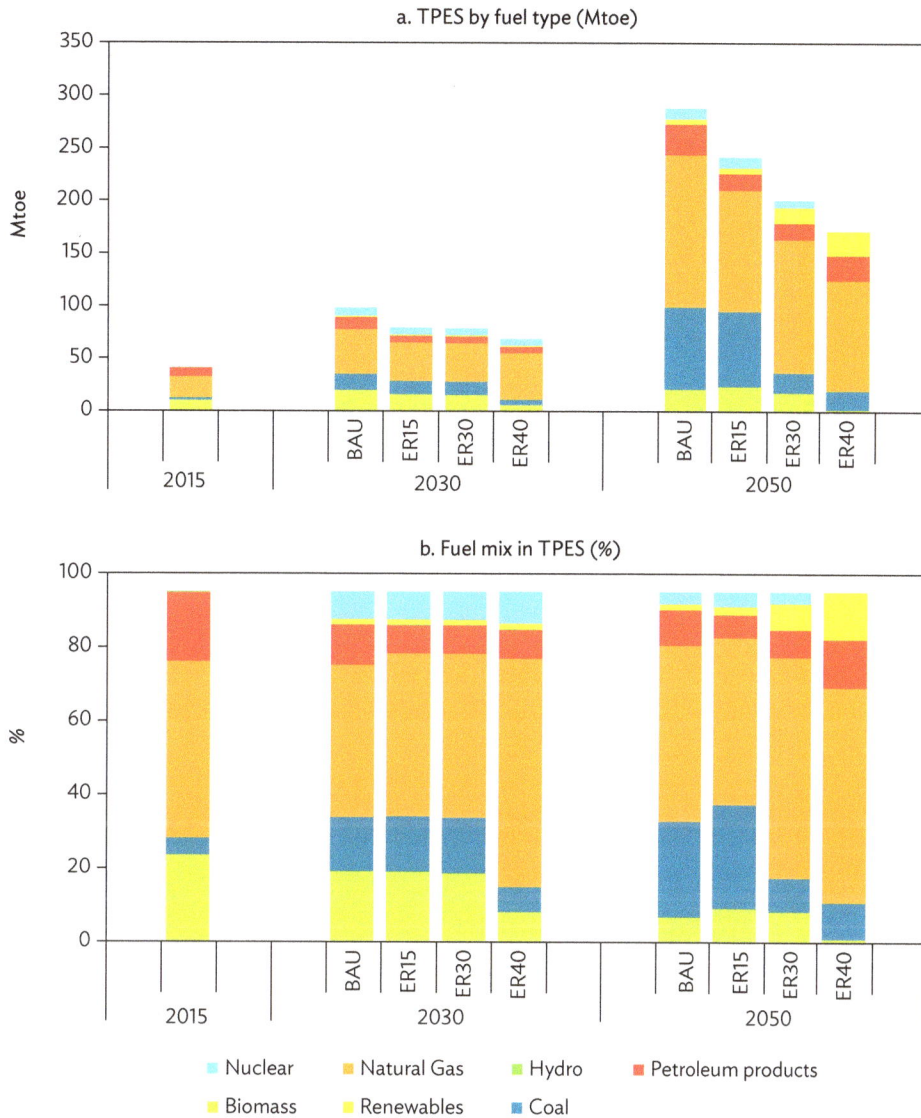

a. TPES by fuel type (Mtoe)

b. Fuel mix in TPES (%)

Legend: Nuclear · Natural Gas · Hydro · Petroleum products · Biomass · Renewables · Coal

BAU = business as usual scenario; ER15 = 15% energy reduction scenario; ER30 = 30% energy reduction scenario; ER40 = 40% energy reduction scenario; Mtoe = million tons of oil equivalent; TPES = total primary energy supply.

Source: Authors.

Figure 5.3: Overall Energy Intensity in Various Scenarios, 2015–2050

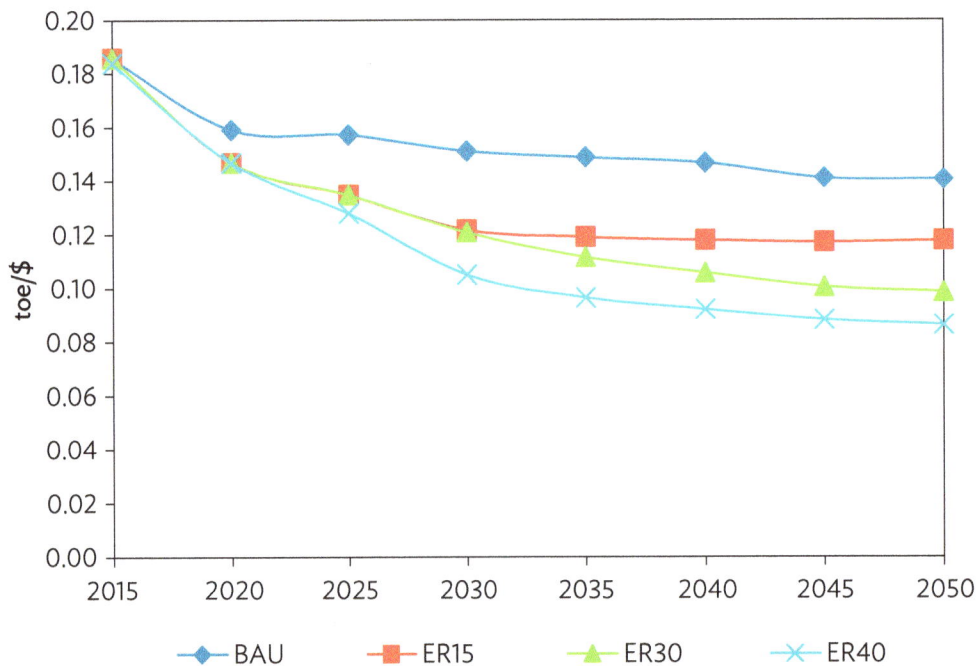

BAU = business as usual scenario; ER15 = 15% energy reduction scenario; ER30 = 30% energy reduction scenario; ER40 = 40% energy reduction scenario; toe = tons of oil equivalent.

Source: Authors.

Electricity Generation

Electricity generation under BAU and energy reduction scenarios are shown in Figure 5.4. The requirement for electricity generation would increase from 65.9 TWh in 2015 to 165.1 TWh in 2030 and 541.8 TWh in 2050 in BAU, i.e., growth at compound annual growth rate (CAGR) of 6.2% during 2015–2050. The electricity generation in energy reduction scenarios would be lower than in BAU because of the use of more energy efficient devices. In 2030, electricity generation in ER30 would be lower than in BAU. In 2050, electricity generation in energy reduction scenarios would be reduced by 21.2% in ER15, 20.7% in ER30, and 11.3% in ER40 than in BAU. The level of electricity generation varies marginally among the three ER scenarios up to 2045. However, the would be a significant difference in electricity generation in 2050 across the ER scenarios: generation level in ER40 would be substantially higher than in ER15 and ER30 due to higher level of electrification in end-use activities in the transport sector.

The cumulative electricity generation during 2015–2050 would be 8,341 TWh in BAU, cumulative generation would be 6,759 TWh in ER15, 19.0% lower than in BAU; and in ER30 and ER40 would be 19.1% and 19.0% lower than in BAU, respectively.

Final Energy Consumption

As expected, the TFEC would decrease in the energy reduction scenarios. In 2030, TFEC would be lower than in BAU by 19.9% in ER15, 20.6% in ER30, and 28.5% in ER40; likewise, the corresponding values in 2050 would be lower by 16.2% in ER15, 20.8% in ER30, and 31.7% in ER40. The changes in final energy consumption at the sector levels are discussed next.

Figure 5.4: Electricity Generation in Business as Usual and Energy Reduction Scenarios

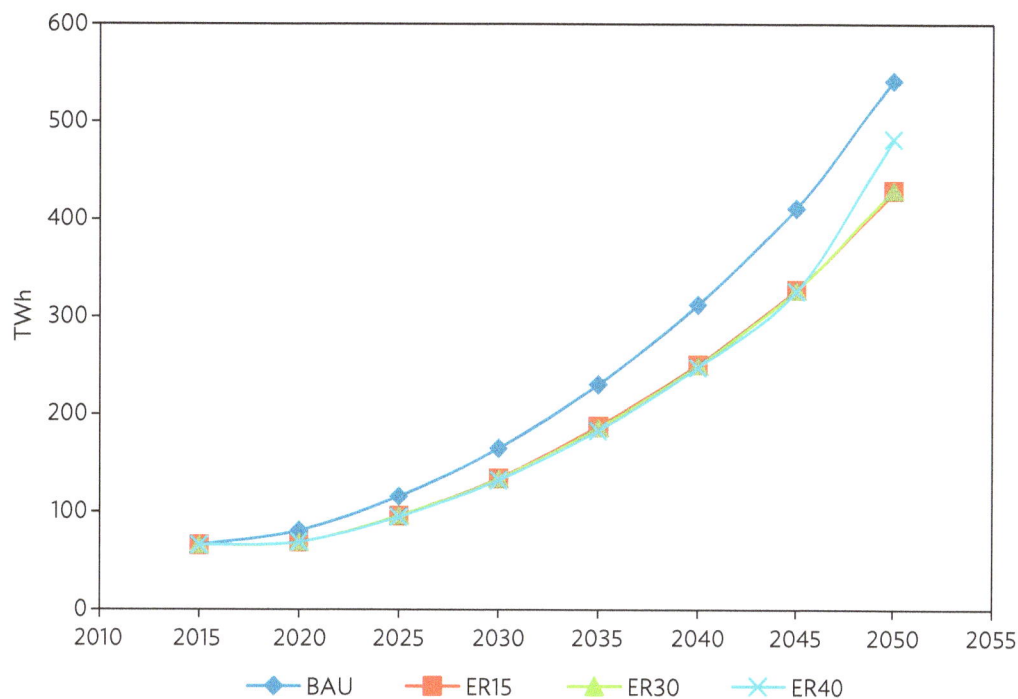

BAU = business as usual scenario; ER15 = 15% energy reduction scenario; ER30 = 30% energy reduction scenario; ER40 = 40% energy reduction scenario, TWh = terawatt-hour.

Source: Authors.

Residential Sector

In 2030, the TFEC of the residential sector would decrease by 20.6%, 22.3%, and 43.2% from the BAU level in ER15, ER30, and ER50 scenarios, respectively; in 2050, the corresponding reductions would be 9.7%, 18.0%, and 32.6%.

In BAU, the shares of natural gas and electricity would increase during 2015–2050. The share of biomass use in the residential sector would decrease; this is, however, due to the assumption of a declining share of traditional biomass with the growing income per capita in the country (Table 5.3).

Natural gas would play a major role in TFEC in both 2030 and 2050 in all energy reduction scenarios. There would be a marked decrease in the share of biomass in 2030 and an increase in the share of natural gas in ER40, because natural gas would replace biomass use for cooking in this scenario. The share of electricity would decrease due to the use of efficient electrical devices in energy reduction scenarios.

In 2050, the share of natural gas in the FEC mix of the residential sector in all energy reduction scenarios would be higher than in BAU. In ER40, the share of natural gas would increase significantly whereas that of biomass would be zero. This is because all biomass use for cooking would be replaced by natural gas. In all energy reduction scenarios, the share of electricity would be lower than in BAU.

Table 5.3: Final Energy Mix in the Residential Sector
(%)

Fuel Type	2015	2030				2050			
		BAU	ER15	ER30	ER40	BAU	ER15	ER30	ER40
Biomass	75.8	66.8	64.4	63.8	32.0	37.0	41.0	34.5	—
Natural gas	12.1	18.6	23.5	24.0	51.8	38.0	42.1	46.9	77.4
Petroleum	0.8	—	—	—	—	—	—	—	—
Electricity	11.3	14.6	12.2	12.3	16.2	25.0	16.9	18.6	22.6
Total	100.0	100.0	100.0	100.0	100.0	100.0	100.0	100.0	100.0

BAU = business as usual scenario; ER15 = 15% energy reduction scenario; ER30 = 30% energy reduction scenario; ER40 = 40% energy reduction scenario.

— = zero or negligible value.

Source: Authors.

Table 5.4: Final Energy Mix in the Commercial Sector
(%)

Fuel Type	2015	2030				2050			
		BAU	ER15	ER30	ER40	BAU	ER15	ER30	ER40
Natural gas	44.2	44.5	55.7	55.7	55.7	44.5	55.9	55.9	—
Petroleum	—	—	—	—	—	—	—	—	47.8
Electricity	55.8	55.5	44.3	44.3	44.3	55.5	44.1	44.1	52.2
Total	100.0	100.0	100.0	100.0	100.0	100.0	100.0	100.0	100.0

BAU = business as usual scenario; ER15 = 15% energy reduction scenario; ER30 = 30% energy reduction scenario; ER40 = 40% energy reduction scenario.

— = zero or negligible value.

Source: Authors.

Table 5.5: Final Energy Mix in the Industry Sector
(%)

Fuel Type	2015	2030				2050			
		BAU	ER15	ER30	ER40	BAU	ER15	ER30	ER40
Biomass	0.0	0.0	2.6	2.6	1.9	0.0	2.9	2.0	2.0
Natural gas	57.8	57.9	49.8	49.9	50.7	53.1	45.6	48.3	49.0
Petroleum	3.3	2.9	2.8	2.8	2.8	2.7	2.6	2.7	2.8
Coal	13.3	18.2	19.9	19.8	19.2	24.5	25.6	22.3	21.1
Electricity	25.6	21.0	24.9	24.9	25.3	19.7	23.3	24.7	25.0
Total	100.0	100.0	100.0	100.0	100.0	100.0	100.0	100.0	100.0

BAU = business as usual scenario; ER15 = 15% energy reduction scenario; ER30 = 30% energy reduction scenario; ER40 = 40% energy reduction scenario.

Source: Authors.

Commercial Sector

The FEC of the commercial sector in 2030 would decrease by about 20% in all energy reduction scenarios. In energy reduction scenarios, energy-efficient technologies would be cost-effective in lighting and cooling. There would be no significant change in the energy consumption and the selection of cost-effective technologies in 2030. In 2050, the sector's FEC would be reduced by 20.3% in ER15 and ER30 and by 32.6% in ER40. There would be lower consumption of electricity in the energy reduction scenarios. In 2050, there would be a switch from natural gas to LPG in ER40. The fuel mix in the commercial sector in 2015, 2030, and 2050 is shown in Table 5.4.

Industry Sector

In BAU, some of the less energy-efficient technologies are considered to be in use in the future . The FEC of the industry sector in 2030 would be 22.5%, 22.6%, and 23.9% lower in ER15, ER30, and ER40 scenarios, respectively. This would happen partly with a decrease in the consumption of natural gas due to increased energy efficiency in the sector. There would also be higher use of electricity, coal, and biomass. Switching to electricity-based technologies is another reason for the decrease in the sector's FEC. Industrial heat pumps would have a major role in the reduction of natural gas consumption and increased use of electricity. In 2050, the sector's FEC would decrease by 23.3% in ER15, by 27.6% in ER30, and by 28.7% in ER40.

The industry sector's final energy mix is shown in Table 5.5. Natural gas would still have a dominant role in the final energy mix in the sector, although its share in energy reduction scenarios would be lower than the BAU level. The share of electricity and coal would increase in energy reduction scenarios compared to their BAU levels in 2030. In 2050, the share of electricity would be higher in all reduction scenarios than in BAU, whereas the share of coal would be lower in ER30 and ER40.

Transport Sector

The FEC of the transport sector in 2030 would be lower by 12.4% each in ER15 and ER30, and by 10% in ER40 compared to BAU. In 2050, the sector's FEC would be reduced by 2.4% and 3.8% in ER15 and ER30, respectively. The FEC would decrease by 44.7% for ER40, due to switching from natural gas to electricity-based technologies. There would be an increase in the use of electricity in ER40 in 2050 compared with BAU, whereas the use of natural gas would be lower.

The final energy mix in the transport sector is shown in Table 5.6. Natural gas would be the dominant fuel in all scenarios in 2030 and 2050 except for ER40 in 2050. Natural gas would be replaced by electricity and petroleum products. Hybrid vehicles operating on petroleum products and fully electric vehicles would have a major role in ER40 scenarios, thus increasing the share of petroleum products and electricity in the final energy mix.

Agriculture Sector

The FEC of the agriculture sector would decrease by 16.1% in all energy reduction scenarios by 2030, driven by reduced use of petroleum products, natural gas, and electricity. This is due to energy-efficiency improvements in irrigation pumps, tillers, and tractors. The same percentage change in FEC would also occur in 2050 for all energy reduction scenarios. There would be no noticeable change in the energy mix of the sector.

Table 5.6: Final Energy Mix in the Transport Sector
(%)

Fuel Type	2015	2030				2050			
		BAU	ER15	ER30	ER40	BAU	ER15	ER30	ER40
Natural gas	32.2	37.6	67.1	67.1	74.6	49.1	80.9	79.9	12.2
Petroleum products	67.3	60.4	30.5	30.5	23.1	49.1	17.9	18.1	64.1
Electricity	0.6	2.0	2.3	2.3	2.3	1.8	1.2	2.0	23.7
Total	100.0	100.0	100.0	100.0	100.0	100.0	100.0	100.0	100.0

BAU = business as usual scenario; ER15 = 15% energy reduction scenario; ER30 = 30% energy reduction scenario; ER40 = 40% energy reduction scenario.

Source: Authors.

Sectoral Contributions to Reductions in Total Final Energy Consumption Under Energy Reduction Scenarios

The contributions of different sectors to reductions in TFEC are given in absolute terms in Figure 5.6 (a) and as percentage shares in Figure 5.6 (b). In 2030, the total reduction in TFEC in ER15, ER30, and ER40 scenarios would be 15.8, 16.4, and 22.7 Mtoe, respectively; in 2050, the corresponding reductions would be 36.3, 46.5, and 71.0 Mtoe.

In 2030, the industry sector would account for the largest share in the reduction of TFEC in ER15 and ER30, while the residential sector would be the largest contributor in ER40. By 2050, the industry sector would have the highest contribution to the reduction of TFEC in all energy reduction scenarios. However, the sector's share in the reduction of TFEC would decrease with the increase in energy reduction targets: accounting for over 75% of the reduction in ER15, about 70% in ER30, and almost 50% in ER40. The residential sector would have the second highest contribution to the reduction in TFEC; its share in the reduction would increase with the level of energy reduction target. The transport sector would have the third largest contribution to the reduction of TFEC in all energy reduction scenarios in both 2030 and 2050, with a substantial share in 2050.

Figure 5.5: Final Energy Consumption in Different Scenarios per Sector

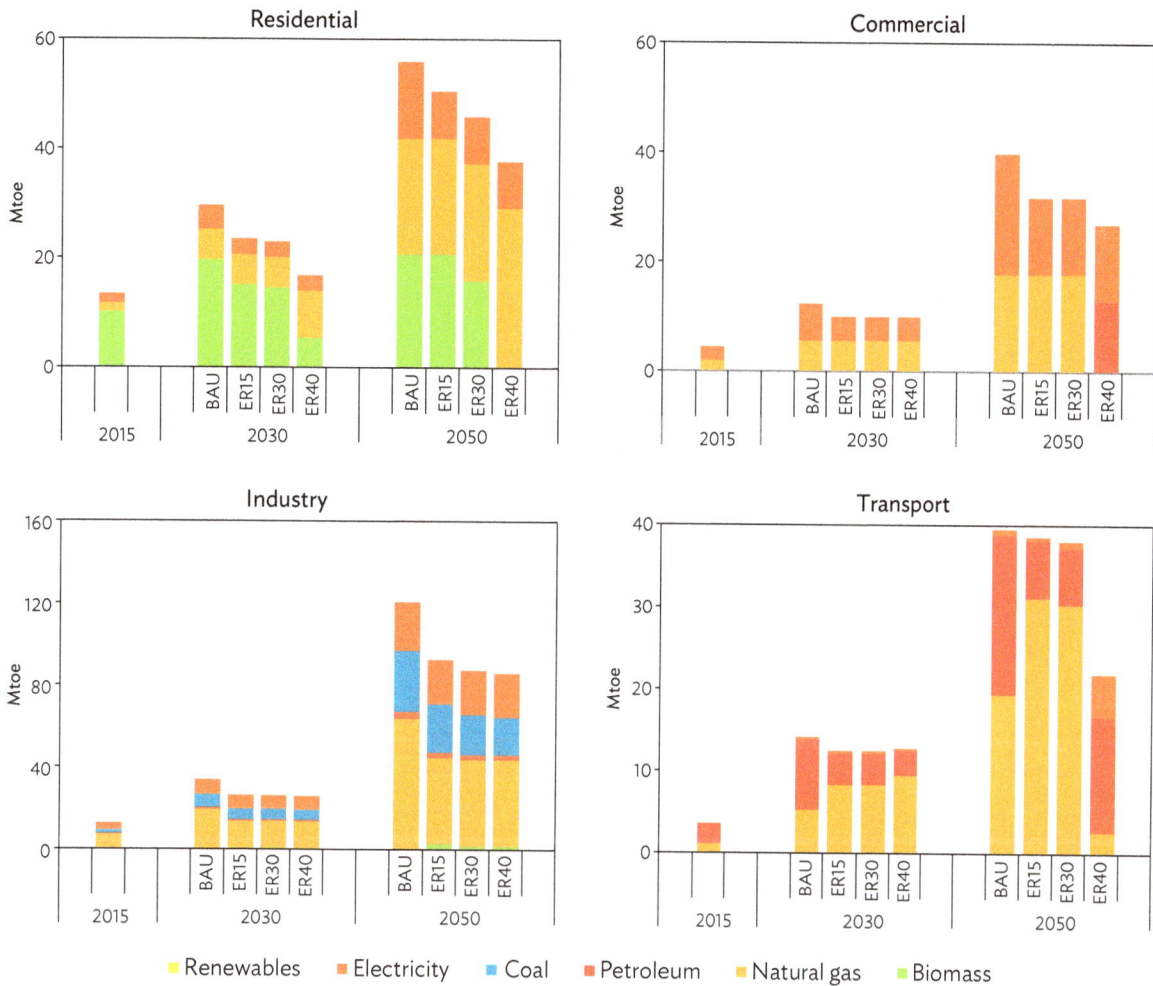

BAU = business as usual scenario; ER15 = 15% energy reduction scenario; ER30 = 30% energy reduction scenario; ER40 = 40% energy reduction scenario; Mtoe = million tons of oil equivalent.

Source: Authors.

Figure 5.6: Sector Contributions in Final Energy Reduction for Energy Reduction Scenarios

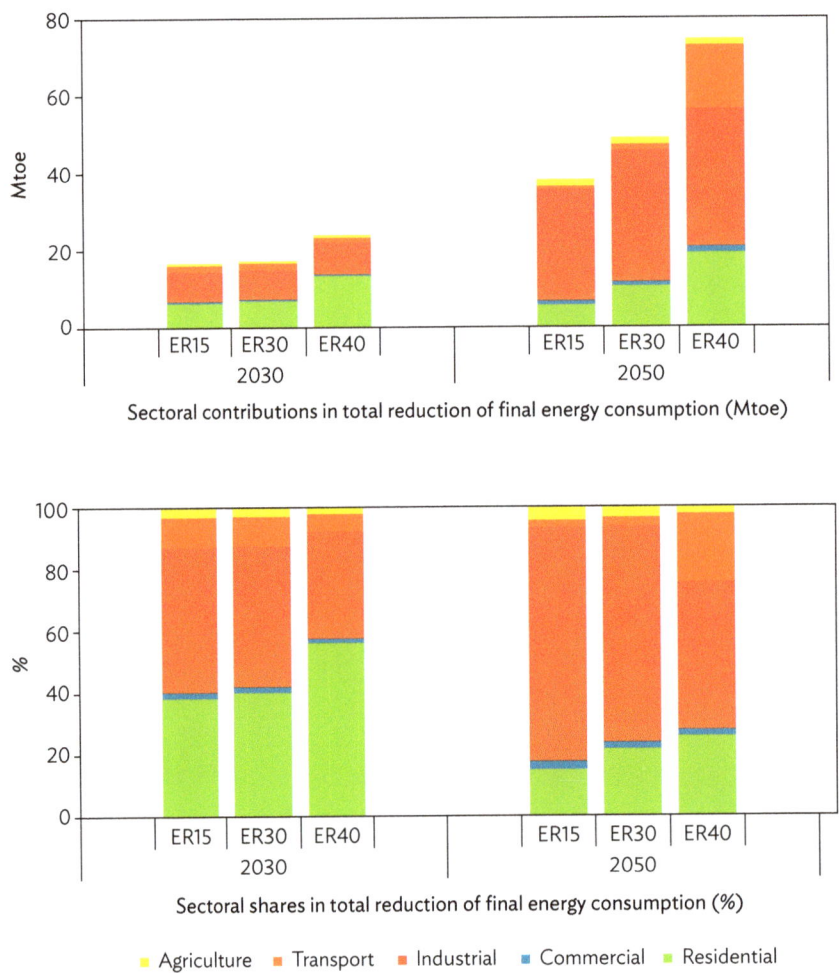

Sectoral contributions in total reduction of final energy consumption (Mtoe)

Sectoral shares in total reduction of final energy consumption (%)

■ Agriculture   ■ Transport   ■ Industrial   ■ Commercial   ■ Residential

BAU = business as usual scenario; ER15 = 15% energy reduction scenario; ER30 = 30% energy reduction scenario; ER40 = 40% energy reduction scenario; Mtoe = million tons of oil equivalent.

Source: Authors.

Overall Efficiency of Energy Conversion and Transmission

Figure 5.7 shows that overall efficiency of energy conversion and transmission in Bangladesh would increase during 2015–2050 in BAU. The overall efficiency in BAU would increase from 74.3% to 81.2% in 2030 and 77.7% in 2050. The decrease in overall efficiency from 2030 to 2050 in BAU is due to the higher share of electricity in FEC in 2050. In 2030, the overall efficiency would be 81.0%, 80.9%, and 83.4% in ER15, ER30, and ER40 scenarios, respectively, due to change in the energy mix in final energy consumption. In 2050, overall efficiency would be 77.5% in ER15, and would increase to 88.3% in ER30 and 89.0% in ER40. The improvement in overall efficiency in ER30 and ER40 in 2050 in the power sector would come from the increased share of other renewables in power generation.

Figure 5.7: Overall Efficiency of Energy Conversion and Transmissioning Different Scenarios in Bangladesh

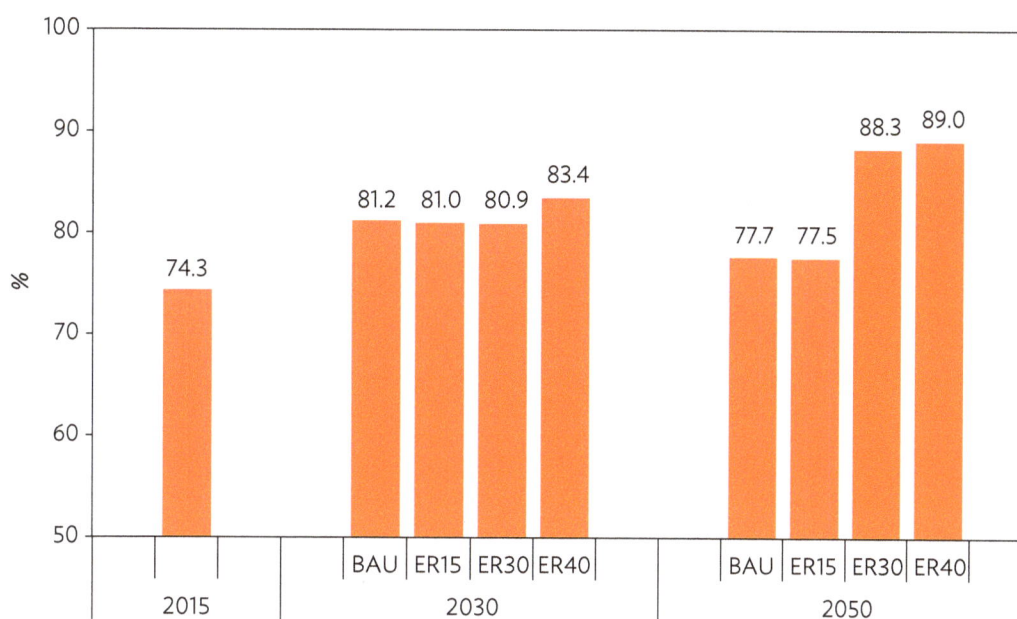

BAU = business as usual scenario; ER15 = 15% energy reduction scenario; ER30 = 30% energy reduction scenario; ER40 = 40% energy reduction scenario.

Source: Authors.

Technology Selection

In the residential sector, energy-efficient electrical devices would be a cost-effective option in all energy reduction scenarios. The improved cook stove (ICS) would be a cost-effective technology option for cooking in ER15.[10] In ER30, AICS would be a cost-effective option, whereas natural gas-based cooking would replace all biomass-based cook stoves in ER40. In the commercial sector, natural gas-based cooking would be replaced by more efficient LPG-based cooking in the ER40 scenario (Akter Lucky and Hossain 2001; Pantangi et al. 2007). Similar to the residential sector, efficient electrical appliances would be cost-effective in the commercial sector in all energy reduction scenarios.

The industry sector offers the highest ESP in all energy reduction scenarios. Textile manufacturing is the major energy-consuming industry subsector. Energy-efficiency improvements in boilers for steam production and gas turbines for power generation in the textile industry have significant ESP in all reduction scenarios. All existing boilers and gas turbines would be replaced with energy efficient ones by 2030. The use of best available stenter technology in the textile industry would also be a cost-effective option in all reduction scenarios. In the steel industry, the best available technology for steel rolling is an economic option in all energy reduction scenarios. Best available technology in steel rolling would replace all conventional steel rolling by 2020.

---

[10] ICS is a type of biomass stove with a higher efficiency than the traditional cook stove but a lower efficiency than AICS.

The brick industry is dominated by zigzag kilns followed by fixed-chimney bull trench kilns. Improved fixed-chimney bull trench kilns are cost-effective in the ER15 scenario, whereas a combination of improved fixed-chimney bull trench kilns and vertical shaft brick kilns would be required to meet the ER30 target. For ER40, all kilns would be replaced by vertical shaft brick kilns.

In the cement industry, vertical mills are cost-effective for raw material grinding in ER15 and ER30 scenarios. Roller mills would be required for raw material grinding for ER40. Long dry kilns in clinker production would be the cost-effective option in the ER15 scenario. In the ER30 scenario, four-stage cyclone suspension preheater kilns in clinker production would be required. For ER40, the combination of four-, five-, and six-stage cyclone suspension preheater kilns is required. By 2050, clinker production would be completely dominated by six-stage cyclone suspension preheater kilns. In the clinker grinding process, vertical mills would be cost-effective for ER15 and ER30; however, for ER40, Horomills would be the cost-effective option.

In the transport sector, the energy reduction scenarios would require the use of light duty full-hybrid and full-electric vehicles, although the contribution of the transport sector would not be very significant unlike for the residential and industry sectors. However, in ER40 the transport sector will play an important role in achieving the energy reduction in 2050 with high penetration of electric and hybrid vehicles.

Investment Requirements and Average Incremental Cost

Figure 5.8 presents the total investment requirement during 2015–2050. The figure compares the investment requirements in two cases: (i) when the modal shares of cars in the passenger transport in energy reduction cases are assumed to be lower than in BAU, with the shares decreasing with an increase in the energy reduction target (Figure 5.8 [a]) and (ii) when the modal shares are maintained at the same level as that in BAU (Figure 5.8 [b]). The total investment (undiscounted) required during 2015–2050 in BAU would be $794 billion. The investment requirement would be 1.8% lower in ER15 than in BAU and 6.0% and 5.4% higher than in BAU in ER30 and ER40, respectively, when the decreasing share of passenger cars is considered. For the same modal share as in BAU, the investment requirement would be higher than BAU by 1.7% in ER15, 21.3% in ER30, and 38.0% in ER40.

The total cost of the energy system in BAU during 2015–2050 would be $3,534 billion (undiscounted). In ER15, ER30, and ER40 scenarios, the cost would be lower than the BAU level by 22.9%, 23.6%, and 23.0%, respectively, when the decreasing share of cars is considered (Figure 5.9). The lower total cost in energy reduction scenarios is because of the no-regret energy-efficient technologies that are not considered to be in use in BAU. That an energy reduction target can be achieved at a lower total cost is also evident from several other studies showing that some energy-efficient technologies would decrease the total cost while providing the same energy services (Subramanyam et al. 2017a, 2017b; Talaei et al. 2018, 2019). Using the same modal share of cars as in BAU, the total cost would be lower than BAU by 21.7% in ER15, 20.0% in ER30, and 15.6% in ER40 scenarios. However, the total cost would increase with increasing energy reduction targets, implying that energy reduction would require a higher total energy system cost.

The average incremental cost (AIC) of energy savings is $855 per kiloton of oil equivalent (ktoe) in ER15, $773/ktoe in ER30, and $542/ktoe in ER40 when the decreasing share of passenger cars is considered (Figure 5.10). The AICs of energy savings for the same modal share of cars as in BAU are $25/ktoe in ER15, $709/ktoe in ER30, and $436/ktoe in ER40.

Figure 5.8: Total Investment Requirement: Effect of Variation in Modal Shares in Passenger Transport, 2015–2050

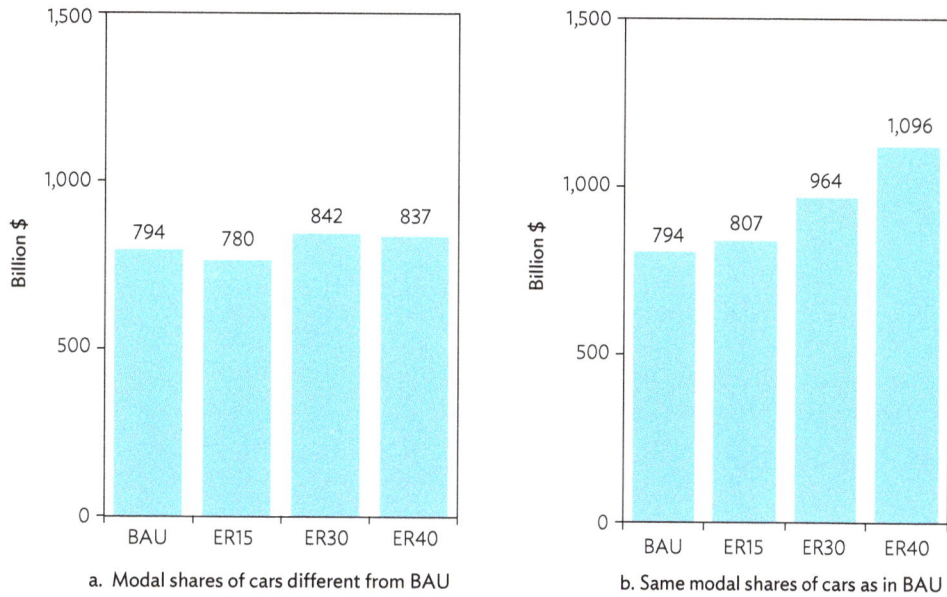

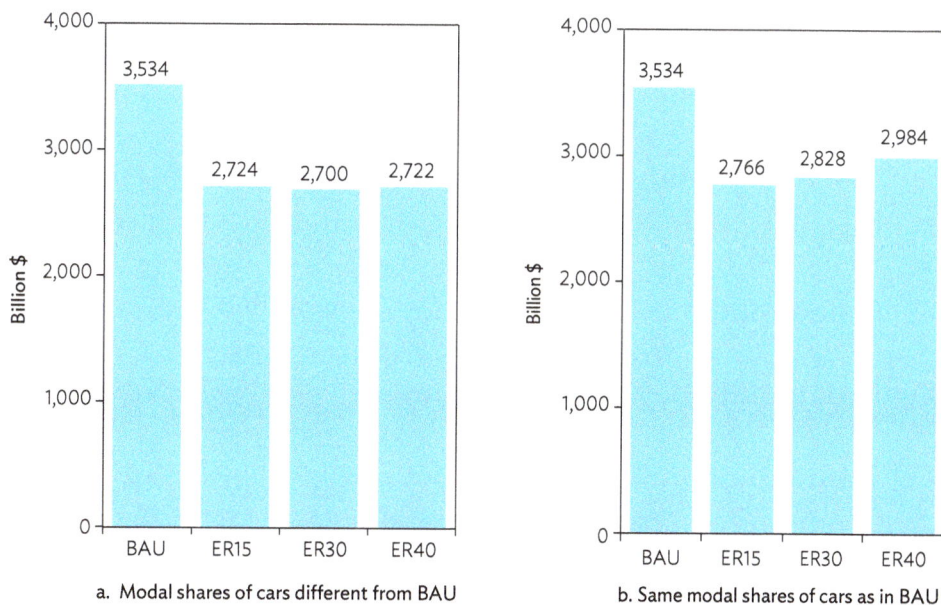

a. Modal shares of cars different from BAU

794, 780, 842, 837 (BAU, ER15, ER30, ER40) — Billion $

b. Same modal shares of cars as in BAU

794, 807, 964, 1,096 (BAU, ER15, ER30, ER40) — Billion $

BAU = business as usual scenario; ER15 = 15% energy reduction scenario; ER30 = 30% energy reduction scenario; ER40 = 40% energy reduction scenario.

Source: Authors.

Figure 5.9: Total Cost of the Energy System: Effect of Variation in Modal Shares in Passenger Transport, 2015–2050

a. Modal shares of cars different from BAU

3,534, 2,724, 2,700, 2,722 (BAU, ER15, ER30, ER40) — Billion $

b. Same modal shares of cars as in BAU

3,534, 2,766, 2,828, 2,984 (BAU, ER15, ER30, ER40) — Billion $

BAU = business as usual scenario; ER15 = 15% energy reduction scenario; ER30 = 30% energy reduction scenario; ER40 = 40% energy reduction scenario.

Source: Authors.

Greenhouse Gas Emissions

Total greenhouse gas (GHG) emissions in the BAU and energy reduction scenarios are presented in Figure 5.11. In BAU, GHG emissions would grow at a compound annual growth rate (CAGR) of 8.4% during 2015–2050. In 2030, GHG emission would be reduced by 20.6% in ER15, 20.8% in ER30, and 30.1% in ER40 scenarios. The industry sector would have the highest share in GHG emissions in the BAU scenario in 2030, followed by the power and transport sectors. The contribution of the residential, commercial, and agriculture sectors would be relatively insignificant compared to other sectors. In ER15 and ER30 scenarios, the power sector would have the highest emission (with a slightly higher share than the industry sector). In ER40, the share of the power sector in total emission would be lower than of the transport sector, mainly due to the high share of other renewables in power generation.

In 2050, GHG emissions would be lower by 17.9% in ER15, 43.6% in ER30, and 48.0% in ER40. In BAU, the power sector would be the major emitter of GHGs followed by the industry and transport sectors, with a similar case for the ER15 scenario. In ER30, the industry sector would be the highest GHG emitting sector, followed by the transport and power sectors. In ER40, the industry sector would be the highest GHG emitting sector, followed by the power and transport sectors.

Figure 5.10: Average Incremental Cost in Energy Reduction Scenarios: Effect of Variation in Modal Shares in Passenger Transport

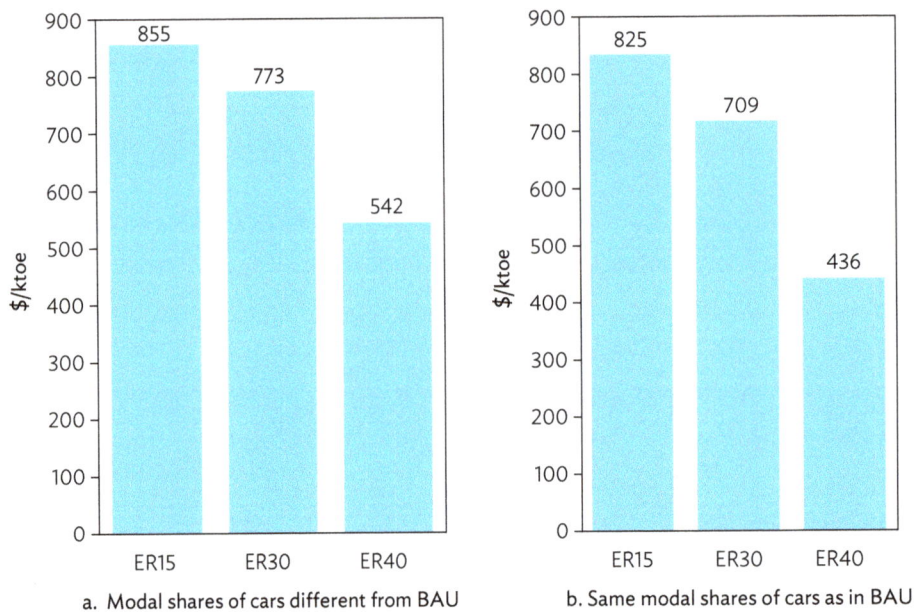

a. Modal shares of cars different from BAU

b. Same modal shares of cars as in BAU

BAU = business as usual scenario; ER15 = 15% energy reduction scenario; ER30 = 30% energy reduction scenario; ER40 = 40% energy reduction scenario.

Source: Authors.

The cumulative GHG emissions in BAU during 2015–2050 would be 10.4 gigatons of carbon dioxide equivalent (GtCO$_2$e) (Figure 5.12). The GHGs would be lower by 19.2% in ER15, 32.6% in ER30, and 38.4% in ER40 scenarios. In BAU, carbon dioxide (CO$_2$) constitutes 97.5% of GHG emission, followed by 1.9% for methane (CH$_4$) and 0.6% for nitrous oxide (N$_2$O). In ER15 and ER30 scenarios, the cumulative GHG would comprise 2.1% methane (CH$_4$) and 0.6% N$_2$O, with the remaining 97.2% being CO$_2$. In ER40, CO$_2$ is 98.6%, CH$_4$ is 0.9%, and N$_2$O is 0.4%.

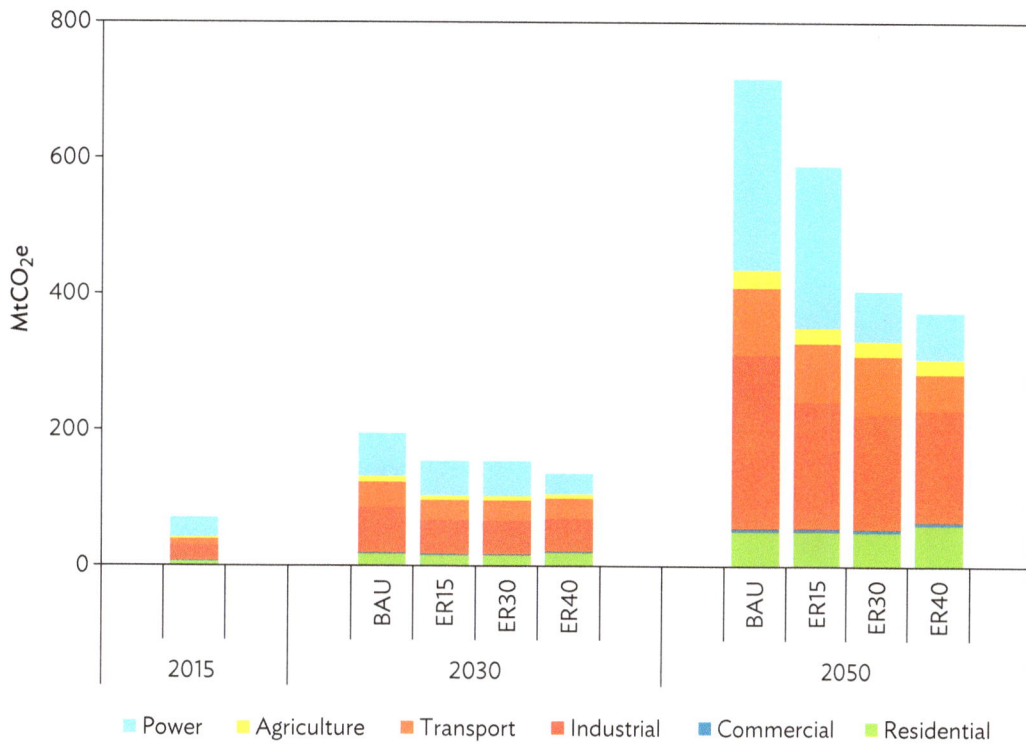

Figure 5.11: Greenhouse Gas Emissions for Business as Usual and Energy Reduction Scenarios, 2030 and 2050

BAU = business as usual scenario; ER15 = 15% energy reduction scenario; ER30 = 30% energy reduction scenario; ER40 = 40% energy reduction scenario.

Source: Authors.

Implication of Transmission and Distribution Efficiency Improvement

The transmission and distribution (T&D) loss during 2015–2050 is assumed to be 11% in BAU and energy reduction scenarios in the base case. Two more T&D loss cases are analyzed (Table 5.2). The base case in Bangladesh is referred to as TDL-11%. Figure 5.13 presents the electricity generation requirement in BAU and energy reduction scenarios for the three different cases. With TDL-10% (i.e., T&D losses of 10%), the level of electricity generation required in 2030 would be lower by 1.1% in BAU, 0.7% in ER15, 0.7% in ER30, and 1.1% in ER40 compared with respective levels with TDL-11% (i.e. base case). With TDL-5%, in 2030, electricity generation would be lower by 5.3% in BAU, 4.5% in ER15, 4.2% in ER30, and 5.1% in ER40 scenarios compared with TDL-11%. In 2050, the electricity generation with TDL-10% would be lower than in TDL-11% by 1.1% in BAU, ER15, and ER30 scenarios, but would be 1.7% higher in ER40. The increase in electricity generation is due to the change in final energy consumption and final energy mix. Electricity use would substitute other fuels in thermal applications. With TDL-5% in 2050, electricity generation would be lower by 5.3% in BAU, 4.3% in ER15, 5.3% in ER30, and 14.2% in ER40.

The cumulative electricity generation in TDL-10% would be lower by 1.1% in BAU, 0.9% in ER15, 1.0% in ER30, and 0.9% in ER40 compared to the respective figures for TDL-11%. In TDL-5%, the cumulative electricity generation would be reduced by 5.3% in BAU, 4.3% in ER15, 5.0% in ER30, and 5.8% in ER40 scenarios compared to TDL-11%.

Figure 5.12: Cumulative Greenhouse Gas Emissions for Business as Usual and Energy Reduction Scenarios by Gas Type, 2015–2050

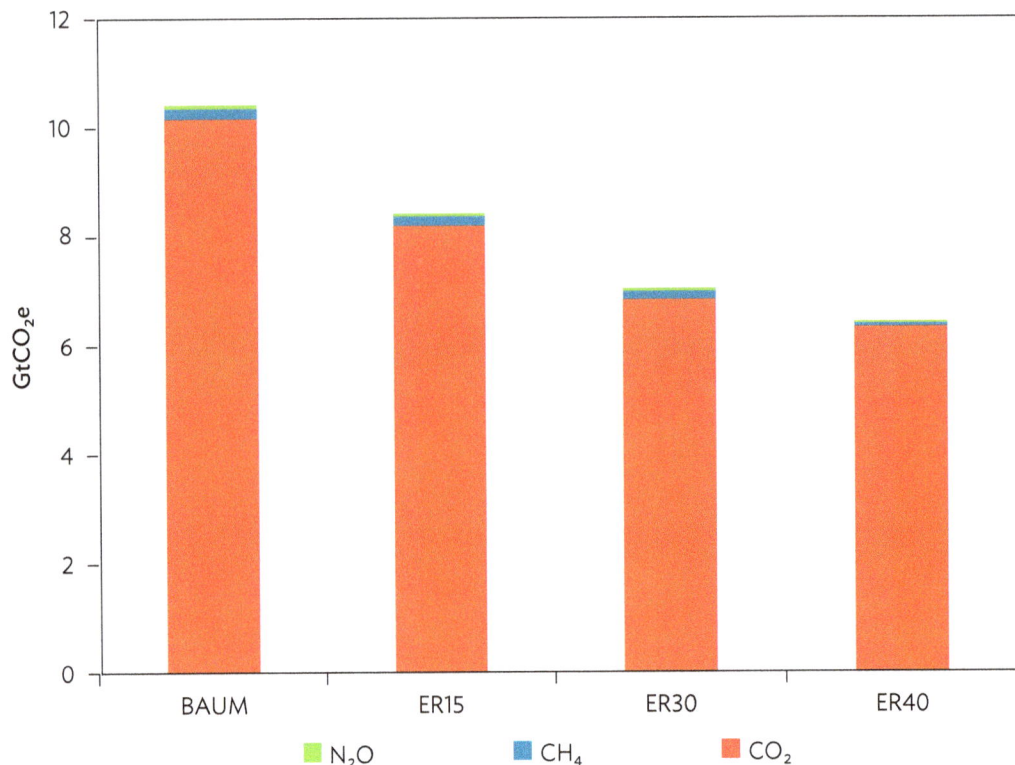

BAU = business as usual scenario; ER15 = 15% energy reduction scenario; ER30 = 30% energy reduction scenario; ER40 = 40% energy reduction scenario; $GtCO_2e$ = gigatons of carbon dioxide equivalent; N_2O = nitrous oxide; CH_4 = methane; CO_2 = carbon dioxide.

Source: Authors.

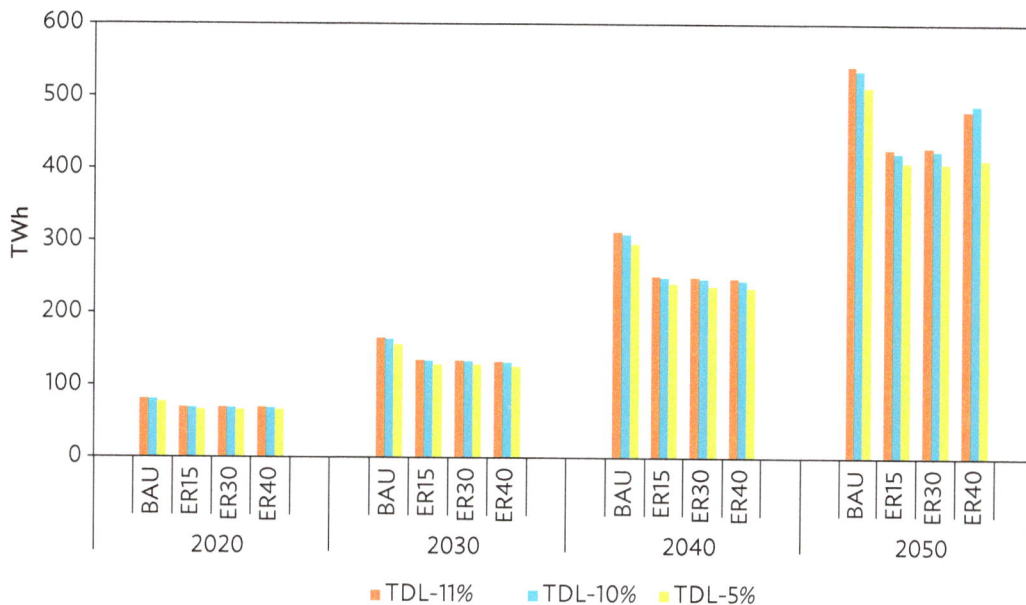

Figure 5.13: Electricity Generation at Various Transmission and Distribution Losses in Bangladesh

BAU = business as usual scenario; ER15 = 15% energy reduction scenario; ER30 = 30% energy reduction scenario; ER40 = 40% energy reduction scenario; TDL-11% = 11% transmission and distribution loss scenario; TDL-10% = 10% transmission and distribution loss scenario; TDL-5% = 5% transmission and distribution loss scenario; TWh = terawatt-hour.

Source: Authors.

Figure 5.14 presents the installed generation capacity requirement with different T&D loss scenarios (i.e., TDL-11%, TDL-10%, and TDL-5%) in BAU and energy reduction scenarios. The overall system generation capacity factor is assumed to be 50.6%, which is the same as that in 2015. In 2030, the installed generation capacity with TDL-10% would be lower than with TDL-11% by 414 MW in BAU, 204 MW in ER15, 203 MW in ER30, and 315 MW in ER40. Similarly, with TDL-5% the installed capacity requirement in BAU, ER15, ER30, and ER40 would be lower by 1,981, 1,377, 1,275, and 1,528 MW, respectively, compared to TDL-11%. In 2050, installed capacity in BAU, ER15, and ER30 for TDL-10% would be 1,358, 1,055, and 1,084 MW higher than for TDL-11%, respectively, but would be 1,802 MW lower for ER40. With TDL-5%, the installed capacity requirement would be reduced by 6,502 MW in BAU, 4,121 MW in ER15, 5114 MW in ER30, and 15,346 MW in ER40 compared to TDL-11%.

The total energy system cost in BAU and energy reduction scenarios in Bangladesh during 2015–2050 with TDL-10% and TDL-5% would be lower compared with TDL-11% levels. With TDL-10%, the total cost would be reduced by 0.2% in BAU and ER15, by 0.4% in ER30, and by 1.3% in ER40 compared with TDL-11%. With TDL-5%, the total cost would be reduced by 1.2% in BAU compared with TDL-11%. Similarly, in ER15, ER30, and ER40 scenarios, the total cost with TDL-5% would be reduced by 1.1%, 1.8%, and 4.0%, respectively, compared with TDL-11%. Note, however, the additional cost of T&D system improvement for TDL-5% is not considered for estimating cost savings.

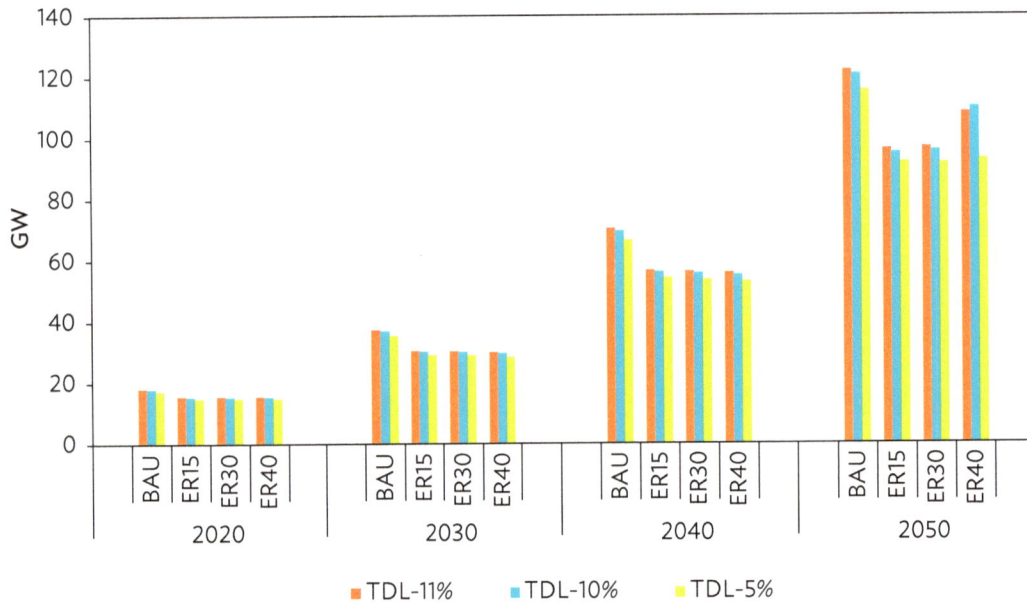

Figure 5.14: Installed Capacity Requirement at Various Transmission and Distribution Losses in Bangladesh

BAU = business as usual scenario; ER15 = 15% energy reduction scenario; ER30 = 30% energy reduction scenario; ER40 = 40% energy reduction scenario; GW = gigawatt; TDL-11% = 11% transmission and distribution loss scenario; TDL-10% = 10% transmission and distribution loss scenario; TDL-5% = 5% transmission and distribution loss scenario.

Source: Authors.

Bhutan

Maximum Energy-Reduction Potential

The study also determined the maximum energy-reduction potential for 2030 and 2050. The values for 2030 and 2050 are 40% and 42.5%, respectively, when the minimum share of cars is lower than in BAU as given in ER40 in Table 5.1. If the minimum share of cars is assumed to be the same as in BAU, the maximum energy-reduction potential would be 38% in 2030 and 41% in 2050.

Total Primary Energy Supply

Figure 5.15 (a) presents the changes in total primary energy supply (TPES) in various scenarios. There would be a decrease in the use of fossil fuels whereas the use of hydro and other renewables would increase during 2020–2050 in all energy reduction scenarios. In 2030, the decrease in the use of coal would result in the most reduction in TPES in ER15 and ER30 scenarios compared with BAU. Decrease in biomass use would be the second highest contributor to the reduction in TPES, followed by petroleum products use. There would be an increase in the use of hydro and other renewables during 2015–2050. In ER40, reduced use of biomass would contribute most to the reduction of TPES in 2030, followed by decreases in consumption of coal and petroleum products. Note that the reduction in biomass use is mainly due to fuel switching in cooking, i.e., from use of solid fuels to more gas and electricity in cooking.

In 2050, there would be a decrease in coal use and this would be the highest contributor to the reduction in TPES in ER15 and ER30 scenarios. However, in ER40, the largest reduction in TPES would come from the decline in use of petroleum products followed by biomass use and coal. Biomass use in TPES would become insignificant by 2050 in ER40. It should be noted that in 2050, the TPES in ER15 is 20.1% lower than that in BAU; i.e., more than the desired reduction in ER15 and is because no-regret options would themselves achieve that level of reduction.

The changes in the shares of different types of energy in TPES are shown in Figure 5.15 (b). The share of biomass would decrease significantly in the BAU scenario during 2015–2050. This is partly due to the assumption that biomass use would decrease over time and also to energy-efficiency improvement in biomass-based technologies. The share of biomass would decrease further in ER30 and ER40 scenarios. In 2030, the share of biomass would be 18.5% in BAU, 18.7% in ER15, 14.3% in ER20, and 4.3% in ER40. Similarly, the share of coal would decrease in all energy reduction scenarios. The shares of petroleum products and hydro in TPES would increase compared to the BAU level in 2030, although the level of consumption of petroleum products would be lower than in BAU. The share of petroleum products would be 33.9% in BAU, 36.0% in ER15, 37.1% in ER30, and 37.8% in ER40; the corresponding shares of hydro would be 27.4%, 31.6%, 36.3%, and 45.3%.

The changes in energy mix are similar in 2050 in all energy reduction scenarios except for petroleum products. The share of petroleum products in BAU would be 42.7%, but reduced by 40.4% in ER15, 37.8% in ER30, and 17.2% in ER40. The share of hydro would increase under the energy reduction targets, ranging from 38.3% in ER15 to 68.2% in ER40.

The changes in energy mix are similar in 2050 in all energy reduction scenarios except for petroleum products. The share of petroleum products in BAU would be 42.7%, but reduced by 40.4% in ER15, 37.8% in ER30, and 17.2% in ER40. The share of hydro would increase under the energy reduction targets, ranging from 38.3% in ER15 to 68.2% in ER40.

Energy Intensity

Figure 5.16 presents the changes in energy intensity in various scenarios. The energy intensity (measured as energy consumption per gross domestic product [GDP]) in BAU would decrease from 0.32 kgoe/$ in 2015 to 0.23 kgoe/$ in 2030 and 0.21 kgoe/$ in 2050. The decrease in energy intensity is partly due to a switch from traditional biomass to modern fuels and also to energy-efficiency improvements. In 2030, energy intensity in ER15, ER30, and ER40 scenarios would be 0.20, 0.18, and 0.16 kgoe/$, respectively, whereas in 2050 it would correspondingly decrease to 0.17, 0.15, and 0.13 kgoe/$. Note, however, that the profiles of energy intensity under the reduction scenarios are based on assumptions made on temporal profiles of energy reduction under the different scenarios.

Figure 5.15: Total Primary Energy Supply in Different Scenarios

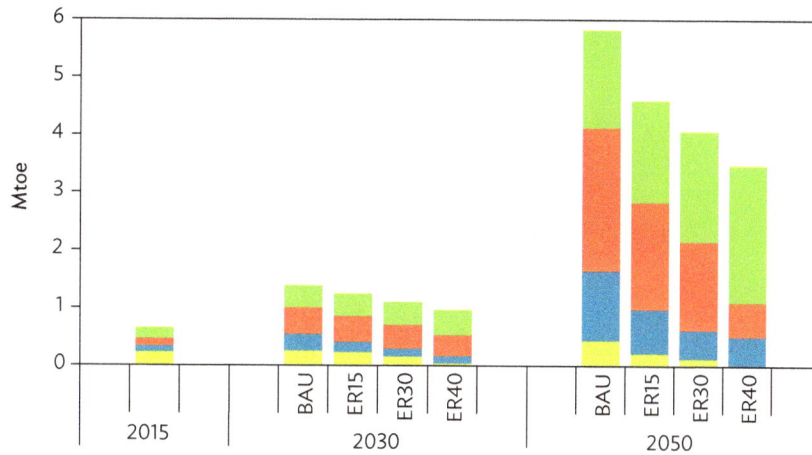

a. TPES by fuel type

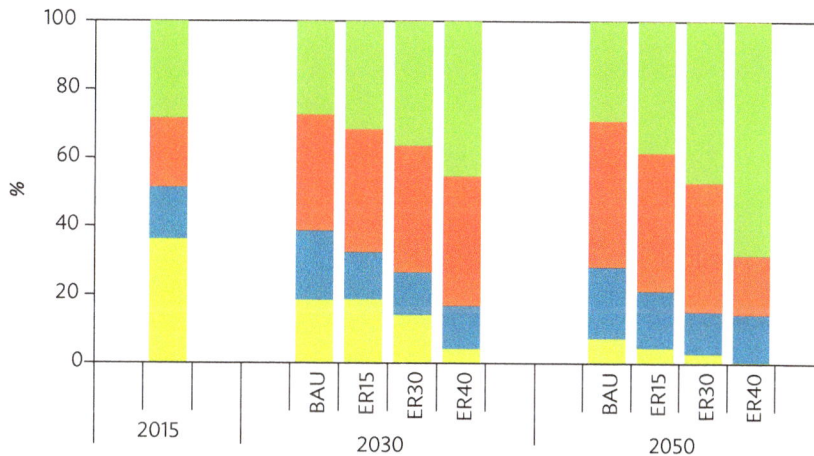

b. Fuel mix in TPES (%)

■ Renewables   ■ Hydro   ■ Petroleum products   ■ Coal   ■ Biomass

BAU = business as usual scenario; ER15 = 15% energy reduction scenario; ER30 = 30% energy reduction scenario; ER40 = 40% energy reduction scenario; Mtoe = million tons of oil equivalent; TPES = total primary energy supply.

Source: Authors.

Figure 5.16: Energy Intensity in Various Scenarios, 2015–2050

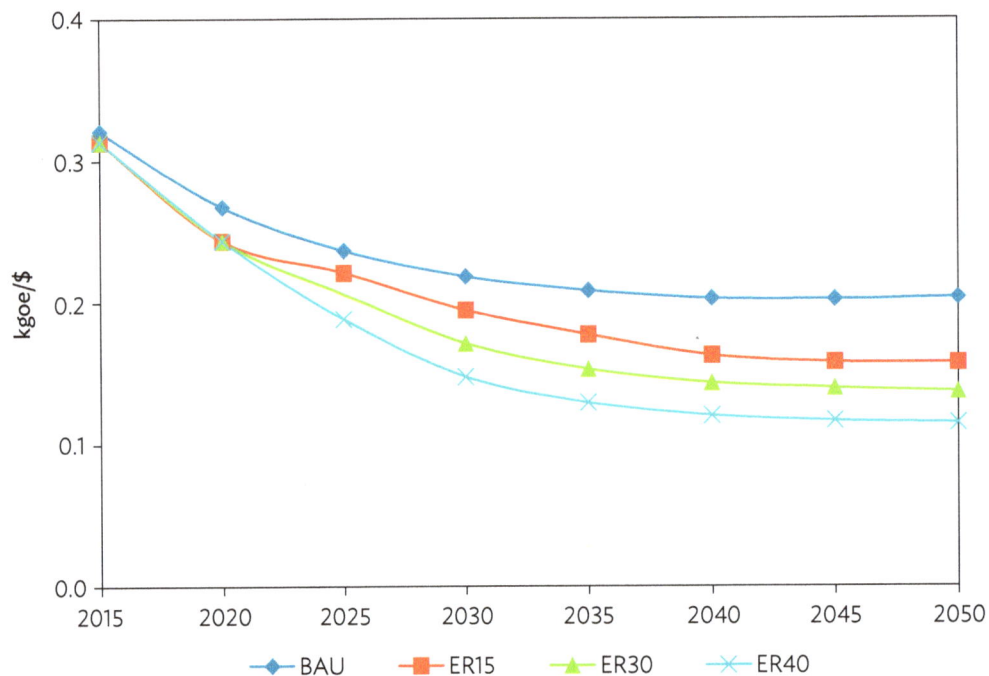

BAU = business as usual scenario; ER15 = 15% energy reduction scenario; ER30 = 30% energy reduction scenario; ER40 = 40% energy reduction scenario; kgoe/$ = kilogram of oil equivalent/United States dollar.

Source: Authors.

Electricity Generation

Electricity generation in BAU and energy reduction scenarios are shown in Figure 5.17. The requirement for electricity generation would increase during 2015–2050 from 2 to 19.8 TWh in BAU, i.e., a compound annual growth rate (CAGR) of 6.6%. In 2030, electricity generation requirements would be higher than in BAU by 3.5% in ER15, 5.8% in ER30, and 15.3% in ER40 scenarios. This is because electricity-based technologies are assumed to replace petroleum products and biomass-based technologies. In 2050, there would also be a higher level of electricity generation in all reduction scenarios than in BAU, with 4.2% higher in E15, 12.9% in ER30, and 40.3% in ER40.

Figure 5.17: Electricity Generation in Business as Usual and Energy Reduction Scenarios

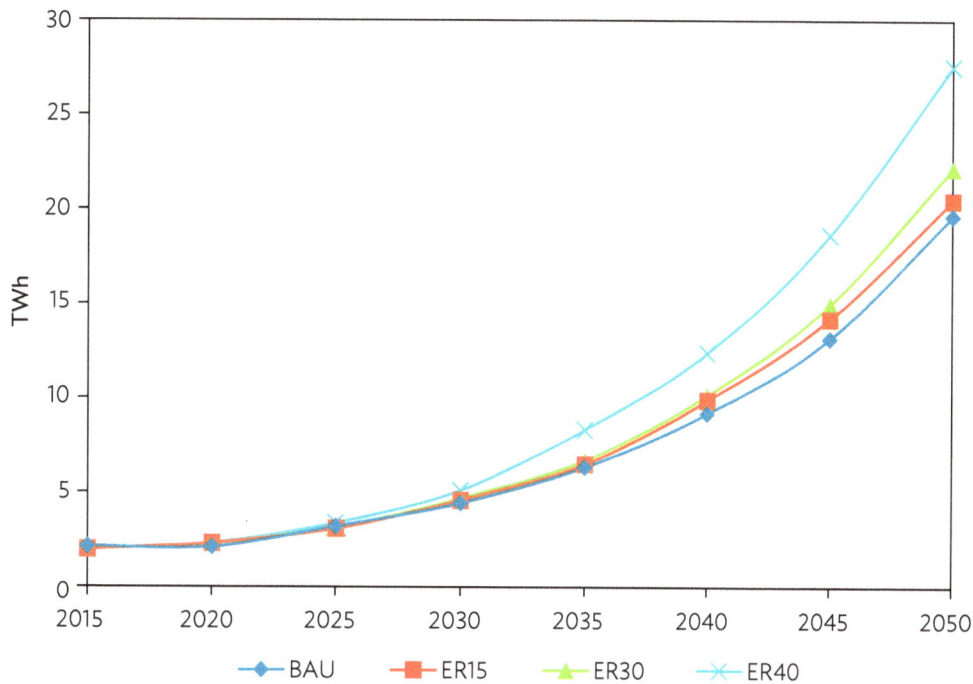

BAU = business as usual scenario; ER15 = 15% energy reduction scenario; ER30 = 30% energy reduction scenario; ER40 = 40% energy reduction scenario; TWh = terawatt-hour.

Source: Authors.

Final Energy Consumption

The final energy consumption (FEC) of all sectors except agriculture would decrease in all energy reduction scenarios. The agriculture sector is mostly reliant on electricity-based technologies in BAU, which are already efficient. Therefore, there would be only negligible changes in the sector's contribution to the TFEC in energy reduction scenarios.

Residential Sector

In 2030, the FEC of the residential sector would decrease by 10.6% in ER15, 23.7% in ER30, and 59.1% in ER50 scenarios; there would be corresponding reductions of 13.3%, 47.4%, and 55.0% in 2050 (Figure 5.18). The consumption of biomass and petroleum products would decrease in all energy reduction scenarios. Electricity consumption would be lower in ER15 than in BAU but would increase in ER30 and ER40.

It is assumed that use of biomass-based technologies in residential sectors would decline over time. Thus, in BAU, the share of biomass in the residential sector would decrease during 2015–2050 but the shares of petroleum, electricity, and renewables (i.e., solar and biogas) would increase. In ER15, the share of biomass in the energy use in 2030 and 2050 would be higher than the BAU level although biomass consumption would be lower than in BAU. The share of biomass in ER15 would be 82.8% in 2030 and 71.8% in 2050, compared to corresponding values of 80.8% and 69.6% in BAU. The share of electricity in the final energy use would be lower than the BAU level in 2030 but higher in 2050. In both years, the electricity consumption would be lower than in BAU.

In the ER30 and ER40 scenarios, the share of electricity, petroleum, and renewables would be higher than in BAU while that of biomass would be lower. In 2050, the share of petroleum products in BAU would be 5.0%, while the share in energy reduction scenarios would become negligible, implying replacement of all petroleum-based technologies by electricity. Similarly, the share of electricity would be 23.9% in BAU, 25.2% in ER15, 66.7% in ER30, and 94.2% in ER40. The shares of renewable would reach 3.0% in ER15, 4.9% in ER30, and 5.8% in ER40 scenarios.

Commercial Sector

The FEC of the commercial sector in 2030 would decrease by 43.0% in all energy reduction scenarios. In 2030, higher reduction targets would have no effect on energy reduction in the commercial sector. In 2050, the sector's FEC would be reduced by 45.4% in both ER15 and ER30 and by 50.4% in ER40.

In all energy reduction scenarios in 2030, consumption of biomass and petroleum products, mainly liquefied petroleum gas (LPG), would decrease while electricity consumption would increase compared with BAU. In 2050, devices based on petroleum products would be completely replaced by electric devices in ER15 and ER30 scenarios. In ER40, biomass-based technologies would also be replaced to a large extent.

In 2030, the share of biomass would be 63.7% in all energy reduction scenarios. In 2050, the share would decrease to around 44.8% in ER15 and ER30, and further decrease to 7.8% in ER40. In 2050, the share of electricity would be 54.7% in both ER15 and ER30 whereas the share of petroleum products would be insignificant. Under ER40, electricity's share in the sector's FEC would increase significantly to 91.7% while that of biomass would be only 7.8%. Similar to 2030, the share of petroleum products in the sector's FEC would be insignificant in 2050, because electricity would replace LPG to a large extent and also replace biomass to some extent in ER40.

Industry Sector

The industry sector's FEC in 2030 would be reduced by 11.8% in ER15, 24.2% in ER30, and 26.8% in ER40 scenarios. This would happen with a decrease in the use of petroleum products, coal, and biomass and an increased use of electricity. In 2050, the sector's FEC would decrease by 18.1% in ER15, by 28.4% in ER30, and 28.7% in ER40.

In BAU, the share of electricity would decrease from 56.3% in 2015 to 50.7% in 2030 and 50% in 2050, whereas the share of coal would increase from 40.8% to 47.0% during 2015–2050. In energy reduction scenarios, the share of electricity would be higher than in BAU. In 2030 and 2050, the share of electricity in ER30 and ER40 would exceed 70%. The share of coal in the sector's FEC would fall in all reduction scenarios during 2020–2050.

Transport Sector

There would be negligible changes in the FEC of the transport sector in ER15 in 2030, whereas the sector's FEC would decrease by 9% in ER30 and by 22% in ER40 compared to BAU. In 2050, the sector's FEC would be reduced by 22.5% in ER15, by 30.7% in ER30, and by over 52% in ER40. The decrease in FEC is due to a switch from internal combustion to electric vehicles with a relatively higher energy conversion efficiency. Note, however, that there can be conversion and T&D losses associated with electricity supply.

Sectoral Contributions to Reductions in Total Final Energy Consumption Under Energy Reduction Scenarios

Figure 5.19 presents the energy reduction by sectors and the sectoral shares in TFEC. In 2030, TFEC would be reduced by 0.1 Mtoe in ER15, 0.3 Mtoe in ER30, and 0.4 Mtoe in ER40 scenarios. In 2050, the reduction would be 1.2 Mtoe in ER15, 1.8 Mtoe in ER30, and 2.4 Mtoe in ER40. The agriculture sector will not contribute to energy reduction. In ER15, the industry sector would offer the maximum reduction potential in 2030, followed by commercial and residential sectors. In ER30 and ER40, the industry sector would have the highest contribution in energy reduction. The residential sector would have the second highest role in ER40, followed by the transport and commercial sectors. The transport sector would provide the major reduction in TFEC, followed by the industry and commercial sectors in all energy reduction scenarios. The transport sector would contribute more than 50% to the reduction of TFEC in ER40, followed by the industry sector with 30.8%.

Figure 5.18: Final Energy Consumption in Different Scenarios per Sector

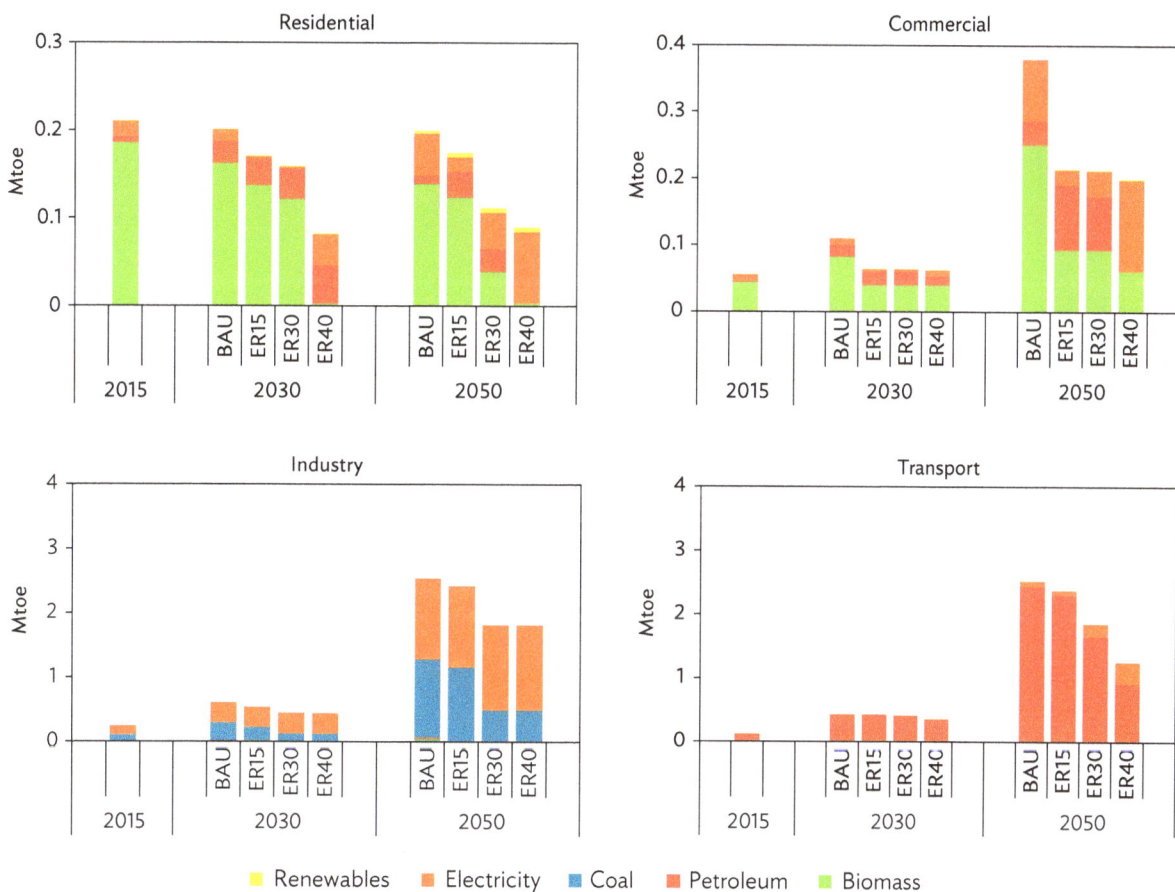

BAU = business as usual scenario; ER15 = 15% energy reduction scenario; ER30 = 30% energy reduction scenario; ER40 = 40% energy reduction scenario; Mtoe = million tons of oil equivalent.

Source: Authors.

Figure 5.19: Sector Contributions in Final Energy Reduction Under Energy Reduction Scenarios

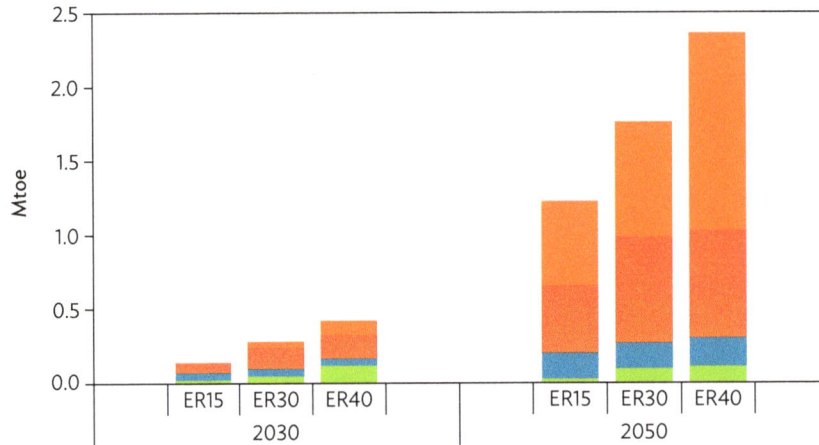

a. Sectoral contributions in total reduction of final energy consumption (Mtoe)

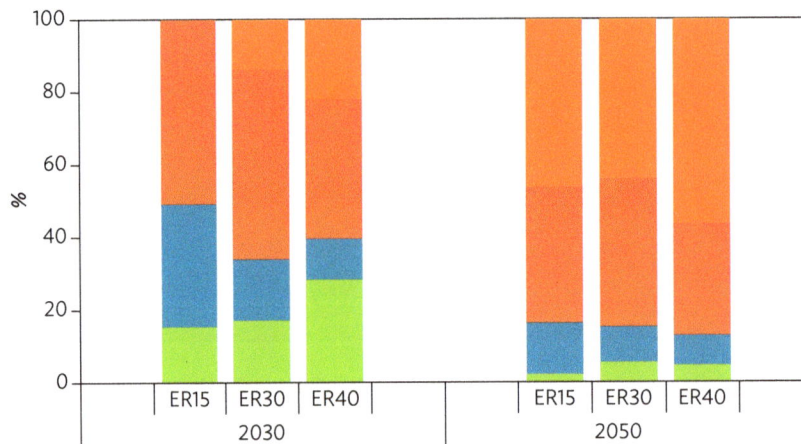

b. Sectoral shares in total reduction of final energy consumption (%)

■ Agriculture   ■ Transport   ■ Industrial   ■ Commercial   ■ Residential

ER15 = 15% energy reduction scenario; ER30 = 30% energy reduction scenario; ER40 = 40% energy reduction scenario; Mtoe = million tons of oil equivalent.

Source: Authors.

Overall Efficiency of Energy Conversion and Transmission

The overall energy conversion efficiency in Bhutan would exceed 99% throughout 2015–2050, due to the heavy reliance on hydro for power generation. In this study, electricity generation from hydro and other renewables is considered to have 100% generation efficiency, i.e., no conversion losses are considered; only T&D losses are accounted for in their cases.

Technology Selection

Residential and commercial sectors. Some of the energy-efficient technologies are found to be cost-effective in BAU; however, our assumptions in BAU restrict the complete replacement of low-efficiency technologies. The improved cook stove (ICS) would be a cost-effective option in the BAU as well as ER15 and ER30 scenarios. The AICS would be cost-effective in the ER30 scenario by 2025. However, in ER40, electric cooking would displace all cooking based on solid and gaseous fuels by 2035. Efficient air-conditioners would be cost-effective in BAU and energy reduction scenarios. In ER40, electric heating would be cost-effective in ER30 and ER40 by 2044 and 2027, respectively. Use of LED lamps would also be cost-effective in BAU and energy reduction scenarios.

Transport sector. Hybrid cars would be cost-effective in ER15 and ER30 scenarios but not in BAU. Electric cars would also be required to meet the ER30 target, but hybrid cars would still have the major share. In ER40, a high level of electric penetration would be needed from 2030 onwards. The combination of diesel-hybrid buses and electric buses would be cost-effective options in the ER40 scenario by 2040 onwards. Electric two-wheelers would be cost-effective options in the BAU scenario. In freight transport, diesel-hybrid trucks would be cost-effective in energy reduction scenarios as well as in BAU by 2021. In ER40, electric trucks would also become cost-effective options by 2030.

Industry sector. Similar to the residential and commercial sectors, some of the energy-efficient technologies and measures that are cost-effective in energy reduction scenarios are also cost-effective in BAU. Energy-efficiency measures would be cost-effective in alloy, carbide, and silicon industries in BAU and energy reduction scenarios. For process heating, electric heat-pump boilers would be cost-effective in all reduction scenarios. Heat-pump boilers would replace all other boilers by 2030. In the cement industry, six-stage cyclone suspension preheater technology in clinker manufacturing would be cost-effective in ER30 and ER40 scenarios.

Agriculture sector. Energy-efficient pumps would be a cost-effective option in BAU as well as energy reduction scenarios.

Investment Requirements and Average Incremental Cost

Figure 5.20 gives the total investment requirement (undiscounted) during 2015–2050 in two cases: with and without modal shift from cars to public mass transport vehicles in the transport sector (Table 5.1). Figure 5.20 (a) shows that total investment requirement is lower by 5.3% in ER15 and 1.7% in ER30 than in BAU. This is partially due to modal shift from cars to public vehicles in the transport sector and also due to lower total cost with energy-efficiency improvement. Note that the study assumes that inefficient technologies would still be prevalent in the BAU scenario despite higher total cost. In the ER40 scenario, the total investment requirement would, however, be 12.1% higher than in BAU.

Figure 5.20: Investment Requirement: Effect of Variation in Modal Shares in Passenger Transport, 2015–2050

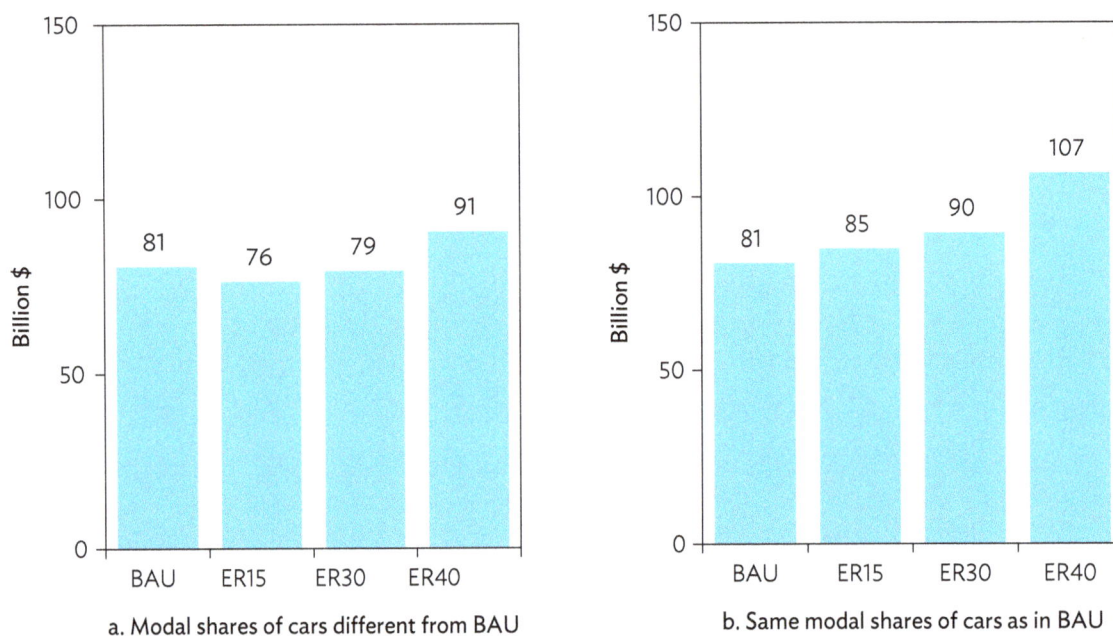

a. Modal shares of cars different from BAU

b. Same modal shares of cars as in BAU

BAU = business as usual scenario; ER15 = 15% energy reduction scenario; ER30 = 30% energy reduction scenario; ER40 = 40% energy reduction scenario.

Source: Authors.

Figure 5.20 (b) shows the investment requirement in the case where the share of cars in passenger demand would be the same as in BAU. The total investment cost would increase with the level of energy reduction targets: by 5.2% in ER15, 10.8% in ER30, and 32.0% in ER40 scenarios.

The total cost of the energy system during 2015–2050 would be $130 billion (undiscounted) in BAU. With a modal shift considered in the transport sector (i.e., from cars to public mass transport vehicles) the total cost in ER15, ER30, and ER40 scenarios would be 11.9%, 11.0%, and 4.5% lower than in BAU, respectively (Figure 5.21 [a]). Note that the lower values of the total cost in energy reduction scenarios are partly because of the lower modal shares of private vehicles considered in the reduction scenarios than in BAU (Table 5.1) and also the use of no-regret technologies.

Figure 5.21: Total Cost of the Energy System: Effect of Variation in Modal Shares in Passenger Transport, 2015–2050

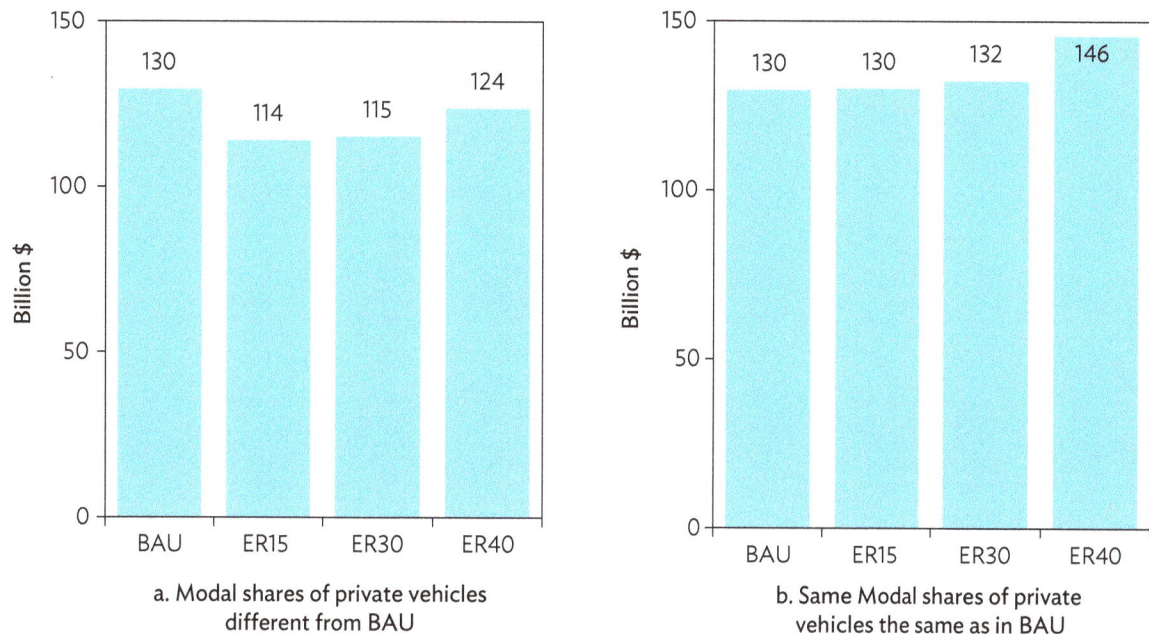

a. Modal shares of private vehicles different from BAU

b. Same Modal shares of private vehicles the same as in BAU

BAU = business as usual scenario; ER15 = 15% energy reduction scenario; ER30 = 30% energy reduction scenario; ER40 = 40% energy reduction scenario.

Source: Authors.

If the minimum shares of private vehicles in all energy reduction scenarios are assumed to be the same as in BAU, the total cost would increase in the energy reduction scenarios (Figure 5.21 [b]) by 0.4% in ER15, 2.2% in ER30, and 12.4% in ER40.

The average incremental cost (AIC) would be negative in all energy reduction scenarios due to the lower total cost in reduction scenarios (Figure 5.22 [a]). Note that we consider modal shift in the transport sector in the reduction scenarios. If the modal shares in the transport sector in all reduction scenarios were to be the same as in BAU, the AIC would be positive and increase with the level of the energy reduction target (Figure 5.22 [b]): it would be $81/ktoe in ER15, $155/ktoe in ER30, and $513/ktoe in ER40.

Figure 5.22: Average Incremental Cost Saving in Energy Reduction Scenarios: Effect of Variation in Modal Shares in Passenger Transport

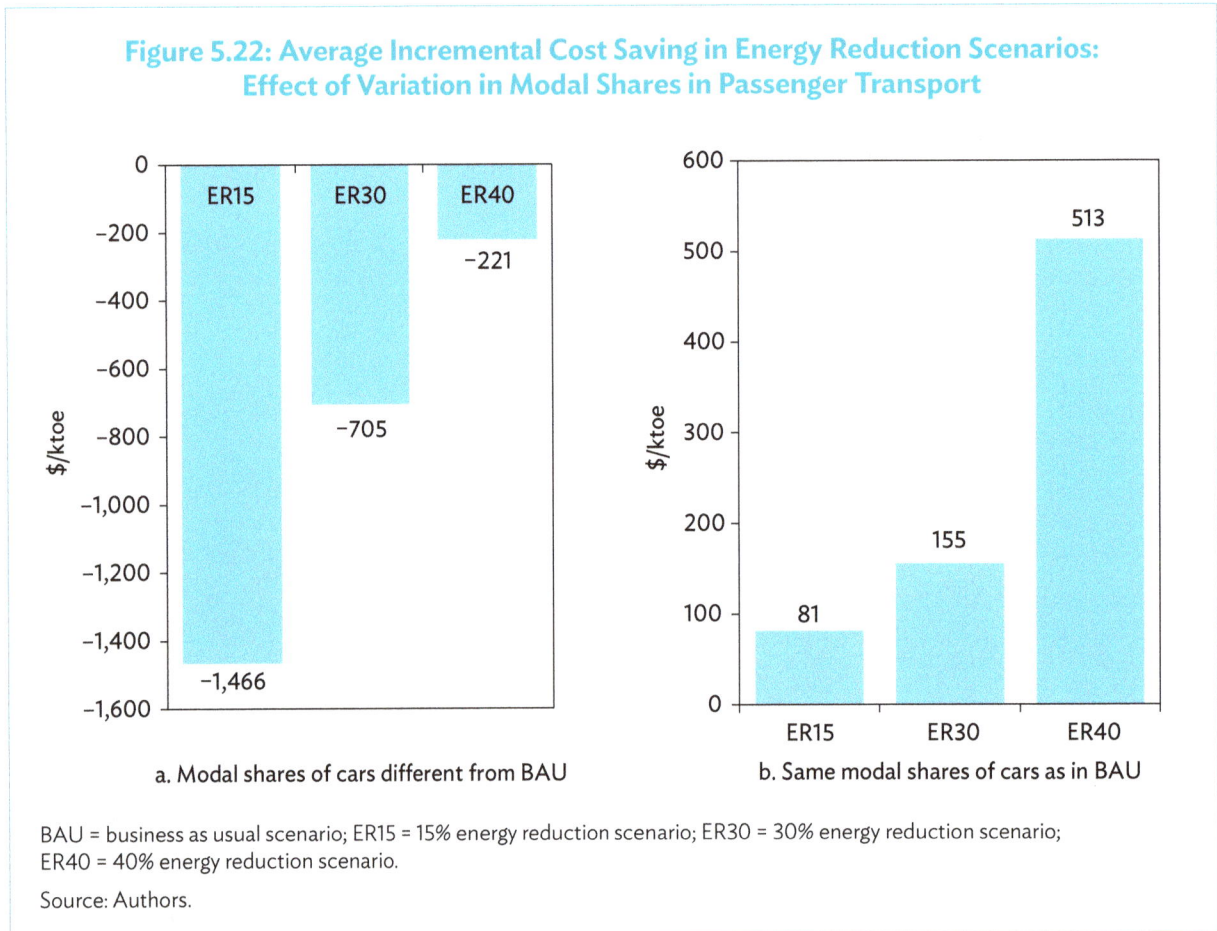

a. Modal shares of cars different from BAU

b. Same modal shares of cars as in BAU

BAU = business as usual scenario; ER15 = 15% energy reduction scenario; ER30 = 30% energy reduction scenario; ER40 = 40% energy reduction scenario.

Source: Authors.

Greenhouse Gas Emissions

Greenhouse gas (GHG) emissions in the BAU and energy reduction scenarios are presented in Figure 5.23. In the BAU scenario, GHG emissions would increase by twice in 2030 compared to 2015 level and by 13.5 times in 2050. In 2030, GHG emission would be reduced by 11.6% in ER15, 27.7% in ER30, and 37.6% in ER40. The transport sector would have the highest share in GHG emissions in all scenarios followed by the industry sector. The contribution of residential, commercial, and agriculture sectors is relatively insignificant compared to that from transport and industry.

In 2050, emissions would be lower by 14.9% in ER15, 43.6% in ER30, and 72.7% in ER40. Interestingly, in ER30 and ER40, percentage reductions in GHG emission would be higher than the percentage reduction in energy consumption. Similarly in 2030, the transport sector would be the major emitter of GHGs, followed by the industry sector in all scenarios; the contribution of agriculture, residential, and commercial sectors would be very small.

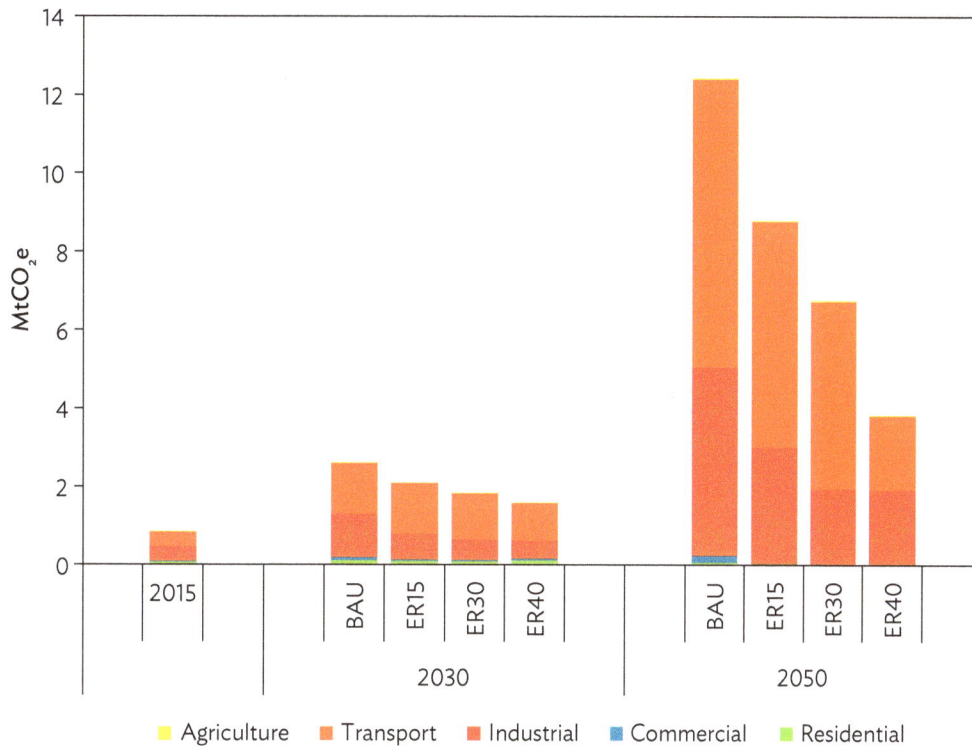

Figure 5.23: Greenhouse Gas Emissions in Business as Usual and Energy Reduction Scenarios, 2030 and 2050

Legend: Agriculture | Transport | Industrial | Commercial | Residential

BAU = business as usual scenario; ER15 = 15% energy reduction scenario; ER30 = 30% energy reduction scenario; ER40 = 40% energy reduction scenario; $MtCO_2e$ = million metric tons of carbon dioxide equivalent.

Source: Authors.

Implications of Transmission and Distribution Efficiency Improvement

The T&D loss in BAU is assumed to be 6% throughout 2015–2050. This study analyzes the effects of reducing T&D loss to 5%. The T&D losses in two cases (Table 5.2) are referred to as TDL-6% and TDL-5%. Figure 5.24 shows the electricity generation requirement at TDL-6% and TDL-5%. In 2030, the electricity generation requirement in TDL-5% would be reduced by 1.0% in BAU, 1.1% in ER15, 1.4% in ER30, and 1.2% in ER40 compared with TDL-6%. In 2050, with TDL-5%, electricity generation requirement would decrease by 1.0% each in BAU and ER15, and would decrease by 1.6% in ER30 and 2.4% in ER40 compared with TDL-6%. The cumulative electricity generation during 2015–2050 with TLD-5% would be reduced by 0.5% in BAU, 1.0% in ER15, 1.3% in ER30, and 1.7% in ER40.

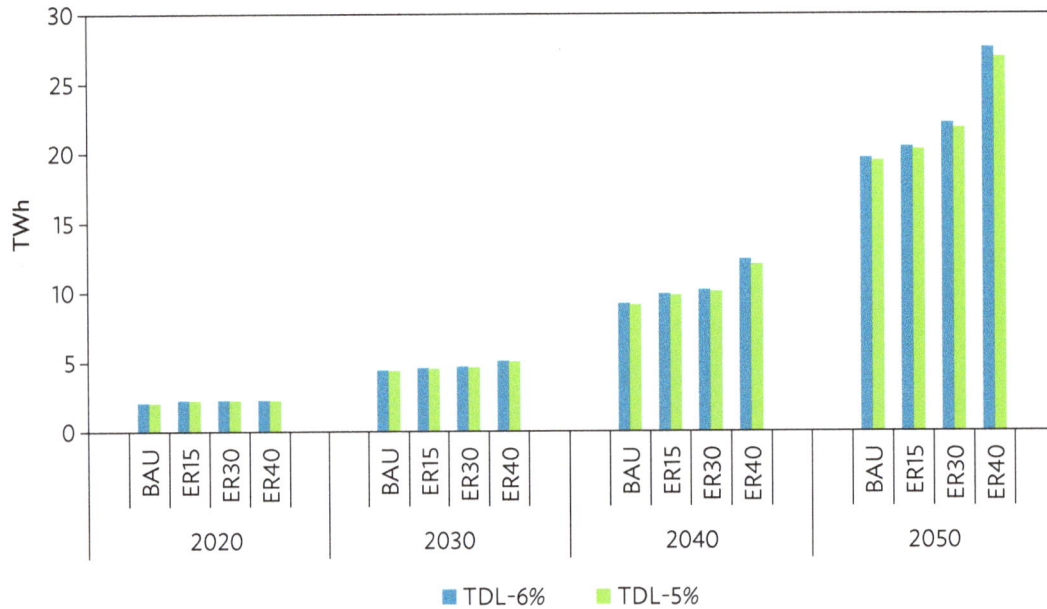

Figure 5.24: Electricity Generation for Various Transmission and Distribution Losses in Bhutan

BAU = business as usual scenario; ER15 = 15% energy reduction scenario; ER30 = 30% energy reduction scenario; ER40 = 40% energy reduction scenario; TDL-6% = 6% transmission and distribution loss scenario; TDL-5% = 5% transmission and distribution loss scenario; TWh = terawatt-hour.

Source: Authors.

The installed capacity requirements in various years in the two cases are presented in Figure 5.25. The capacity factor is assumed to be 55.0% throughout the period, based on the system capacity factor in 2015. In 2030, the installed generation capacity requirement with TDL-5% would decrease by 9.3 MW in BAU, 10.6 MW in ER15, 13.4 MW in ER30, and 13.0 MW in ER40. In 2050, the installed capacity requirement would be reduced by 42 MW in BAU, 43 MW in ER15, 72 MW in ER30, and 140 MW in ER40.

Figure 5.25: Installed Capacity Requirement for Various Transmission and Distribution Losses in Bhutan

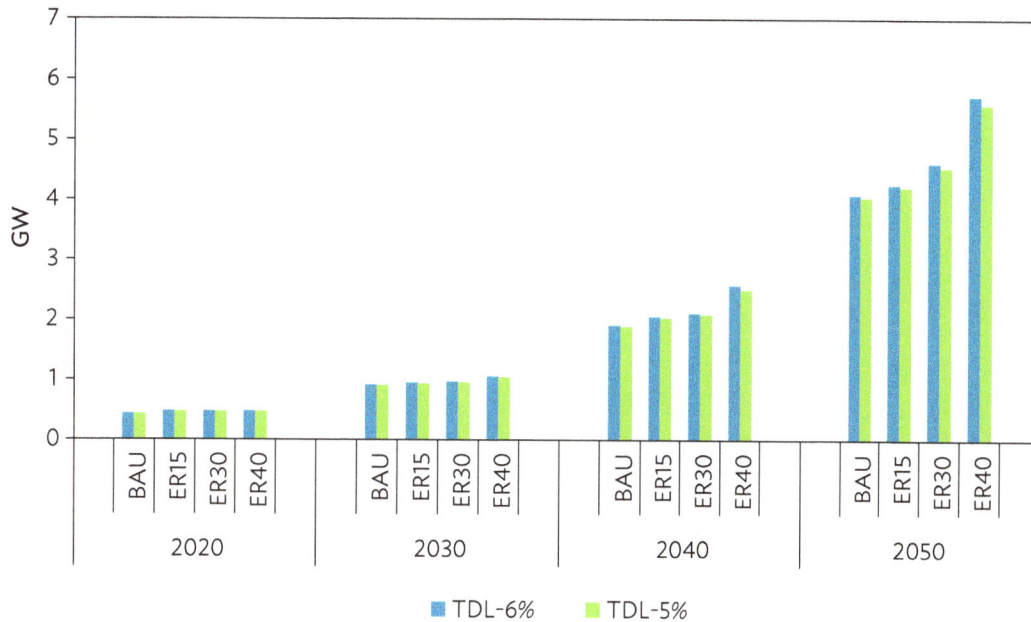

BAU = business as usual scenario; ER15 = 15% energy reduction scenario; ER30 = 30% energy reduction scenario; ER40 = 40% energy reduction scenario; GW = Gigawatt hours; TDL-6% = 6% transmission and distribution loss scenario; TDL-5% = 5% transmission and distribution loss scenario.

Source: Authors.

The total system cost would decrease with TDL-5% in BAU and energy reduction scenarios compared to TDL-6% levels. The decrease in total cost is not significant; the cost would be lower by 0.1% in BAU, 0.04% in ER15, 0.1% in ER30, and 0.6% in ER40. Note, however, the additional cost of T&D system improvement for TDL-5% is not considered in estimating cost savings here.

Nepal

Determination of Maximum Energy-Reduction Potential in 2030 and 2050

The study found that the maximum potential for reduction of total primary energy supply (TPES) to be 54.0% in 2030 compared with BAU when the minimum shares of cars are as shown in Table 5.1. However, if the shares of passenger cars were the same as in BAU, the maximum energy-reduction potential would be slightly lower (i.e., 53.7%). In 2050, the maximum reduction potential would be 51.0% when considering the different shares of cars. If shares of cars were the same as in BAU, the maximum energy-reduction potential would be 50.1%.

Total Primary Energy Supply

Figure 5.26 (a) presents TPES in selected years in various scenarios. There would be a decrease in the use of fossil fuels and traditional biomass, and an increase in the use of hydro and other renewables, in all energy reduction scenarios compared with BAU. In 2030, lower use of biomass contributes to the highest reduction in TPES in all energy reduction scenarios. The reduction in the use of petroleum products would account for the second highest reduction in TPES in ER15, followed by a lower use of coal. In ER30 and ER40, there would be more reduction in the use of coal than petroleum products. In 2030, there would be higher usage of hydro and other renewables in energy reduction scenarios than in BAU.

In 2050, the consumption of petroleum products in ER40 would be higher than in ER15 and ER30. This is mainly due to the shift from lower-efficiency biomass technologies to more efficient LPG-based technologies in the residential sector.

Decrease in biomass use would be the highest contributor to the reduction in TPES in ER15 scenario in 2050, followed by petroleum products and coal. In ER30 and ER40, decrease in biomass use would be the major contributor to reduction in TPES. There would be a decline in the use of petroleum products and coal in all reduction scenarios; however, their contribution in energy reduction would be less significant than that of biomass. The second largest reduction in TPES would be due to decline in the use of petroleum products in ER30 and ER40. Decreased use of coal would account for the third highest reduction in TPES in energy reduction scenarios in 2050. The use of hydro and other renewables would increase in all reduction scenarios.

The shares of different types of energy in TPES in different scenarios are shown in Figure 5.26 (b). Biomass share would decrease significantly in the BAU scenario during 2015–2050. In 2030, biomass share would fall slightly in ER15 and ER30 compared with BAU but would decrease significantly in ER40. In ER15, petroleum products would have a lower share in TPES than in BAU. However, in ER30 and ER40 the share of petroleum products would be higher than in BAU although the level of consumption of the fuels would be lower than in BAU. The role of coal is smaller than BAU in reduction scenarios in that it would have a lower share in TPES. Additionally, the share of coal would not change significantly in BAU and reduction scenarios. Hydroelectricity has an important role in energy reduction. There would be higher shares of hydro and other renewables in TPES in energy reduction scenarios than in BAU.

In 2050, the share of biomass in BAU and ER15 would not be much different; however, their shares would fall significantly in ER30, and drop further in ER50; from 34.6% in BAU to 32.8% in ER15, 15.5% in ER30, and 2.2% in ER40. The share of petroleum products in ER15 would be lower than in BAU; however, their share in ER30 would be higher than in ER15. The share of petroleum products in ER40 would be higher than in BAU; the share would be 25.3% in BAU, 19.0% in ER15, 24.9% in ER30, and 29.0% in ER40. It is noteworthy that although the share of petroleum products in ER40 is higher than in BAU, the level of their consumption would still be lower than in BAU. Hydropower would become increasingly important to meet the rising energy reduction targets; its share in TPES would increase from 35.9% in ER15 to 54.9% in ER40. The share of coal would be little affected for the energy reduction targets considered and remain in the range of 11.1%–13.8%.

Figure 5.26: Total Primary Energy Supply in Different Scenarios

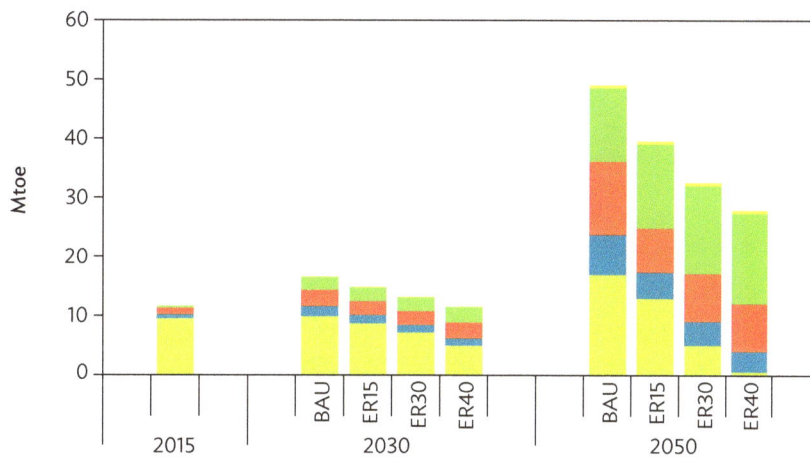

a. TPES by fuel type

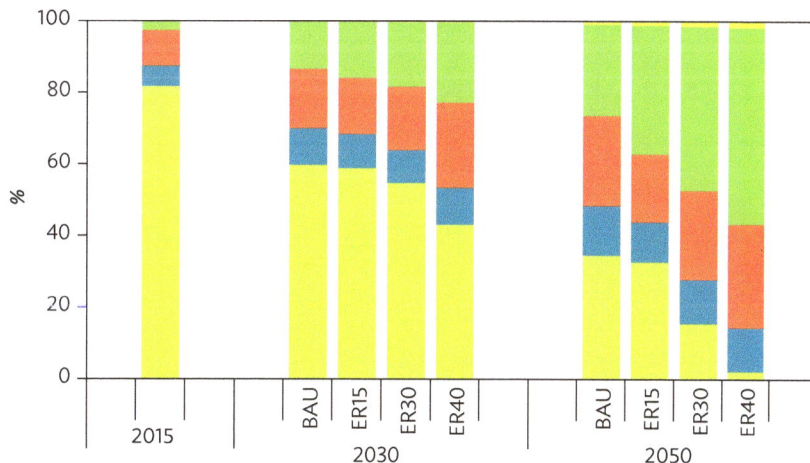

b. Fuel mix in TPES (%)

Renewables   Hydro   Petroleum products   Coal   Biomass

BAU = business as usual scenario; ER15 = 15% energy reduction scenario; ER30 = 30% energy reduction scenario; ER40 = 40% energy reduction scenario; Mtoe = million tons of oil equivalent; TPES = total primary energy supply.

Source: Authors.

Energy Intensity

Figure 5.27 presents the changes in overall energy intensity (measured as energy consumption per unit of GDP) in various scenarios. The overall energy intensity in BAU would decrease from 0.55 kgoe/$ in 2015 to 0.30 kgoe/$ in 2030 and 0.18 kgoe/$ in 2050. The decrease in energy intensity for energy reduction scenarios is due partly to a switch from traditional biomass fuels to modern fuels and partly to energy-efficiency improvements in different sectors.

Figure 5.27: Energy Intensity in Various Scenarios, 2015–2050

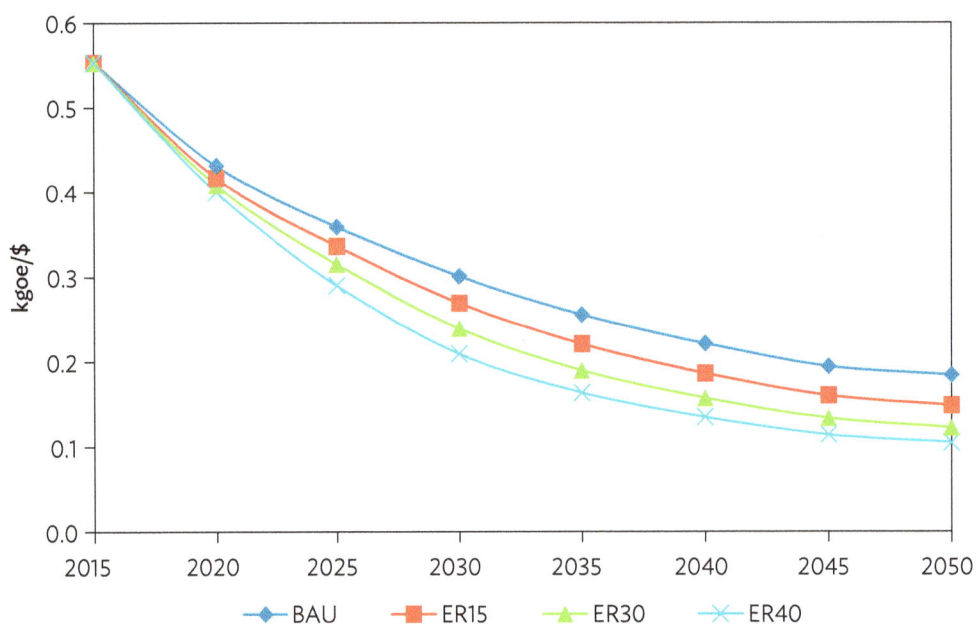

BAU = business as usual scenario; ER15 = 15% energy reduction scenario; ER30 = 30% energy reduction scenario; ER40 = 40% energy reduction scenario; kgoe/$ = kilogram of oil equivalent/United States dollar.

Source: Authors.

Electricity Generation

Electricity generation in BAU and energy reduction scenarios is shown in Figure 5.28. In BAU, the electricity generation requirement would increase from 5.6 TWh in 2015 to 25.1 TWh in 2030 and to 147.4 TWh in 2050, i.e., a compound annual growth rate (CAGR) of 9.8% during 2015–2050. In energy reduction scenarios, electricity generation in 2020 would be lower than in BAU, due to decreasing electricity consumption driven by energy-efficiency improvements. In BAU, it is assumed that certain less efficient technologies (e.g., incandescent bulbs and electrical devices) will still be in use despite their higher life-cycle cost, while in energy reduction scenarios no such constraints are imposed on technology selection. From 2025 onwards, there would be a higher level of electricity generation in all energy reduction scenarios than in BAU due to fuel switching to electricity-based technologies. Electricity generation would be higher by 6.3% in ER15, 9.4% in ER30, and 19.0% in ER40 in 2030 than in BAU. In 2050, electricity generation requirement would be 13.8% higher in E15, 19.5% higher in ER30, and 22.8% higher in ER40.

The cumulative electricity generation during 2015–2050 would be 1,760 TWh in BAU. It would be lower than in BAU by 10.8% in ER15, 16.4% in ER30, and 20.7% in ER40 scenarios.

Figure 5.28: Electricity Generation in Business as Usual and Energy Reduction Scenarios

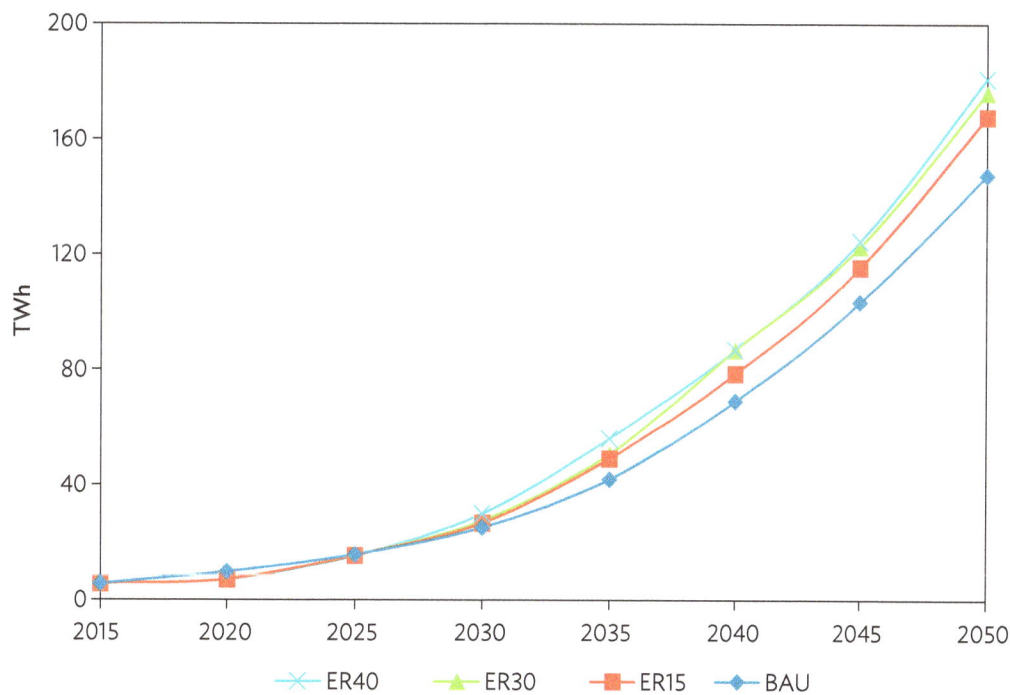

BAU = business as usual scenario; ER15 = 15% energy reduction scenario; ER30 = 30% energy reduction scenario; ER40 = 40% energy reduction scenario; TWh = terawatt-hour.

Source: Authors.

Final Energy Consumption

Residential Sector

The FEC in all sectors would decrease in all energy reduction scenarios (Figure 5.29). In 2030, FEC of the residential sector would decrease by 7.9% in ER15, 20.0% in ER30, and 34.4% in ER50; similarly, in 2050, there would be corresponding reductions of 7.4%, 37.1%, and 49.5%.

In BAU, the share of biomass in the residential sector would decrease during 2015–2050 due partly to the assumption that use of traditional biomass would decrease over time and partly because of an increasing switch to modern fuels, e.g., electricity and petroleum products. As such, the shares of petroleum products and electricity would increase.

Figure 5.29: Final Energy Consumption in Different Scenarios per Sector

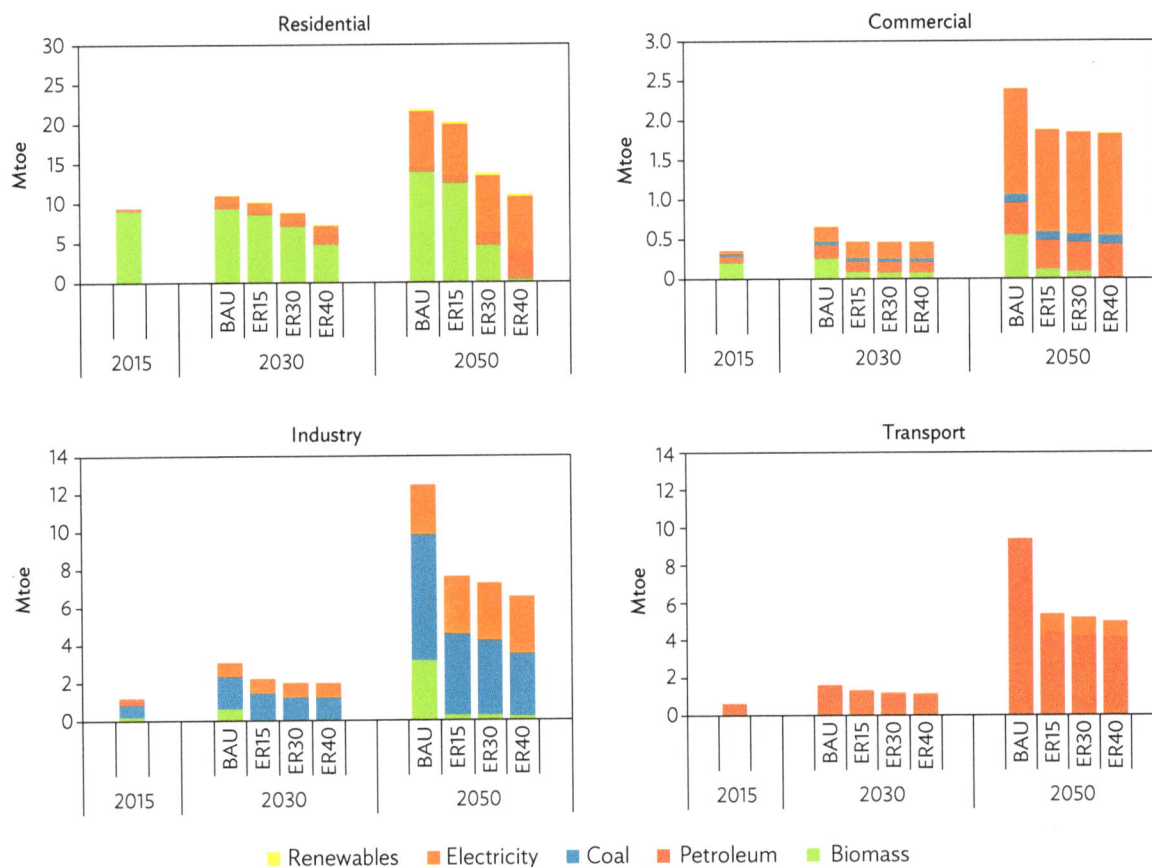

BAU = business as usual scenario; ER15 = 15% energy reduction scenario; ER30 = 30% energy reduction scenario; ER40 = 40% energy reduction scenario; Mtoe = million tons of oil equivalent.

Source: Authors.

In 2030, biomass use would decrease with increases in energy reduction targets. The use of petroleum products would be lower in ER15 and ER30 and higher in ER40 than in BAU. The higher use of petroleum products in ER40 is due to a shift from biomass to LPG-based technologies. Electricity consumption would increase slightly in ER15 and ER30 but increase significantly in ER40 in 2030. The fuel mix in ER15 and ER30 would be almost the same as in BAU. The situation would differ for ER40 in that there would be a marked decrease in the share of biomass and an increase in the share of petroleum products. The share of petroleum products would be 5.4% in BAU and increase to 6.0% in ER15, 8.9% in ER30, and 17.3% in ER40.

In 2050, there would be a massive reduction in the use of biomass in ER30 and ER40. The consumption of electricity and petroleum products would increase significantly in ER40 compared to other scenarios. The share of biomass in FEC in the residential sector would fall slightly from 64.0% in BAU to 62.2% in ER15, and would drop significantly to 34.1% in ER30 and 3.6% in ER40. The share of petroleum products in the sector's FEC would be rather low: 2.6% in BAU, 4.5% in ER15, and 11.3% in ER30; however, their share would increase significantly to 31.4% in ER40. In contrast, electricity would have a very significant share in the sector's FEC: 32.3% in BAU, 32.1% in ER15, 52.9% in ER30, and 62.8% in ER40. The shares of renewables would reach 1.2% in ER15, 1.6% in ER30, and 2.1% in ER40 scenarios.

Commercial Sector

The FEC of the commercial sector in 2030 would decrease by 28.3% in ER15 and by 29.0% in both ER30 and ER40 scenarios. Likewise, in 2050, the sector's FEC would decrease by 21.5% in ER15, 22.9% in ER30, and 23.6% in ER40. In energy reduction scenarios, there would be a decrease in the consumption of petroleum products (mainly LPG) and biomass, while electricity consumption would increase.

In 2030, the share of biomass in the FEC of the commercial sector would decrease to the range of 17.9%–19.0% in energy reduction scenarios compared to almost 40% in BAU, whereas the share of petroleum products would not change significantly. The share of coal would be 6.1% in BAU and would increase to the range of 8.5%–8.6% in reduction scenarios. There would be a major fuel switching (i.e., toward use of electricity), with electricity's share increasing to 45.2% in ER15, 46.2% in ER30, and 46.4% in ER40 scenarios compared to less than 30% in BAU.

In 2050, the use of biomass would decrease significantly in energy reduction scenarios. This is due to energy-efficiency improvement and substitution of biomass by LPG and electricity in thermal applications like cooking and heating. There would be higher consumption of petroleum products in ER40 than in ER15 and ER30. Further, there would be a partial substitution of electricity with LPG in the sector; this is because the cost of electricity supply would increase with the increase in electricity generation thereby making electricity more expensive than LPG for cooking. The share of electricity in the FEC of the sector would be 68.4% in ER15, 69.4% in ER30, and 70.4% in ER40 compared to 55.6% in BAU.

Industry Sector

In 2030, the FEC of the industry sector would be lower by 27.6% in ER15, 34.8% in ER30, and 35.5% in ER40 scenarios. This would happen with a decrease in the use of biomass, petroleum products, and coal and increased use of electricity. There would be a major reduction in the use of biomass and only minor reductions in coal and petroleum products. In 2050, the sector's FEC would decrease by 38.7% in ER15, 41.6% in ER30, and 47.4% in ER40. These decreases in FEC are due to improvements in energy efficiency as well as fuel switching (from biomass and oil to electricity). Electricity based heat-pump technology would have an important role in substitution of biomass boilers for providing process heat.

The share of electricity in the industry sector would increase from 22.9% in BAU to 34.3% in ER15, 37.8% in ER30, and 38.1% in ER40 in 2030. In reduction scenarios, the share of biomass would lie within 3.0%–3.3%. In 2050, electricity would account for 36.3% of the FEC in ER15, 37.5% in ER30, and 41.8% in ER40 whereas biomass would represent 3.2%–3.7% of the sector FEC in all reduction scenarios. Note that coal would have the highest contribution to the sector's FEC in BAU as well as energy reduction scenarios during 2020–2050.

Transport Sector

In the transport sector, the FEC in energy reduction cases would be lower than in BAU; in 2030 it would be lower by 3.0% in ER15, 4.1% in ER30, and 4.8% in ER40. The share of petroleum products in FEC would drop from 99.3% in BAU to 97.2% in ER15, 91.8% in ER30, and 92.2% in ER40 in 2030. In 2050, the sector's FEC would decrease more significantly: by 42.8% in ER15, 45.1% in ER30, and 55.7% in ER40. The share of petroleum products would decrease to 81.4% in ER15, 80.9% in ER30, and 61.8% in ER40. Electricity use in the sector would increase significantly; representing 18.6% of FEC in ER15, 19.1% in ER30, and 38.2% in ER40 compared to 0.3% in BAU.

Agriculture Sector

In 2030, the FEC of the agriculture sector would decrease by 10.0% in all energy reduction scenarios compared with BAU. The share of petroleum products in FEC would decrease from 92.4% in BAU to 86.0% in energy reduction scenarios. In 2050, the sector's FEC would decrease by 5.8% in ER15, 5.3% in ER30, and 17.0% in ER40. The share of petroleum products in the sector's FEC would be 84.0% in BAU, 81.1% in ER15, 86.1% in ER30, and 79.4% in ER40. Electricity would substitute petroleum products in the agriculture sector.

Sectoral Contributions to Reductions in Total Final Energy Consumption Under Energy Reduction Scenarios

The contribution of different sectors to the reduction of TFEC in absolute terms is given in Figure 5.30 (a) and in percentage shares in Figure 5.30 (b). In 2030, the total reduction in TFEC in would be 1.9 Mtoe in ER15, 3.9 Mtoe in ER30, and 5.6 Mtoe in ER40 scenarios; in 2050, the corresponding reductions would be 11.1, 18.2, and 22.9 Mtoe. In 2030, the residential sector would be the major contributor to the reduction in TFEC in ER15, followed by the industry, commercial, and agriculture sectors. In ER30 and ER40 scenarios, the residential sector would have the highest potential to reduce TFEC, followed by the industry, transport, and commercial sectors. In 2050, the industry sector would make the highest contribution to reduction of TFEC in ER15. In ER30 and ER40, the residential sector which would play the greatest role in reducing TFEC, followed by the industry, transport, and commercial sectors.

Figure 5.30: Sector Contributions in Final Energy Reduction under Energy Reduction Scenarios

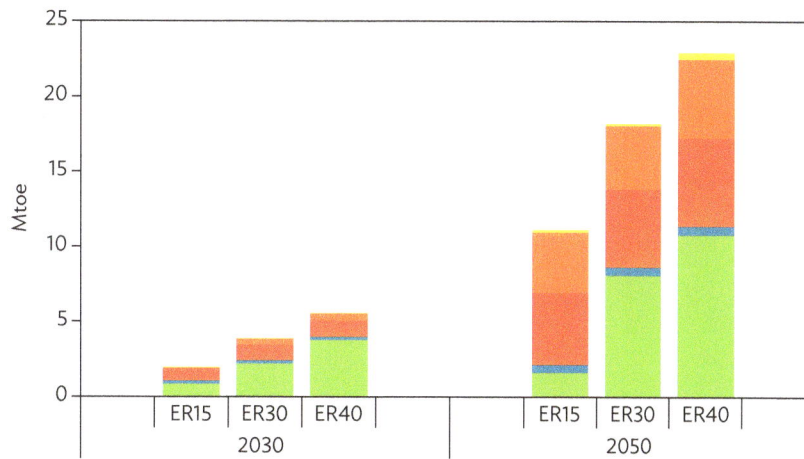

a. Sectoral contributions in total reduction of final energy consumption (Mtoe)

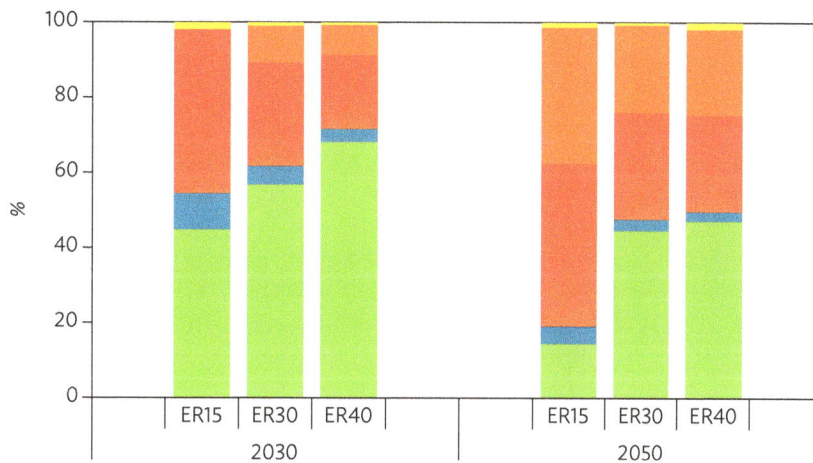

b. Sectoral shares in total reduction of final energy consumption (%)

Agriculture   Transport   Industrial   Commercial   Residential

ER15 = 15% energy reduction scenario; ER30 = 30% energy reduction scenario; ER40 = 40% energy reduction scenario; Mtoe = million tons of oil equivalent.

Source: Authors.

Overall Efficiency of Energy Conversion and Transmission

The overall energy efficiency of the energy system in Nepal would exceed 95% throughout 2015–2050, due to the country's high reliance on hydro for power generation and biomass in the residential sector. The losses are mainly due to transmission and distribution (T&D) losses in power sector. The T&D losses are relatively high but the effect on overall efficiency is not significant due to the low share of electricity in TFEC.

Technology Selection

The residential sector has the largest share in the TFEC, with cooking accounting for the highest share of this. Improved cook stoves (ICS) would be a cost-effective option in all energy reduction scenarios. By 2050, advanced improved cook stoves (AICS) would be a cost-effective option in ER15 and ER30. In ER40, energy-efficient LPG stoves would replace all solid fuel-based cooking (i.e., AICS) by 2045. Energy-efficient LPG stoves would be economically attractive compared to conventional LPG stoves throughout 2015–2050. For lighting throughout 2015–2050, light emitting diode (LED) bulbs would be the least-cost option. In addition, energy-efficient electrical devices such as LED bulbs for lighting, efficient air-conditioners, and efficient fans, would be cost-effective in all energy reduction scenarios in both residential and commercial sectors. In the commercial sector, electric cooking would be cost-effective following 2040 in ER15, 2039 in ER30, and 2038 in ER40.

In the brick industry, improved fixed-chimney bull trench kilns would be cost-effective in all energy reduction scenarios. However, from 2044 onwards, vertical shaft brick kilns would partially penetrate the brick industry in ER40. For process heat in industries, energy-efficient coal and diesel boilers would be cost-effective in all reduction scenarios. From 2021 onwards, heat-pump boilers would also be a cost-effective option in all reduction scenarios. In the cement industry, four-stage cyclone suspension preheater type rotary kilns would be cost-effective for clinker production in all reduction scenarios. From 2025 onwards, five-stage cyclone suspension preheaters with calciners and high-efficiency cooler type rotary kilns would be cost-effective in ER30 and ER40 scenarios, whereas in ER40, this would be the cost-effective option following 2034. For raw material grinding in the cement industry, vertical mills would be a cost-effective option from 2020 onwards in all energy reduction scenarios. In the cement grinding process, vertical mills would be cost-effective following 2021 in all reduction scenarios. For motive power application in industries, ultra-premium efficiency type IE5 motors would be cost-effective throughout the period for motors of all sizes. In the case of lighting, LED lamps would be the least-cost option in all scenarios including BAU.

In the agriculture sector, efficient electric pumps would be cost-effective in all energy reduction scenarios during 2015–2050. In the case of threshing in agriculture, efficient gasoline threshers would be cost-effective. However, efficient electric threshers would be cost-effective by 2036 in ER15 and by 2034 in ER40.

In the transport sector, electric two-wheelers would be cost-effective from 2029 onwards in ER15, and from 2026 onwards in ER30 and ER40. Diesel-hybrid cars would be cost-effective following 2019 in all energy reduction scenarios. Small electric cars would penetrate following 2030 in ER15, 2027 in ER30, and 2025 in ER40. In ER40, diesel-hybrid buses would be cost-effective from 2044 onwards. In freight transport, diesel-hybrid trucks and pick-ups would be cost-effective in all energy reduction scenarios. Electric trucks would penetrate in ER15 from 2035, in ER30 from 2027, and in ER40 from 2026. Electric pick-ups would be cost-effective following 2037 in ER15, 2028 in ER30, and 2027 in ER40. In freight transport, it is assumed that trucks and pick-ups do not substitute each other completely, i.e., minimum shares of both are defined.

Investment Requirements and Average Incremental Cost

Total investment requirements of meeting the energy reduction targets during 2015–2050 compared with BAU are shown in Figure 5.31. The figure compares the investment requirements in two cases: (i) when the modal shares of private vehicles in the passenger transport in energy reduction cases are assumed to be lower than in BAU, with the shares decreasing with an increase in the energy reduction target (Figure 5.27 [a]), and (ii) when the modal shares are maintained at the same level as that in BAU (Figure 5.27 [b]). Note that with the modal share of private vehicles in energy reduction scenarios considered to be the same as in BAU, the investment cost would be higher than when the modal shares are assumed to decrease with reduction targets. However, the total cost of the energy system during 2015–2050 in ER15 and ER30 would be lower than the $758 billion (undiscounted) in BAU.

Figure 5.31: Total Investment Requirement: Effect of Variation in Modal Shares in Passenger Transport, 2015–2050

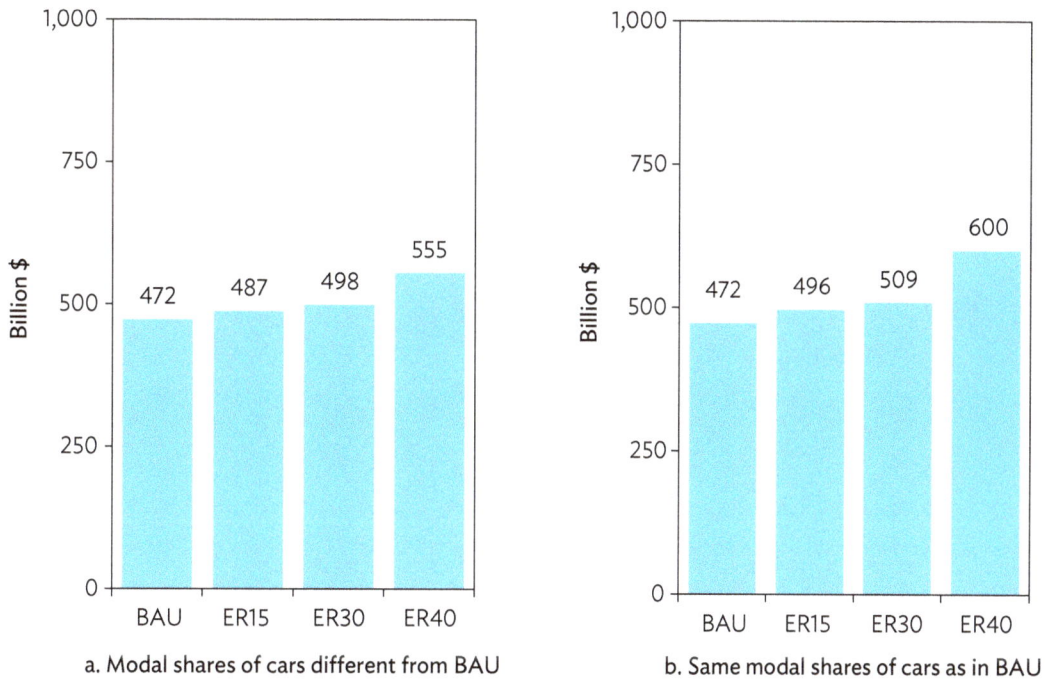

a. Modal shares of cars different from BAU

b. Same modal shares of cars as in BAU

BAU = business as usual scenario; ER15 = 15% energy reduction scenario; ER30 = 30% energy reduction scenario; ER40 = 40% energy reduction scenario.

Source: Authors.

When lower modal shares of private cars are considered, the total cost would be lower by 4.8% in ER15 and 2.3% in ER30; however, in ER40, the total cost would be 7.1% higher (Figure 5.32 [a]). The lower values of the total cost in ER15 and ER30 scenarios are partially because of the lower modal shares of private vehicles considered in the reduction scenarios than in BAU and also because of the assumption of the continuation in use of some less efficient technologies in BAU. The higher total cost in the ER40 scenario is due to increased investment in hydro development as well as in more expensive electricity-based technologies such as electric vehicles.

Therefore, some low-efficiency technologies would continue to be in use despite their higher total cost. When the modal share of private cars is considered to be the same in BAU and energy reduction scenarios, the total system cost would be lower by 3.1% in ER15 and 0.5% in ER30 but 14.3% higher in ER40 (Figure 5.27 [b]).

Figure 5.32: Total Cost of the Energy System: Effect of Variation in Modal Shares in Passenger Transport, 2015–2050

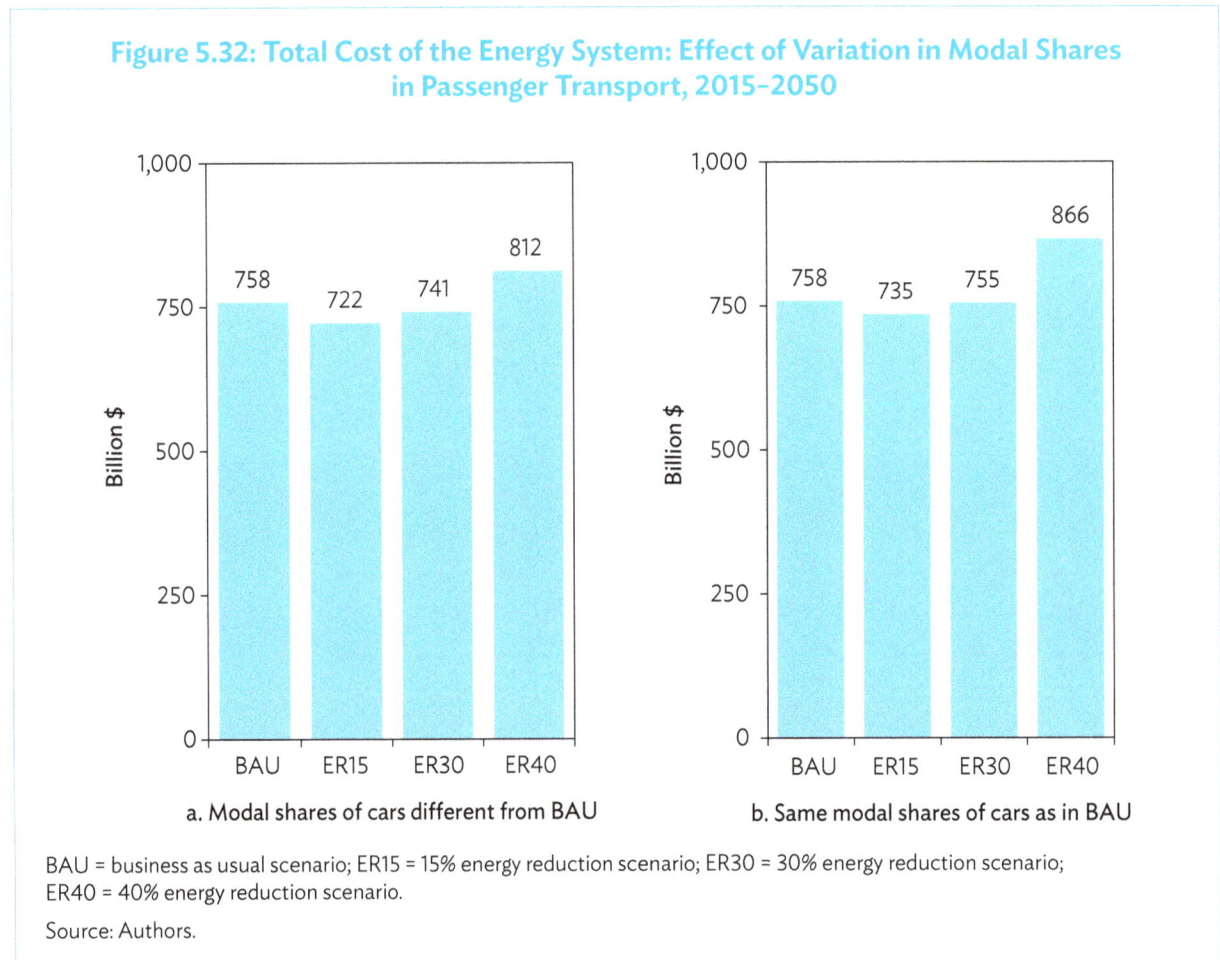

a. Modal shares of cars different from BAU

b. Same modal shares of cars as in BAU

BAU = business as usual scenario; ER15 = 15% energy reduction scenario; ER30 = 30% energy reduction scenario; ER40 = 40% energy reduction scenario.

Source: Authors.

Figure 5.33 presents the average incremental cost (AIC) for the energy reduction scenarios. The AIC would be positive in ER15 and ER30 but negative in ER40. This implies that there is a net increase in the total cost to achieve the ER40 target. If the modal shares in the transport sector in all reduction scenarios are assumed to be the same as in BAU, AIC would be positive in ER15 but negative in ER30 and ER40.

Greenhouse Gas Emissions

Greenhouse gas (GHG) emissions in the BAU and energy reduction scenarios are presented in Figure 5.34. In the BAU scenario, GHG emissions would increase at a compound annual growth rate (CAGR) of 6.0% during 2015–2050. The cumulative GHG emissions in BAU during this period would be 913 MtCO$_2$e. The cumulative emissions would be lower than the BAU level by 24.6% in ER15, 27.9% in ER30, and 29.4% in ER40 scenarios.

Figure 5.33: Average Incremental Cost Saving in Energy Reduction Scenarios: Effect of Variation in Modal Shares in Passenger Transport

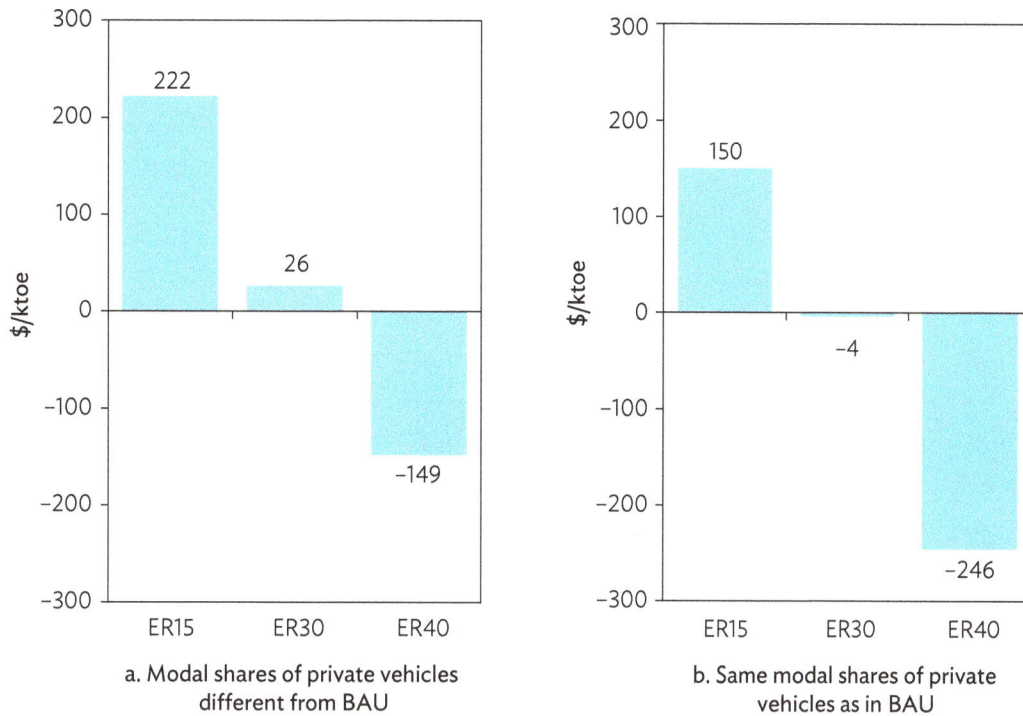

a. Modal shares of private vehicles
different from BAU

b. Same modal shares of private
vehicles as in BAU

ER15 = 15% energy reduction scenario; ER30 = 30% energy reduction scenario; ER40 = 40% energy reduction scenario; ktoe= kiloton of oil equivalent.

Source: Authors.

In 2030, GHG emission would be reduced by 15.3% in ER15, 22.5% in ER30, and 21.0% in ER40. The industry sector would have the highest share in GHG emissions in all reduction scenarios in 2030. The contribution of the commercial and agriculture sectors would be relatively insignificant compared to the residential, transport, and industry sectors. In ER15, the industry sector is followed by the transport and residential sectors. In ER30 and ER40, the residential sector is the second highest emitter, followed by the transport sector.

In 2050, GHG emissions would be lower than the BAU level by 36.0% in ER15, 39.4% in ER30, and 46.2% in ER40. The transport sector would be the largest GHG emitter, followed by the industry sector in BAU. However, in the energy reduction scenarios, the industry sector is the highest emitter, followed in order by the transport, agriculture, and residential sectors. The contribution to GHG emissions of the agriculture, residential, and commercial sectors would be very small in reduction scenarios in 2050.

Figure 5.34: Greenhouse Gas Emissions in Business as Usual and Energy Reduction Scenarios, 2030 and 2050

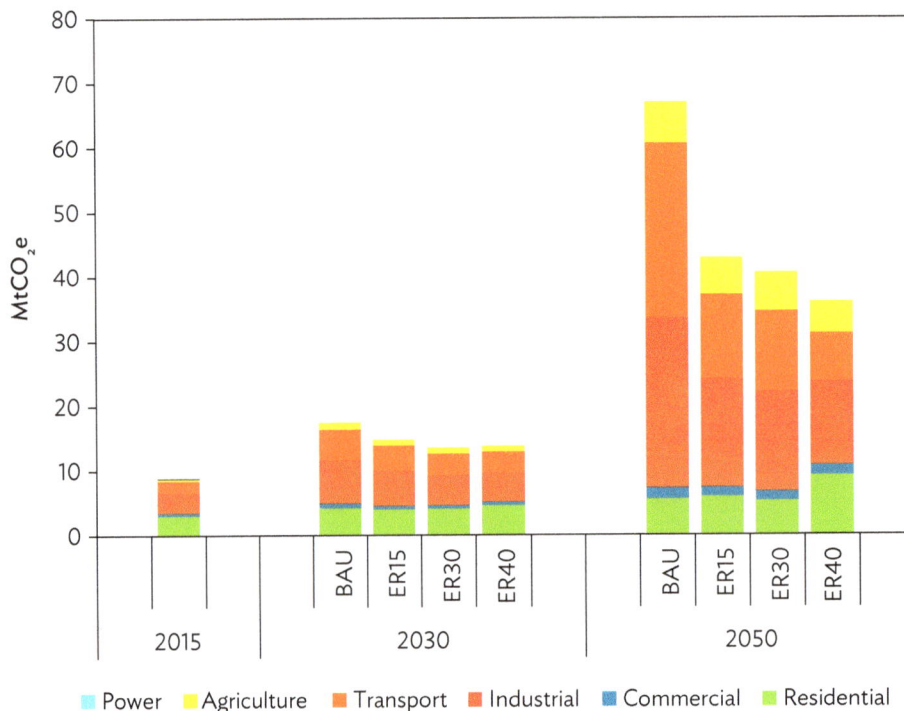

BAU = business as usual scenario; ER15 = 15% energy reduction scenario; ER30 = 30% energy reduction scenario; ER40 = 40% energy reduction scenario; $MtCO_2e$ = million metric tons of carbon dioxide equivalent.

Source: Authors.

Implications of Efficiency Improvement in Transmission and Distribution

The effect of reduction in T&D losses in power generation is presented in Figure 5.35. The T&D in BAU is assumed to drop from 25% in 2015 to 15% by 2020 and remain at 15% until 2050. Two more cases with T&D losses of 10% and 5% are also analyzed. Three T&D loss cases are considered: TDL-15%, TDL-10%, and TDL-5% (Table 5.2). The reduction in T&D loss would not necessarily reduce the electricity generation in the case of Nepal. In 2030, electricity generation in ER40 for TDL-10% would be 4.8% higher than for TDL-15%. This is due to a change in final energy consumption and final energy mix because the reduction in T&D loss would make electricity more cost-effective mostly in thermal applications. Similarly, electricity generation in ER40 would be 6.5% higher for TDL-5% than TDL-15%. In 2050, electricity generation in BAU would be 0.5% higher for TDL-5% than TDL-15%.

Figure 5.35: Electricity Generation for Various Transmission and Distribution Losses in Nepal

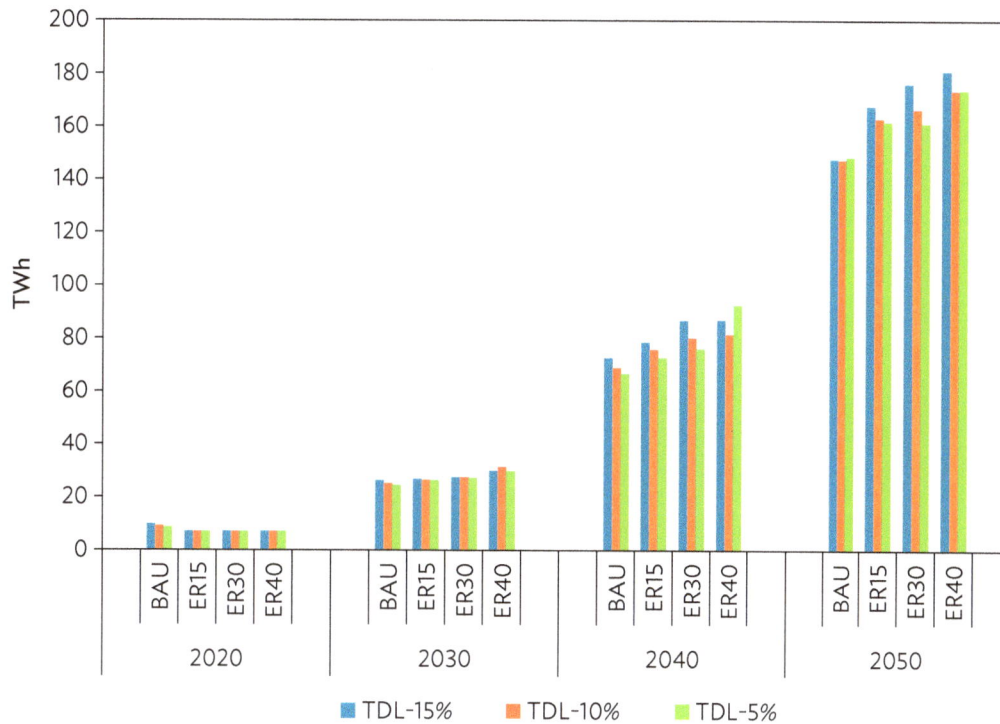

BAU = business as usual scenario; ER15 = 15% energy reduction scenario; ER30 = 30% energy reduction scenario; ER40 = 40% energy reduction scenario; TDL-15% = 15% transmission and distribution loss scenario; TDL-10% = 10% transmission and distribution loss scenario; TDL-5% = 5% transmission and distribution loss scenario; TWh = terawatt-hour.

Source: Authors.

The cumulative electricity generation for TDL-10% would be lower than for TDL-15% in BAU and energy reduction scenarios: by 2.4% in BAU, 3.0% in ER15, 5.4% in ER30, and 4.1% in ER40. For TDL-5%, electricity generation would be lower by 4.5% in BAU, 5.3% in ER15, and 7.4% in ER30 compared with TDL-15%, but slightly higher (by 0.3%) in ER40.

Figure 5.36 presents the electricity generation capacity in various scenarios with the three different levels of T&D loss. The capacity factor is assumed to be 52.7% in all cases in BAU and energy reduction scenarios. In 2050, there would be a lower installed capacity requirement in all reduction scenarios for TDL-10% and TDL-5% compared to TDL-15%. For TDL-5%, installed capacity requirement in BAU would be 164 MW higher than for TDL-15%.

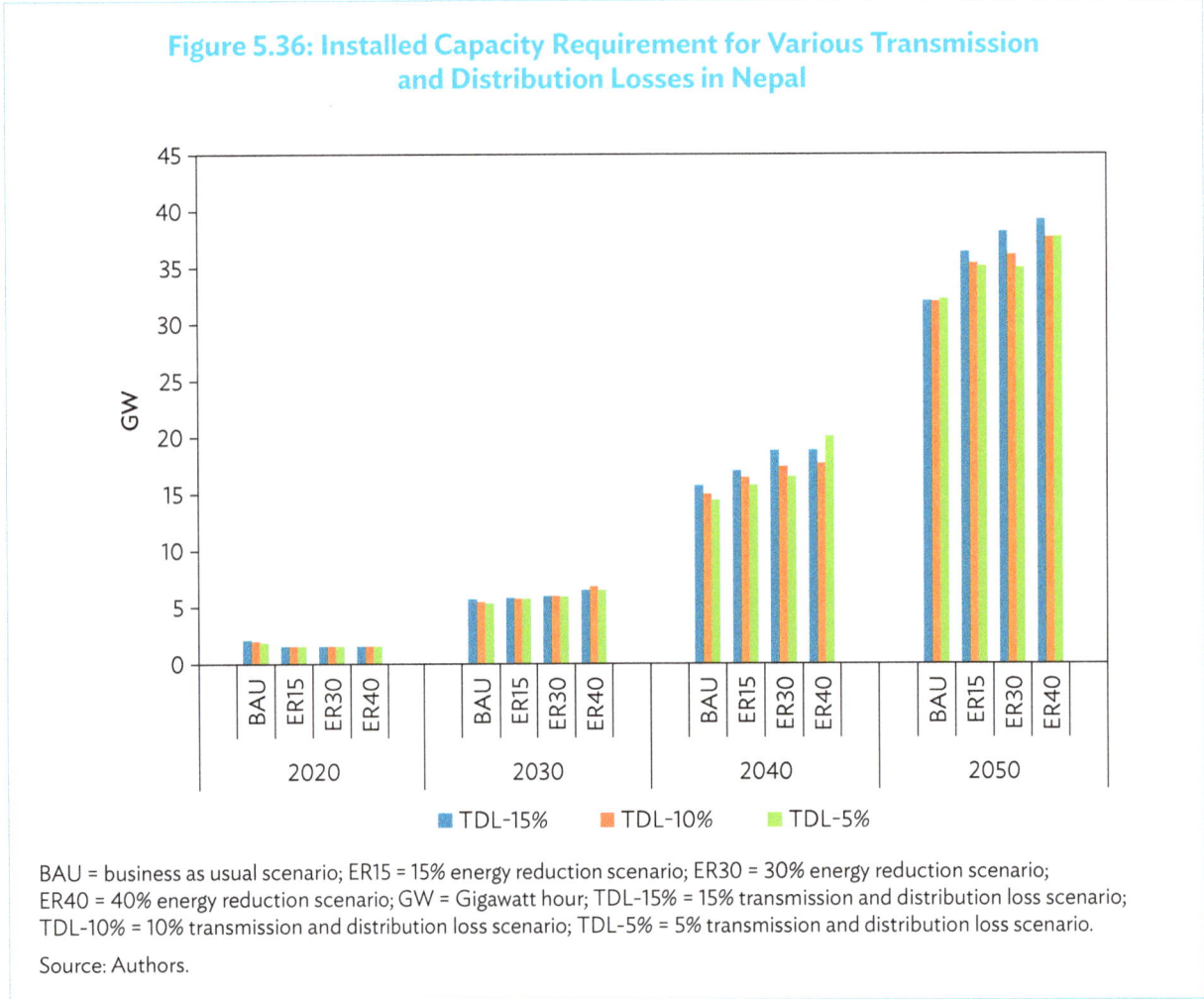

Figure 5.36: Installed Capacity Requirement for Various Transmission and Distribution Losses in Nepal

BAU = business as usual scenario; ER15 = 15% energy reduction scenario; ER30 = 30% energy reduction scenario; ER40 = 40% energy reduction scenario; GW = Gigawatt hour; TDL-15% = 15% transmission and distribution loss scenario; TDL-10% = 10% transmission and distribution loss scenario; TDL-5% = 5% transmission and distribution loss scenario.

Source: Authors.

The total system cost in BAU and energy reduction scenarios during 2015–2050 would be reduced for TDL-10% compared with TDL-15%, and would decrease further for TDL-5%. For TDL-10%, the total system cost (excluding the cost associated with T&D loss reduction) would decline by 0.4% in BAU, 0.8% in ER15, 1.1% in ER30, and 3.7% in ER40; corresponding declines for TDL-5% would be 0.8%, 1.4%, 1.9%, and 5.4%.

Sri Lanka

Maximum Energy-Reduction Potential

The maximum potential for reduction in total primary energy requirement is 52.5% in 2030 and 56% in 2050, when the minimum share of cars is as given in Table 5.1. The maximum potential for the reduction in total primary energy requirement is slightly lower, i.e., 52.0% in 2030 and 53% in 2050 when the minimum share of cars is assumed to be as in BAU.

Total Primary Energy Supply

The changes in total primary energy supply (TPES) in various scenarios are presented in Figure 5.37 (a). The TPES would be reduced by 3.2 Mtoe in ER15, 4.5 Mtoe ER30, and 6.8 Mtoe in ER40 scenarios in 2030. Reduced use of biomass and petroleum products would mainly contribute to the reduction in TPES in all energy reduction scenarios. The use of coal in all reduction scenarios would, however, be higher than that in BAU. There would also be a higher level of usage of natural gas, other renewables (solar and wind), and hydro (including small hydro) in the energy reduction scenarios than in BAU. Their shares in TPES would, however, be very small.

In 2050, the TPES would decrease by 7.8 Mtoe in ER15, 15.8 Mtoe in ER30, and 21.0 Mtoe in ER40. The decrease in the use of petroleum products, natural gas, and biomass would be the major cause for the reduction in TPES in reduction scenarios. There would be higher usage of coal in ER15 and ER30 scenarios than in BAU, whereas coal use would be slightly lower in ER40 than BAU. Use of other renewables would increase significantly under ER40 but their role would not be substantial in ER15 and ER30.

Figure 5.37 (b) shows the shares of different types of energy in TPES under different scenarios. In energy reduction scenarios, in 2030, the percent share of petroleum products and biomass in the primary energy mix would be lower than in BAU, whereas the share of other renewables, hydro, natural gas, and coal would be higher than in BAU.

In 2050, the share of biomass in the primary energy mix would be higher in ER30 than in BAU, but lower in ER15 and ER40. The share of biomass would change from 25.4% in BAU to 22.8% in ER15, 27.4% in ER30, and 22.1% in ER40. Petroleum products would play the biggest role in the primary energy supply for all scenarios: 50.0% in BAU, 40.5% in ER15, 35.0% in ER30, and 38.1% in ER40. The share of coal would increase significantly in all reduction scenarios compared with BAU. The shares of other renewables and hydro would also increase with the increase in energy reduction targets.

Figure 5.37: Total Primary Energy Supply in Different Scenarios

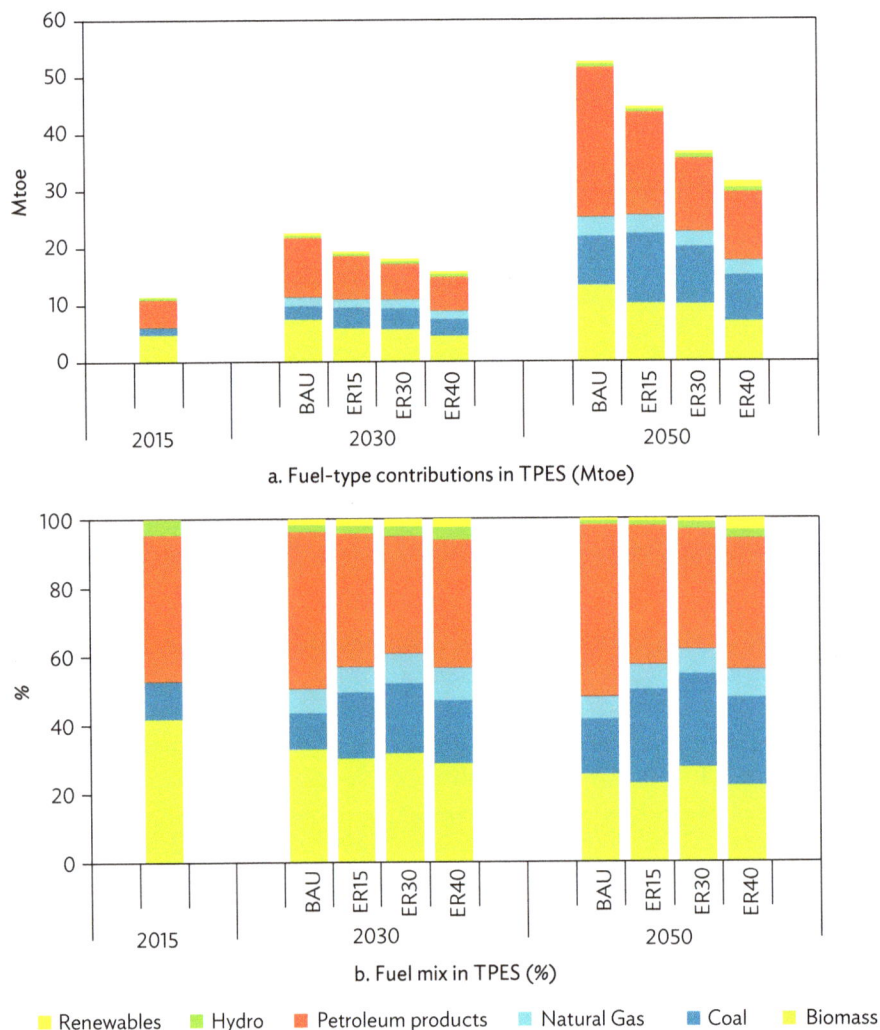

a. Fuel-type contributions in TPES (Mtoe)

b. Fuel mix in TPES (%)

■ Renewables   ■ Hydro   ■ Petroleum products   ■ Natural Gas   ■ Coal   ■ Biomass

BAU = business as usual scenario; ER15 = 15% energy reduction scenario; ER30 = 30% energy reduction scenario; ER40 = 40% energy reduction scenario; Mtoe = million tons of oil equivalent; TPES = total primary energy supply.

Source: Authors.

Energy Intensity

The changes in the energy intensity in different scenarios are shown in Figure 5.38. In BAU, the energy intensity would decrease from 0.142 kgoe/$ in 2010 to 0.118 kgoe/$ in 2030 and 0.115 kgoe/$ in 2050. In 2030, energy intensity would be 0.102, 0.095, and 0.083 kgoe/$ in ER15, ER30, and ER40 scenarios, respectively; whereas corresponding values would be 0.098, 0.081, and 0.069 kgoe/$ in 2050.

Figure 5.38: Energy Intensity for Various Scenarios, 2015–2050

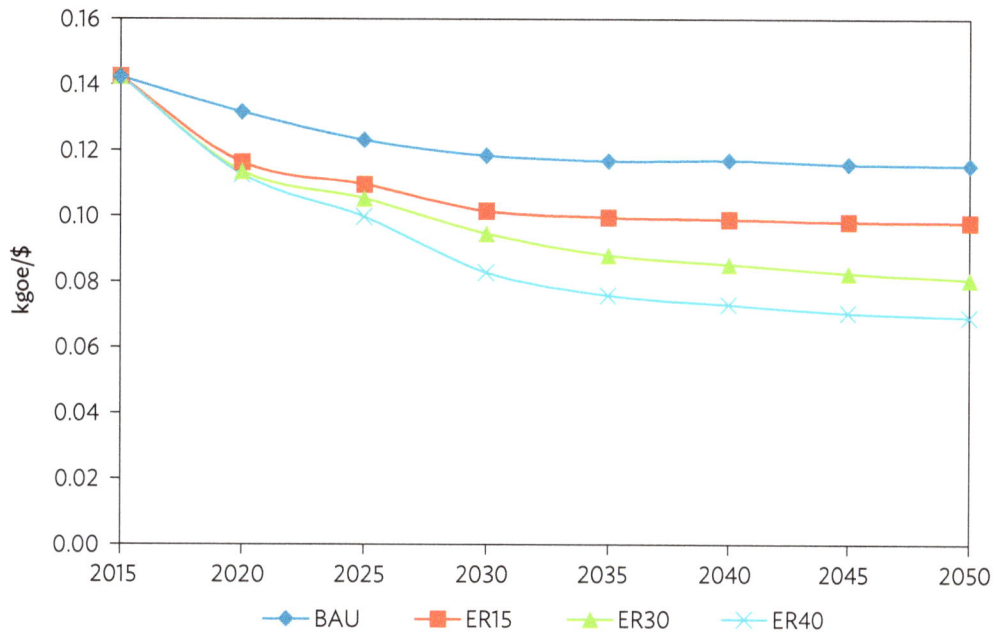

BAU = business as usual scenario; ER15 = 15% energy reduction scenario; ER30 = 30% energy reduction scenario; ER40 = 40% energy reduction scenario; kgoe/$ = kilogram of oil equivalent.

Source: Authors.

Electricity Generation

Electricity generation in different scenarios is shown in Figure 5.39. Electricity generation requirement would grow at a CAGR of 4.8% during 2015–2050 in BAU: from 12.6 TWh in 2015 to 30.0 TWh in 2030 and 65.1 TWh in 2050. Electricity generation in energy reduction scenarios would be lower during 2015–2025 due to energy-efficiency improvement in electrical devices. Electricity generation requirement in ER15 would remain lower than in BAU during 2015–2050. Electricity generation in ER30 and ER40 would be higher than in BAU by 2030, due to higher use a well as shift to electricity-based technologies.

In 2030, electricity generation in the ER15 scenario would be 9.9% lower than in BAU, but would be 4.0% higher in ER30 and 16.3% higher in ER40. Similarly, in 2050, electricity generation would be 5.9% lower in ER15 than BAU but 4.5% higher in ER30 and 5.1% higher in ER40. The major reason for the increase in electricity generation in ER30 and ER40 is higher usage of electric vehicles in the transport sector and greater use of heat-pump boilers in the industry sector.

Figure 5.39: Electricity Generation in Business as Usual and Energy Reduction Scenarios

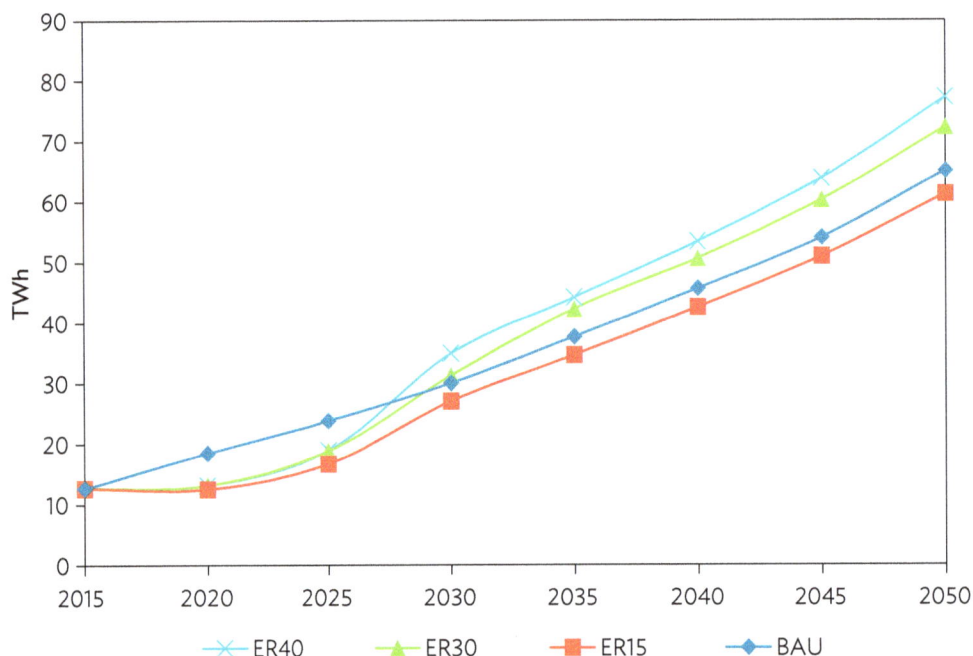

BAU = business as usual scenario; ER15 = 15% energy reduction scenario; ER30 = 30% energy reduction scenario; ER40 = 40% energy reduction scenario; TWh = terawatt-hour.

Source: Authors.

Final Energy Consumption

The changes in the sector-wise final energy consumption under different scenarios are described in this section.

Residential Sector

In BAU, FEC in the residential sector would decrease from 3.1 Mtoe in 2015 to 2.9 Mtoe in 2030 and to 3.1 Mtoe in 2050 (Figure 5.40). In 2030, FEC of the sector would decrease by 11.0% in ER15 and by 13.7% in both ER30 and ER40 scenarios. Similarly, in 2050, FEC would be reduced by 6.1% in ER15 and by 8.6% in both ER30 and ER40. There would be lower consumption of electricity, biomass (traditional), and petroleum products in the energy reduction scenarios in 2030 and 2050 compared to BAU, whereas the level of use of renewables would be higher in all reduction scenarios.

In BAU, the share of biomass use in the residential sector would decrease during 2015–2050, directly due to the assumption of declining share of traditional biomass with the growing income per capita in the country. Biomass would still have a major role in final energy mix in 2030. In 2050, electricity would be the major source of final energy consumption. The share of renewables would increase significantly in energy reduction scenarios in both 2030 and 2050.

Commercial Sector

The FEC of the commercial sector would decrease by 17.3% in 2030 and by 12.9% in 2050 in all energy reduction scenarios. There would be a decrease in the use of all fuels in reduction scenarios, mostly due to the use of more efficient technologies. In 2030, electricity would have the highest share in the FEC mix of the sector, followed by biomass and petroleum products. In 2050, electricity would have the dominant share in the sector's final energy mix, followed by petroleum products.

Industry Sector

The FEC of the industry sector in 2030 would be 6.1% lower for ER15, 13.3% for ER30, and 42.7% for ER40 scenarios. In 2030, there would be a decrease in consumption of biomass and petroleum products and increased use of coal in ER15 and ER30. For ER40, use of biomass, petroleum products, and coal would decrease while that of electricity would increase. There would be high penetration of heat-pump technology for process heating in the sector in ER40. In 2050, the sector's FEC would decrease by 5.8% in ER15, by 25.0% in ER30, and by 45.2% in ER40. The use of biomass and petroleum products would decrease compared with BAU. Consumption of coal would increase in all scenarios, but would decrease with the energy reduction target. The use of electricity in reduction scenarios would be higher than in BAU, and would increase with the level of the energy reduction target. In ER30 and ER40, electricity would have the second highest share in the FEC mix of the sector. Biomass would have a major share in the industry sector's final energy consumption in BAU and energy reduction scenarios.

Transport Sector

The FEC in the transport sector would increase from 2.9 Mtoe in 2015 to 8.4 Mtoe in 2030 and 21.6 Mtoe in 2050 in BAU. Petroleum products would be the predominant fuel in the sector; the share of electricity in the sector's FEC, although relatively small, would increase with the level of energy reduction target. In 2030, the FEC would be lower by 21.1% in ER15, 33.9% in ER30, and 37.5% in ER40. The share of electricity in FEC of the transport sector would be 0.5% in ER15, 4.2% in ER30, and 4.4% in ER40 in 2030 compared to 0.1% in BAU.

In 2050, the sector's FEC in would be reduced by 26.4% in ER15, 48.6% in ER30, and 52.5% in ER40 scenarios compared with BAU. Electricity's share in the sector's FEC mix would be nearly 1% in ER15, 5.9% in ER30, and 6.3% in ER40.

Sectoral Contributions to Reductions in Total Final Energy Consumption Under Energy Reduction Scenarios

The contribution of different sectors to the reduction of TFEC are given in absolute terms in Figure 5.41 (a) and as percentage shares in Figure 5.41 (b). In 2030, the total reduction in TFEC in ER15, ER30, and ER40 scenarios would be 2.8, 4.5, and 6.9 Mtoe, respectively; the corresponding reductions in 2050 would be 7.3, 15.4, and 19.6 Mtoe. In 2030, the transport sector would be the major contributor to the reduction in TFEC, followed by the industry sector; the case would be similar for 2050. In 2030, the residential sector would have a higher share in total FEC reduction than the commercial sector in all energy reduction scenarios; however, in 2050, the commercial sector would have a greater role than the residential sector.

Figure 5.40: Final Energy Consumption in Different Scenarios per Sector

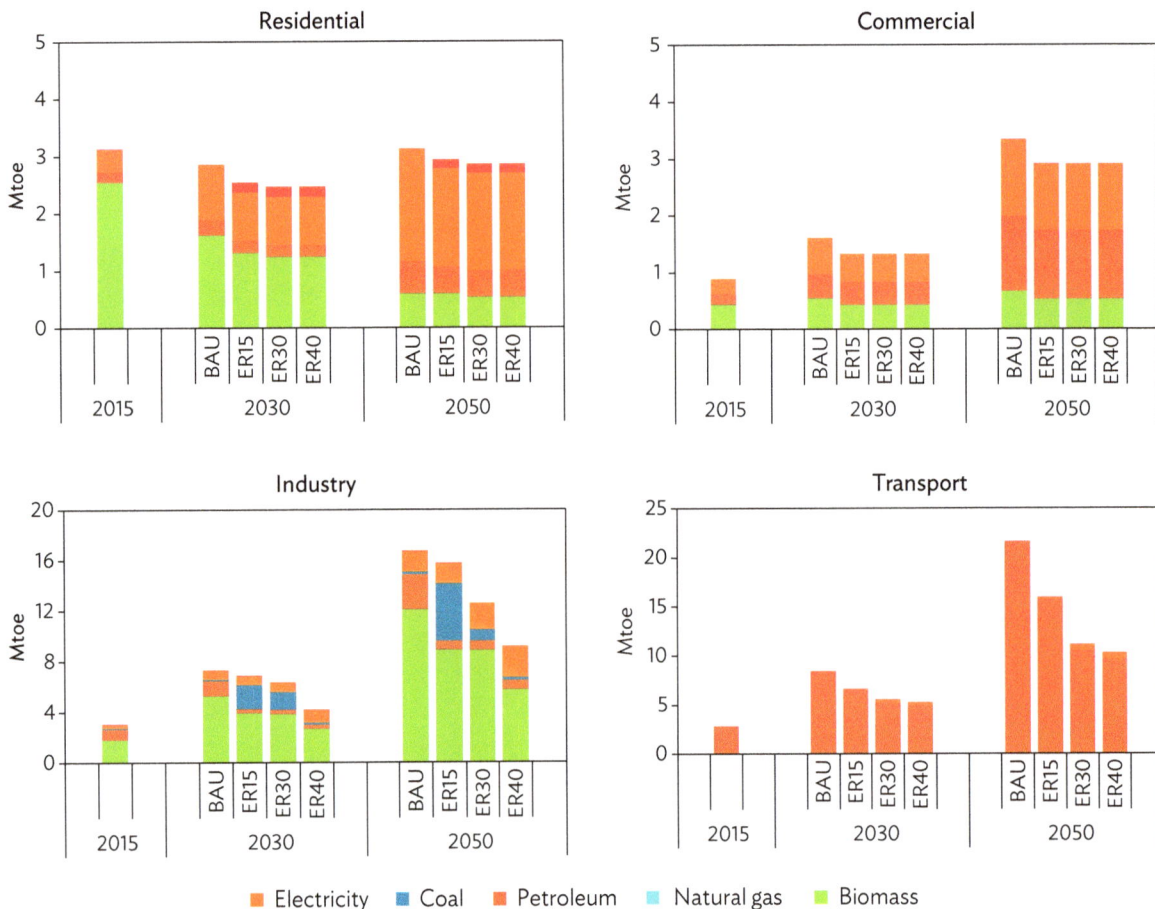

BAU = business as usual scenario; ER15 = 15% energy reduction scenario; ER30 = 30% energy reduction scenario; ER40 = 40% energy reduction scenario; Mtoe = million tons of oil equivalent.

Source: Authors.

Figure 5.41: Sector Contributions in Final Energy Reduction for Energy Reduction Scenarios

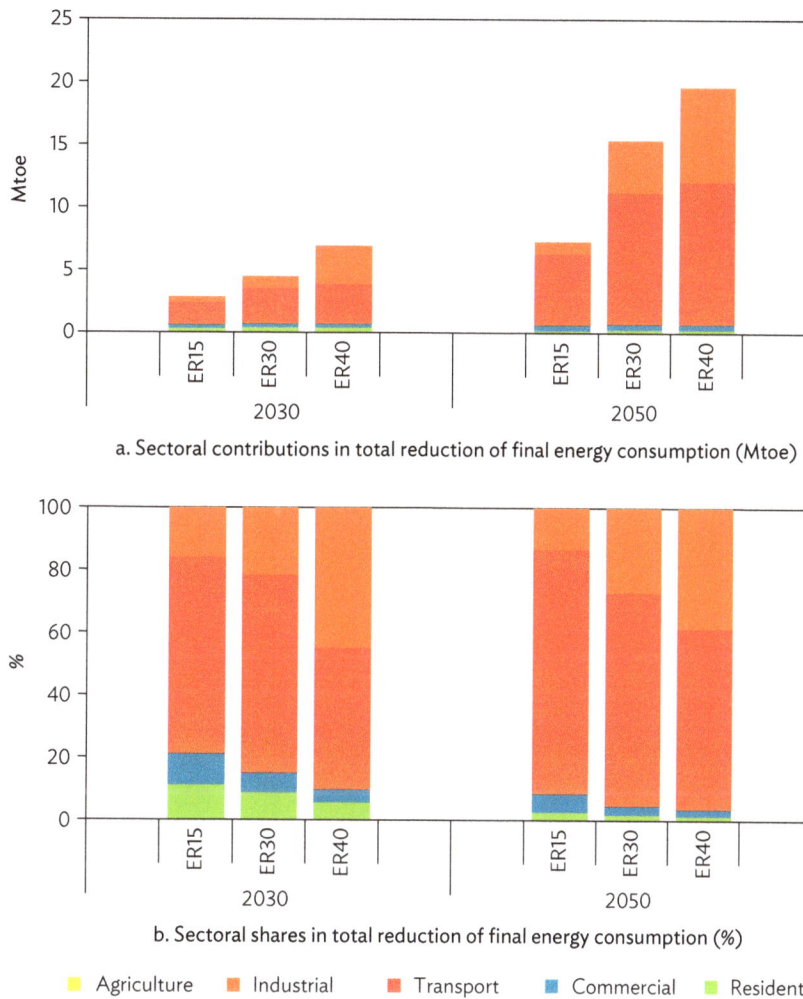

a. Sectoral contributions in total reduction of final energy consumption (Mtoe)

b. Sectoral shares in total reduction of final energy consumption (%)

Agriculture   Industrial   Transport   Commercial   Residential

ER15 = 15% energy reduction scenario; ER30 = 30% energy reduction scenario; ER40 = 40% energy reduction scenario; Mtoe = million tons of oil equivalent.

Source: Authors.

Overall Efficiency of Energy Conversion and Transmission

The overall efficiency of energy conversion and transformation under different scenarios in selected years is presented in Figure 5.42. In BAU, the overall efficiency would increase from 86.8% in 2015 to 89.4% in 2030, and decrease to 85.4% by 2050. This is due to the increase in overall electricity generation efficiency in the power sector in 2030. The decrease in the overall energy efficiency in 2050 compared to 2015 is due to the higher share of electricity in TFEC. With energy reduction targets, the overall efficiency would be 89.6% in ER15, 86.8% in ER30, and 83.6% in ER40 scenarios in 2030. The higher efficiency in ER15 is due to a lower share of electricity in the FEC than in BAU; therefore, conversion losses would also be lower. In 2050, the overall efficiency in the energy reduction scenarios would be lower than in BAU: 84.2% in ER15, 80.2% in ER30, and 80.1% in ER40. This is due to the higher share of electricity in FEC in 2050 in reduction scenarios than in BAU.

Figure 5.42: Overall Efficiency of Energy Conversion and Transmission for Different Scenarios

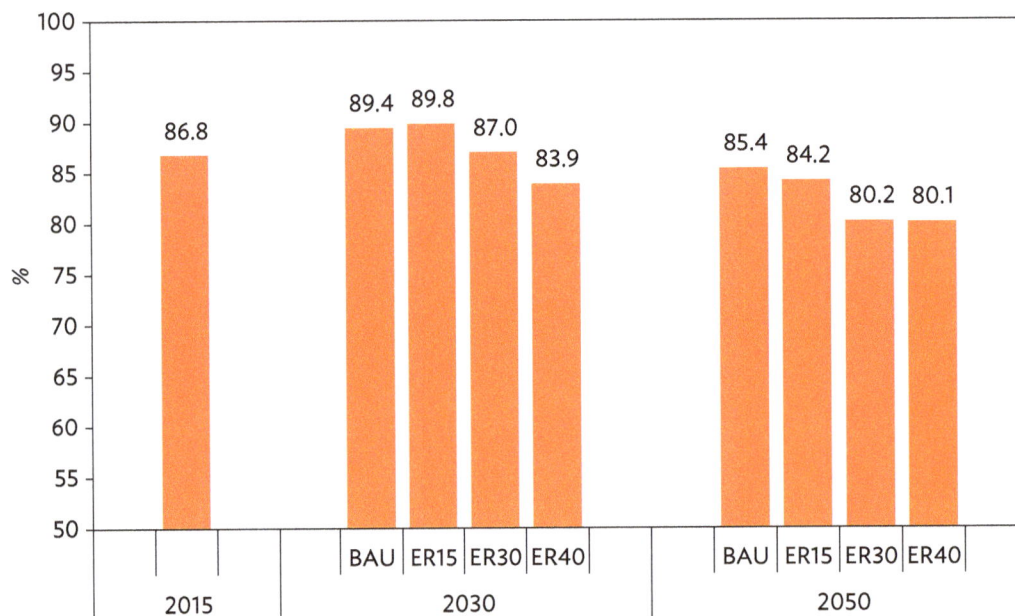

BAU = business as usual scenario; ER15 = 15% energy reduction scenario; ER30 = 30% energy reduction scenario; ER40 = 40% energy reduction scenario.

Source: Authors.

Technology Selection

Residential and commercial sectors. Most of the energy-efficient technologies in these sectors would be cost-effective in BAU; therefore, there is no significant difference between the BAU and energy reduction scenarios in terms of technology choice. In both the sectors, light emitting diode (LED) lamps are cost-effective in all scenarios. Energy-efficient electric devices such as fans, air-conditioners, and televisions would be cost-effective in all energy reduction scenarios in these sectors. Besides biogas-based cooking would be a cost-effective option in energy reduction scenarios. Improved cook stoves (ICS) would be cost-effective over traditional cook stoves (TCS) in the BAU as well as all reduction scenarios in the case of the residential sector.

Transport sector. Energy reduction in the transport sector for reduction scenarios would take place mainly due to modal shift from private cars to mass transport, i.e., buses. In addition, electric two-wheelers and diesel-hybrid trucks would be cost-effective from 2020 onwards in all reduction scenarios. Diesel-hybrid cars would be cost-effective following 2032 in ER40 and 2035 in ER30.

Industry sector. In the industry sector, heat pumps for process heat are a cost-effective measure from 2028 in ER40 and from 2034 in the ER30 scenario. Other measures in energy reduction scenarios include energy-efficiency improvements in existing facilities such as downsizing motors to match loads, use of variable-speed drives, improving the combustion efficiency by controlling the air flow rate, and adding insulation to reduce heat losses in thermal systems. In the cement industry, deployment of vertical mills for raw material processing and for clinker grinding would be cost-effective in the reduction scenarios. In clinker production, six-stage cyclone suspension preheaters with calciners and high-efficiency cooler type rotary kilns would be economically attractive options from 2029 onwards in ER40, from 2034 in ER30, and from 2042 in ER40. The use of improved fixed-chimney bull trench kilns in the brick industry would be cost-effective in all energy reduction scenarios.

Investment Requirements and Average Incremental Cost

Figure 5.43 (a) presents the investment requirement (undiscounted) when modal shares of cars in the transport sector in energy reduction scenarios differ from that in BAU, whereas Figure 5.43 (b) shows the investment requirement when the modal shares are the same in all scenarios (Table 5.1 shows the minimum shares of cars). The investment requirements in energy reduction scenarios are lower than in BAU due to the lower share of cars in passenger transport than in BAU (Figure 5.43 [a]). The investment required in energy reduction cases would be lower than in BAU: by 14.3% in ER15, 8.4% in ER30, and 11.0% in ER40. The total investment cost in ER30 would be higher than in ER15 due to the introduction of costlier energy-efficient technologies and the shift to electricity-based technologies in transport (e.g., electric vehicles) and industry (e.g., heat pump), which would also require higher investment in the power sector. However, the investment requirement would be lower in ER40 than ER30 due to a lower share of cars for ER40. When the same modal share of cars as in BAU is assumed in reduction scenarios, the investment cost compared to the BAU level would be reduced by 10.4% in ER15, but increased by 0.3% in ER30 and 4.3% in ER40.

Figure 5.43: Investment Requirement: Effect of Variation in Modal Shares in Passenger Transport, 2015–2050

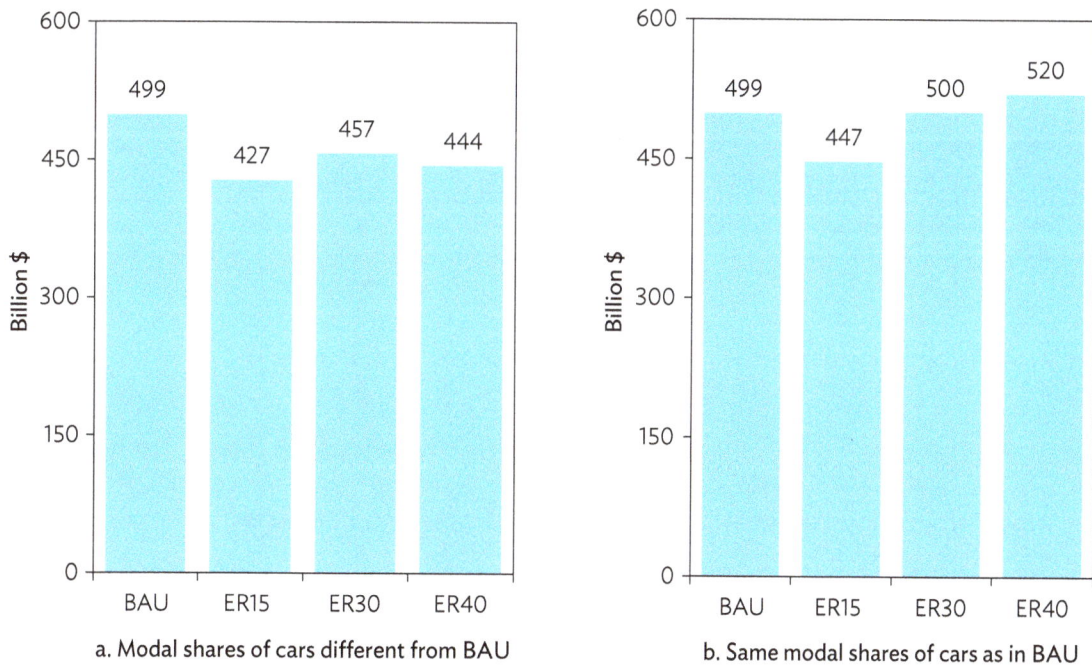

a. Modal shares of cars different from BAU

b. Same modal shares of cars as in BAU

BAU = business as usual scenario; ER15 = 15% energy reduction scenario; ER30 = 30% energy reduction scenario; ER40 = 40% energy reduction scenario.

Source: Authors.

The total energy system cost during 2015–2050 would be $1,309 billion (undiscounted) in BAU. When lower shares of cars than in BAU are considered, the total cost would decrease by 20.0% in ER15, 27.2% in ER30, and 29.9% in ER40 scenarios (Figure 5.44). The lower total costs in energy reduction scenarios is due to the modal shift in the transport sector and the use of cost-effective energy efficient options in other sectors for reduction cases compared to BAU. When the same share of cars is considered in both BAU and reduction scenarios, total cost would be lower by 17.0% in ER15, 22.4% in ER30, and 21.6% in ER40.

Figure 5.44: Total Cost of the Energy System: Effect of Variation in Modal Shares in Passenger Transport, 2015–2050

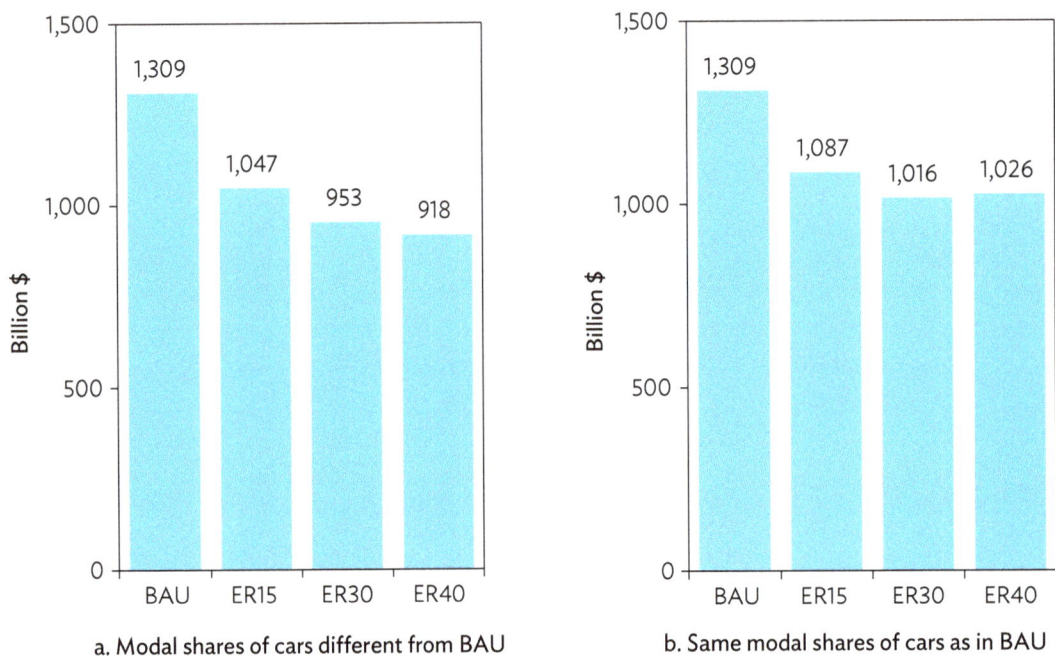

a. Modal shares of cars different from BAU

b. Same modal shares of cars as in BAU

BAU = business as usual scenario; ER15 = 15% energy reduction scenario; ER30 = 30% energy reduction scenario; ER40 = 40% energy reduction scenario.

Source: Authors.

The average incremental cost (AIC) of energy saving in energy reduction scenarios is presented in Figure 5.45. The AIC per ktoe would be $1,205 in ER15, $1,192 in ER30, and $1,061 in ER40, when a modal shift in transport sector is considered in reduction scenarios. When the modal shares in reduction cases are the same as in BAU, the AIC per ktoe would be $941 in ER15, $1,054 in ER30, and $808 in ER40.

Figure 5.45: Average Incremental Cost of Energy Saving in Energy Reduction Scenarios: Effect of Variation in Modal Shares in Passenger Transport

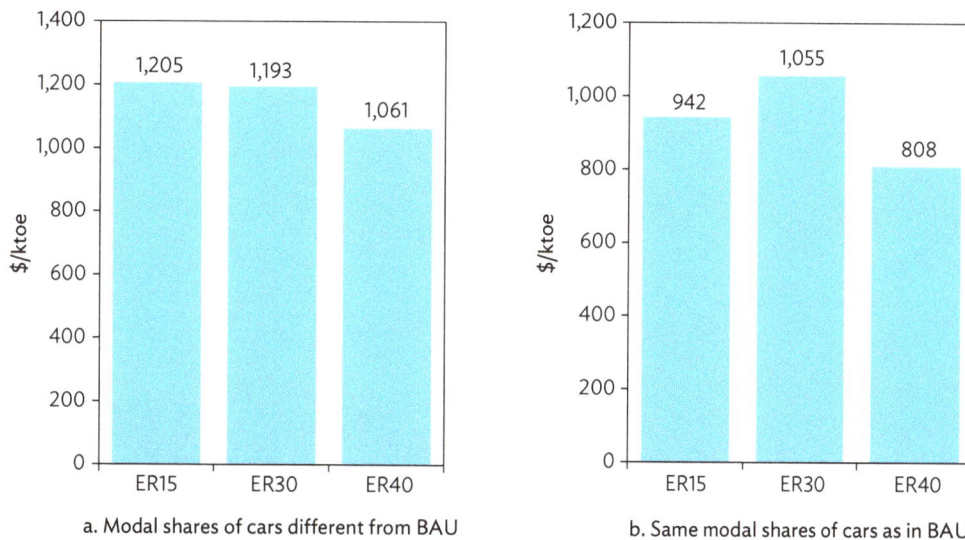

a. Modal shares of cars different from BAU

b. Same modal shares of cars as in BAU

ER15 = 15% energy reduction scenario; ER30 = 30% energy reduction scenario; ER40 = 40% energy reduction scenario; $/ktoe = dollar per kilogram of oil equivalent.

Source: Authors.

Greenhouse Gas Emissions

Emission of greenhouse gases (GHGs) would increase by 1.2 times in 2030 and 4.7 times in 2050 in BAU compared to 2015 (Figure 5.46). Under the energy reduction targets, GHG emissions would decrease by 16.8% in ER15, 18.8% in ER30, and 23.8% in ER40 in 2030 compared with BAU. In 2050, the emissions would be reduced by 17.3% in ER15, 28.2% in ER30, and 37.1% in ER40.

In ER15, the transport sector would be the greatest emitter of GHGs during 2015–2050, followed by the power and industry sectors. However, in ER30 and ER40, the power sector would be the highest emitter, followed by transport and industry sectors. Emissions from the residential and commercial sectors would be relatively less significant.

The cumulative GHG emissions in BAU during 2015–2050 would be 2,174 $MtCO_2e$. The GHG emissions would be lower than the BAU level by 15.9% in ER15, 21.9% in ER30, and 29.7% in ER40 scenarios.

Implications of Efficiency Improvement in Transmission and Distribution

The transmission and distribution (T&D) loss is assumed to be 10% during 2015–2050 in BAU and energy reduction scenarios. However, the present study also analyzed the effect of lowering the T&D loss on electricity generation to 5%. The T&D losses in two cases are referred to as TDL-10% and TDL-5% (Table 5.2). The electricity generation requirement in 2030 would be reduced by 5.3% in BAU, 5.2% in ER15, 3.0% in ER30, and 6.6% in ER40 when T&D loss is reduced from 10% to 5% (Figure 5.47). The cumulative electricity generation during 2015–2050 with TDL-5% cases would decrease by 5.1% in BAU, 5.2% in ER15, 5.0% in ER30, and 4.8% in ER40.

Figure 5.46: Greenhouse Gas Emissions in Business as Usual and Energy Reduction Scenarios

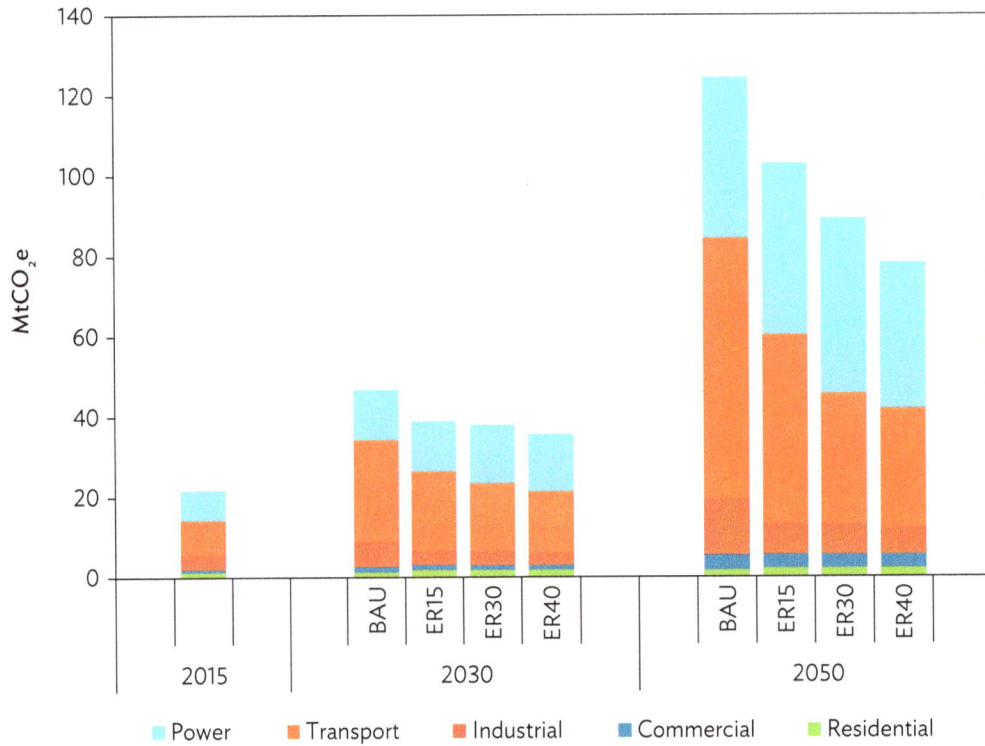

BAU = business as usual scenario; ER15 = 15% energy reduction scenario; ER30 = 30% energy reduction scenario; ER40 = 40% energy reduction scenario; $MtCO_2e$ = million metric tons of carbon dioxide equivalent.

Source: Authors.

Figure 5.48 presents the installed capacity requirement in two cases. With TDL-5%, a lower level of installed capacity would be needed in all scenarios. The installed capacity requirement would decrease by 440 MW in BAU, 434 MW in ER15, 260 MW in ER30, and 641 MW in ER40 in 2030; in 2050, the corresponding reductions would be 954, 1,004, 1,100, and 1,105 MW.

The total system cost would be lower due to the improvement in T&D loss. The system costs (excluding that associated with T&D system improvement) would decrease with TDL-5% by 0.4% in BAU, 0.5% in ER15, 0.6% in ER30, and 0.7% in ER40 scenarios compared with TDL-10%.

Figure 5.47: Electricity Generation for Various Transmission and Distribution Losses in Sri Lanka

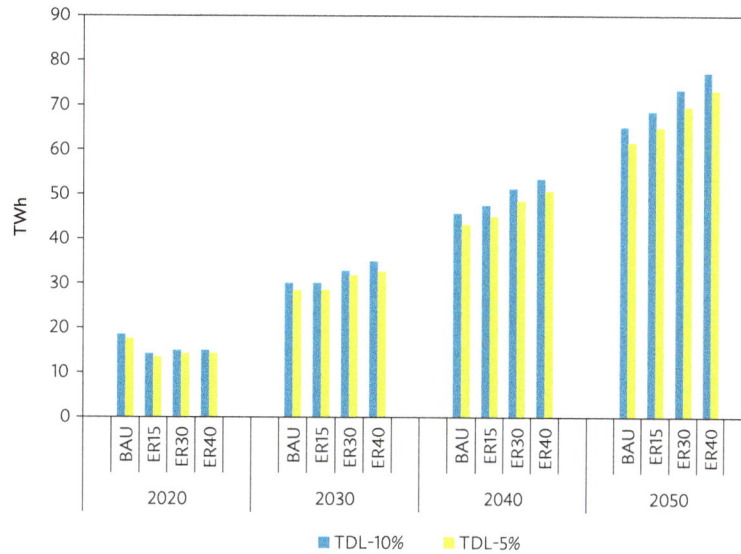

BAU = business as usual scenario; ER15 = 15% energy reduction scenario; ER30 = 30% energy reduction scenario; ER40 = 40% energy reduction scenario; TDL-10% = 10% transmission and distribution loss scenario; TDL-5% = 5% transmission and distribution loss scenario; TWh = terawatt-hour.

Source: Authors.

Figure 5.48: Installed Capacity Requirement for Various Transmission and Distribution Losses in Sri Lanka

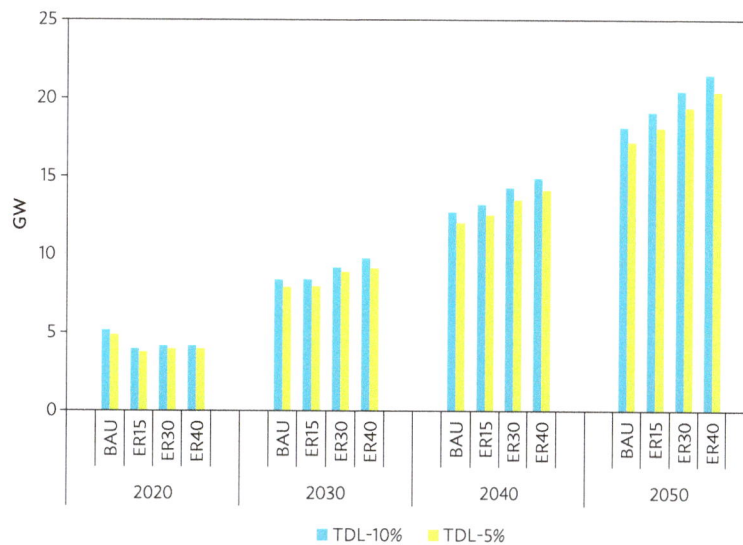

BAU = business as usual scenario; ER15 = 15% energy reduction scenario; ER30 = 30% energy reduction scenario; ER40 = 40% energy reduction scenario; GW = Gigawatt hour; TDL-10% = 10% transmission and distribution loss scenario; TDL-5% = 5% transmission and distribution loss scenario.

Source: Authors.

India

The analysis so far in the case of Bangladesh, Bhutan, Nepal, and Sri Lanka has focused on the assessment of the implications of alternative energy reduction targets on the energy- and technology-mix in different sectors of those countries. The analysis used a long-term national energy system model of each country developed for this study. In the case of India, no such modeling was carried out, so the discussion focuses on the information available from the relevant literature. More specifically, this section highlights the effects of targets set by the Government of India on energy-efficiency improvement in selected sectors or subsectors under its Perform Achieve and Trade (PAT) scheme. It further discusses the implications for energy savings, technology-mix, and energy mix of GHG emission intensity targets under India's intended nationally determined contributions (INDCs) compared with the BAU scenario.

As mentioned in Chapter 4, PAT is a scheme imposed on major industries of India by the government through the Bureau of Energy Efficiency (BEE). The PAT scheme, through its various cycles, not only aims to expand its coverage of the sectors and subsectors but it also makes the energy-efficiency targets increasingly stringent; BEE 2018e has more details. Table 5.7 shows four different PAT cycles with their respective energy-saving target, implementation period number of sectors covered, and total number of "designated consumers" (i.e., production units or plants). The PAT cycle 1 focused on eight major industry subsectors including thermal power plants; it involved 478 designated consumers and set a total energy-saving target of 4%. However, by the end of its implementation period, PAT cycle 1 achieved a total reduction in energy consumption of 5.3% (about 8.7 Mtoe), exceeding the target by more than 30%. Table 5.8 shows details of the sector-wise (or subsector-wise) energy-saving targets and corresponding achievements by the end of the cycle. Except for the thermal power plant subsector, all other subsectors overachieved their respective targets. Evaluation of performance under PAT cycle 2 is yet to be carried out, but the implementation of other cycles is ongoing.

The BEE carried out the projection of PAT cycle 1 until 2030, which shows that energy intensity of selected designated consumers will be 95.95 toe/$ million under the PAT scheme from the average baseline[11] energy intensity of 156.66 toe/$ million. This shows an energy intensity improvement projection of 39%, which is around 3% less than that in BAU (98.65 toe/$ million) in 2030.

---

[11] Baseline year is 2007–2010 as per Government of India, Bureau of Energy Efficiency. 2018. Enhancing Energy Effiency Through Industry Partnership (Outcome & Way Forward). New Delhi. https://beeindia.gov.in/sites/default/files/press_releases/Consolidated%20Report.pdf.

Table 5.7: Perform Achieve and Trade Cycles and their Respective Targets and Achievements

PAT Cycles	Period	Designated Consumers	Sectors	Energy Saving Target (Mtoe)
PAT cycle 1	2012–2015	478	8	6.7
PAT cycle 2	2016–2019	621	11	8.9
PAT cycle 3	2017–2020	116	6	1.1
PAT cycle 4	2018–2021	109	8	0.7

PAT = Perform Achieve and Trade; Mtoe = million tons of oil equivalent.

Source: Government of India, Bureau of Energy Efficiency. 2018. Enhancing Energy Effiency Through Industry Partnership (Outcome & Way Forward). New Delhi. https://beeindia.gov.in/sites/default/files/press_releases/Consolidated%20Report.pdf.

Table 5.8: Energy Savings Achieved by Each Participating Designated Consumers in Perform Achieve and Trade Cycle 1

	Sector	Designated Consumers	Energy Saving Target (Mtoe)	Energy Savings Achieved (Mtoe)	Achievement Over the Target (%)
1.	Thermal power plant	144	3.21	3.06	(5)
2.	Textile	90	0.07	0.13	95
3.	Cement	85	0.81	1.48	82
4.	Iron and steel	67	1.49	2.10	41
5.	Pulp and paper	31	0.12	0.29	143
6.	Fertilizer	29	0.48	0.78	64
7.	Chlor-Alkali	22	0.05	0.09	72
8.	Aluminium	10	0.46	0.73	60

Mtoe = million tons of oil equivalent.

Source: Government of India, Bureau of Energy Efficiency. 2018. Enhancing Energy Effiency Through Industry Partnership (Outcome & Way Forward). New Delhi. https://beeindia.gov.in/sites/default/files/press_releases/Consolidated%20Report.pdf.

A review of the existing energy literature on India revealed a lack of studies focused directly on the implications of energy reduction targets on energy mix and technology-mix over the long term. There exist some studies that focus on the effects of nationally determined contributions (NDCs) and emission reduction target (IEA 2015a, 2015b; Mitra et al. 2017; Niti Aayog 2017; Vishwanathan et al. 2017; CSTEP 2018; Dhar et al. 2018; Thambi et al. 2018). In the absence of studies on energy reduction targets, discussion of relevant results of Vishwanathan et al. (2017) on emission reduction targets is included in this section. A discussion of the effects of emission reduction targets could still be interesting as an emission reduction target in an economy dominated by fossil fuels like India is also likely to result in reduced overall energy consumption. The study by Vishwanathan et al. assumes two scenarios: the baseline scenario (i.e., BAU), which assumes continuity of current economic dynamics and policies along with adaptation of long-term policy interventions related to services and energy technology in every major sector; and the INDC scenario, based upon India's emission intensity reduction target of 33%–35% from the 2005 level by 2030. In the subsequent sections, the energy implications of the INDC based on Vishwanathan et al. (2017) are discussed.

Energy Implications Under Business as Usual and Intended Nationally Determined Contribution Scenarios

Total Primary Energy Demand
The total primary energy demand for India during 2000–2050 shows that primary energy demand under the INDC scenario would be reduced by 6% in 2030 and 10.4% in 2050 compared to the BAU scenario (Vishwanathan et al. 2017).

Total Final Energy Consumption
Vishwanathan et al. (2017) estimates that the TFEC under the INDC scenario would be reduced by 7% in 2030 and 14% in 2050 from the BAU scenario.

The study also shows that the fuel mix in final energy consumption under the INDC scenario would be dominated by coal and oil for 2020, 2030, and 2050 although the share of fossil fuels would decrease. In 2050, the combined share of coal and oil in the INDC scenario is estimated to decrease from 58% to 55% under the INDC scenario compared to BAU in 2050. The share of solar energy would increase from 1% in 2000 to 9% in 2050 in both scenarios. Electricity's share would increase by 6% in BAU and by 8% in the INDC scenario during 2000–2050.

Energy Saving Potential Under the Intended Nationally Determined Contribution Scenario

This section discusses the energy saving potential (ESP) under the INDC scenario of the power, industry, residential, agriculture, and transport sectors based on Vishwanathan et al. (2017).

Power Sector
Table 5.9 shows the energy savings from different options with the substitution of subcritical technologies in the power sector during 2015–2020. Supercritical power plants, improvement in aggregate commercial and technical losses,[12] and renewables (mainly solar) show potential to save energy. After 2021, smart grids are also selected in the power sector.

---

[12] "Aggregate technical and commercial losses … is [a] combination of energy loss (technical loss + theft + inefficiency in billing) and commercial loss (default in payment + inefficiency in collection)". Government of India, National Power Portal. Glossary of Terms. https://npp.gov.in/glossary.

Table 5.9: Energy Savings with Respect to Sub-critical Technologies

Period	High Impact Opportunities[a]	Energy Savings (ktoe)[b]
2015–2020	Super-critical power plants in place of sub-critical	23,980
	AT&C losses	12,898
	Renewables (solar, wind) in place of coal-sub-critical	30,859
2021–2030	Super-critical / ultra-super-critical in place of sub-critical	232,206
	AT&C losses	17,197
	Renewables (solar, wind) in place of coal-sub-critical	147,392
	Smart grid	2,508
2031–2050	Super-critical power plants in place of sub-critical	689,262
	AT&C losses	28,662
	Renewables (solar, wind) in place of coal-sub-critical	738,703
	Smart grid	49,441

AT&C = aggregate technical and commercial; ktoe = kiloton of oil equivalent.

[a] High impact opportunities are defined as "specific actions that can advance the sustainable energy of a country within the larger global initiative of achieving sustainable energy for all through energy access, improving energy efficiency and encouraging renewable forms of energy." S. S. Vishwanathan et al. 2017. Enhancing Energy Efficiency in India: Assessment of Sectoral Potentials. Copenhagen Center on Energy Efficiency, UNEP DTU Partnership, Copenhagen. p. 14.
[b] Originally reported in Peta Joules (PJ); 1 PJ = 23.8846 ktoe.

Source: S. S. Vishwanathan et al. 2017. Enhancing Energy Efficiency in India: Assessment of Sectoral Potentials. Copenhagen Center on Energy Efficiency, UNEP DTU Partnership, Copenhagen.

Industry Sector

Vishwanathan et al. (2017) considered improvements in specific energy consumption (SEC) of different industries in BAU in a similar manner as in the PAT scheme. In the INDC scenario, they consider mostly higher level of improvements in SEC of the industries than in BAU. Table 5.10 shows the ESP of the industries during 2015–2050. The fertilizer industry has the highest ESP, accounting for 83% in 2015–2020 and 41% in 2021–2030 of the total industry sector ESP. During 2031–2050, the cement industry has the highest ESP, i.e., 57% of total ESP in the industry sector.

Vishwanathan et al. (2017) also identified energy-efficient technologies in the industry sector that are cost-effective under the INDC scenario (Table 5.11).

Table 5.10: Energy Saving Potential for Different Industries in Intended Nationally Determined Contributions Scenario for India, 2015–2050

Period	Industry	Energy Savings with Respect to BAU (ktoe)[a]
2015–2020	Aluminum	0
	Cement	2,059
	Chlor Alkali	0
	Fertilizer	13,581
	Iron and Steel	0
	Paper and Pulp	707
	Textiles	0
	Total (Industrial sector)	16,347
2021–2030	Aluminum	2,116
	Cement	60,323
	Chlor Alkali	143
	Fertilizer	66,585
	Iron and Steel	19,077
	Paper and Pulp	13,089
	Textiles	103
	Total (Industrial sector)	161,436
2031–2050	Aluminum	5,632
	Cement	513,679
	Chlor Alkali	2,916
	Fertilizer	129,863
	Iron and Steel	129,459
	Paper and Pulp	114,343
	Textiles	2,983
	Total (Industrial sector)	898,875

BAU = business as usual; ktoe = kiloton of oil equivalent.
[a] Originally reported in Peta Joules (PJ); 1 PJ = 23.8846 ktoe.
Source: S. S. Vishwanathan et al. Enhancing Energy Efficiency in India: Assessment of Sectoral Potentials. Copenhagen Center on Energy Efficiency, UNEP DTU Partnership, Copenhagen.

Table 5.11: Energy Efficient Technologies in the Industrial Sector

Sector	Energy Efficient Technologies
Aluminum	Improved Soderberg Process Improved Bayer Process Improved pre-baked process
Cement	Dry process Semi-dry process
Chlor Alkali	Oxygen depolarized Cathode Zero gap membrane
Fertilizer	Natural Gas Naptha
Iron and Steel	DRI-EAF (coal-based) Scrap-EAF DRI-EAF (gas-based)
Paper and Pulp	Blow heat recovery Co-generation
Textiles	Drying process New spinning process

DRI-EAF = direct reduced iron in electric arc furnace; EAF = electric arc furnace.

Source: S. S. Vishwanathan et al. 2017. Enhancing Energy Efficiency in India: Assessment of Sectoral Potentials. Copenhagen Center on Energy Efficiency, UNEP DTU Partnership, Copenhagen.

Table 5.12: Energy Savings in Different Periods in Residential and Commercial, Agricultural, and Transport Sector in the Intended Nationally Determined Contributions Scenario

Period	Technology Shift		Energy Savings due to Replacement (ktoe)[a]
	From	To	
2015–2020	Electric pumps	Energy-efficient pumps	2,627
	CFL	LED	1,791
	Incandescent bulb	LED	3,009
	Fluorescent tubes	LED	1,218
	AC	AC (5-star)	1,481
	Advanced biomass stoves	Cleaner cooking stoves	3,320
	4-wheelers	Metro	1,791
2020–2030	Electric pumps	Energy-efficient pumps	14,140
	Energy-efficient fans	Super energy-efficient fans	27,587
	AC	AC (5-star)	4,275
	AC 5 star	AC (Advanced)	3,057
	LPG stoves	Cleaner cooking stoves	4,920
	4-wheelers	Metro	5,613
2030–2050	Electric pumps	Energy-efficient pumps	10,820
	Energy-efficient fans	Super energy-efficient fans	13,065
	2030: AC (5-star)	AC (Advanced)	6,019
	2040: AC (Advanced)	AC (Advanced) with cool roof	12,635
	4-wheelers	Metro	94,010

AC = air conditioners; CFL = compact fluorescent lamp; ktoe = kiloton of oil equivalent; LED = light emitting diode; LPG = liquefied petroleum gas.

[a] Originally reported in Peta Joules (PJ); 1 PJ = 23.8846 ktoe.

Source: S. S. Vishwanathan et al. 2017. Enhancing Energy Efficiency in India: Assessment of Sectoral Potentials. Copenhagen Center on Energy Efficiency, UNEP DTU Partnership, Copenhagen.

Other Sectors

Other sectors include residential and commercial, agriculture, and transport sectors. The ESP of different end-use services in these sectors is shown in Table 5.12. Use of LED bulbs, air-conditioners (five-star and advanced), cleaner cooking stoves, and efficient fans in the residential and energy-efficient pumps in the agriculture sector help in energy savings in short, medium, and long terms. In the transport sector, for urban areas, introduction of metro-rail is an energy-efficient alternative to private vehicles (Vishwanathan et al. 2017).

5.5 Concluding Remarks and Policy Implications

This study assessed the maximum energy-reduction potential for two cases: the minimum share of passenger cars being the same as in BAU and being lower than in BAU (i.e. modal shift from cars to mass transport such as bus). It should be kept in mind that the maximum potential is still underestimated in this study. It is assumed that passenger cars would have minimum share of 20% of total passenger service demand in 2050. The full potential of modal shift from private vehicles (cars and two-wheelers) to mass transport (bus and rail) in the transport sector is not considered in the study. The maximum energy-reduction potential in Bangladesh is 46.5% in 2030 and 40.03% in 2050 when the minimum share of cars is assumed to be as for the ER40 scenario (Table 5.1). Without the modal shift (i.e., when the minimum share of cars is assumed to be the same as in BAU), the maximum reduction potential would be 46.0% in 2030 and 38.2% in 2050. The maximum energy-reduction potential in Bhutan would be 40.0% in 2030 and 42.5% in 2050, with a minimum share of cars assumed to be lower than in BAU. If the minimum share of cars is assumed to be as in BAU, the maximum energy-reduction potential in Bhutan would be 38.0% in 2030 and 41.0% in 2050. In Nepal, the maximum potential for the reduction of total primary energy supply (TPES) would be 54.0% in 2030 and 51.0% when the minimum share of cars is lower than in BAU. However, if the share of passenger cars is the same as in BAU, the maximum energy-reduction potential would be slightly lower: 53.7% in 2030 and 50.1% in 2050. In Sri Lanka, the maximum energy-reduction potential would be 52.5% in 2030 and 56.0% in 2050 when modal shift is considered. The maximum potential for the reduction in total primary energy requirement is slightly lower when the minimum share of cars is assumed to be as in BAU: 52.0% in 2030 and 53.0% in 2050.

In the three energy-reduction scenarios, the study identifies the energy reduction potential from each sector to meet the respective energy reduction targets. The study focuses on 2 snapshot years. In Bangladesh, major reductions in TFEC in ER15 and ER30 scenarios in 2030 would come from the industry sector, whereas the residential sector would be the major contributor in ER40. In 2050, the industry sector would have the biggest role in energy reduction followed by the residential sector in all energy reduction scenarios. In the case of Bhutan, the industry sector would contribute most to the reduction of TFEC in 2030 in ER15, followed by the commercial and residential sectors. In ER30 and ER40, industry would have the highest contribution to energy reduction followed by the residential sector. In 2050, the transport sector would provide the highest contribution in ER15 and ER40, followed by the industry and commercial sectors. In ER30, the industry and transport sectors would have the major roles in energy reduction. For Nepal, residential and industry sectors would be the major contributors to reduction in TFEC in 2030, whereas the transport sector would also have a significant share in 2050. In Sri Lanka, the transport sector would be the major contributor to the reduction in TFEC in both 2030 and 2050 and the industry sector would contribute second most in the reduction of TFEC in both 2030 and 2050.

Furthermore, the study also identifies the necessary energy-efficient devices and fuel-switching options in each sector. In the cases of Bhutan and Nepal, there would be greater use of electricity in energy reduction scenarios. The power sector is almost dependent on hydro in these two countries. Switching from petroleum and biomass to electricity based end-use technologies in Nepal and Bhutan has a major role in energy reduction. For Bangladesh, electricity use would be lower in energy reduction targets due to a higher dependence on fossil fuels for power generation. In Sri Lanka, there would be higher power generation requirements in ER30 and ER40 scenarios than in BAU in the long term. In higher energy-reduction targets, biomass-based cooking in rural areas would be replaced by cooking based on petroleum and electricity.

Energy-efficient electrical devices such as efficient air-conditioners and fans are cost-effective options to meet energy reduction targets in the residential and commercial sectors in all countries. In the transport sector, a shift from cars to mass transport such as buses would have a major role in reducing energy consumption. In addition, the use of hybrid and electric vehicles would also decrease the transport FEC, especially for Bhutan and Nepal. Energy-efficiency measures and the use of efficient technologies in the industry sector also provide significant reduction potential in all countries. Ultra-premium efficiency type IE5 motors would be cost-effective for motive power. Vertical mills and six-stage cyclone suspension preheater kilns are needed in the cement industry. Heat-pump technology for producing process heat could be a promising technology in the industry sector in future. In the brick industry, vertical shaft brick kilns are an attractive option to meet energy reduction targets.

This study also revealed that energy-efficiency improvements in the residential, commercial, and industry sectors offer opportunities for significant energy reductions at lower costs. For example, traditional cook stoves (TCS) are still in use despite having higher operating costs. Similarly, incandescent lamps are still used despite having cost-effective options like compact fluorescent lamps (CFLs) and LED lamps. Therefore, effective energy policies and promotion of energy-efficient technologies would make a big contribution in energy saving and reduction of GHG emissions from energy use. Also, policies to promote modal shift (i.e., from cars to buses) would significantly contribute to energy reductions.

6 Energy Efficiency-Related Institutional Arrangements

I t is imperative for countries to have robust regulations and an effective institutional structure to translate their energy efficiency and conservation (EEC) initiatives into action. This chapter discusses the government institutions concerned with EEC that have been established or are in the process of being established in each of the five countries under study.

6.1 Bangladesh

A number of institutions are either directly or indirectly linked to issues of energy efficiency in Bangladesh. The following are the key institutions:

- Ministry of Power, Energy and Mineral Resources (MPEMR)
- Sustainable and Renewable Energy Development Authority (SREDA)
- Bangladesh Energy and Power Research Council
- Bangladesh Energy Regulatory Commission
- Infrastructure Development Company Limited (IDCOL)

Ministry of Power, Energy and Mineral Resources. MPEMR is the government's main body responsible for planning, developing, implementing, and overall management of Bangladesh's energy sector. The Power Division of MPEMR is responsible for the promotion of energy efficiency through the formulation of policy, regulations, incentive mechanisms, as well as research and development (R&D).

Sustainable and Renewable Energy Development Authority. SREDA was established as a nodal agency to promote, facilitate, and disseminate renewable energy and energy efficiency to ensure the country's energy security. The SREDA functions under the Power Division of MPEMR and acts as a coordinating body between government agencies and nongovernment organizations working in renewable energy and energy-efficiency sectors. The SREDA also acts as an implementing body to promote EEC and monitors nationwide energy consumption and implementation of EEC programs (MPEMR 2018).

Bangladesh Energy and Power Research Council. This is an apex body that coordinates, monitors, and evaluates energy- and power-related research activities. It also encourages and coordinates private research institutes to carry out energy and electric power research. The council lists EEC as one of its thrust areas of research (The Independent 2015).

Bangladesh Energy Regulatory Commission. This the country's regulatory body. It has the mandate for petroleum, electricity, and gas markets. The commission was established in April 2004 through a legislative act. Besides general functions performed by a typical regulator, the commission has the responsibility of determining efficiency standards of energy-consuming machinery and appliances. It is mandated to ensure efficiency in the use of energy through energy audits as well as verification, monitoring, and analysis of energy data (BERC 2019).

Infrastructure Development Company Limited. IDCOL is a nonbank finance institution created to bridge the finance gap for developing infrastructure and renewable energy projects. The main objective of IDCOL is to stimulate and optimize private sector investment in renewable energy and energy efficiency through public–private partnership initiatives (IDCOL 2014).

Bangladesh's master plan on EEC (MPEMR and SREDA 2015) lists several other organizations with crucial roles on EEC. The Bangladesh Standardization and Testing Institute is responsible for the development of Bangladesh Standards on energy efficiency. The roles and responsibility of the institute are "a. Issuance of Bangladesh Standards related to the Energy Efficiency Labeling Program; b. Conduct of energy efficiency tests required for the Energy Efficiency Labeling Program" (SREDA 2015; p. 3-3). The Ministry of Industry cooperates with SREDA in energy management and labeling programs. More importantly, the Bangladesh Accreditation Board is an accreditation body for ISO 9000, 14001, and 50001 certifications. It is also expected to handle accreditation of laboratories for energy-efficiency measurement tests, which are responsible for the Energy Efficiency Labeling Program and the energy manager and auditor licensing system.

The Ministry of Finance is responsible for preparing budgets for EEC policy promotion, while the Ministry of Housing and Public Works implements the Bangladesh National Building Code in the housing and building sector.

According to the EEC master plan (MoPEMR and SREDA 2015), local governments and utilities are also expected to play important roles. Local governments are mandated to administer national building code and green building guidelines. The utilities are supposed to be responsible for improving the efficiency of power generation and transmission as well as to incentivize EEC.

6.2 Bhutan

The Ministry of Economic Affairs (MoEA) and the Ministry of Agriculture and Forests are the government ministries mainly involved in planning and coordinating activities related to energy in Bhutan.

The Ministry of Agriculture and Forests focuses on administration of biomass resources and planning and designing policy for utilization and maintenance of forest resources. The MoEA is responsible for planning, coordination, and implementation of power generation from both conventional and renewable sources. Other polices related to energy consumption and exports as well as import of fossil fuels are also formulated by MoEA. The Department of Renewable Energy (DoRE), under MoEA, serves as the central coordinating agency and the nodal agency of the Royal Government of Bhutan on energy-efficiency initiatives and renewable energy development. The DoRE is composed of the Alternate Energy, Planning and Coordination, and Research and Development divisions.

The Planning and Coordination Division is associated with the formulation of policies and regulations for EEC and renewable energy. The division is also responsible for planning and coordination of programs and initiatives and handles administration and implementation of subsidies associated with energy efficiency (DoRE 2016).

Research and development related to energy-efficiency technologies are carried out by the Research and Development Division. In addition to renewable energy, the division is responsible for the following EEC activities:

- Promotion of EEC improvement measures
- Initiation of standard and labeling program
- Establishment of testing and certification procedures
- Development of necessary testing facilities
- Promote innovative financing of energy-efficiency projects
- Prepare educational curriculum on EEC

Recognizing the need for cooperation from multisector agencies for executing EEC programs, DoRE's road map on EEC (DoRE 2018) outlines relevant agencies along with their roles and responsibilities (Table 6.1).

Table 6.1: Key Agencies for the Implementation of the Energy Efficiency and Conservation Roadmap per Sector

Sector	Lead Agency	Collaborating Agencies
Building	Ministry of Works and Human Settlements Bhutan Standards Bureau	Department of Renewable Energy (DoRE) Municipalities National Housing and Development Corporation Limited Private sectors
Appliances	DoRE Bhutan Standards Bureau (BSB)	Department of Trade, Ministry of Economic Affairs (MoEA) Private sector Bhutan Chamber of Commerce and Industry
Industry	DoRE Department of Industry, MoEA Department of Cottage and Small Industry, MoEA	Bhutan Electricity Authority Bhutan Power Corporation Limited Bhutan Chamber of Commerce and Industry Bhutan Standards Bureau Association of Bhutanese Industries
Cross-cutting	Ministry of Finance Gross National Happiness Commission National Environment Commission	Financial Institutions Royal University of Bhutan

Source: DoRE. 2018. Energy Effiency Roadmap (Draft Report). http://www.moea.gov.bt/wp-content/uploads/2018/07/EE-Roadmap-Draft.pdf.

According to the EEC road map, the Ministry of Finance will handle energy-efficiency financing instruments forwarded by DoRE. The ministry will seek endorsement for fiscal incentives from Bhutan's parliament and make necessary arrangements to incorporate energy-efficiency aspects into a public procurement system. The Gross National Happiness Commission will periodically review the implementation status and overall effectiveness of adopted EEC measures. The Department of Trade, under MoEA, is responsible for monitoring of imported energy-consuming devices to check for substandard energy-efficiency products.

According to the EEC road map, the Bhutan Standards Bureau will be responsible for certification of the performance of energy-efficient appliances. The Ministry of Works and Human Settlements will develop building codes in coordination with DoRE. In the electricity sector, the Bhutan Electricity Authority is responsible for promoting energy-efficiency measures.

6.3 **India**

In India, the following government ministries are involved in the energy sector:

- Ministry of Power (MoP)
- Ministry of New and Renewable Energy
- Ministry of Coal
- Ministry of Petroleum and Natural Gas

India's Energy Conservation Act, 2001 came into effect in March 2002. Consequently, institutions were established both at the central and state levels to implement the act. The Bureau of Energy Efficiency (BEE) is the nodal agency at the central level and the State Designated Agencies (SDAs) work at the state level. These institutions are provided with regulatory and enforcement authorities.

The BEE is the nodal agency on energy efficiency in India. The mission of BEE is to assist in the development of policy and strategy to reduce energy intensity of the economy with emphasis on self-regulation and following market principles. Additionally, BEE is empowered with promotional roles such as information dissemination, awareness creation, and promotion of R&D to mainstream energy efficiency.

The SDAs are responsible for expanding energy-efficiency initiatives at the state level. They are also provided with developmental, facilitation, and regulatory roles; more details can be found in Sengupta and Kumar (n.d.).

Besides BEE and SDAs, which are regulatory institutions, corporate institutions have been created to expand the energy-efficiency market in the country. The most prominent among them is Energy Efficiency Services Limited (EESL), which is a joint venture of public sector undertakings under the Ministry of Power. This institution was established to implement energy-efficiency projects and create and sustain the energy-efficiency market as well as attract private sector investment in energy efficiency (EESL 2018b). There are also energy service companies (ESCOs) that provide the following energy-saving solutions to their clients (BEE 2015d):

- Technical services such as identifying ESPs, designing, retrofitting, and implementing projects on EEC
- Guarantee the performance of such EEC projects and undertake risk (technical, financial, and operational) management
- Other services such as energy auditing, financing, monitoring, and maintenance

ESCOs perform in-depth analyses of energy consumption of the clients and design energy-efficient solutions if there is ESP. They then install required retrofits or new devices. The ESCOs also play the role of monitoring and maintenance so that returns generated from the project sufficiently pay back the investment made in EEC. In cases where some projects fail to deliver the returns on the investments, ESCOs often pay the difference. The ESCOs are enlisted by BEE through a grading process based on assessment of the financial and technical strength, market position, and human resource availability of the firm and other relevant criteria (BEE 2015d).

The Central Electricity Regulatory Commission is the regulator of the country's electricity market. Aside from the roles performed by a typical electricity regulator, the commission performs advisory functions to promote efficiency in the power industry. The commission also issues trading regulations for energy-saving certificates in the Perform Achieve and Trade (PAT) scheme.

6.4 **Nepal**

The Ministry of Energy, Water Resources and Irrigation is responsible for developing policies, plans, and strategies relevant to energy as well as water resources in Nepal. The Government of Nepal launched the National Energy Efficiency Strategy (MoEWRI 2018), which explicitly states that a government institution will be created specifically to promote, develop, and carry out energy-efficiency measures in the country. Other than acting as a regulator in the market, the institution will be responsible for coordinating relevant entities, implementing energy-efficiency strategies, developing a future road map, and monitoring and evaluating associated progress. Recently, the government designated the Alternative Energy Promotion Centre as the nodal agency for energy efficiency—this is a government institution initially formed as the nodal agency for the promotion of renewable and alternative energy technologies in Nepal (NEEP 2019). According to the National Energy Efficiency Strategy, separate energy-efficiency strategies will be created for all listed or identified entities and their institutional structure will also incorporate a dedicated monitoring unit to ensure smooth coordination and monitoring of relevant entities.

Nepal recently established the Nepal Electricity Regulatory Commission following enactment of the Nepal Electricity Regulatory Commission Act 2017. The commission is responsible for specifying the standards and other regulations for generation plants, transmission lines, and distribution networks. It is also responsible for regulating electricity tariffs.

6.5 **Sri Lanka**

The Ministry of Power and Renewable Energy is responsible for formulating polices and regulations on power generation and utilization of renewable energy resources. It is also mandated to develop energy-efficiency policies (MoPRE 2012).

The Sri Lanka Sustainable Energy Authority (SLSEA), an organization under the Ministry of Power and Renewable Energy, was established in 2007 following the enactment of the Sri Lanka Sustainable Energy Authority Act No. 35 of 2007. The SLSEA is an apex institution formed to improve energy efficiency in the country (SLSEA 2018).

The Public Utilities Commission of Sri Lanka is the regulatory body established by the Public Utilities Commission of Sri Lanka Act No. 35 of 2002 to regulate public utility industries. The commission commenced regulating the electricity sector after 2009 with the enactment of the Sri Lanka Electricity Act No. 20 of 2009. According to this act, the commission is responsible for the following (PUCSL 2014):

- Promoting the efficient use of electricity supplied to premises
- Directing distribution licensees to ensure efficient use of electricity at consumer level
- Collecting information regarding the level of performance attained by distribution licensees in connection with the promotion of efficient use of electricity by consumers

7 Energy Efficiency Policies, Initiatives, and Programs

This chapter provides a country-wise summary of acts, regulations, policies, programs, and initiatives that are directly or closely related to energy efficiency and conservation (EEC). The chapter begins with regional comparison of laws dedicated to EEC as well as other energy acts related to EEC. It is then followed by discussion of existing energy polices and initiatives related to EEC per country.

7.1 Acts and Regulations Related to the Energy Sector and Energy Efficiency

Regulations and acts concerning EEC provide the necessary foundation to build upon and shape the course of a country's future energy scenario. The following sections briefly describe the existing acts and regulations on EEC in South Asian economies and highlight their key features.

Energy Efficiency and Conservation Acts

Among the South Asian countries, only India and Bangladesh have a dedicated act on EEC. India's Energy Conservation Act 2001 was passed by the Indian Parliament in September 2001 and was later amended in 2010 (MoLJ 2010). As discussed in Chapter 6, both the BEE and SDAs were established to implement the provisions of the act. The BEE is the nodal agency at the federal level and SDAs function at the state level. The act allows the Government of India and, in some cases, state governments to do the following (MoLJ 2010):

(i)   In relation to devices and appliances

- Define energy consumption standards for devices and appliances
- Conduct mandatory display of labels on specified equipment and appliances
- Prevent the manufacture, sale, purchase, and import of specified equipment and appliances not in line with standards

(ii) In the buildings sector

- Prepare the Energy Conservation Building Code (ECBC) for EEC in commercial buildings
- Amend the ECBC to suit regional and local climatic conditions
- Instruct owners or tenants of commercial buildings to comply with the ECBC provisions

(iii) In the industry sector

- Identify and list high-energy consuming industries, commercial buildings, and other entities as designated consumers

- Develop and designate energy consumption norms and standards for designated consumers
  Instruct designated consumers to (i) designate or appoint certified energy managers in charge of
  EEC, (ii) get energy audits carried out by an accredited energy auditor in a prescribed manner,
  (iii) provide information on energy consumption and measures adopted as per the recommendations
  of accredited energy auditor, and (iv) adhere to energy consumption norms and standards

In Bangladesh, Energy Efficiency and Conservation Rules 2016 (Act No. 189) (EECRs) which represents the major act on EEC was enacted in 2016 (SREDA 2019). The Sustainable and Renewable Energy Development Authority Act No. 48 was passed in 2012, which formally established the Sustainable and Renewable Energy Development Authority (SREDA) in May 2014. The SREDA coordinates, facilitates, and promotes development of renewable energy and energy efficiency in Bangladesh.

Although Sri Lanka does not have a dedicated act related to EEC, the country has passed an act to establish a government organization to carry out functions related to EEC and sustainable growth of the energy sector. Sri Lanka's Sustainable Energy Authority (SLSEA) Act No. 35 of 2007 led to formation of the SLSEA. A major objective of SLSEA is energy-efficiency improvement and energy conservation in the country (Wickramasinghe 2010).

Bhutan and Nepal are yet to enact dedicated laws governing EEC. In Nepal's case, a draft version of an act called Energy Efficiency and Conservation Act, 2076 is currently being reviewed by stakeholders at the province level. The draft act envisions formation of a Board of Energy Efficiency and Conservation of Nepal and a special bureau to carry out tasks and activities as instructed by the board. The draft act also has a provision to establish a fund for EEC activities, which can be accessed by public and private institutions as well as individuals to improve their EEC status.

Table 7.1 presents a list of acts dedicated to EEC as well as those indirectly related to EEC.

Table 7.1: Acts Dedicated to Energy Efficiency and Conservation and Other Related Acts

Type of Act	Bangladesh	Bhutan	India	Nepal	Sri Lanka
Energy Efficiency and Conservation Acts or Rules	Energy Efficiency and Conservation Rules 2016	None	Energy Conservation Act 2001 (MoLJ, 2010)	None	None
Other Acts related to EEC	• The Sustainable and Renewable Energy Development Authority Act, 2012 (MoLJPA, 2012) • Bangladesh Energy Regulatory Commission Act 2003 (MoPEMRD, 2003) • Electricity Act 1910 (Under revision) (Dhaka Tribune, 2017) • Gas Act 2010 (CRC Trust, 2010)	• Electricity Act 2001 (NAB, 2001)	• Electricity Act 2003 (MoLJ, 2003) • Electricity Regulatory Commissions Act, 1998 (GoI, 1998) • The Electricity Supply Act, 1948 (GoI, 1948)	• Electricity Act 2049 (GoN, 1992) • Nepal Electricity Authority Act (GoN, 1984) • Electricity Regulatory Commission Act	• Sri Lanka Electricity Act No. 20 of 2009 (GoS, 2009) • Sri Lanka Sustainable Energy Authority Act No. 35 of 2007 (GoS, 2007) • Public Utilities Commission of Sri Lanka act No. 35 of 2002 (GoS, 2007)

NAB = National Assembly of Bhutan; GoN = Government of Nepal; GoS = Government of Sri Lanka; GoI = Government of India; MoLJ = Ministry of Law and Justice; MoLJPA = Ministry of Law, Justice and Parliamentary Affairs; MoPEMRD = Ministry of Power, Energy and Mineral Resources Energy and Mineral Resources Division; CRC = Chancery Law Chronicles.

Source: Authors.

In Bangladesh, EECRs stipulate institutional arrangements to carry out EEC initiatives and identify relevant sector-wise strategies. They state SREDA as the nodal agency to lead EEC-related activities. Moreover, they identify designated consumers and state minimum energy performance standards. For the improvement of energy efficiency in energy-consuming appliances in the residential and commercial sectors, EECRs provide a phase-wise list of such appliances to be covered by the Energy Labelling Program SREDA (2019). The EECRs also allow SREDA to develop and recommend minimum energy performance standards. For the industry sector, EECR has identified large energy-consuming subsectors for voluntary or compulsory energy audit requirements. As for energy conservation in buildings, EECRs identified several energy-efficiency measures applicable for the country. The EECRs also authorize SREDA to determine thresholds for buildings to be regulated under the act.

The Sustainable and Renewable Energy Development Authority Act was enacted to form SREDA. The responsibilities and functions of SREDA in relation to energy efficiency as stipulated by the act include the following (SREDA 2012):

(i)   taking actions to create public awareness and encouragement for the efficient use of energy;

(ii)   encouraging the use of energy-efficient equipment and taking steps for standardization and labeling of energy-using equipment and appliances;

(iii)   establishing testing laboratories or providing assistance in establishing laboratories for testing and certification of energy-using equipment;

(iv)   encouraging EEC-related R&D, identifying innovative financing for implementation of projects, and arranging necessary training;

(v)   assisting the government in developing and implementing an energy-efficiency building code;

(vi)   making regulations for qualification and competence of energy managers and energy auditors and selection of accredited energy auditor firms;

(vii)   coordinating the EEC implementation activities in government, semi-government, and autonomous organizations and creating commercial markets for sustainable energy in the private sector through demonstration;

(viii) assisting the government to make necessary laws, rules, and regulations for sustainable energy development;

(ix)   identifying low-efficiency equipment and taking steps to stop their production, import, and sale; and

(x)   taking steps to declare designated consumers.

Energy Efficiency and Conservation Building Code for Commercial and Residential Buildings

India and Sri Lanka already have in place building codes on EEC. In 2017, India revised its older version of the Energy Conservation Building Code prepared in 2007. Similarly, Sri Lanka is revising its existing building code for energy efficiency called Code of Practice For Energy Efficient Buildings in Sri Lanka-2008 and is planning to release an updated version (MoPRE 2017). Bangladesh and Bhutan are planning to prepare their first-ever code on building EEC. In Nepal's case, the existing building code (MoUD 2015) mainly considers safety aspects of buildings and not EEC.

Bangladesh. The Ministry of Housing and Public Works initiated the enactment of a new version of the Bangladesh National Building Code (HBRI 2015) and the Green Building Guidelines to promote EEC in the building sector (SREDA 2015). The new building code is expected to consider EEC in buildings. The Green Building Guidelines, on the other hand, are voluntary. The guidelines provide recommendations on energy and water consumption efficiency and environmental impact caused due to building construction, use, and decommissioning. This guideline is expected to be ready by 2025 (SREDA 2015).

Bhutan. Bhutan does not yet have an energy-efficiency building code. However, its road map on EEC states that using the provisions of EEC policy (DoRE 2017), the Ministry of Works and Human Settlements and DoRE would develop building codes for new buildings as well as retrofits in existing buildings (DoRE 2018). Several studies are reportedly ongoing to that end. The government planned to carry out energy audits of a number of buildings by the end of 2019 to provide baseline energy consumption data. This baseline is to be used to formulate energy-efficiency building codes.

Also, based on the Indian ECBC, PricewaterhouseCoopers prepared the Bhutan Building Energy Efficiency Code to provide guidelines for use by building professionals (PwC n.d.). Similarly, another guideline titled "Bhutan Green Design Guidelines" (MoWHS 2013) was also issued by the government in 2013 with the primary motive of encouraging adoption and implementation of green design and construction practices in the country.

India. In India, the ECBC was first prepared in 2007 under the Energy Conservation Act, 2001. The ECBC sets the minimum energy performance level for large new commercial buildings.[13] Although ECBC is developed at the central government level, the authority for its enforcement lies with the states, and they can also modify the code to meet regional or local requirements. The code comes into effect and becomes mandatory only when a state or local government accepts and implements it in its jurisdiction (Yu et al. 2017). More details on tasks and responsibilities of the central, state, and local governments for mainstreaming ECBC are provided in United Nations Development Program (UNDP) and BEE (2016). The ECBC prescribes standards for:

- building envelope (walls, roofs, and windows);
- lighting (outdoor and indoor);
- heating, ventilation, and air-conditioning systems;
- solar hot water heating; and
- electrical systems.

In 2017, the Government of India released an updated building code titled Energy Conservation Building Code 2017. The code provides energy performance standards for new commercial buildings. With its implementation in commercial buildings, energy consumption is expected to decline by 50%. The updated code incorporates futuristic advancements in building technology to improve energy efficiency and sets parameters to integrate renewable energy in building design (Government of India, Press Information Bureau [PIB] 2017).

In a further extension, the government launched the Energy Conservation Building Code for Residential Buildings in 2018 to enhance energy efficiency in the residential sector (PIB 2018a). The code is designed with an objective to help designers, architects, and builders associated in construction of residential buildings throughout the country. In December 2018, BEE released the part of the code concerned with the design of energy-efficient building envelopes for residential buildings (BEE 2018b).

Nepal. As stated earlier, Nepal has a building code that considers the structural safety of buildings with no focus on EEC (MoUD 2015).

Sri Lanka. Sri Lanka's first energy-efficiency building code was prepared by the Ceylon Electricity Board (CEB) in 2000. Later, to incorporate the latest technology advancements and modern requirements, the Code of Practice for Energy Efficient Buildings in Sri Lanka 2008 was prepared by SLSEA under the Sri Lanka Sustainable Energy Authority Act (SLSEA 2009). The SLSEA plans to replace this with a new code, which will be performance based unlike the existing code that is based on a prescriptive approach (MoPRE 2017). This new code will be mandatory

---

[13]   Buildings having connected load of 100 kW or with contract demand of 120 kVA and above.

for commercial buildings. To make it easier for participants to comply with the code, Sri Lanka is preparing the Guideline for Sustainable Energy Residences in Sri Lanka, which focuses on energy efficiency and sustainability (ODSM Operation Demand Side Management 2018).

7.2 Energy Efficiency Plans, Policies, and Programs

South Asian countries vary widely in terms of policies, programs, and initiatives designed to promote EEC. Among the countries, India already has vast experience and several success stories in these areas. Other countries in the subregion are at various stages of energy efficiency policy and program development. This section briefly discusses the existing EEC policies, programs, and initiatives in each country.

National Energy Efficiency and Conservation Policy and Strategies

In India, the major policy initiative was the enactment of Energy Conservation Act. The act served as the basis for institutionalization of the BEE and mandates it to set standards on EEC. India's National Electricity Policy (MoP 2005) governs the entire electricity sector and was introduced by the government in 2005. In 2008, the government formulated the National Action Plan on Climate Change, which explicitly includes the National Mission for Enhanced Energy Efficiency as one of its eight missions. The basic elements of the National Mission for Enhanced Energy Efficiency include market-based mechanisms to improve energy efficiency, accelerating the transition to use of energy-efficient appliances in designated sectors, making energy-efficient products affordable, and providing financial stimulus to decrease capital cost of energy-efficient technologies (Jain et al. 2019). The MoP and BEE are responsible for preparation of the implementation plan of the National Mission for Enhanced Energy Efficiency.

The Government of Bhutan endorsed the National Energy Efficiency and Conservation Policy in November 2019 (Ministry of Economic Affairs [MoEA] 2019). All EEC measures in Bhutan are governed by this policy, which states that DoRE (under MoEA) is a nodal agency and outlines the institutional roles and responsibilities of other agencies. It presents sector-wise strategies to improve energy efficiency in the building, industry, and transport sectors in the country. It also outlines the institutional arrangements to carry out EEC activities along with the roles and responsibilities of relevant agencies. In relation to the fiscal measures to promote EEC, the policy authorizes the DoRE to use the Renewable Energy Development Fund established under the Alternative Renewable Energy Policy 2013 in two ways: technical assistance and lending for programs.

Nepal recently launched its first-ever strategy document titled "National Energy Efficiency Strategy 2075" (Ministry of Energy, Water Resources and Irrigation [MoEWRI] 2018) on EEC in 2018, which states time-bound sector-wise strategies, targets, and responsible institutions as well as financing strategies. It also identifies challenges and possible opportunities related to EEC. More importantly, it envisages the creation of a nodal governmental agency to carry out the following functions:

- execution of EEC initiatives,
- coordination with relevant agencies,
- creation of a national master plan on EEC,
- monitoring and evaluation of EEC performance, and
- performing regulatory roles related to EEC.

Sri Lanka's National Energy Policy and Strategies (NEPS) 2008 (MoPE 2008) is regarded as the country's first-ever comprehensive energy policy covering all players in the energy sector. The NEPS specify implementation strategies as well as specific targets and milestones[14] and institutional responsibilities. One of the major objectives of NEPS is the promotion of EEC. The NEPS provide some listed strategies for efficient utilization of energy in the supply- and demand-side as follows:

- Creating incentive and disincentive measures such as labeling, building codes, and energy audits
- Identifying financing mechanisms to continuously improve EEC
- Entrusting the Energy Conservation Fund to coordinate all activities related to EEC
- Lowering power generation and network losses to lowest possible
- Shifting toward a more efficient and larger-capacity vehicular transport system

The Government of Sri Lanka set a target of 100% energy self-sufficiency by 2030 through a plan document titled Sri Lanka Energy Sector Development Plan for a Knowledge-Based Economy: 2015–2025 (MoPRE 2015). This document states that EEC is one thrust area and a "national priority." The plan identifies the following strategies to improve EEC across the value chain in the country (MoPRE 2015):

- Enhancing the efficiency of electricity generation and petroleum refineries
- Reducing electricity transmission and distribution losses and petroleum distribution losses to acceptable norms
- Promoting energy-efficient modes in the transport sector
- Improving efficiency among end-users of electricity and petroleum products
- Promoting sustainable and environmentally friendly building concepts in urban development

Furthermore, the document states the following key programs for implementation of the plan:

- Energy conservation in the transport, industry, and commercial sectors
- Standardization and automation of street lighting
- Introduction of time-of-use meters and tariffs
- Smart cities and green buildings
- Sustainable energy zone programs

The latest master plan of Bangladesh aims to improve the country's energy intensity (i.e., total primary energy consumption per unit of GDP) by 15% by 2021 and 20% by 2030 from that of the base year 2013–2014 (SREDA 2015).

Energy Efficiency Master Plans and Road Maps

Among the South Asian countries, Bangladesh and Bhutan have a dedicated master plan or road map on EEC. In Bangladesh, the Energy Efficiency and Conservation Master Plan up to 2030 was prepared in 2015 by SREDA and the Japan International Cooperation Agency (JICA). The master plan presents a road map and an action plan up to 2030 as well as a legal, institutional, and operational framework for its effective implementation (SREDA 2015). In Bhutan, DoRE prepared the Energy Efficiency Roadmap in 2018, which illustrates the energy savings potential and its potential impacts on GHG emission. It also states the key interventions needed, roles of relevant institutions, and financial requirements (DoRE 2018).

---

[14]   For T&D loss reduction, electrification of households, and generation from renewable sources.

Although other countries are yet to have an integrated national masterplan on energy efficiency, there are national energy-efficiency strategies and various sectoral schemes or programs for energy efficiency improvements. In India, the energy-efficiency schemes include the Perform Achieve and Trade (PAT) scheme for the industry sector as well as demand-side management programs targeted to various sectors. The country has also enacted the Energy Conservation Building Code. In Sri Lanka, the NEPS include strategies for EEC in a broader term. Additionally, the country has launched different activities dedicated to EEC in the past; including programs on efficient cook stoves, energy labeling, reduction of losses in electricity supply, national energy conservation, utility driven CFLs, and enactment of energy-efficiency building codes.

Nepal recently announced its National Energy Efficiency Strategy in addition to having implemented energy-efficiency programs focused on promotion of improved cook stoves and efficient lamps. A supporting study for the National Energy Efficiency Strategy titled Background Document for Nepal Energy Efficiency Strategy was prepared by NEEP with support from the German International Cooperation in 2015. The study highlights policy gaps and discusses how other countries have addressed such gaps. It also presents feasibility, expected benefits, as well as cost implications of adopting proposed energy-efficiency measures in Nepal based on a techno-economic modeling analysis. More recently, a study carried out under an ADB technical assistance program[15] aimed at formulating an investment pipeline for EEC activities for the next 5 years. The study is based on actual energy audit reports of 57 buildings and factories. It also aimed to identify demand-side EEC technologies that are economically feasible. Among the feasible technologies, the study attempted to identify those that do not require advanced engineering and to develop a pipeline of investment projects with such technologies.

Major Energy Efficiency Schemes and Programs

Energy Standard and Labeling

Setting standards and labeling (S&L) for energy-consuming devices has existed in developed countries for some time. Some developing countries have also adopted similar programs. Generally, an S&L program provides consumers with information on the ESP of the device they want to purchase. Commonly, star ratings are provided to the devices, with more stars indicating the devices have higher efficiency. Countries in South Asia vary widely in terms of energy S&L.

Standards and Labeling in Bangladesh
In line with the Sustainable and Renewable Energy Development Authority Act of 2012, the Government of Bangladesh released a draft regulation on S&L titled "SREDA Standard and Labeling (Appliance & Equipment) Regulation 2018." It establishes the rules and procedures for prescribing minimum energy performance S&L of appliances and devices based on their energy-efficiency performance (SREDA 2018).

Standards and Labeling in Bhutan
Bhutan is yet to start an S&L program.

Internationally, it is a more common practice to set S&L to suit a country's own interests. Since most of the appliances and equipment used in Bhutan are imported, the national policy makers face the challenge of determining the appropriate kind of standard that should be adopted for the country.

There also seems to be a challenge of inter-organizational coordination in setting an effective S&L program and lack of sufficient resources for such a program in Bhutan as is the case in most other countries of South Asia.

---

[15] ADB. Regional: Improving Institutional Capacity on Preparing Energy Efficiency Investments. https://www.adb.org/projects/50294-001/main.

Standard and Labeling Program in India

In the residential and commercial sectors, India has made significant achievements in S&L. Initiated in 2006 with an objective of removing information barriers to consumers on energy savings from efficient appliances, the program helps consumers make more rational informed purchases. Under this program, star labeling is assigned to appliances on a comparative basis, with a higher number of stars referring to a more efficient device and higher energy savings. The program covered a total of 25 electrical appliances by 2018 (BEE 2018a). In 2010, mandatory labeling was also introduced with the intention of phasing out energy-inefficient appliances. Mandatory labeling started with room air-conditioners, fluorescent tube lights, frost-free refrigerators, and distribution transformers. As of 2019, labeling became mandatory for 10 appliances: room air-conditioners, frost-free refrigerators, tubular fluorescent lamps, distribution transformers (cassette and floor standing), direct cool refrigerators, color televisions, electric geysers, variable capacity inverter air-conditioners, and light emitting diode (LED) lamps. Furthermore, BEE prepared the Super-Efficient Equipment Programme, under which appliances exceeding the five-star label will be promoted along with financial incentives (BEE 2018d). Under this program, super-efficient ceiling fans were selected as the first appliances to be adopted, and consultations with stakeholders have been completed to finalize the technical specifications. Currently, selection and procurement of an entity responsible for monitoring and verification is in process (BEE 2020a).

Standard and Labeling Program in Nepal

In Nepal, the Alternative Energy Promotion Centre (AEPC) in collaboration with the Nepal Bureau of Standards and Metrology has started a project titled Preparation of Energy Efficiency Standards for Selected Electrical Appliances and Equipments and Appliances with the aim to prepare energy efficiency standards for fans, refrigerators, room air-conditioners, induction motors, and pump sets (AEPC 2020). The project is in its initial stage and a firm has been awarded the contract to study and determine energy efficiency standards.

Standards and Labeling in Sri Lanka

In Sri Lanka, a labeling scheme was first initiated in 2000 for CFLs by the CEB in association with the Sri Lanka Standards Institute and the National Engineering Research and Development Centre. Establishment of the Sri Lanka Sustainable Energy Authority (SLSEA) further boosted the program and since then SLSEA has prepared energy-efficiency standards for several widely used residential and commercial devices, with few of these standards being revised. Table 7.2 illustrates the status and progress of S&L in Sri Lanka.

Table 7.2: Status and Progress of Standards and Labelling Programs in Sri Lanka

Device	Standard	Regulation	Current Status
CFLs	Yes	Draft regulation for revised standards was prepared.	Mandatory energy label exists.
ACs	Draft energy labelling standards has been prepared	—	Public comments solicited on draft standards
Refrigerators	Yes	—	Consumption benchmarks for refrigerators are being revised
LED lamps	Yes	—	Voluntary MEPS label
Computers	Draft energy labelling standards has been prepared	—	
Ceiling fans	Yes	Yes	Mandatory energy label

— = not available; AC = Air-conditioner; AEPC= Alternative Energy Promotion Centre; CFL = compact fluorescent lamps; LED = light emitting diode; MEPS = Minimum Energy Performance Standard.

Source: Compiled from MoPRE (2017) and ODSM (2017).

Perform Achieve and Trade Scheme for Energy Efficiency of the Industry Sector in India

The PAT scheme under the National Mission for Enhanced Energy Efficiency in India is a highly successful program. The scheme was launched in 2008 with an objective to ramp up the overall efficiency of the industry sector in a cost-effective manner. The scheme uses regulatory as well as market-based mechanisms to create a robust incentive-based scheme (BEE 2011).

On the regulatory side, the scheme imposes legal obligations on designated consumers to reduce specific energy consumption within a pre-specified time frame.[16] The reduction targets are set in such a way that the industries with the best energy-efficiency status receive a lower target and vice versa. The Energy Conservation Act authorizes the central government to issue Energy Savings Certificates (ESCerts) to over-performing designated consumers at the end of the compliance period. An interesting part of this scheme is that the ESCerts are tradable in exchanges. Thus, an under-performing designated consumer can comply with their obligation by purchasing ESCerts or by paying a specified penalty.

The first cycle of the PAT scheme (2012–2015) covered over 400 energy-intensive utilities and industries, and the scheme managed to reduce energy consumption by 5.3%. The first cycle targeted eight major energy-intensive subsectors: aluminum, cement, chlor-alkali, fertilizer, iron and steel, paper and pulp, thermal power plants, and textile. Except for thermal power plants, all designated consumers surpassed their targets (IEA 2018b). The energy reduction target for the first cycle was set at 6.68 Mtoe, but the actual savings surpassed this comfortably and saved 8.67 Mtoe (BEE 2017b).[17]

The second cycle of PAT operated during 2016–2019. Its coverage was extended to 11 subsectors with a total of 621 designated consumers and a total energy consumption of around 227 Mtoe. The three additional subsectors covered in this cycle were petroleum refineries, railways, and electricity distribution companies. The overall reduction target was 8.869 Mtoe (BEE 2017b).

The third cycle was announced on 30 March 2017. Targets on specific energy consumption were assigned to 116 designated consumers with a total energy consumption of 35 Mtoe from six subsectors: pulp and paper, cement, iron and steel, textile, thermal power plants, and aluminum. It aims to decrease the overall energy consumption of these subsectors by 1.06 Mtoe. The third cycle is proposed to be implemented on a rolling basis by which new designated consumers are included annually (BEE 2017c). The fourth cycle is planned to include commercial buildings of 24-hour usage and the petrochemical sector (BEE 2017c).

To make the PAT scheme even more effective, the Government of India introduced finance instruments to support participating entities. The Partial Risk Guarantee Fund for Energy Efficiency provides risk-sharing services to financing institutions that provide loans for energy-efficiency projects; BEE (2017a) has more details. The Partial Risk Guarantee Fund for Energy Efficiency supports financing of EEC projects by undertaking the following:

- Addressing the risks faced and/or perceived by the financing institutions seeking to fund EEC projects
- Building capacity of participating finance institutions to finance EEC projects on a commercially sustainable basis

---

[16] The Energy Conservation Act authorizes the central government to select designated customers based on the yearly energy consumption of the industry and compared to the prescribed sector-wise threshold limit.

[17] Garnaik (2014) lists major entities involved in the scheme having direct and indirect participation and discusses how the targets were set and what sort of challenges were faced in the first PAT cycle.

Similarly, to provide equity support to energy-efficiency projects and initiatives, the government initiated the Venture Capital Fund for Energy Efficiency; BEE (2015f) has more details. The main beneficiaries are Energy Service Companies (ESCOs) and other companies planning to carry out EEC projects.

On the technical side, BEE has prepared the Energy Conservation Guidelines for Industries to ensure smooth implementation of the scheme. The objective of the guidelines is to guide the management and operators of participating entities to manage energy consumption by standardizing the performance of various energy-consuming equipment and systems in manufacturing processes (BEE 2018c).

Targeted End-Use Specific Energy Efficiency Programs

Efficient Cook Stove Programs

Improved Cook Stove Program of Infrastructure Development Company Limited in Bangladesh

The Infrastructure Development Company Limited (IDCOL) in Bangladesh has undertaken the IDCOL Improved Cook Stove Program, funded by the World Bank and the Government of Bangladesh. The program aimed to distribute one million improved cook stoves (ICS) by the end of 2018 by adopting a market-based approach. However, the program achieved its goal of distributing one million ICS in January 2017, nearly 2 years before the targeted time. A new target was set to distribute five million ICS by 2021 (IDCOL 2017).

Efficient Cook Stove Programs in Bhutan

The Bhutan Sustainable Rural Biomass Energy Project was implemented for the promotion and dissemination of energy-efficient cook stoves in rural regions of Bhutan. The project ran during 2012–2015 and was supported by the Global Environment Facility, the Royal Government of Bhutan, the United Nations Development Programme, and other funding partners.

Efficient Cook Stove Programs in India

A national program on ICS, the National Programme for Improved Chulha, was launched in India in 1984. It was a long-term effort to promote research as well as development and dissemination of efficient stoves in the country. The main objective was to decrease the demand for fuel wood, and the program focused on the development of a variety of cook stoves. It was funded in 23 states and five union territories of India. By 2001, the program had successfully reached 32.77 million households, which was 27% of the total potential (Hanbar and Karve 2002).

The National Biomass Cook Stoves Programme was launched by the Ministry of New and Renewable Energy in December 2009 with the following primary objectives:

- Enhancing the use of biomass in cook stoves
- Mitigating climate change by lowering the black carbon as well as other emissions released from burning biomass for cooking
- Mitigating drudgery of women and children using traditional stoves for cooking

To achieve these objectives, the program focused on designing very efficient, cost-effective, durable, and ergonomic cook stoves. The program aimed to disseminate 2.75 million ICSs by the end of the 12th plan period (MoNRE 2019).

A program named "Unnat Chulha Abhiyan" was launched in 2014 for the promotion of improved biomass cook stoves. This program was responsible for disseminating 36,940 ICSs of family type and 849 of community type by March 2018 (PIB 2018c).

Efficient Cook Stove Programs in Nepal

The Government of Nepal launched the Nepal Energy Efficiency Programme (NEEP) in 2010.[18] The NEEP is a bilateral technical cooperation between the government and the German International Cooperation. The program started with an objective of improving the plan for energy-efficiency enhancement and its basic conditions for implementation; its two phases were completed by 2017. The first phase of the program focused on introducing market-based energy efficiency services and introducing efficient biomass-based cook stoves. More importantly, the program also assisted the government in establishing policy and institutional framework to boost EEC. The second phase of NEEP focused on horizontal and vertical expansion of the energy-efficiency market.

Efficient Cook Stoves (Anagi Stove) Programme of the Ceylon Electricity Board, Sri Lanka

According to Wickramasinghe (2010), the efficient stove program promoting the Anagi Stove was started in 1986 in Sri Lanka and has successfully delivered more than 1.76 million ICSs until 2009. It was a joint project implemented by CEB and the Intermediate Technology Development Group. The success of this ICS program in urban areas led to its popularity in rural areas as well, through initiatives of organizations like the Integrated Development Association (IDEA). An interesting lesson from this program concerns the successful role of IDEA itself. IDEA did not take part in all aspects of the project, rather it focused on identifying gaps in the value chain of stoves. IDEA was involved in giving technical training and providing promotional and marketing skills to poor rural potters including women. Many traditional potters received training on ICS manufacturing through the efforts of IDEA. As a result, the cook stove manufacturing industry was upscaled from a cottage to a medium-scale industry (Wickramasinghe 20010).

Energy Efficient Lighting and Cooling Programs

The Unnat Jyoti by Affordable LEDs for All Program in India for Efficient Lighting and Fans

In 2010, the Government of India initiated the program called "Bachat Lamp Yojana" which was based on the Clean Development Mechanism under the Kyoto Protocol of United Nations Framework Convention on Climate Change (BEE 2015b). The purpose of the program was to improve lighting efficiency in the residential sector by shifting away from incandescent lamps toward compact fluorescent lamps. This program went through a series of enhancements over time; starting from 2015 it was replaced by the National LED Program, which was renamed "Unnat Jyoti by Affordable LEDs for All" in 2016. With an innovative business model based on demand aggregation, mass campaigning, and mass procurement, this program emerged as the largest subsidy-free domestic lighting scheme in the world in a span of 3 years (EESL 2018a). The program claims to have distributed more than 321 million LEDs by January 2019, consequently saving over 41,000 GWh annually (EESL 2019). This program was further extended to cover energy-efficient tube lamps and fans and was renamed "Unnat Jeevan by

---

[18] Government of Nepal, Town Development Fund. Energy Efficiency. http://tdf.org.np/energy-efficiency/.

Affordable LEDs and Appliances for All." The implementing agency of the program, Energy Efficiency Services Limited (EESL), played a crucial role; it procured appliances in bulk and made them available to consumers at a rate much below the market price. Under the program each household could only purchase 10 LED bulbs if purchased upfront and 4 if purchased on a monthly installment basis. Interestingly, the program did not involve any subsidy or exchange of old bulbs.

Ujyalo Nepal Abhiyan (Brighter Nepal Campaign)

The Nepal Electricity Authority, the state electricity utility, has a plan to distribute 20 million LED bulbs, potentially saving around 200 megawatts (MW) of electricity. The government allowed the authority to purchase LED lamps from EESL in India (My Republica 2017).

Presidential Task Force on Energy Demand-Side Management in Sri Lanka

The Operation Demand-side Management program was initiated to reduce the consumption of electricity in nine selected areas. The program aimed at avoiding the need for 500 MW of installed capacity within 5 years (ODSM 2017a). The thrust areas of the program are as follows:

- Elimination of incandescent lamps (domestic)
- Efficient chillers
- Efficient refrigerators
- Efficient motors
- Efficient fans
- Efficient lighting
- Efficient air-conditioners
- Commercial and industrial green buildings
- Smart homes

Efficient Lighting Initiatives of Bangladesh Program

The Efficient Lighting Initiatives of Bangladesh program was initiated by the Ministry of Power, Energy and Mineral Resources and the Rural Electrification Board, with the support of the World Bank in early 2009. The aim of the program was large-scale deployment of CFLs to increase energy efficiency in the lighting sector. The program was developed under the Clean Development Mechanism, which allowed it to earn carbon revenue. Through IDCOL, the World Bank helped in registering it as a Clean Development Mechanism program for earning carbon revenue for the emission reduction credits generated. The program also set a world record by distributing the most (five million) CFLs in one day (World Bank 2016).

Voluntary Programs on Building Energy Efficiency

There are several voluntary programs on building energy-efficiency improvements in India. The voluntary programs exist beside the regulatory programs required by the ECBC. The voluntary programs include the following:

- **Scheme for star rating of office buildings:** This voluntary labeling program is based on the performance of buildings in terms of specific energy usage (kilowatt hour [kWh])/square meters/year) and is executed by BEE. It rates existing office buildings on a scale of 1–5 stars, from least to most efficient (BEE 2009). Around 184 buildings were rated under this scheme by 2015 (BEE 2015c).

- **Green Rating for Integrated Habitat Assessment:** This is another widely implemented voluntary building rating program, pertinent to new buildings with floor space exceeding 2,500 square meters. Evaluation of a building is based on its performance over the life cycle and nationally accepted energy and environmental principles (Yu et al. 2017). More than 1,200 projects have reportedly been rated under the Green Rating for Integrated Habitat Assessment labeling (GRIHA 2018).

- **Leadership in Energy and Environmental Design:** This certification system is an internationally recognized rating system for buildings. In addition to energy efficiency, this rating is based on several other aspects including sustainability, water usage, and resources. The certification is applicable to all types of buildings (Yu et al. 2017).

Financing Schemes for Energy Efficiency

The financing schemes on energy-efficiency programs in each of the South Asian countries are briefly discussed here.

Bangladesh. In Bangladesh, IDCOL approved Tk750 million (i.e., about $8.8 million in July 2020) of debt financing to enhance energy efficiency of brick manufacturing plants. IDCOL also has a plan to finance energy-efficient boilers and other machinery in the industry sector (IDCOL 2017). The Energy Efficiency and Conservation Project Promotion Financing Program—a JICA-funded project—provides soft loans to factories that can promote EEC through IDCOL and the Bangladesh Infrastructure Finance Fund Limited. JICA provides a concessional loan to the Government of Bangladesh at 0.1% and the eligible companies receive the amount as loans under the JICA-funded project at an interest rate of 4%. The Government of Japan has extended a loan of Tk8.57 billion million (about $101 million in July 2020) to the Government of Bangladesh to promote energy efficiency in the country (The Independent 2017).

Nepal. The Financing Energy Efficiency Programme Nepal provides grants up to 39% for implementation of energy efficiency measures in industries in the country (Adelphi n.d.). The grant is disbursed by Rastriya Banijya Bank Limited on the basis of a financing agreement with the German development bank KfW. The size of the grant depends on industry size, possession of an ISO certificate, and route of application.

India. As mentioned earlier, the Partial Risk Guarantee Fund for Energy Efficiency and the Venture Capital Fund for Energy Efficiency operate under the BEE in India. There are several other financing schemes on energy efficiency in the country, such as the financing schemes of Indian Renewable Energy Development Agency Limited (IREDA 2018), Clean Technology Fund (CTF n.d.), and the Japanese ODA Loan Project (Onishi 2013).

In 2012, ADB collaborated with ICICI Bank to provide a $100 million credit line deal for renewable energy and EEC projects for small- and medium-sized industries in India. The credit line aimed to catalyze financing of renewable energy and EEC projects by more local banks. Specifically, the credit line was aimed to enhance energy efficiency in co-generation and waste-heat recovery; replacement of inefficient motors, pumps, and fans in industry; as well as manufacturing and deployment of CFLs or LED lights (ADB 2012).

The Energy Conservation Act 2001 requires the state governments in India to establish a State Energy Conservation Fund for the promotion of EEC, which is managed by the State Designated Agencies. In India, 28 states have constituted these funds, of which 24 have also provided matching contributions (BEE 2015g).

Sri Lanka. In 2016, the Commercial Bank of Ceylon launched Green Development Loans. The objective of this scheme was to make business operations eco-friendlier in Sri Lanka (The Island 2016). Green Development Loans are available for the following:

- Projects that aim to reduce a minimum of 10% energy consumption over current usage
- Projects with directly identifiable expenses relating to energy reducing measures, for example, solar power and solar net metering systems
- LED lighting arrangements or specialized units designed for EEC, and expenditure related to upgrading of waste management systems

Sri Lanka drafted the Energy Conservation Fund Act in 1985. However, this act was repealed by the Sri Lanka Sustainable Energy Authority Act, 2007. The Energy Conservation Fund was created within the Ministry of Irrigation and Power to bridge the funding gaps in implementing EEC projects. The main objective of the fund was to finance, stimulate, and initiate tasks and projects for the enhancement of energy demand management and conservation programs in the country (Wickramasinghe 2010). The Energy Conservation Fund executed several initiatives, such as variable-speed drives in tea withering, micro hydro-powered community electrification, and inclusion of energy conservation as a subject in school curricula (Wickramasinghe 2010). Other key financing programs include JICA-supported loan schemes E-Friends I implemented in 1998 and E-Friends II implemented in 2004. These programs offered very low interest rates of 6.5%–8.5%. They covered more than 16 energy savings projects, mostly in the plantation sector (Wickramasinghe 2010).

Establishment of Energy Management System

Sri Lanka introduced an energy management system in the aftermath of the oil crisis in the 1980s, which severely affected the Sri Lankan economy. The Sri Lanka Energy Managers Association was established in 1984 to carry out EEC project activities (Wickramasinghe 2010). The SLSEA currently facilitates EEC in the industry sector through the introduction of the ISO50001 Energy Management System. According to MoPRE (2017), more than 200 energy managers in the private sector and around 16 energy auditors were accredited, and around 150 energy management officers were appointed in the public sector.

Other Policies and Programs

Energy Efficiency Programs on Agricultural Pumps in India
The Agriculture Demand-side Management scheme of BEE was started in India with an objective of reducing the energy intensity of agricultural water pumping by replacing old inefficient pumps with star-labeled energy efficient pumps. This scheme was initiated during the ninth plan in 11 distribution companies of selected eight[19] agriculture intensive states (BEE 2015a).

---

[19] Maharashtra, Haryana, Punjab, Rajasthan, Gujarat, Andhra Pradesh, Madhya Pradesh, and Karnataka.

The State of Haryana implemented a scheme on energy conservation in the agriculture sector. This scheme provides subsidies on pump sets with energy efficiency rated at four stars and above. Under this scheme, all farmers of Haryana who are installing new tube well connection or upgrading pump sets with a higher capacity are encouraged to install at least four-star rated (BEE Star rating) pump sets and would be eligible for the state subsidy. Farmers, who own older non-ISI[20] motors and want to replace them with at least four-star rated motors, would also be eligible under this scheme (IREEED 2015).

Training Program on Efficient Use of Energy in Sri Lankan Tea Industries

Sri Lanka has launched a program on efficient use of energy in tea industries. More than 300 factory officers in tea industries were trained for a week on improved utilization of energy in manufacturing. The program covered 14% of the entire tea-manufacturing sector. The program was attributed with reducing energy consumption by around 15% in some cases (Wickramasinghe 20010).

Tax and Subsidies on Electric and Hybrid Vehicles

There are tax and subsidy policies favoring electric and hybrid vehicles in the five South Asian countries under this study. The following gives the country-specific highlights of the policies.

Bangladesh. Bangladesh has been promoting hybrid vehicles by providing substantial tax incentives.[21] The government also provides various tax exemptions for electric vehicles (electric two-wheelers, light duty vehicles, and heavy-duty vehicles) (IDCOL 2019). In 2018, the Bangladesh Road Transport Authority drafted guidelines on electric vehicles making registration, fitness certificates, and tax tokens mandatory (Bdnews24 2019).

Bhutan. The Bhutan Sustainable Low-Emission Urban Transport System project, which received a grant of $2.6 million by the Global Environment Facility Trust Fund, was initiated in 2019 to facilitate low-carbon transition in the country's urban transport sector by fostering the growth of low-emission vehicles, particularly electric vehicles (GEF 2019). The project offers incentives to taxi drivers switching to electric vehicles and tax waivers to the general population who switch to electric vehicles. Furthermore, Bhutan has increased the loan–to–value ratio for electric vehicles from the existing 30% to 50% (Business Bhutan 2019).

India: In India, the Department of Heavy Industry implemented the Faster Adoption and Manufacturing of (Hybrid &) Electric Vehicles (FAME) scheme in April 2015 to promote the manufacturing of electric vehicles and to maintain their sustainable growth. It is a part of the National Electric Mobility Mission Plan launched in 2015. This scheme pushed penetration of electric vehicles in public transportation by creating a market and by aggregating demand as well as by enabling their large-scale purchase. Phase I of this scheme provided incentives to electric scooters, three-wheelers, electric cars, hybrid cars, and electric buses in the form of upfront reduction in purchase price. Phase I lasted until 31 March 2019, which saw 278,000 electric vehicles[22] supported by the scheme; in addition 465 buses were also sanctioned to various cities and states (PIB 2018b). Furthermore, the FAME scheme envisages a holistic growth of the electric vehicle sector. The focus areas of the FAME scheme also include development of charging infrastructure, technology development, demand creation, and pilot projects (PIB 2018b). As such, in Phase I of FAME, grants were also sanctioned for specific projects under pilot projects, R&D or technology development, and public charging infrastructure. Phase II of the FAME scheme was made official in March 2019; it is planned to be implemented over a period of 3 years. Phase I utilized approximately Rs5.29 billion (about $70 million in July 2020) (PIB 2018b) and Phase II is expected to have a fund requirement of approximately Rs100 billion (about $1.3 billion in July 2020) (DHI 2019).

---

[20] ISI mark is a mark for industrial products in India, which certifies that a product conforms to the Indian Standard.
[21] Duty on the import of hybrid cars varies, starting from 25% and going up to 60%.
[22] Electric and hybrid vehicles.

Nepal. The Government of Nepal has significantly reduced customs duty on electric vehicles to 1% for public vehicles and 10% for private vehicles. The government has also exempted the road tax on electric vehicles. Furthermore, lending regulations have been amended to support growth of electric vehicles; for example their loan-to-value ratio has been increased to 80% compared to 60% for fossil fuel-based vehicles (GGGI 2018). However, Nepal does not yet have any subsidy or other government incentives to promote electric vehicles.

Sri Lanka. Sri Lanka has increased the loan–to–value ratio on electric vehicles to promote the use of vehicles powered by non fossil fuels. The loan–to–value ratio is up to 90% for electric vehicles, and is 70% for hybrid cars (MoF 2018).

Training Programs for Energy Auditors

In India, the Energy Conservation Act 2001 mandates energy audit of designated consumers by accredited energy auditors. The auditors also play a major role in the PAT scheme. The BEE carries out the accreditation of energy auditors and designs training modules and national level examination required for the certification process. Up to now, 596 energy auditors have been certified (BEE 2020b).

The first program for energy auditor training in Sri Lanka was as early as 1984. By 2010, 300 energy sector professionals were trained. The creation of the Sri Lanka Energy Managers Association, a strong network of energy professionals for the promotion of energy efficiency and rational use of energy, was also associated with this program (Wickramasinghe 2010; SLEMA 2017). The Sustainable Energy Authority Act No. 35 of 2007 in Sri Lanka, stipulates an accreditation scheme for energy managers and energy auditors. It specifies the minimum qualification and requirements for accreditation of energy managers and auditors such as periodic examination requirements and training required (PDSRSL 2007).

In Nepal, the Energy Efficiency Centre provides training courses on EEC that are closely modeled on those of the BEE, India. The center basically provides two types of courses: energy auditor and energy manager training courses. The first provides skills and expertise on energy auditing in industry, the second is designed to provide professional knowledge on energy management and energy efficiency in the industry (EEC 2016).

Energy Efficiency Improvement in Nationally Determined Contributions of South Asian Countries

All of the South Asian countries have mentioned energy efficiency as a part of their respective nationally determined contributions (NDCs) under the Paris Agreement on Climate Change in 2015. Bangladesh and India pledged to focus on the power sector and upgrade coal power plants to supercritical technology. Bangladesh, Bhutan, India, and Sri Lanka have included industrial energy-efficiency improvement as an element of their NDCs. The major focus of all South Asian countries is the transport sector, particularly electric mobility. Each South Asian country has shown interest in promoting electric vehicles and changing the mode of transportation. In the residential sector, both Bangladesh and Nepal have plans to promote improved cook stoves to achieve efficient use of energy.

Details of measures on energy efficiency as stated in NDCs of South Asian countries are presented in Appendix 6.

8 Regional Cooperation on Energy Efficiency and Energy Conservation

One form of regional cooperation on energy could be the opening up of the market for providers of energy services or commodities across the countries in the region. However, regional cooperation does not need to be limited to provision of energy commodities or services. Exchange of knowledge can be another form of regional cooperation in that member states that have significantly advanced know-how and experience can share those who lack them. There is huge potential for such cooperation in South Asia. However, not much has been achieved except for a few bilateral electricity trade agreements between India and neighboring countries. This chapter begins with a brief description of status of regional cooperation in energy. It is then followed by identification of potential areas for future regional collaboration.

8.1 Status of Regional Cooperation on Energy in South Asia

Existing Arrangements for Regional Cooperation

The Bay of Bengal Initiative for Multi-Sectoral Technical and Economic Cooperation

The Bay of Bengal Initiative for Multi-Sectoral Technical and Economic Cooperation (BIMSTEC) is a regional organization consisting of Bangladesh, Bhutan, India, Nepal, Sri Lanka, Myanmar, and Thailand, which was institutionalized through the Bangkok Declaration on 6 June 1997 (BIMSTEC 2019a). This collaboration is aimed at bridging the gap between South Asian and South East Asian economies. It was established as a platform for intra-regional cooperation between the Association of Southeast Asian Nations and the South Asian Association for Regional Cooperation (SAARC) members.

The energy sector was identified as a priority area for regional cooperation by the organization, and a BIMSTEC Grid Interconnection Program is envisioned. Through this program, it is planned to expand trading of energy among the member states and accelerate the development of new hydropower projects, natural gas grids, and renewable energy projects. In relation to energy efficiency, sharing of expertise, experience, knowledge, and information on energy-efficiency programs has been identified as a BIMSTEC key thrust area (BIMSTEC 2019).

South Asian Association for Regional Cooperation

There are eight SAARC member states: Afghanistan, Bangladesh, Bhutan, India, Maldives, Nepal, Pakistan, and Sri Lanka. It was formed with the signing of the SAARC Charter in Dhaka on 8 December 1985 (SAARC 2018a). The energy sector is one area of cooperation; the initiative on energy cooperation began in January 2000 with the formation of a Technical Committee on Energy. In January 2004, a specialized Working Group on Energy was formed. This group consists of expert groups on oil and gas, electricity, renewable energy, and technology and knowledge sharing (including energy efficiency and coal). The group has met eight times since its formation (SAARC 2018b).

A big step in achieving energy cooperation in South Asia was the SAARC Framework Agreement for Regional Energy Cooperation, which was signed in 2014.[23] One of the highlights of the agreement is the promotion of energy efficiency in the region. For scaling up of cooperation in energy efficiency, Article 12 of the agreement authorizes member states to enable and stimulate knowledge sharing and joint research in the domain of energy efficiency.

Intra-Regional Cooperation

Cross-border trading of electricity exists in the region; however, it is not significant when compared with its potential. India shares most of the trade volume and the existing arrangements are based on government-to-government agreements for simple bilateral electricity trading (Dhakal et al. 2019). India has arrangements for bilateral trading of electricity with Bangladesh, Bhutan and Nepal. However, few initiatives have been taken recently to realize a multilateral mode of power trading in the region. In 2018, Nepal and Bangladesh signed a memorandum of understanding to explore the possibility of electricity trade between the two countries (The Kathmandu Post 2018). However, if such trade is to materialize, there has to be a trilateral agreement among Bangladesh, India and Nepal to use the power transmission network of India. Although the earlier version of guidelines on electricity trading issued by the Ministry of Power, in 2016 failed to envision such trilateral agreements (MoP 2016), the recently amended guidelines has made some provisions to allow for trilateral trade after signing the agreement and getting due approvals from relevant entities (MoP 2018).

Existing Institutions for Cooperation in Energy Efficiency

South Asian Association for Regional Cooperation Energy Centre

The SAARC Energy Centre was created as a special purpose vehicle to boost energy cooperation in South Asia in 2005. It is a regional institution formed to provide a platform for experts, officials, nongovernment organizations, and academia to realize the potential of regional energy cooperation (SEC 2020).

South Asia Regional Initiative for Energy

The South Asia Regional Initiative for Energy (SARI/E) is funded by the US Agency for International Development to strengthen energy security in South Asia. Energy-efficiency standard and labeling (S&L) for appliances is one of the four building blocks of SARI/E. During the initial phases, a team of experts from the US, India, and Sri Lanka was involved in coordinating S&L programs in the region. The focus of the S&L activities was on alignment of technical specifications of participating countries with each other for certification of energy efficiency for widely used devices (Mcneil & Berkeley, n.d.).[24]

---

[23] Government of Nepal, MoEWRI. 2014. SAARC Framework Agreement on Energy Cooperation (Electricity) https://www.moewri.gov.np/storage/listies/May2020/saarc-framework-agreement.pdf.

[24] Alignment can be of multiple forms: one form can be the use of technically equivalent testing procedures to define device efficiency by participating countries; another can be setting the same definitions on standards, labels, or minimum requirements of device categories.

ADB's South Asia Subregional Economic Cooperation Program

The South Asia Subregional Economic Cooperation (SASEC) program—member countries being Bangladesh, Bhutan, India, Maldives, Myanmar, Nepal, and Sri Lanka—was created to promote regional prosperity, improve economic opportunities, and enhance the quality of life of people (SASEC 2019). ADB supports the SASEC program mainly through the following:

- Institutional strengthening and capacity building activities
- Funding projects and technical assistance
- Initiatives on regional cooperation

ADB Efforts to Assist SASEC Members to Improve EEC

In October 2011, during the Energy Working Group Meeting of SASEC held in Bangkok, a list of programs was endorsed by the stakeholders for regional cooperation on energy. More importantly, the stakeholders requested ADB for technical assistance to promote energy-efficiency practices, and sharing of best practice, experience, and expertise. In response, ADB provided technical assistance under the SASEC Subregional Energy Efficiency Initiative to develop a regional energy-efficiency database of barriers, energy-efficiency policies, potential investments, and technology available locally. Another output of this initiative was a technical report with road map and action plan for harmonizing energy-efficiency S&L, measurement, verification protocols, and energy-efficiency indicator benchmarking (SASEC 2011). A SASEC Energy Working Group Meeting held in Thimpu in 2012 endorsed the road map for Energy Efficiency in SASEC; the road map proposed implementation of phase-wise interventions by ADB. One short-term action plan recommended in the road map was to support EEC policy and reforms. In response, ADB provided technical assistance[25] for the preparation of energy-efficiency policies and guidelines for Bhutan and Nepal (ADB 2015).

Other Key Bilateral Activities Supported by ADB for SASEC Members

In November 2019, ADB approved a loan of $250 million to Energy Efficiency Services Limited (EESL), a government-owned energy service company (ESCO), to increase energy-efficiency investment in India. EESL leverages the loan to fund emerging energy-efficiency opportunities, which were not the focus of traditional ESCO investments, such as smart electricity meters, distributed solar photovoltaic systems, and electric vehicle programs. Also, the project targets raising awareness of energy-efficient technologies among stakeholders. Local organizations are to be engaged in knowledge-sharing and training, and women electricity consumers were to be a special focus (ADB 2019a). ADB previously approved a loan to EESL in September 2016 for the Demand-side Energy Efficiency Sector Project. The loan covered high priority areas under EESL's ESCO business, such as growth in use of more efficient LEDs for municipal street lighting equipped with remote operating technology, more efficient domestic lighting through replacement of incandescent lamps with LEDs, and higher energy-efficiency agricultural water pumps. Another activity of the project was to demonstrate the scalability of the ESCO model for realizing further energy savings in India (ADB 2016).

In Bangladesh, an ADB project was approved in 2011 to support a program to improve demand-side energy efficiency in industry.[26] ADB provided assistance under two components: (i) a $30 million loan facility to be disbursed to participating finance institutions for them to lend to eligible industrial energy-efficiency projects, and (ii) a technical assistance program to identify bankable energy-efficiency projects in target industries

---

[25] The technical assistance project was the Preparation of Energy Efficiency Policies and Guidelines for Bhutan and Nepal.

[26] ADB. Bangladesh: Industrial Energy Efficiency Finance Program. https://www.adb.org/projects/45916-012/main.

(textiles, steel, cement, ceramics, chemicals, and agro-industries). The technical assistance program also contributed to growth in expertise among financiers of the projects and technical solution providers (ADB 2011).

In Sri Lanka, a project preparatory technical assistance[27] for the Green Power Development and Energy Efficiency Improvement Investment Program[28] was funded by ADB. The aim of the program was to help decrease the technical and commercial losses of electricity networks. The project preparatory technical assistance identified investment needs to support the program. The program was completed in 2014 (ADB 2013).

In Nepal, ADB provided a loan for the Energy Access and Efficiency Improvement Project aimed to increase energy access, increase energy efficiency, and promote renewable energy and capacity building. Besides construction of transmission and distribution infrastructure, the other outcomes of the project relate to EEC improvement and include energy-efficiency improvement with capacitor banks and countrywide delivery of CFLs (ADB 2019b).

8.2 Possible Areas for Regional Cooperation in Energy Efficiency

This section points out key areas in which there are possibilities for regional cooperation among South Asian countries for enhancing energy efficiency. The potential areas of regional collaboration include exchange of know-how, sharing of experience, capacity building, regional funding mechanism, research, and development among the participating nations.

Standard and Labeling Program

Harmonization of the S&L program is characterized by the application of the same testing process, mutual recognition of test results, and setting the same performance standard level and labeling criteria for appliances. Such measures have been taken in several regional groups such as Asia-Pacific Economic Cooperation, the Pan American Standards Commission, the Association of Southeast Asian Nations, and the North American Energy Working Group, and even in the South Asia region (Weil and McMahon 2005).

As stated earlier, the idea of aligning energy-efficiency regulations and standards is not new to the region. The SARI/E initiated the alignment of S&L programs in the region in early 2000. It focused on harmonization of technical specifications for certification of energy-efficiency related to most commonly-used appliances. The program even aimed to evaluate the advantages of establishing regional testing facilities (Mcneil and Berkeley n.d.).

Harmonization of the S&L program can also lead to significant cost savings. If an exporting country's testing protocol differs from that of an importing one, multiple testing protocols would have to be performed. Even more, in the worst case, an entire new testing facility may be required. Such additional expenditure may even act as a barrier to export products. Regionally recognized standards following the same protocols would prevent such additional investment and time consumed in the process.

---

[27] ADB. Sri Lanka: Green Power Development and Energy Efficiency Improvement Investment Program. https://www.adb.org/projects/47037-002/main.

[28] ADB. Sri Lanka: Green Power Development and Energy Efficiency Improvement Investment Program. https://www.adb.org/projects/47037-003/main.

Bangladesh has explicitly stated in its master plan that it will join the harmonization movement and prepare its S&L program by analyzing neighboring countries and global trends (SREDA 2015). Following Bangladesh's footsteps, other countries could also examine the prospect for S&L harmonization.

There are, however, some challenges to the harmonization of S&L across the region:

- With the exception of India, which has well-developed domestic appliance manufacturing sector, other countries in the region have relied on imports of such appliances. So, drafting a common standard or label applicable for the entire region may be a challenging task.

- Harmonization and coordination are required between relevant agencies involved in S&L programs of participating countries, which may not be an easy task.

- Appropriate institutions, laboratory with adequate facilities, and sufficient skilled human resource capacity are needed to execute the program. They may not be available in some of the countries.

- Continual funding will be required either from the governments or international funding agencies.

- For effective regional collaboration on S&L, all participating governments should politically and economically prioritize the program.

Building Energy Code

Among the South Asian countries, India has successfully implemented its building code in numerous states, with more states to implement the code in future. It even has voluntary schemes in operation such as BEE's building labeling program, Green Rating for Integrated Habitat Assessment rating, and Leadership in Energy and Environmental Design certification. Sri Lanka is now revising its old building code to accommodate new technologies and modern requirements. Similarly, Bangladesh is also working on its national building codes.

Unlike the case of appliances and devices, for which harmonization and alignment of codes and standards is possible, building energy codes can be unique to each country and so alignment of codes may be impractical. However, experience and knowledge gained by other countries in designing, testing, and implementation could be valuable for those countries trying to develop their own national building code. Establishing a regional knowledge-sharing platform could expedite the process and also save additional investment on research and development (R&D).

Bulk Procurement and Distribution of Energy-Efficient Appliances

India's Unnat Jyoti by Affordable LEDs for All scheme for LED lamps was based on an innovative approach taken by EESL regarding bulk procurement of lamps and their effective distribution. The approach drove down LED lamp prices in India well below the market price and made LED lamps ubiquitous. This approach was also replicated for energy-efficient tube lamps and fans. Adoption of similar schemes by other countries would need know-how on institutional setups as well as their roles, appropriate country-specific financing schemes, and other protocols.

Regional Operation of Energy Service Companies

ESCOs are specialized in the development and implementation of energy-efficiency projects. Some ESCOs can also finance the project costs and their clients (i.e., the enterprises, who are the ESCO clients) pay the ESCOs back over time using their energy cost savings. The ESCOs prepare energy-saving performance contracts for an EEC project and bear most of the risk. If the projected energy savings are not realized, ESCOs may bear a loss in their revenue. Thus, ESCOs can play a major role in the promotion of energy efficiency by offering business solutions for potential EEC investments and taking the performance risk associated with energy efficiency programs. At present, services provided by these entities are limited to their parent countries. Expansion of services of experienced and advanced ESCOs would help in the exchange of the latest knowledge on energy-efficiency measures and technologies to potential customers in other countries. Cross-country operation of major ESCOs operating in a South Asian country could be a kind of regional cooperation. However, amendment of acts and regulations may be needed to allow an ESCO based in one country to provide its services in another.

Regional Fund on Energy Efficiency

Improvement of energy efficiency requires additional investment. The high initial cost is considered a barrier to adoption of energy-efficient devices. Lack of funds to finance energy-efficient technologies poses an additional challenge in promoting EEC in many South Asian countries. Regional funds with an objective to invest in EEC projects could bridge investment-related gaps in the South Asia region.

There can be opportunities for a regional fund to attract financing from existing global funds that have a policy to promote EEC. The Global Energy Efficiency and Renewable Energy Fund (GEEREF) was launched in 2008, funded by the European Union and Norway (GEEREF 2018). The GEEREF is a global public–private partnership that invests in private equity funds, which would in turn invest in special renewable energy and EEC projects in emerging and developing economies (EIB 2016). By the end of 2018, GEEREF had invested in 13 funds spanning Asia, Africa, Latin America, and the Caribbean (GEEREF 2018). Similarly, in Europe, the European Energy Efficiency Fund facilitates investments in public sectors, especially those hindered by budgetary restrictions (EEEF 2019).

Another important strategy may be linking of regional funds with climate funds such as the Green Climate Fund and the Climate Investment Fund. Further access to climate funds could channelize additional investments. The Green Climate Fund has funded numerous projects, which are diverse in nature and are related to energy efficiency, such as the following:

- Providing loan to energy-efficient heating appliances and housing products in Mongolia (GCF 2018d)
- Scaling up energy-efficiency investment in Vietnam to reduce energy intensity (GCF 2018c)
- Generating enabling environment for energy-efficiency investments by small and medium enterprises (GCF 2018a)
- Promoting risk mitigation instruments and finance for renewable energy and energy-efficiency investments (GCF 2018b)

Financing Institutions

India has institutionalized a number of agencies and launched several key programs with the important task of financing EEC projects. For example, the Energy Efficiency Financing Platform was launched to provide a platform for finance institutions and project developers to interact for the implementation of projects (BEE 2015a). The platform was initiated with the following objectives:

- ensure availability of finance at reasonable rates for energy-efficiency projects
- create demand for energy-efficiency products and services
- promote ESCO companies and performance-based contracting
- conduct capacity building of banks and financing institutions
- help establish credible monitoring and verification protocols to confirm energy savings

Also, the Partial Risk Guarantee Fund for Energy Efficiency in India provides risk-sharing facilities to lenders (BEE 2017). The Venture Capital Fund for Energy Efficiency was created to provide last-mile equity support for EEC projects (BEE 2015b). Establishing similar institutions is imperative for the energy-efficiency market to grow in the region. The experience and know-how gained by Indian energy-efficiency funding entities could be a valuable basis for neighboring countries in establishing similar financing institutions. Exchanging the know-how and experience gained from such success stories in a regional platform could assist and expedite energy-efficiency financing programs at the regional level.

Perform Achieve Trade Scheme

The experience and know-how gained by India through successful implementation of its Perform Achieve Trade (PAT) scheme could be valuable for other countries, who are considering implementing similar schemes. Extensive research and expertise would be required to implement a scheme like PAT. They would be needed for activities such as determining baseline specific energy consumption, setting fair energy reduction targets for diverse participating entities, setting up trading platforms, and imposing penalties (Garnaik 2014). Collaborations in the form of customized training programs, regional workshops, and peer exchanges could prove useful in developing necessary capacity in other countries.

Collaboration in Research and Development on Energy Efficiency and Formation of a Regional Center

A dedicated regional organization that could provide advice on strategies, identify appropriate technologies, and enhance national capacities in regard to energy efficiency could significantly help in promoting energy efficiency in the South Asian countries. Such an organization could also serve as a regional platform for R&D on energy efficiency and for sharing knowledge and technology data. Also, such an organization could play a meaningful role concerning harmonization of policy and regulations such as the S&L program.

An example of such a regional center elsewhere is the Southern Africa Development Community Centre for Renewable Energy and Energy Efficiency in Southern Africa; its objectives include introduction of best-practices, provision of technical know-how, mobilizing investment, and building institutional frameworks on renewable energy and energy-efficiency measures (SACREEE 2018). Another example is the Regional Centre for Renewable Energy and Energy Efficiency (RCREEE), which was also established to diffuse cost-effective renewable energy and energy-efficiency polices, strategies, and technologies in the Arab region (RCREEE 2019).

South Asian countries could also benefit from the establishment of a regional center for enhancing their energy efficiency. Such a center could help to establish a sustainable energy-efficiency market and to gain access to EEC expertise in the region. It could be a primary go-to organization for facilitation of funding as well and act as an advisory platform on technical matters pertaining to EEC. Such a regional institution could also help improve the legal and regulatory framework of South Asian countries, ensure coherence of EEC policies, and facilitate in the harmonization of activities related to EEC. Even international best-practices on EEC could be promoted in the region through such a center.

Appendixes

1 Factor Decomposition Model to Analyze the Effects of Factors Behind a Change in Energy Consumption of Different Productive Sectors of Economy

Let,

E_{ij}	=	Consumption of fuel type i by sector j
E_i	=	Total energy consumption by sector j
Y_j	=	Value added by sector j ("sectoral GDP" of sector j)
Y	=	Total GDP
S_j	=	Share of sector j in GDP
I_j	=	Energy intensity of sector j
M_{ij}	=	Share of fuel type i in the energy consumption of sector j

Total consumption of energy in the productive sector of economy can be expressed as:

E = Sum of energy consumption by fuel type for all productive sectors

$$= \sum_{j} E_{ij}$$

$$= \sum_{j} \sum_{i} Y \cdot \frac{Y_j}{Y} \cdot \frac{E_j}{Y_j} \cdot \frac{E_{ij}}{E_j} \tag{A1.1}$$

$$= \sum_{j} \sum_{i} Y \cdot S_j \cdot I_j \cdot M_{ij} \tag{A1.2}$$

$$= \sum_{j} \sum_{i} \begin{pmatrix} Total \\ activity \end{pmatrix} \times \begin{pmatrix} Share\ of \\ sector\ j \\ in\ GDP \end{pmatrix} \times \begin{pmatrix} Energy \\ intensity\ of \\ sector\ j \end{pmatrix} \times \begin{pmatrix} Share\ of\ fuel \\ type\ i\ in\ energy \\ consumption \\ of\ sector\ j \end{pmatrix}$$

Based on Equation (A1.2), the change in total energy consumption from year 0 to year T can be decomposed into changes due to four factors: i.e., change in total output, change in output share of a sector, change in energy intensity of a sector, and change in consumption of fuel type i in sector j.

That is, a change in total energy consumption from year 0 to year T (ΔE_{Total}) can be expressed as:

$$\Delta E_{Total} = E^T - E \tag{A1.3}$$

$$= \Delta E_{Activity} + \Delta E_{Structure} + \Delta E_{Intensity} + \Delta E_{Fuelmix} \tag{A1.4}$$

where,

$\Delta E_{Activity}$ = Effect due to changes in total output (activity effect)

$\Delta E_{Structure}$ = Effect due to changes in output share of a sector (structural effect)

$\Delta E_{Intensity}$ = Effect due to changes in energy intensity of a sector (energy intensity effect)

$\Delta E_{Fuelmix}$ = Effect due to changes in consumption of fuel type in a sector (fuel mix effect)

Following Ang (2006) and Shrestha et al. (2009), the above effects are expressed as:

$$\Delta E_{Activity} = \widetilde{w}_{total} \ln \frac{Y^T}{Y^0} \tag{A1.5}$$

$$\Delta E_{Structure} = \sum_j \widetilde{w}_j \ln \frac{S_j^T}{S_j^0} \tag{A1.6}$$

$$\Delta E_{Intensity} = \sum_j \widetilde{w}_j \ln \frac{I_j^T}{I_j^0} \tag{A1.7}$$

$$\Delta E_{Fuelmix} = \sum_j \sum_i \widetilde{w}_{ij} \ln \frac{M_{ij}^T}{M_{ij}^0} \tag{A1.8}$$

where,

$$\widetilde{w}_{ij} = \frac{E_{ij}^T - E_{ij}^0}{\ln E_{ij}^T - \ln E_{ij}^0} \tag{A1.9}$$

$$\widetilde{w}_j = \sum_j \widetilde{w}_{ij}$$

$$\widetilde{w}_{total} = \sum_j \widetilde{w}_j \tag{A1.10}$$

2 Factor Decomposition Model to Analyze the Effects of Factors Behind a Change in Energy Consumption of Power Sector

Let,

E_i =   Total energy consumption for power generation based on fuel type i

G_i =   Generation of electricity based on fuel type i

G =   Total generation of electricity

C =   Total demand for electricity

C' =   Total demand of electricity net of "imported electricity" and including "own use of electricity by power plants"

S_i =   Share of generation based on fuel type i in total generation

T&D   =   Transmission and distribution efficiency

FI_i =   Electricity generation efficiency of generation based on fuel type i

Total consumption of energy in the sector can be expressed as:

E =   Sum of energy consumption of all subsectors

$$= \sum_i E_i$$

$$= \sum_i C' \cdot \frac{G}{C'} \cdot \frac{G_i}{G} \cdot \frac{E_i}{G_i} \tag{A2.1}$$

$$= \sum_i C' \cdot TnD.S_i \cdot FI_i \tag{A2.2}$$

$$= \sum_i \left(\begin{array}{c} \text{Total final} \\ \text{electricity} \\ \text{consumption} \\ \text{met} \\ \text{by domestic} \\ \text{generation} \end{array} \right) \times \left(\begin{array}{c} \text{Transmission} \\ \text{and} \\ \text{distribrition} \\ \text{efficeincy} \end{array} \right) \times \left(\begin{array}{c} \text{Fuel mix} \\ \text{of} \\ \text{fuel } i \end{array} \right) \times \left(\begin{array}{c} \text{Electricity} \\ \text{generation} \\ \text{efficiency} \\ \text{by fuel } i \end{array} \right)$$

Based on Equation (A2.2), the change in total energy consumption from year 0 to year T can be decomposed into changes in four factors: final electricity consumption, transmission and distribution efficiency, fuel mix, and electricity generation efficiency of a power plant.

That is, a change in total energy consumption from year 0 to year T (ΔE_{Total}) can be expressed as:

$$\Delta E_{total} = E^T - E \tag{A2.3}$$

$$= \Delta E_{Output} + \Delta E_{TnD} + \Delta E_{Structure} + \Delta E_{Intensity} \tag{A2.4}$$

where,

ΔE_{Output} = Effect due to changes in total final electricity consumption (final electricity consumption effect)

ΔE_{TnD} = Effect due to changes in transmission and distribution efficiency (transmission and distribution efficiency effect)

$\Delta E_{Structure}$ = Effect due to changes in the fuel mix (fuel mix effect)

$\Delta E_{Intensity}$ = Effect due to changes in the electricity generation efficiency (electricity generation efficiency effect)

Following Ang (2006) and Shrestha et al. (2009), the above effects are expressed as:

$$\Delta E_{Output} = \tilde{w}_{total} \ln \frac{C'^T}{C'^0} \tag{A2.5}$$

$$\Delta E_{TnD} = \tilde{w}_{total} \ln \frac{TnD^T}{TnD^0} \tag{A2.6}$$

$$\Delta E_{Structure} = \sum_j \tilde{w}_i \ln \frac{S_i^T}{S_i^0} \tag{A2.7}$$

$$\Delta E_{Intensity} = \sum_j \tilde{w}_i \ln \frac{Fli_i^T}{Fl_i^0} \tag{A2.8}$$

where,

$$\tilde{w}_i = \frac{E_i^T - E_i^0}{\ln E_i^T - \ln E_i^0} \tag{A2.9}$$

$$\tilde{w}_{total} = \sum_i \tilde{w}_i \tag{A2.10}$$

3 Classification of Sectors, Subsectors, and Services in AIM/Enduse Models

Table A3: Classification of Sectors, Sub-sectors, and Services

Sector and Final Service	Service Unit	Bangladesh	Bhutan	Nepal	Sri Lanka
Agriculture					
Irrigation (Pump)	toe	✓	✓	✓	✓
Threshing (Thresher)	toe	✓	✓	✓	✓
Harvesting (Tractor)	1,000 units	✓	✓	✓	✓
Transportation—Road passenger					
Taxi	10^6 passenger kilometers	✓	✓	✓	✓
Van and pickup	10^6 passenger kilometers	✓	✓	✓	✓
Bus	10^6 passenger kilometers	✓	✓	✓	✓
Passenger car	10^6 passenger kilometers	✓	✓	✓	✓
Micro bus and pickup	10^6 passenger kilometers	✓	✓	✓	✓
Motorcycle	10^6 passenger kilometers	✓	✓	✓	✓
Motor tricycle	10^6 passenger kilometers	✓	✓	✓	✓
Transportation—Freight					
Pickup	10^6 ton kilometers	✓	✓	✓	✓
Truck	10^6 ton kilometers	✓	✓	✓	✓
Transportation—Rail					
Passenger	10^6 passenger kilometers	✓	✓	✓	✓
Freight	10^6 ton kilometers	✓	✓	✓	✓
Transportation—Air					
Air passenger	10^9 passenger kilometers			✓	
Transportation—Water					
Freight	10^9 ton kilometers	✓	✓	✓	✓
Residential—Urban					
Cooking	toe	✓	✓	✓	✓
Lighting	Billion lumen hours	✓	✓	✓	✓
Cooling (fan, air-conditioning)	1,000 units	✓	✓	✓	✓
Water heating	toe		✓	✓	
Refrigeration	1,000 units	✓	✓	✓	✓
Television	1,000 units	✓	✓	✓	✓
Ironing	1,000 units	✓	✓	✓	✓

Sector and Final Service	Service Unit	Bangladesh	Bhutan	Nepal	Sri Lanka
Other electrical appliances	1,000 units	✓	✓	✓	✓
Residential—Rural					
Cooking	toe	✓	✓	✓	✓
Lighting	Billion lumen hours	✓	✓	✓	✓
Cooling (fan)	1,000 units	✓	✓	✓	✓
Refrigeration	1,000 units	✓	✓	✓	✓
Water heating	toe		✓	✓	
Television	1,000 units	✓	✓	✓	✓
Ironing	1,000 units	✓	✓	✓	✓
Other electrical appliances	1,000 units	✓	✓	✓	✓
Commercial sector					
Cooking	toe				
Lighting	Billion lumen hours	✓	✓	✓	✓
Air conditioning	1,000 units	✓	✓	✓	✓
Refrigeration	toe	✓	✓	✓	✓
Thermal use	toe	✓	✓	✓	✓
Electricity, others (except refrigeration)	toe	✓	✓	✓	✓
Industry—Brick					
Brick	1,000 units	✓		✓	
Industry—Cement					
Ground limestone	1,000 tons	✓	✓	✓	✓
Clinker	1,000 tons	✓	✓	✓	✓
Cement	1000 tons	✓	✓	✓	✓
Industry—Alloy					
Alloy	1,000 tons		✓		
Industry—Silicon					
Silicon	1,000 tons		✓		
Industry—Carbide					
Carbide	1,000 tons		✓		
Industry—Chemical Fertilizer					
Chemical fertilizer	1,000 tons	✓			
Industry—Iron and Steel					
Rolled steel	1,000 tons	✓			
Final products	1,000 tons	✓		✓	
Industry—Textile					
Steam	toe	✓			✓
Yarn	1,000 tons	✓			✓

Sector and Final Service	Service Unit	Bangladesh	Bhutan	Nepal	Sri Lanka
Fabric	1,000 tons	✓			✓
Industry—Tea					
Sorted tea	tons				✓
Rolled tea	tons				✓
Dried tea	tons				✓
Industry—Rice Production					
Final product—rice	tons				✓
Industry—Water treatment and Supply					
Final product—water	Million cubic meters				✓
Industry—Garment					
Garment	Million meters	✓			✓
Industry—Motive Power					
Small size motor (<0.75 kW)	toe	✓	✓	✓	✓
Medium size motor (0.75 kW–375kW)	toe	✓	✓	✓	✓
Large size motor (375 kW)	toe	✓	✓	✓	✓
Industry—Process Heat					
Thermal heat	toe	✓	✓	✓	✓
Conversion and supply					
Electricity generation	toe	✓	✓	✓	✓
Electricity	toe	✓	✓	✓	✓

kW = kilowatt; toe = tons of oil equivalent.
Source: Authors.

4 Technologies in AIM/Enduse Models

Agriculture Sector

There are altogether 15 technologies in agriculture. In this study, the agriculture sector is not considered for Sri Lanka.

Table A4.1: Technologies in the Agriculture Sector

	End-use Device Options	Fuel Options	Service	Bangladesh	Bhutan	Nepal	Sri Lanka
1	Conventional tractor	Diesel	Tilling	✓	✓	✓	
2	Efficient tractor	Diesel	Tilling	✓	✓	✓	
3	Pump with standard motor	Electricity	Irrigation	✓	✓	✓	
4	Pump with efficient motor	Electricity	Irrigation	✓	✓	✓	
5	Pump with standard diesel engine	Diesel	Irrigation	✓	✓	✓	
6	Pump with efficient diesel engine	Diesel	Irrigation	✓	✓	✓	
7	Pump with standard gasoline engine	Gasoline	Irrigation	✓	✓	✓	
8	Pump with efficient gasoline engine	Gasoline	Irrigation	✓	✓	✓	
9	Solar pump	Solar	Irrigation	✓	✓	✓	
10	Thresher with standard motor	Electricity	Threshing	✓	✓	✓	
11	Thresher with efficient motor	Electricity	Threshing	✓	✓	✓	
12	Thresher with standard diesel engine	Diesel	Threshing	✓	✓	✓	
13	Thresher with efficient diesel engine	Diesel	Threshing	✓	✓	✓	
14	Thresher with standard gasoline engine	Gasoline	Threshing	✓	✓	✓	
15	Thresher with efficient gasoline engine	Gasoline	Threshing	✓	✓	✓	

Source: Authors.

Residential and Commercial Sector

There are altogether 38 technologies in the residential sector. Space heating and water heating in the residential sector are not considered in the case of Bangladesh and Sri Lanka. Natural gas-based technologies are considered only in the case of Bangladesh.

Table A4.2: Technologies in Residential and Commercial Sectors

	End-use Device Options	Fuel Options	Service	Bangladesh	Bhutan	Nepal	Sri Lanka
1	Traditional Cook Stove (TCS)	Biomass	Cooking	✓	✓	✓	✓
2	Improved Cook Stove (ICS)	Biomass		✓	✓	✓	✓
3	Advanced ICS (AICS)	Biomass		✓	✓	✓	✓
4	LPG Stove	LPG		✓	✓	✓	✓
5	Energy Efficient LPG Stove	LPG		✓	✓	✓	✓
6	Natural gas stove	Natural gas		✓			
7	Biogas stove	Biogas		✓	✓	✓	✓
8	Electric Stove	Electricity		✓	✓	✓	✓
9	Efficient Electric Stove	Electricity		✓	✓	✓	✓
10	Briquette stove	Briquette		✓	✓	✓	✓
11	Solar Cooker	Solar		✓	✓	✓	✓
12	Incandescent lamp	Electricity	Lighting	✓	✓	✓	✓
13	Compact fluorescent lamp	Electricity		✓	✓	✓	✓
14	Fluorescent tube lamp	Electricity		✓	✓	✓	✓
15	LED lamp	Electricity		✓	✓	✓	✓
16	Kerosene lamp	Kerosene			✓	✓	
17	Fan (Standard)	Electricity	Space cooling by fan[a]	✓	✓	✓	✓
18	Fan (Efficient)	Electricity		✓	✓	✓	✓
19	Air-Conditioner (AC) (SEER 13)	Electricity	Space cooling/ heating by AC[a]	✓	✓	✓	✓
20	Air-Conditioner (SEER 20.5)	Electricity		✓	✓	✓	✓
21	Air-Conditioner (SEER 25.6)	Electricity		✓	✓	✓	✓
22	Air-Conditioner (SEER 28.2)	Electricity		✓	✓	✓	✓
23	Electric heater	Electricity	Space heating[a]		✓	✓	
24	LPG heater	LPG			✓	✓	
25	Kerosene heater	Kerosene			✓	✓	
26	Biomass heater	Biomass			✓	✓	

	End-use Device Options	Fuel Options	Service	Bangladesh	Bhutan	Nepal	Sri Lanka
27	Electric water heater	Electricity	Water heating		✓	✓	
28	Biomass water heater	Biomass			✓	✓	
29	LPG Geyser	LPG			✓	✓	
30	Solar water heater	Solar			✓	✓	
31	Refrigerator (standard)	Electricity	Refrigeration	✓	✓	✓	✓
32	Refrigerator (energy efficient)	Electricity		✓	✓	✓	✓
33	Conventional TV	Electricity	Television	✓	✓	✓	✓
34	LCD TV	Electricity		✓	✓	✓	✓
35	LED TV	Electricity		✓	✓	✓	✓
36	Desktop computer	Electricity	Computer	✓	✓	✓	✓
37	Laptop computer	Electricity		✓	✓	✓	✓
38	Other electrical devices	Electricity	Electrical devices	✓	✓	✓	✓

LCD = liquid crystal display; LED = light emitting diode; LPG = liquefied petroleum gas; SEER = seasonal energy efficiency ratio.

[a] Fan and air-conditioner both provide space cooling services. A fan is a basic means of cooling. More advanced is the air-conditioner, which can reduce the temperature to give thermal comfort. Air-conditioners are also used for space heating. In this study, space cooling by fans and space cooling by air-conditioners are treated separately due to the differences in their services. The services are estimated based on the number of AC units. In space heating, the services by the use of air-conditioners are also treated separately into air-conditioner services.

Source: Authors.

Transport Sector

Table A4.3: Technologies in the Transport Sector

	End-use Device Options	Fuel Options	Bangladesh	Bhutan	Nepal	Sri Lanka
	Passenger Transport					
1	Diesel bus	Diesel	✓	✓	✓	✓
2	Electric bus	Electricity	✓	✓	✓	✓
3	Biofuel bus	B5, B10	✓	✓	✓	✓
4	Diesel-hybrid bus	Diesel	✓	✓	✓	✓
5	Fuel cell bus	Hydrogen	✓	✓	✓	✓
6	Trolley bus	Electricity	✓	✓	✓	✓
7	CNG bus	CNG	✓			
8	Diesel mini-bus	Diesel	✓	✓	✓	✓
9	Biofuel mini-bus	B5, B10	✓	✓	✓	✓
10	Electric mini-bus	Electricity	✓	✓	✓	✓
11	CNG mini-bus	CNG	✓			
12	Diesel micro-bus	Diesel	✓	✓	✓	✓

	End-use Device Options	Fuel Options	Bangladesh	Bhutan	Nepal	Sri Lanka
13	Biofuel micro-bus	B5, B10	✓	✓	✓	✓
14	LPG micro-bus	LPG	✓	✓	✓	✓
15	Electric micro-bus	Electricity	✓	✓	✓	✓
16	CNG micro-bus	CNG	✓			
17	Gasoline taxi	Gasoline	✓	✓	✓	✓
18	Gasohol taxi	E5, E10	✓	✓	✓	✓
19	Electric taxi	Electricity	✓	✓	✓	✓
20	Gasoline hybrid taxi	Gasoline	✓	✓	✓	✓
21	Fuel cell taxi	Hydrogen	✓	✓	✓	✓
22	CNG taxi	CNG	✓			
23	Diesel three-wheeler	Diesel	✓	✓	✓	✓
24	Gasoline three-wheeler	Gasoline	✓	✓	✓	✓
25	LPG three-wheeler	LPG	✓	✓	✓	✓
26	Natural gas three-wheeler	Natural gas	✓	✓	✓	✓
27	Electric three-wheeler	Electricity	✓	✓	✓	✓
28	CNG three-wheeler	CNG	✓			
29	Gasoline car	Gasoline	✓	✓	✓	✓
30	Diesel car	Diesel	✓	✓	✓	✓
31	Biodiesel car	B5, B10	✓	✓	✓	✓
32	Bioethanol car	E5, E10	✓	✓	✓	✓
33	Flexi-fuel car	E85	✓	✓	✓	✓
34	Electric car – short distance	Electricity	✓	✓	✓	✓
35	Electric car – long distance	Electricity	✓	✓	✓	✓
36	Gasoline hybrid car	Gasoline	✓	✓	✓	✓
37	Diesel hybrid car	Diesel	✓	✓	✓	✓
38	CNG car	CNG	✓			
39	Two-wheeler	Gasoline	✓	✓	✓	✓
40	Hybrid two-wheeler	Gasoline	✓	✓	✓	✓
41	Electric two-wheeler	Electricity	✓	✓	✓	✓
42	Passenger train	Diesel	✓	✓	✓	✓
43	Electric train	Electricity	✓	✓	✓	✓
44	Mass rapid transit	Electricity	✓	✓	✓	✓
	Freight transport					
45	Truck	Diesel	✓	✓	✓	✓
46	Hybrid truck	Diesel	✓	✓	✓	✓
47	Biodiesel truck	B5, B10	✓	✓	✓	✓

	End-use Device Options	Fuel Options	Bangladesh	Bhutan	Nepal	Sri Lanka
48	Fuel cell truck	Hydrogen	✓	✓	✓	✓
49	Electric truck short-haul	Electricity	✓	✓	✓	✓
50	Electric truck long-haul	Electricity	✓	✓	✓	✓
51	CNG truck	CNG	✓			
52	Pick-up	Diesel	✓	✓	✓	✓
53	Hybrid pick-up	Diesel	✓	✓	✓	✓
54	Biodiesel pick-up	B5, B10	✓	✓	✓	✓
55	Electric pick-up	Electricity	✓	✓	✓	✓
56	Fuel cell pick-up	Hydrogen	✓	✓	✓	✓
57	CNG pick-up	CNG	✓			
58	Tractor	Diesel	✓	✓	✓	✓
59	Biodiesel tractor	B5, B10	✓	✓	✓	✓
60	Electric tractor	Electricity	✓	✓	✓	✓
61	Freight ropeway	Electricity	✓	✓	✓	✓
62	Freight rail	Diesel	✓	✓	✓	✓
63	Electric freight rail	Electricity	✓	✓	✓	✓

B5 = blend of 5% biodiesel and 95% petrodiesel; B10 = blend of 10% biodiesel and 90% petrodiesel; CNG = compressed natural gas; E5 = Blend of 5% ethanol and 95% gasoline; E10 = blend of 10% ethanol and 90% gasoline; E85 = blend of 85% ethanol and 15% gasoline; LPG = liquefied petroleum gas.

Source: Authors.

Table A4.4: Technologies in the Industry Sector

	End-use Device Options	Fuel Options	Bangladesh	Bhutan	Nepal	Sri Lanka
	Brick industry					
1	Clamp kiln	Coal, biomass	✓		✓	✓
2	Fixed chimney – bull trench kiln (BTK)	Coal, biomass	✓		✓	✓
3	Improved fixed chimney – BTK	Coal, biomass	✓		✓	✓
4	Hoffman kiln	Coal, biomass	✓		✓	✓
5	Moving chimney – BTK	Coal, biomass	✓		✓	✓
6	Vertical shaft brick kiln	Coal, biomass	✓		✓	✓
7	Zigzag kiln	Coal, biomass	✓		✓	✓
	Cement industry					
	Cement—raw material grinding					
8	Ball mill with pre-grinding	Electricity	✓	✓	✓	✓
9	Ball mill without pre-grinding	Electricity	✓	✓	✓	✓
10	Vertical mill	Electricity	✓	✓	✓	✓
11	Roller mill	Electricity	✓	✓	✓	✓

	End-use Device Options	Fuel Options	Bangladesh	Bhutan	Nepal	Sri Lanka
	Cement—clinker production kilns					
12	Wet	Electricity, coal, biomass, natural gas[a]	✓	✓	✓	✓
13	Long dry		✓	✓	✓	✓
14	1-stage cyclone suspension preheater		✓	✓	✓	✓
15	2-stage cyclone suspension preheater		✓	✓	✓	✓
16	3-stage cyclone suspension preheater		✓	✓	✓	✓
17	4-stage cyclone suspension preheater		✓	✓	✓	✓
18	5-stage cyclone suspension preheater plus high-efficiency cooler		✓	✓	✓	✓
19	6-stage cyclone suspension preheater plus high-efficiency cooler		✓	✓	✓	✓
	Cement—finish grinding					
20	Ball mill	Electricity	✓	✓	✓	✓
21	Vertical mill		✓	✓	✓	✓
22	Roller press		✓	✓	✓	✓
23	Horomill		✓	✓	✓	✓
	Paper and pulp industry					
	Pulp preparation					
24	Kraft process	Electricity, heat[b]			✓	
25	Soda process				✓	
26	Secondary fiber pulping process				✓	
27	Kraft process and continuous digester				✓	
	Pulp bleaching					
28	Conventional – small mill	Electricity, heat			✓	
29	Conventional – large mill				✓	
30	Displacement bleaching				✓	
	Stock preparation					
31	Small mill	Electricity, heat			✓	
32	Large mill				✓	
	Conversion to paper					
33	Small mill	Electricity, heat			✓	
34	Large mill				✓	
35	Small mill with improved evaporator				✓	
36	Large mill with improved evaporator				✓	

[a] Natural gas has been considered in the case of Bangladesh only.
[b] Heat and steam are produced in the boiler and heat pump.
Source: Authors.

Table A4.5: Gross Domestic Product Growth Rate
(%)

Country	2018–2020	2020–2025	2025–2030	2030–2035	2035–2040	2040–2045	2045–2050
Bangladesh[a]	7.3	7.3	7.05	6.8	6.2	5.60	5.60
Bhutan[b]	7.8	7.8	7.80	7.8	7.8	7.80	7.80
Nepal[c]	6.0	7.0	7.50	8.0	8.5	8.25	8.00
Sri Lanka[d]	4.5	5.5	6.00	6.5	6.8	6.50	6.00

Values are close to gross domestic product growth rates in:

[a] Bangladesh Planning Commission. 2017. Bangladesh Delta Plan 2100. General Economics Division. https://oldweb.lged.gov.bd/UploadedDocument/UnitPublication/17/624/Bangladesh%20Delta%20Plan%202100%20Draft%20Report.pdf.

[b] World Bank. 2016. Bhutan Economic Update. https://openknowledge.worldbank.org/bitstream/handle/10986/26004/Bhutan12-16.pdf?sequence=1.

[c] Water and Energy Commission Secretariat. 2017. Electricity Demand Forecast Report (2015–2040). Kathmandu.

[d] Presidential Expert Committee. 2019. Sustainable Sri Lanka 2030 Vision and Strategic Path. http://www.presidentsoffice.gov.lk/wp-content/uploads/2019/05/Final-v2.4-Typeset-MM-v12F-Cov3.pdf.

Source: Authors' estimates.

Table A4.6: Gross Domestic Product
($'000,000,000 2015)

Country	2015	2020	2025	2030	2035	2040	2045	2050
Bangladesh	220.0	313.0	446.0	627.0	871.0	1,176.0	1,544.0	2,028.0
Bhutan	2.0	2.9	4.2	6.2	9.0	13.0	19.0	27.7
Nepal	21.4	27.4	38.4	55.2	81.1	121.9	181.2	266.2
Sri Lanka	80.0	105.0	142.0	190.0	247.0	307.0	374.0	455.0

Sources: World Bank. 2018. World Bank Database. https://data.worldbank.org/ (accessed 3 September 2019). Authors' calculation based on GDP growth rates presented in Table A4 (e).

Table A4.7: Population
('000,000)

Country	2015	2020	2025	2030	2035	2040	2045	2050
Bangladesh	161.00	170.00	178.00	186.00	192.00	196.00	200.00	202.00
Bhutan	0.79	0.84	0.88	0.91	0.94	0.97	0.98	0.99
Nepal	28.70	30.30	31.80	33.20	34.20	35.10	35.70	36.10
Sri Lanka	20.90	21.60	21.90	22.00	22.00	21.90	21.70	21.30

Source: United Nations, Department of Economic and Social Affairs, Population Division (UN DESA PD). 2017. World Population Prospects 2017. New York.

Table A4.8: Population Growth Rate
(%)

Country	2018–2020	2020–2025	2025–2030	2030–2035	2035–2040	2040–2045	2045–2050
Bangladesh	1.02	0.99	0.83	0.64	0.49	0.35	0.22
Bhutan	1.18	1.01	0.81	0.63	0.46	0.35	0.24
Nepal	1.09	1.00	0.83	0.64	0.47	0.35	0.23
Sri Lanka	0.39	0.26	0.11	0.01	(0.08)	(0.20)	(0.34)

Source: United Nations, Department of Economic and Social Affairs, Population Division (UN DESA PD). 2017. World Population Prospects 2017. New York.

Table A4.9: Share of Urban Population
(%)

Country	2015	2020	2025	2030	2035	2040	2045	2050
Bangladesh	34.3	38.0	41.6	44.9	47.9	50.5	53.1	55.7
Bhutan	38.6	39.4	40.1	40.8	41.5	42.2	42.8	43.5
Nepal	18.6	20.2	22.2	24.5	27.0	29.7	32.7	36.0
Sri Lanka	18.3	18.9	19.6	20.9	22.7	25.0	27.5	30.4

Source: United Nations, Department of Economic and Social Affairs, Population Division (UN DESA PD). 2019. World Urbanization Prospects: The 2018 Revision. New York.

Table A4.10: Technological Specifications in the Residential and Commercial Sectors

Technology	Lifetime of New Equipment (year)	Technology Efficiency Unit	Technology Efficiency
Cooking[a,b]			
Coal cook stove	15	%	40.2
Gas Hob	15	%	70.3
Gas oven	15	%	80.3
Electric hobs	10	%	80.2
Electric oven	10	%	90.4
Biomass traditional cook stove (TCS)	1	%	10.0
Biomass improved cook stove (ICS)	3	%	20.0
Biomass advanced ICS	5	%	35.0
Lighting[c]			
Incandescent bulb	3	lumen/Watt	13.0
Fluorescent bulb	2	lumen/Watt	100.0
CFL bulb	4	lumen/Watt	60.0
LED	8	lumen/Watt	100.0
Space heating or cooling[d]			
LPG Heater	8	%	80.0
Biomass Heater	5	%	30.0
Briquette Heater	5	%	37.0
Electric Heater	8	%	100.0
Kerosene Heater	8	%	65.0
Air-Conditioners_SEER13	15	SEER(BTU/hr/W)	13.0
Air-Conditioners_SEER20.5	15	SEER(BTU/hr/W)	20.5
Air-Conditioners_SEER25.6	15	SEER(BTU/hr/W)	25.6
Air-Conditioners_SEER28.2	15	SEER(BTU/hr/W)	28.2

BTU/hr/W = British thermal unit per hour/Watt; CFL = compact fluorescent lamps; LED = light emitting diode; LPG = liquefied petroleum gas; SEER = seasonal energy efficiency ratio.

[a] Technology data based on direct communication with Winrock International Nepal.
[b] International Energy Agency (IEA). 2014. World Energy Investment Outlook 2014.
[c] Energy Efficiency Investment Assumption Tables. Paris.
[d] IEA. 2019. Tracking Buildings. Paris. https://www.iea.org/reports/tracking-buildings; dIEA. 2018c. The Future of Cooling. Paris. https://www.iea.org/reports/the-future-of-cooling.

Source: Authors' estimates.

Table A4.11: Technological Specifications in the Cement Industry

Process	Electricity (toe/1,000 tons)	Thermal energy (toe/1,000 tons)
Raw Material Grinding		
Ball Mill (G)	3.2	
– without pregrinding	0.0	
– with pregrinding	(1.3)	
Vertical Mill (G)	2.3	
Roller Mill (G)	1.9	
Clinker Production		
Wet kiln	2.5	143.3
Long Dry	2.5	109.9
1-stage cyclone suspension preheater	2.5	99.8
2-stage cyclone suspension preheater	2.5	90.0
3-stage cyclone suspension preheater	2.5	84.8
4-stage cyclone suspension preheater	2.5	75.0
5-stage cyclone suspension preheater	2.5	71.9
6-stage cyclone suspension preheater	2.5	70.0
Finish Grinding		
Ball Mill	3.1	
Vertical Mill	2.3	
Roller Press	2.1	
Horomill	2.0	

G = toe/1,000 tons; toe = tons of oil equivalent.

Notes: The negative value indicates energy saving with the application of the technology.

Source: International Finance Corporation (IFC). 2017. Improving Thermal and Electric Energy Efficiency at Cement Plants: International Best Practice. Washington D.C.

Table A4.12: Technological Specifications in the Brick Industry

Technology (Kiln) Type	Life	Thermal Energy Consumption (toe/million bricks)
Fixed Chimney Bull Trench Kiln	15	60.60
Improved Fixed Chimney Bull Trench Kiln	15	46.70
Hoffman Kiln	15	60.60
Moving Chimney Bull Trench Kiln	15	72.70
Vertical Shaft Brick Kiln	15	34.90
Clamp Kiln	1	114.43
ZigZag Kiln	15	55.60

toe = tons of oil equivalent.

Source: S. Maithel, S. Kumar, and D. Lalchandani. 2014. Factsheets about Brick Kilns in South and South-east Asia. Greentech Knowledge Solutions Pvt Ltd, New Delhi.

Table A4.13: Technological Specifications of the Motors Considered in the Study

Motive Power	
Small size motor (<0.75 kW)	Efficiency
Standard efficiency	68.0
Premium efficiency	76.0
Premium efficiency	80.0
Super premium efficiency	83.0
Ultra premium efficiency	87.0
Medium size motor (0.75 kW–375.00 kW)	
Standard efficiency	78.0
Premium efficiency	84.0
Premium efficiency	86.0
Super premium efficiency	89.0
Ultra premium efficiency	92.0
Large size motor (>375 kW)	
Standard efficiency	94.0
Premium efficiency	95.0
Premium efficiency	96.0
Super premium efficiency	96.5
Ultra premium efficiency	97.0

kW = kilowatt.

Source: United Nations Environment Programme. 2017. Accelerating the Global Adoption of Energy-Efficient Electric Motors and Motor Systems. Paris.

5 Transmission and Distribution Loss Profiles

Transmission and distribution (T&D) loss profiles for Bangladesh, Bhutan, Nepal, and Sri Lanka in this study are presented in Figure A5. The T&D loss is assumed to be same during 2015–2050 in the case of Bangladesh, Bhutan, and Sri Lanka. In case of Nepal, T&D loss would drop from 25% in 2015 to 15% in 2020 and remain the same during 2020–2050.

Figure A5: Transmission and Distribution Loss Profiles

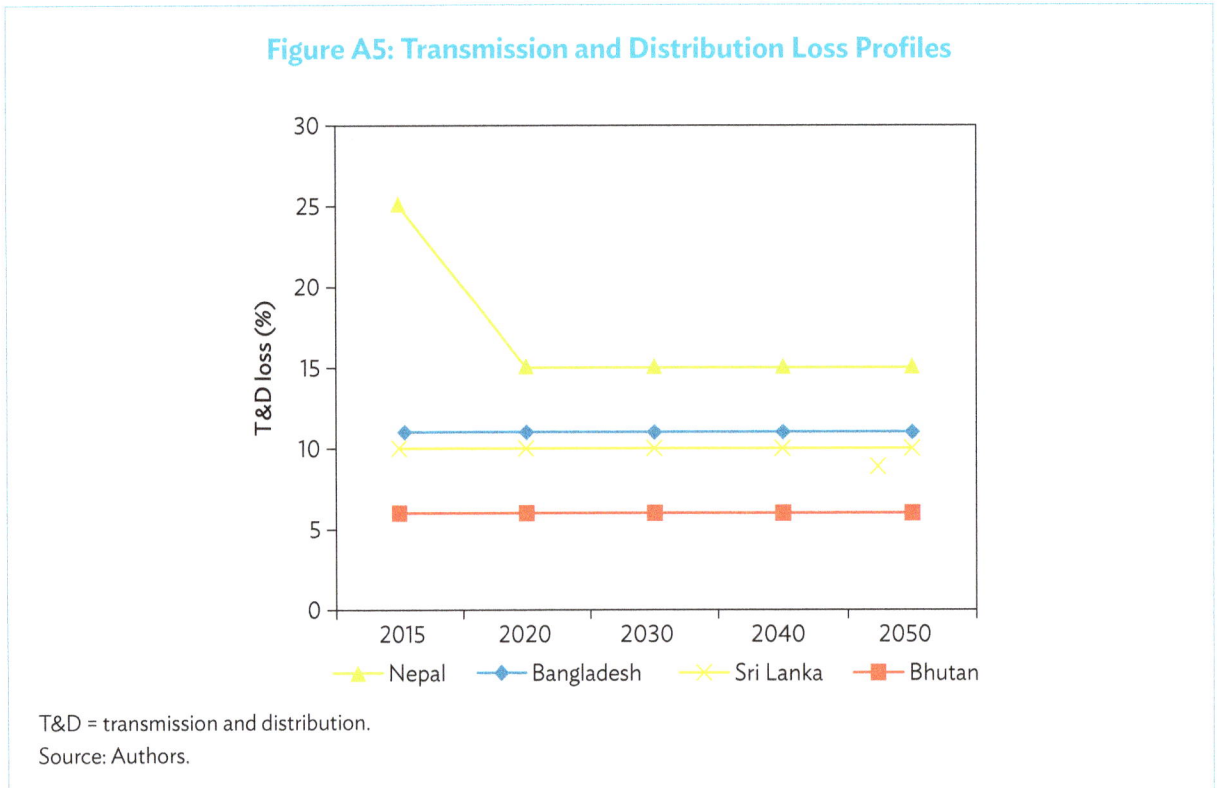

T&D = transmission and distribution.
Source: Authors.

6 Nationally Determined Contribution Targets of the South Asian Countries

Bangladesh (MOEF 2015)

- By 2030, 100% coal power plant using supercritical technology
- By 2030, efficient running of vehicles will lead to 15% improvement in efficiency of vehicles
- 10% energy consumption reduction in the industry sector compared to business as usual by 2030
- 70% and 20% market share of improved biomass cook stoves and improved gas stoves by 2030
- Overall energy consumption of the commercial sector will be reduced by 25% compared to business as usual.

Bhutan (NEC 2015)

- Improving efficiency in freight transport and existing vehicles through standards and capacity building
- Promoting nonfossil fuel-powered and nonmotorized transport such as fuel cell and electric vehicles
- Improvement of manufacturing processes and technologies in existing industries
- Promoting energy efficiency in appliances and buildings

India (UNFCCC 2015)

- To save 10% of energy consumption by 2019 compared to 2015
- Promoting ultra-supercritical technology for coal power plants
- Promoting energy efficiency in buildings, appliances, transport, and industry
- Zero Effect, Zero Defect with Make in India campaign to enhance energy and resource efficiency, pollution control, use of renewable energy, and waste management etc.
- To promote faster adoption and manufacturing of hybrid and electric vehicles in the country by providing incentives under the National Electric Mobility Mission Plan 2020
- To improve fuel standards by switching from Bharat Stage IV fuels to Bharat Stages V and VI across the country in the near future

Nepal (MoPE 2016)

- Promote clean energy and energy-efficient technology
- 20% increment in the share of electric vehicles by 2020 compared to 2010 vehicle stock
- Promote public transport systems and bicycle use
- Promote improved cooking stoves by around 475,000 stoves to improve energy efficiency in cooking.

Sri Lanka (MMDE 2016)

- National priority to improve the fuel economy and energy efficiency in the transport sector
- Improved fuel economy of transport (liter/passenger km or liter/tkm) by enhancing the engine performance of vehicles, deploying new technologies such as electrification of vehicles, using lightweight materials, increasing passenger occupancy rates, and freight load factors
- By 2030, environmentally sustainable and energy-efficient transport systems will be established
- Enhance the quality and efficiency of public transport modes
- Improve efficiency of industrial energy, water, and raw materials
- Highly efficient motors will be introduced for the entire industry sector

References

Adelphi. (n.d.). Financing Energy Efficiency (EE) Programme Nepal. https://energy-efficiency-nepal.com/sites/energy-efficiency-nepal.com/files/documents/fc_neep_flyer_rbb.pdf.

R. Akter Lucky and I. Hossain. 2001. Efficiency Study of Bangladeshi Cookstoves With an Emphasis on Gas Cookstoves. *Energy*. 26 (3). pp. 221–237.

Alternative Energy Promotion Center (AEPC). 2020. Selection of Consulting Services for "Preparation of Energy Efficiency Standards for Selected Electrical Equipments and Appliances." Kathmandu. https://www.aepc.gov.np/uploads/docs/selection-of-consulting-services-for-preparation-of-energy-efficiency-standards-for-selected-electrical-equipments-and-appliances-1580803276.pdf.

B.W. Ang. 2006. Monitoring Changes in Economy-Wide Energy Efficiency: From Energy-GDP Ratio to Composite Efficiency Index. *Energy Policy*. 34 (5). pp. 574–582. https://doi.org/10.1016/j.enpol.2005.11.011.

Asian Development Bank (ADB). 2011. Proposed Loan Facility and Technical Assistance Industrial and Infrastructure Development Finance Company and Other Financial Institutions Industrial Energy Efficiency Finance Program (Bangladesh). Manila. https://www.adb.org/sites/default/files/project-document/60531/45916-01-ban-rrp.pdf.

ADB. 2012. ADB Provides Credit Line to Finance Renewable Energy and Energy Efficiency Projects in India. News release. 29 March. https://www.adb.org/news/adb-provides-credit-line-finance-renewable-energy-and-energy-efficiency-projects-india.

——— 2013. *Preparing the Green Power Development and Energy Efficiency Improvement Investment Program*. Manila. https://www.adb.org/projects/documents/green-power-development-and-energy-efficiency-improvement-investment-program-pptar.

——— 2015. *Technical Assistance Completion Report: Preparation of Energy Efficiency Policies and Guidelines for Bhutan and Nepal*. Manila. https://www.adb.org/projects/documents/energy-efficiency-policies-and-guidelines-for-bhu-and-nep-tcr?fbclid=IwAR2YBqTZay6Q056QutoEWtEgzpRZzdMHgSjXdfvAhdItQ2TDN8YHTrKmZpA.

——— 2016. India: Demand-Side Energy Efficiency Sector Project. Manila. https://www.adb.org/projects/48224-002/main#project-pds.

——— 2018. *Key Indicators for Asia and the Pacific 2017*. Manila. https://www.adb.org/publications/key-indicators-asia-and-pacific-2017.

——— 2019a. ADB Provides $250 Million to Expand Energy Efficiency Investments in India. Manila. https://www.adb.org/news/adb-provides-250-million-expand-energy-efficiency-investments-india.

———— 2019b. Nepal: Energy Access and Efficiency Improvement Project. Manila. https://www.adb.org/documents/nepal-energy-access-and-efficiency-improvement-project.

Bangladesh Energy Regulatory Commission (BERC). 2019. Welcome to BERC. Dhaka. https://berc.portal.gov.bd/site/page/e77bd7df-b6d3-4b7c-a00e-685eb130a25c/-.

Bangladesh Planning Commission. 2017. Bangladesh Delta Plan 2100. General Economics Division. https://oldweb.lged.gov.bd/UploadedDocument/UnitPublication/17/624/Bangladesh%20Delta%20Plan%202100%20Draft%20Report.pdf.

Bangladesh Power Development Board (BPDB). 2016. *Annual Report 2015–2016*. Dhaka.

BPDB. 2017. *Annual Report 2016–2017*. Dhaka. http://www.bpdb.gov.bd/download/annual_report/Annual%20Report%202016-17%20(2).pdf.

BPDB. 2019. Annual Report 2018-19. Dhaka. https://www.bpdb.gov.bd/bpdb_new/resourcefile/annualreports/annualreport_1574325376_Annual_Report_2018-19.pdf.

Bay of Bengal Initiative for Multi-Sectoral Technical and Economic Cooperation (BIMSTEC). 2019a. About BIMSTEC. Dhaka. https://bimstec.org/?page_id=189.

BIMSTEC. 2019b. Energy Sector. Dhaka. https://bimstec.org/?page_id=268.

Bdnews24. 2019. Bangladesh Moves to Charge Electric Car Revolution with Legal Cover. https://bdnews24.com/bangladesh/2019/01/24/bangladesh-moves-to-charge-electric-car-revolution-with-legal-cover.

K. Bhardwaj and E. Gupta. 2017. Analyzing the "Energy-Efficiency Gap": An Empirical Analysis of Air Conditioners in the Household Sector of Delhi. Indian Growth and Development Review. 10 (2). pp. 66–88.

Bhutan Power Company Limited (BPC) 2017. Annual Report. Thimphu. https://www.bpc.bt/wp-content/uploads/2018/06/Final-BPC-Report-2017.pdf.

BPC. 2018. Meeting Bhutan's Electricity Needs. Thimphu. https://www.bpc.bt/wp-content/themes/2020/assets/downloads/BPC-Annual-Report-2018.pdf?

Broin, E. Ó. et al. 2015. Quantification of the Energy Efficiency Gap in the Swedish Residential Sector. *Energy Efficiency*. 8 (5). pp. 975–993.

Bureau of Energy Efficiency (BEE). 2009. Scheme for BEE Star Rating for Office Buildings. Details of the Scheme for Rating of Office Buildings. New Delhi. https://beeindia.gov.in/sites/default/files/BEE Star Rating for existing Office Buildings.pdf.

BEE. 2011. Perform Achieve and Trade (PAT) Mechanism. New Delhi.

———— 2015a. Agriculture DSM. New Delhi. https://beeindia.gov.in/content/agriculture-dsm-0.

———— 2015b. Bachat Lamp Yojana. New Delhi. https://beeindia.gov.in/content/bly-1.

———— 2015c. Energy Professionals. New Delhi. https://beeindia.gov.in/content/energy-professionals.

———— 2015d. ESCOs. New Delhi. https://www.beeindia.gov.in/content/escos-0.

———— 2015e. Existing Building. New Delhi. https://beeindia.gov.in/content/existing-building.

———— 2015f. Venture Capital Fund for Energy Efficiency (VCFEE). New Delhi. https://beeindia.gov.in/sites/default/files/VCFEE_0.PDF.

———— 2015g. SDAs. New Delhi. https://www.beeindia.gov.in/content/sdas-0.

———— 2017a. Partial Risk Guarantee Fund-Brochure. New Delhi. https://beeindia.gov.in/sites/default/files/PRGFEE 8 pages Brochure for printing by HyEJE revised %281%29.pdf.

———— 2017b. Achievements under Perform Achieve and Trade (PAT). New Delhi. https://beeindia.gov.in/sites/default/files/Booklet_Achievements under PAT_May 2017.pdf.

———— 2017c. BEE Booklet. New Delhi. https://beeindia.gov.in/sites/default/files/Final Booklet 29-9-2017.pdf.

———— 2018a. BEE Star Label. New Delhi. https://www.beestarlabel.com/.

———— 2018b. Eco-Niwas Samhita 2018 (Energy Conservation Building Code for Residential Buildings) Part I: Building Envelope. New Delhi. https://www.beeindia.gov.in/sites/default/files/ECBC_BOOK_Web.pdf.

———— 2018c. Energy Conservation Guidelines for Industries. New Delhi. https://www.beeindia.gov.in/sites/default/files/Energy conservation guidelines for industries.pdf.

———— 2018d. SEEP. New Delhi. https://www.beeindia.gov.in/content/seep-0.

———— 2018e. Enhancing Energy Efficiency Through Industry Partnership (Outcome & Way Forward). New Delhi. https://beeindia.gov.in/sites/default/files/press_releases/Consolidated%20Report.pdf.

———— 2020a. Super-efficient Equipment Programme (SEEP). New Delhi. https://beeindia.gov.in/content/seep-0.

———— 2020b. Energy Auditors. New Delhi. https://beeindia.gov.in/content/energy-auditors.

Business Bhutan. 2019. A Major Push to Promote Electric Vehicles. https://www.businessbhutan.bt/2019/01/29/a-major-push-to-promote-electric-vehicles/.

Center for Study of Science, Technology and Policy (CSTEP). 2018. Roadmap for Achieving India's NDC Pledge. Bangalore.

Central Statistics Office (CSO). 2012. Energy Statistics 2012 (Nineteenth Issue). New Delhi. http://www.mospi.gov.in/sites/default/files/publication_reports/Energy_Statistics_2012_28mar.pdf.

CSO. 2018. Energy Statistics 2018 (Twenty Fifth Issue). New Delhi. http://www.mospi.gov.in/sites/default/files/publication_reports/Energy_Statistics_2018.pdf.

Clean Technology Fund (CTF). Investment Plan for Clean Technology Fund. http://www.moef.nic.in/sites/default/files/IP-CTF-2011.pdf.

CRC Trust. 2010. The Bangladesh Gas Act, 2010 - Chancery Law Chronicles. http://www.clcbd.org/document/602.html.

S. Dhakal, P. Karki, and S. Shrestha. 2019. Cross-Border Electricity Trade for Nepal: A SWOT-AHP Analysis of Barriers and Opportunities Based on Stakeholders' Perception. *International Journal of Water Resources Development*. https://doi.org/10.1080/07900627.2019.1648240.

S. Dhar, M. Pathak, and P. R. Shukla. 2018. Role of Energy Efficiency for Low Carbon Transformation of India. *Chemical Engineering Transactions*. 63. pp. 307–312.

Department of Energy (DoE). 2007. Bhutan Energy Data Directory 2005. Thimphu.

Department of Heavy Industries (DHI). 2019. Notification- Phase II of FAME India Scheme. New Delhi. https://dhi.nic.in/writereaddata/UploadFile/publicationNotificationFAME II 8March2019.pdf.

Department of Renewable Energy (DoRE). 2016. Bhutan Energy Data Directory 2015. Thimphu. https://www.moea.gov.bt/wp-content/uploads/2018/07/Bhutan-Energy-Data-Directory-2015.pdf.

DoRE. 2017. National Energy Efficiency & Conservation Policy (Final). Thimphu. https://www.gnhc.gov.bt/en/wp-content/uploads/2017/05/EEC-Final-Draft-Policy-2017-Final-1.pdf.

——— 2018. Energy Efficiency Roadmap (Draft Report). Thimphu. http://www.moea.gov.bt/wp-content/uploads/2018/07/EE-Roadmap-Draft.pdf.

Energy Efficiency Centre (EEC). 2016. Training. Kathmandu. http://www.eec-fncci.org/content-training.

Energy Efficiency Services Limited (EESL). 2018a. About UJALA. New Delhi. https://eeslindia.org/content/raj/eesl/en/Programmes/UJALA/About-UJALA.html.

EESL. 2018b. Home. New Delhi. https://eeslindia.org/content/raj/eesl/en/home.html.

——— 2019. National Ujala Dashboard. New Delhi. http://ujala.gov.in/.

European Energy Efficiency Fund (EEEF). 2019. Objective of the Fund. https://www.eeef.eu/objective-of-the-fund.html.

S. P. Garnaik. 2014. Perform Achieve & Trade (PAT): An Innovative Mechanism for Enhancing Energy Efficiency of Industrial Sector in India. 36th Industrial Energy Technology Conference. New Orleans, Louisiana, 20–23 May. pp. 1–8.

Global Energy Efficiency and Renewable Energy Fund (GEEREF). What GEEREF Is. https://geeref.com/about/what-geeref-is.html.

Global Environment Facility (GEF). 2019. Bhutan Sustainable Low-emission Urban Transport Systems. https://www.thegef.org/project/bhutan-sustainable-low-emission-urban-transport-systems.

Global Green Growth Institute (GGGI). 2018. Accelerating Implementation of Nepal's Nationally Determined Contribution National Action Plan for Electric Mobility. Seoul.

Government of India. 1948. The Electricity (Supply) Act. Gazette of India: New Delhi. http://www.cercind.gov.in/ElectSupplyAct1948.pdf.

Government of India. 1998. The Electricity Regulatory Commissions Act. New Delhi. http://www.cercind.gov.in/ElectReguCommiAct1998.pdf.

Government of Nepal. 1984. Nepal Electricity Authority Act, 2041 (1984). Nepal Gazette: Kathmandu. http://www.moewri.gov.np/images/category/nepal-electricity-authority-act-2041-1984.pdf.

Government of Nepal. 1992. Electricity Act, 2049. Nepal Gazette: Kathmandu. https://www.nea.org.np/admin/assets/uploads/supportive_docs/Electricity Act.pdf.

Government of Sri Lanka. 2007. Sri Lanka Sustainable Energy Authority Act, No. 35 of 2007. Gazette of the Democratic Socialist Republic of Sri Lanka: Colombo. http://www.energy.gov.lk/document/SLSEA Act-E.pdf.

Government of Sri Lanka. 2009. Sri Lanka Electricity Act, No. 20 of 2009. Gazette of the Democratic Socialist Republic of Sri Lanka: Colombo. http://www.pucsl.gov.lk/english/wp-content/themes/pucsl/pdfs/ electricity_act_2009.pdf.

Green Climate Fund (GCF). 2018a. Promoting Private Sector Investments in Energy Efficiency in the Industrial Sector and in Paraguay. https://www.greenclimate.fund/project/fp063?inheritRedirect=true&redire ct=/what-we-do/projects-programmes%3Fp_p_id%3D101_INSTANCE_Hreg2cAkDEHL%26p_p_ lifecycle%3D0%26p_p_state%3Dnormal%26p_p_mode%3Dview%26p_p_col_id%3D_118_ INSTANCE_4ZRnUzRWpEqO__colum.

GCF. 2018b. Promoting Risk Mitigation Instruments and Finance for Renewable Energy and Energy Efficiency Investments. https://www.greenclimate.fund/projects/fp064?inheritRedirect=true&redirect=%2Fw hat-we-do%2Fprojects-programmes%3Fp_p_id%3D101_INSTANCE_Hreg2cAkDEHL%26p_p_ lifecycle%3D0%26p_p_state%3Dnormal%26p_p_mode%3Dview%26p_p_col_id%3D_118_ INSTANCE_4ZRnUzRWpEqO__colum.

———— 2018c. Scaling Up Energy Efficiency for Industrial Enterprises in Vietnam. https://www.greenclimate.fund/ projects/fp071?inheritRedirect=true&redirect=%2Fwhat-we-do%2Fprojects-programmes.

———— 2018d. Energy Efficient Consumption Loan Programme. https://www.greenclimate.fund/project/sap004?i nheritRedirect=true&redirect=/what-we-do/projects-programmes.

Green Rating for Integrated Habitat Assessment (GRIHA). 2018. Home. New Delhi. http://www.grihaindia. org/?T=griha_council&#&griha_council.

R. D. Hanbar and P. Karve. 2002. National Programme on Improved Chulha (NPIC) of the Government of India: an overview. *Energy for Sustainable Development.* 6 (2). pp. 49–55. https://doi.org/10.1016/S0973-0826(08)60313-0.

Housing and Building Research Institute (HBRI). 2015. Bangladesh National Building Code. Dhaka. http://www. ovice.or.kr/filebank/construction/OVIC16032003/OVIC16032003.pdf.

Indian Renewable Energy Development Agency Limited (IREDA). 2018. Energy Efficiency and Conservation. New Delhi. https://www.ireda.in/energy-efficiency-conservation.

Indian Renewable Energy and Energy Efficiency Policy Database (IREEED). 2015. http://www.ireeed.gov.in/ summarytableee.

Infrastructure Development Company Limited (IDCOL). Dhaka. http://idcol.org/home/about.

IDCOL. 2017. IDCOL Energy Efficiency. Dhaka. http://www.idcol.org/old/bd-map_ics/bangladesh_map/.

———— 2019. Enabling Ecosystem for Electric Mobility in Bangladesh. Bangladesh Clean Energy Summit 2019. Dhaka. http://idcol.org/bces-2019/assets/newsevents/knowledgepapers/Enabling ecosystem for Electric Mobility in Bangladesh.pdf.

International Energy Agency (IEA). 2014. *World Energy Investment Outlook 2014: Energy Efficiency Investment Assumption Tables.* Paris.

IEA. 2015a. *Energy Efficiency Outlook for India: Sizing up the Opportunity*. Paris.

———— 2015b. *India Energy Outlook*. Paris.

———— IEA Online Database. Paris. https://www.iea.org/data-and-statistics/data-tables? (accessed 18 August 2019).

———— 2018a. IEA - India-Perform Achieve and Trade (PAT) Scheme. Paris. https://www.iea.org/policies/1780-perform-achieve-trade-pat-scheme.

———— 2018b. *The Future of Cooling*. Paris. https://www.iea.org/reports/the-future-of-cooling.

———— 2019. *Tracking Buildings*. Paris. https://www.iea.org/reports/tracking-buildings.

International Finance Corporation (IFC). 2017. *Improving Thermal and Electric Energy Efficiency at Cement Plants: International Best Practice*. Washington D.C.

M. Jain, A.B. Rao, and A. Patwardhan. 2019. Energy Efficiency Policies in India: Implications for Climate Change Mitigation. In C. Venkataraman, T. Mishra, S. Ghosh, and S. Karmakar, eds. Climate Change Signals and Response (pp. 289–303). Springer, Singapore. https://doi.org/10.1007/978-981-13-0280-0_18.

M. Kainuma, Y. Matsuoka, and T. Morita, eds. 2003. Climate Policy Assessment: AIM/Enduse model. Springer, Tokyo. https://doi.org/10.1007/978-4-431-53985-8.

S. Maithel, S. Kumar, and D. Lalchandani. 2014. Factsheets about Brick Kilns in South and South-east Asia. Greentech Knowledge Solutions Pvt Ltd, New Delhi.

Mitra, A. et al. 2017. Pathways for Meeting India's Climate Goals. Washington, D.C: World Resources Institute.

Ministry of Economic Affairs (MoEA). 2019. National Energy Efficiency and Conservation Policy. Bhutan. https://www.moea.gov.bt/wp-content/uploads/2017/07/Final-EEC-Policy.pdf.

Ministry of Energy, Water Resources and Irrigation (MoEWRI). 2018. National Energy Efficiency Strategy 2018. Nepal. http://www.moewri.gov.np/images/category/National-Energy-Efficiency-Strategy-2075.pdf.

Ministry of Environment and Forests (MOEF). 2015. Intended Nationally Determined Contributions (INDC). Bangladesh. https://www4.unfccc.int/sites/ndcstaging/PublishedDocuments/Bangladesh%20First/INDC_2015_of_Bangladesh.pdf.

Ministry of Finance (MoF). 2018. New Vehicle Price Tax Gazette Sri Lanka 2018. Colombo. https://www.gazette.lk/2018/08/new-vehicle-price-tax-gazette-sri-lanka-2018.html.

Ministry of Law and Justice (MoLJ). 2003. The Electricity Act, 2003. India. http://www.cercind.gov.in/Act-with-amendment.pdf.

MoLJ. 2010. The Energy Conservation (Amendment) Act, 2010. India. http://www.mercindia.org.in/pdf/Order 58 42/The Energy Conservation (Amendment) Act, 2010.pdf.

Ministry of Law, Justice and Parliamentary Affairs (MoLJPA). 2012. The Sustainable and Renewable Energy Development Authority Act, 2012 (Act No. 48 of 2012). Legislative and Parliamentary Affairs Division: Dhaka, Bangladesh. http://www.dpp.gov.bd/upload_file/gazettes/10720_39500.pdf.

Ministry of Mahaweli Development and Environment (MMDE). 2016. Nationally Determined Contributions.: Sri Lanka. https://www4.unfccc.int/sites/ndcstaging/PublishedDocuments/Sri%20Lanka%20First/NDCs%20 of%20Sri%20Lanka.pdf.

Ministry of Population and Environment (MoPE). 2016. Nationally Determined Contributions.: Nepal. https:// www4.unfccc.int/sites/ndcstaging/PublishedDocuments/Nepal%20First/Nepal%20First%20NDC.pdf.

Ministry of Power (MoP). 2005. National Electricity Policy. India. https://powermin.nic.in/en/content/national-electricity-policy.

MoP. 2016. Guidelines on Cross Border Trade of Electricity. India.

—— 2018. Guidelines for Import/Export (Cross Border) of Electricity - 2018. India.

Ministry of Power and Energy (MoPRE). 2008. National Energy Policy & Strategies of Sri Lanka. Gazette of the Democratic Socialist Republic of Sri Lanka. Colombo.

MoPRE. The Ministry. http://powermin.gov.lk/english/?page_id=1222.

—— 2015. Sri Lanka Energy Sector Development Plan for a Knowledge-Based Economy: 2015–2025. Sri Lanka. http://powermin.gov.lk/sinhala/wp-content/uploads/2015/03/ENERGY_EMPOWERED_ NATION_2015_2025.pdf.

—— 2017. Performance 2017 and Programmes for 2018. Sri Lanka. http://powermin.gov.lk/english/wp-content/ uploads/2017/10/MoPRE-2017.2018-03-English.pdf.

Ministry of Power, Energy and Mineral Resources (MPEMR). 2012. Energy Efficiency and Conservation Rules, Initial Draft 22 October 2012. Bangladesh. http://www.asialeds.org/sites/default/files/resource/file/30.pdf.

MPEMR. 2018. Sustainable and Renewable Energy Development Authority (SREDA). Bangladesh. https:// mpemr.gov.bd/power/details/26.

Ministry of Power, Energy and Mineral Resources Energy and Mineral Resources Division (MoPEMRD). 2003. Act No 14 of 2003. Bangladesh. http://www.sreda.gov.bd/d3pbs_uploads/files/acts_2_bangladesh_energy_ regulatory_commission_act_2003.pdf.

Ministry of Urban Development (MoUD). 2015. Nepal National Building Code. http://www.moud.gov.np/images/ category/NBC_206_2015_ARCHITECTURAL_DESIGN_REQUIREMENTS1.pdf.

Ministry of Works and Human Settlement (MoWHS). 2013. Bhutan Green Building Design Guidelines. http:// www.mowhs.gov.bt/wp-content/uploads/2014/05/Bhutan-GREEN-Building-Design-Guidelines-PDF-for-website-FI.pdf.

National Assembly of Bhutan (NAB). 2001. Electricity Act of Bhutan Year 2001. Thimphu. http://www.nab.gov. bt/assets/uploads/docs/acts/2014/Electricity_act_2001_Eng.pdf.

National Environment Commission (NEC). 2015. Intended Nationally Determined Contribution. Thimphu. https://www4.unfccc.int/sites/ndcstaging/PublishedDocuments/Bhutan%20First/Bhutan-INDC-20150930.pdf.

National Power Portal (NPP). Glossary of Terms. https://npp.gov.in/glossary.

Nepal Electricity Authority (NEA). 2001. Annual Report FY 2000/2001 A Year in Review. Kathmandu. http://www.nea.org.np/admin/assets/uploads/supportive_docs/Nepal%20Electricity-compressed.pdf.

NEA. 2019. A Year in Review - Fiscal Year 2018/2019. Kathmandu: Nepal Electricity Authority (NEA). Kathmandu. http://www.nea.org.np/admin/assets/uploads/supportive_docs/90599295.pdf.

Nepal Energy Efficiency Programme (NEEP). 2019. AEPC to promote Energy Efficiency. Kathmandu. http://energyefficiency.gov.np/newspage-44-AEPC to promote Energy Efficiency.

Y. Onishi. 2013. India Ex-Post Evaluation of Japanese ODA Loan Project Micro, Small and Medium Enterprises Energy Saving Project. https://www2.jica.go.jp/en/evaluation/pdf/2012_ID-P200_4.pdf.

Operation Demand Side Management (ODSM). 2017a. About Us. Presidential Task Force on Energy Demand Side Management, Sri Lanka. http://www.energy.gov.lk/ODSM/About-Us.html.

ODSM. 2017b. Standards and Regulations. Presidential Task Force on Energy Demand Side Management, Sri Lanka. http://www.energy.gov.lk/ODSM/Standards-and-Regulations.html.

——— 2018. Residential Building Code. Presidential Task Force on Energy Demand Side Management, Sri Lanka. http://www.energy.gov.lk/ODSM/Residential-Buildingcode.html.

Pangeni, R. 2017. NEA Chief says LED Lamps Instrumental for Demand-side Management. MyRepublica. 10 May. https://myrepublica.nagariknetwork.com/news/ghising-says-led-bulbs-instrumental-for-demand-side-management/.

V. K. Pantangi et al. 2007. Performance Analysis of Domestic LPG Cooking Stoves With Porous Media. *International Energy Journal.* 8 (2). pp. 139–144.

K.S. Parikh and J.K. Parikh. 2016. Realizing Potential Savings of Energy and Emissions From Efficient Household Appliances in India. *Energy Policy.* 97 (October). pp. 102–111.

Government of Sri Lanka. 2007. Sri Lanka Sustainable Energy Authority Act, No. 35 of 2007. Gazette of the Democratic Socialist Republic of Sri Lanka. http://www.energy.gov.lk/document/SLSEA Act-E.pdf.

Presidential Expert Committee. 2019. Sustainable Sri Lanka 2030 Vision and Strategic Path. http://www.presidentsoffice.gov.lk/wp-content/uploads/2019/05/Final-v2.4-Typeset-MM-v12F-Cov3.pdf.

Press Information Bureau (PIB). 2017. Shri Piyush Goyal Launches Energy Conservation Building Code 2017. India. http://pib.nic.in/newsite/PrintRelease.aspx?relid=165748.

PIB. 2018a. ECO Niwas Samhita 2018 - an Energy Conservation Building Code for Residential Buildings Launched. India. http://pib.nic.in/newsite/PrintRelease.aspx?relid=186406.

——— 2018b. FAME-India Scheme. India. http://pib.nic.in/newsite/PrintRelease.aspx?relid=186277.

——— 2018c. Government Making Efforts to Reduce Dependence on Traditional Biomass Cooking. India https://pib.gov.in/PressReleaseIframePage.aspx?PRID=1525934.

Public Utilities Commission of Sri Lanka (PUCSL). 2014. Public Utilities Commission of Sri Lanka- Regulatory Manual. http://www.pucsl.gov.lk/english/wp-content/uploads/2014/05/Regulatory-Manual-March-2013-Version-3.pdf.

PwC. (n.d.). Bhutan Building Energy Efficiency Code. PwC. www.pwc.com.

Rasel, A. R. 2017. Legislation of New Electricity Act Stuck in Red Tape. *Dhaka Tribune*. https://www.dhakatribune. com/bangladesh/power-energy/2017/02/27/new-electricity-act-limbo.

Regional Center for Renewable Energy and Energy Efficiency (RCREEE). 2019. Who We Are. http://www.rcreee. org/content/who-we-are.

SAARC Energy Centre (SEC). 2020. About us. Islamabad. https://www.saarcenergy.org/about-us/.

SADC Centre for Renewable Energy and Energy Efficiency (SACREEE). 2018. Our Partners. https://www.sacreee. org/content/our-partners.

South Asia Subregional Economic Cooperation (SASEC). 2011. SASEC Subregional Energy Efficiency Initiative. https://www.sasec.asia/index.php?page=project&pid=68&url=sasec-subregional-energy-efficiency-initiative. SASEC.

SASEC. 2019. What is SASEC? South Asia Subregional Economic Cooperation (SASEC). https://www.sasec.asia/ index.php?page=what-is-sasec.

South Asian Association for Regional Cooperation (SAARC). About Us. http://saarc-sec.org/about-saarc.

SAARC. 2018. Energy Transport Science and Technology. http://saarc-sec.org/areas_of_cooperation/area_ detail/energy-transport-science-and-technology/click-for-details_10.

A. Sengupta and S. Kumar. 2011. Roadmap for India in Energy Efficiency. *The Atlantic Energy Efficiency Policy Briefs*. http://environmentportal.in/files/file/India_Sengupta.pdf.

S.R. Shakya and R.M. Shrestha. 2011. Transport Sector Electrification in a Hydropower Resource Rich Developing Country: Energy Security, Environmental and Climate Change Co-Benefits. *Energy for Sustainable Development*. 15 (2). pp. 147–159.

R.M. Shrestha, G. Anandarajah, and M. H. Liyanage. 2009. Factors Affecting CO_2 Emission From the Power Sector of Selected Countries in Asia and the Pacific. *Energy Policy*. 37. June. pp. 2375–2384.

R. M. Shrestha et al. 2012. Atmospheric Brown Cloud (ABC) Emission Inventory Manual. United Nations Environment Programme, Nairobi, Kenya.

R.M. Shrestha and S. Rajbhandari. 2010. Energy and Environmental Implications of Carbon Emission Reduction Targets: Case of Kathmandu Valley, Nepal. *Energy Policy*. 38 (9). pp. 4818–4827.

Sri Lanka Energy Managers Association (SLEMA). 2017. Our Story. Colombo. http://www.slema.lk/.

Sri Lanka Sustainable Energy Authority (SLSEA). 2009. Code of Practice for Energy Efficient Buildings in Sri Lanka-2008. Colombo. http://www.energy.gov.lk/images/energy-management/residential-building-code. pdf.

SLSEA. 2018. Inception. Colombo. http://www.energy.gov.lk/en/about-us/inception.

V. Subramanyam, M. Ahiduzzaman, and A. Kumar. 2017a. Greenhouse Gas Emissions Mitigation Potential in the Commercial and Institutional Sector. *Energy and Buildings*. 140. April. pp. 295–304.

V. Subramanyam et al. 2017b. Energy Efficiency Improvement Opportunities and Associated Greenhouse Gas Abatement Costs for the Residential Sector. *Energy*. 118. January. pp. 795–807.

Sustainable and Renewable Energy Development Authority (SREDA). 2012. The Sustainable and Renewable Energy Development Authority Act, 2012 (Act No. 48 of 2012). Bangladesh. http://www.dpp.gov.bd/upload_file/gazettes/10720_39500.pdf.

SREDA. 2015. Energy Efficiency and Conservation Master Plan up to 2030. Bangladesh. http://open_jicareport.jica.go.jp/pdf/12231247.pdf.

—— 2018. SREDA Standard and Labeling (Appliance & Equipments) Regulation-2018. Bangladesh. http://www.sreda.gov.bd/files/Standard and labeling regulation Draft 1_08_2018.pdf.

—— 2019. Acts, Policies & Rules. Bangladesh. http://www.sreda.gov.bd/index.php/site/page/cd84-f74c-6e7a-8b20-16a5-73a9-ff7e-fb95-66d8-6fd4V.

A. Talaei, M. Ahiduzzaman, and A. Kumar. 2018. Assessment of Long-Term Energy Efficiency Improvement and Greenhouse Gas Emissions Mitigation Potentials in the Chemical Sector. *Energy*. 153 (June). pp. 231–247.

A. Talaei et al. 2019. Assessment of Long-Term Energy Efficiency Improvement and Greenhouse Gas Emissions Mitigation Options for the Cement Industry. *Energy*. 170 (March). pp. 1051–1066.

S. Thambi, A. Bhatacharya, and O. Fricko. 2018. India's Energy and Emissions Outlook: Results from India Energy Model. Niti Ayog, New Delhi.

The Independent. 2015. Energy Research Council Selects Areas to Work. http://www.theindependentbd.com/printversion/details/5295.

The Independent. 2017. 4 Companies Get Govt Nod. http://www.theindependentbd.com/post/96251.

The Island. 2016. Commercial Bank launches Green Development Loans to Support Country's Sustainability Agenda. http://www.island.lk/index.php?page_cat=article-details&page=article-details&code_title=135343.

The Kathmandu Post. 2018. Nepal, Bangladesh sign power cooperation deal. http://kathmandupost.ekantipur.com/news/2018-08-11/nepal-bangladesh-sign-power-cooperation-deal.html.

United Nations, Department of Economic and Social Affairs, Population Division (UN DESA PD). 2017. World Population Prospects 2017. New York.

UN DESA PD. 2019. World Urbanization Prospects: The 2018 Revision. New York.

United Nations Environment Programme. 2017. Accelerating the Global Adoption of Energy-Efficient Electric Motors and Motor Systems. Paris.

United Nations Environment Programme and BEE. 2016. Rolling Out Energy Conservation Building Code (ECBC), 6. http://www.in.undp.org/content/dam/india/docs/pub-EnE/Rolling out ECBC Codes.pdf.

United Nations Framework Convention on Climate Change. 2015. India's Intended Nationally Determined Contribution: Working Towards Climate Justice. https://www4.unfccc.int/sites/ndcstaging/PublishedDocuments/India%20First/INDIA%20INDC%20TO%20UNFCCC.pdf.

O. van de Riet, G. de Jong, and W. Walker. 2008. Drivers of Freight Transport Demand and Their Policy Implications. In A. Perrels, V. Himanen, and M. L. Gosseling, eds. *Building Blocks for Sustainable Transport* (pp. 73–102). Emerald Group Publishing Limited.

S. S. Vishwanathan et al. 2017. Enhancing Energy Efficiency in India: Assessment of Sectoral Potentials. Copenhagen Center on Energy Efficiency, UNEP DTU Partnership, Copenhagen.

Water and Energy Commission Secretariat. 2017. Electricity Demand Forecast Report (2015–2040). Kathmandu.

S. Weil and J.E. McMahon. 2005. Energy Efficiency Labels and Standards: A Guidebook for Appliances, Equipment and Lighting. Lawrence Berkeley National Laboratory. http://escholarship.org/uc/item/2rj0w00t.

H. Wickramasinghe. 2010. Sri Lanka Country Report on Energy Efficiency Improvement & Conservation, (August). http://www.saarcenergy.org/wp-content/uploads/2016/02/SriLankaCountryReport.pdf.

World Bank. 2016. Bhutan Economic Update. https://openknowledge.worldbank.org/bitstream/handle/10986/26004/Bhutan12-16.pdf?sequence=1.

World Bank. 2016. Energy – Bangladesh Sets a World Record: 5 Million CFLs in One Day! http://web.worldbank.org/WBSITE/EXTERNAL/TOPICS/EXTENERGY2/0,,contentMDK:22647135~pagePK:210058~piPK:210062~theSitePK:4114200,00.html.

World Bank. 2018. World Bank Database. https://data.worldbank.org/. Accessed 3 September 2019.

S. Yu et al. 2017. Improving Building Energy Efficiency in India: State-Level Analysis of Building Energy Efficiency Policies. *Energy Policy*. 110. July. pp. 331–341. https://doi.org/10.1016/j.enpol.2017.07.013.

www.ingramcontent.com/pod-product-compliance
Lightning Source LLC
Chambersburg PA
CBHW041428270326
41932CB00031B/3496